CULTS AND NONCONVENTIONAL RELIGIOUS GROUPS

A Collection of Outstanding Dissertations and Monographs

Edited by
J. GORDON MELTON
Institute for the Study of American Religion

A GARLAND SERIES

THE ESOTERIC SCENE, CULTIC MILIEU, AND OCCULT TAROT

DANNY L. JORGENSEN

GARLAND PUBLISHING, INC.
New York & London
1992

Library of Congress Cataloging-in-Publication Data

Jorgensen, Danny L.
The esoteric scene, cultic milieu, and occult tarot / Danny L. Jorgensen.
p. cm. — (Cults and nonconventional religious groups)
Includes bibliographical references and index.
ISBN 0-8153-0769-1
1. Occultism—United States. 2. Occultism—Social aspects—United States. 3. Tarot—United States. I. Title. II. Series
BP1434.U6J67 1992
133—dc20 92-15862
CIP

Printed on acid-free, 250-year-life paper

MANUFACTURED IN THE UNITED STATES OF AMERICA

CONTENTS

LIST OF FIGURES

LIST OF ILLUSTRATIONS

Illustration

LIST OF TABLES

PREFACE

This book deals with beliefs, practices, and activities described as mystical, psychical, magical, spiritual, metaphysical, theosophical, esoteric, occult, and/or pagan, among other possible labels, by their American disciples. I began observing and participating in believers' activities in 1975 while living in a metropolitan area of the northcentral United States. Through a methodology of participant observation (Jorgensen, 1989), as discussed in Chapter One, I experienced and described the meanings of these beliefs, practices, and activities from the perspectives of adherents. Later in the year I moved to an urban center in the southwestern United States referred to here as the "Valley." Fieldwork, based primarily on participant observation, was conducted in the Valley between 1975 and 1978.

In the course of this investigation I was labeled a "seeker." I subsequently performed other membership roles (Adler and Adler, 1987) as a "client" of divinatory practitioners, and as an initiate or "student" of the occult tarot. Eventually I became a "tarot card reader" and, thereby, a fully participating member of a geographically dispersed "esoteric community" in the Valley, as discussed in Chapter Five. Participant observation was supplemented by several other methods. I interviewed groups and practitioners in the Valley by telephone, and collected flyers, advertisements, and related documents. Indepth interviews with tarot diviners in the community were conducted primarily by Lin Jorgensen. I employed several assistants—Tina Walton, David Kurtz, Heidi Griffin, and Lin Jorgensen—for the purpose of gathering divinatory readings of the tarot.

Before leaving the field in 1978 I reviewed scholarly literature related to this topic for the purpose of analyzing, interpreting, and presenting findings in the form of a doctoral dissertation. This report, "Tarot Divination in the Valley of the Sun: An Existential Sociology of the Esoteric and Occult" (Jorgensen, 1979), was completed after moving to an urbanized area of the southeastern United States in 1978. Over the next five years these materials were analyzed and interpreted further, resulting in the publication of four additional reports. They focused specifically on the esoteric community and related cultic milieu in the Valley (Jorgensen, 1982), the social meanings of occultism as exemplified by members of the esoteric community (Jorgensen and Jorgensen, 1982), solidarity and networks of occultists in the community, partly as illustrated by psychic fairs (Jorgensen, 1983), and community members' use of the occult tarot for divination (Jorgensen, 1984).

Since 1978 I have continued to review pertinent scholarly literature, as well as esoteric and occult writings by way of library research. In 1985 I made two trips to Chicago for the purpose of examining and collecting documents about esotericism and occultism from the archives of the Institute for the Study of American religion. This heretofore unpublished scholarship supports a more comprehensive theoretical interpretation of esoteric and occult knowledge.While living in the southeastern United States I have studied particular beliefs, practices, and groups, less formally and systematically, through media reports, casual observation, and the investigative reports of students. All of these researches are drawn together in this work. This book is based on my earlier studies and reports. However, it includes new findings, as well as a substantially different analysis and interpretation of my previous work.

I describe, analyze, and interpret social meanings of "esoteric culture" as it is experienced, defined, distributed, structured, organized, and enacted by societal members. My analysis concentrates on members' definitions of esoteric knowledge, the manner in which they organize their activities socially, and the procedures they employ to achieve a sense of having accomplished occult knowledge. This interpretation informs and is facilitated by a "grounded" theory of esoteric culture (see Glazer and Strauss, 1967). Although the idea of "esoteric culture" derives from the work of Edward A. Tiryakian (1973, 1974), my use of it differs substantially from his insightful formulation.

Chapter Two presents this theory of esoteric culture, including the "cultic milieu" (Campbell, 1972), whereby it is sustained and organized socially. I discuss meanings and sources of esoteric knowledge in Western societies, focusing specifically on its manifestations, historically, in American society. Drawing on John Irwin's (1977) concept of a "social scene," I argue that esoteric culture and the related cultic milieu emerged to form an esoteric scene in the United States during the late 1960's. This concept is useful for subsequently distinguishing the esoteric community from other esoteric activities and organizations in the Valley. Although this scene has declined during the 1980's, esoteric culture remains visible in all large American cities today.

Chapters Three and Four describe, analyze, and interpret the esoteric scene in the Valley. I focus on the social organization of members' activities by way of elaborate networks of social relationship among seekers, clients, practitioners, and cultic groups. Much of this activity is seen by members as constituting an esoteric community in the Valley. Within this community networks of social relationship are partitioned or segmented to constitute particular factions of groups and participants. These alliances reflect somewhat different social meanings and orientations to esoteric knowledge. In spite of tremendous diversity and factionalism, members of this community sustain a sense of solidarity by way of relations with a sometimes hostile exoteric society, an ethos and ethics, as well as shared activities, such as psychic fairs.

Chapters Six, Seven, and Eight discuss the social construction of the occult tarot, related theosophies, and methods for interpreting the symbolic images represented by these unique cards. I examine the historical process whereby the tarot was appropriated by occultists and defined as the symbolic key to all arcane (secret, esoteric) wisdom. Occult interpretation of these cards resulted in the creation of elaborate theories of meaning, or theosophies whereby the tarot and its symbolic images were systemically interrelated with other bodies of esoteric knowledge. I argue that the occult tarot may be seen, interpretatively, as a human text. This text constitutes an occult language composed of grammars and vocabularies of meaning. Interpreting the tarot involves reading this text. The theosophical language of the occult tarot is used for scholarly-like studies, meditation, divination, and sometimes ritual. I focus special attention on the manner in which the occult tarot is used by diviners and querents to achieve a sense that they have accomplished an extraordinary knowledge of reality.

By way of conclusion, Chapter Nine explores the sociological significance of esoteric culture as a formulation of alternative sociocultural realities. Esoteric culture is viewed interpretatively as a product of human efforts to make life meaningful in an otherwise absurd world. This book aims to provide a sociological understanding of esoteric culture and the cultic milieu, particularly its contemporary manifestations as an esoteric scene in America. My focus on the occult tarot reflects a special concern for understanding, sociologically, how occult claims to knowledge are accomplished and enacted socially.

What I am about here is reflected by the ***Prince of Swords***.

—Danny L. Jorgensen

ACKNOWLEDGEMENTS

John M. Johnson and David L. Altheide provided invaluable assistance and direction during my fieldwork in the Valley. They also have supported me in countless other ways over the last fifteen years. They continue to share responsibility in this matter, but I no longer hold them responsible for this research or its products. Tina Walton, David Kurtz, Heidi Griffin, and Lin Jorgensen received divinatory readings of the tarot from members of the esoteric community in the Valley. I appreciate their willingness to collect these materials and share them with me. Val and Steve Crowley, Heidi Griffin, and Lin Jorgensen were very helpful in transcribing tarot card readings for analysis and interpretation.

Lin Jorgensen participated fully as a co-worker in field research. Indepth interviews with tarot diviners in the Valley primarily were conducted by Lin. Her considerable skill with informal interviewing is opulently reflected in these materials. I benefitted tremendously from countless debriefing and brainstorming sessions with Lin during our fieldwork, and from many, many hours of subsequent analysis and interpretation of these materials. She also is hereby acknowledged as the co-author of a previous report based on this research that informs this book (Jorgensen and Jorgensen, 1982).

My research in the Valley would have been impossible without the trust and cooperation of members of the esoteric community. In keeping with traditions of fieldwork I have not revealed the actual identities of any of the people or groups serving as the basis for this report. I regret being unable to acknowledge them by name, particularly several special friends and trusted informants.

Participant observational research in the Valley served as the basis for my doctoral dissertation, *Tarot Divination in the Valley of the Sun: An Existential Sociology of the Esoteric and Occult* (The Ohio State University, 1979). I appreciate the assistance of my doctoral committee, Gisela and Roscoe Hinkle, Richard Lundman, and George Demko, with this project. Gia Hinkle, in particular, brilliantly framed the original analysis of tarot divination, and her many insights are apparent in my subsequent interpretations.

J. Gordon Melton was a gracious host during two visits to the Institute for the Study of American Religion in Chicago during 1985. He suggested that I submit this work to Garland Publishing. I appreciate his support of its publication as well as his helpful comments on the manuscript.

The permission of Samuel Weiser, Incorported to quote from Aleister Crowley's *The Book of Thoth* (York Beach, ME: Samuel Weiser, Inc., 1974), pp. 3-4, 42, is gratefully acknowledged. I appreciate the permission of Taplinger Publishing Company, Incorporated to quote from Alfred Douglas' *The Tarot* (NY: Taplinger, 1972).

AGMüller, The Church of Light, William J. Hurley, Lotus Light Publications, Naipes y Especialidades Graficas, S.A., and U.S. Games Systems, Incorporated, all very kindly granted me permission to reproduce tarot cards on which they hold copyrights. These materials are used here as illustrations only, and they in no way imply any endorsement for or against related beliefs, practices, or enterprises. I am solely responsible for the manner in which these illustrations are employed.

I appreciate Jack Hurley's efforts to educate me about recent developments with the tarot. Late in this project he provided a wide variety of important information, much of which I have been unable to integrate with the existing analysis and interpretation. To my surprise, he has stimulated my interest in pursuing many of these issues in subsequent works.

I am grateful to the University of South Florida's College of Social and Behavioral Sciences for a small research and travel grant that supported one of my visits to Chicago in 1985.

Khaleah Bryant read and commented on drafts of this book. I very much appreciate her comments and editorial assistance. The final product, consequently, was greatly improved. Mike Wright provided various forms of assistance with the preparation of the manuscript, including construction of several figures and tables, as well as the transformation of basic format.

This book is dedicated to Julie, Greta, Adrean, Eric, and now Mikkey, all of whom endured parts of its research and writing.

THE ESOTERIC SCENE, CULTIC MILIEU, AND OCCULT TAROT

Chapter 1

Observing and Participating in the Cultic Milieu

In 1975 I began looking for Americans who were making extraordinary claims to knowledge on the basis of unconventional practices. Eventually, I encountered expansive networks of practitioners performing what they called "magic," "clairvoyance," "divination," "mediumship," "meditation," "witchcraft," and "healing," as well as other, rather extraordinary practices and rituals.[1] They most commonly described their doctrines and beliefs as "psychic," "esoteric," "spiritual," and "religious"; but, they also employed the words "occult," "mystic," "magic," "metaphysical," "theosophical," "intuitive," "hermetic," "new age," "pagan," "scientific," and "philosophical," among others, in this way. Although these Americans were geographically dispersed throughout a large metropolitan center referred to here as "the Valley," they envisioned their activities in terms of a "esoteric," "psychic," or "spiritual community." Over the next three years I studied these peoples' beliefs and activities by way of a methodology of participant observation (see Jorgensen, 1989).

The fundamental goals of this inquiry were to observe, experience, and describe this sociocultural world in terms of the meanings ascribed to it by members, natives, or insiders. Since 1978 I have collected other pertinent information, and concentrated on analyzing and interpreting my findings. The results are reported in this book. It describes, analyzes, and interprets what Tiryakian (1973, 1974) called "**esoteric culture**." This includes bodies of knowledge, especially theosophies, constructed and used by believers to define "reality" in ultimately meaningful ways, as well as practices, like meditation and divination, employed by practitioners to enact and accomplish their images of reality. Esoteric culture exists in marked contrast with the socially dominant exoteric culture, and it is distinguishable in terms of a lack of socially sanctioned legitimacy in Western societies. The **occult tarot** serves as a concrete illustration of a theosophically constituted body of esoteric knowledge, while its use by occultists for hermetic study, meditation, and divination exemplifies occult practices. Esoteric culture is distributed, structured, and organized, I argue, in the form of what Campbell (1972) called the "**cultic milieu.**" This social environment contains publics and collective behavioral audiences, as well as elaborate networks of seekers, practitioners, cults, sects, and collective movements.

A METHODOLOGY OF PARTICIPANT OBSERVATION

The methodology of participant observation I employed consists of principles and strategies for describing, analyzing, and interpreting human existence (Jorgensen, 1989; also see Bruyn, 1966; Speier, 1973; Johnson, 1975; Douglas, 1976; Marcus and Fisher, 1986; Denzin, 1989a). It takes as the paramount reality to be studied the experiences, meanings, and interactions of members (insiders or natives) of concrete situations and settings as viewed from their perspectives (see Schutz, 1967; Berger and Luckmann, 1966; Blumer, 1969; Douglas and Johnson, 1977). Participant observational inquiry is loosely focused and guided by general theoretical interests, casual, open-ended questions, and perhaps suspicions that constantly are subject to modification and change based on fieldwork. Specific preconceptions, prejudices, operational measures, as well as formal, definitive concepts, hypotheses, and explanatory theories are avoided, deliberately.

The researcher observes, interviews, and gathers rich, dense, highly detailed qualitative information in other ways, while cultivating trusting relationships, participating, and performing membership roles (see Adler and Adler, 1987; Geertz, 1973). Thick, descriptive interpretations, personal experiences, and other information, such as documents and artifacts, are recorded by way of fieldnotes, journals, analytic files, and other similar strategies. These materials are analyzed and interpreted constantly by way of an open-ended, dialectical process whereby study problems are defined, observed, analyzed, and interpreted repeatedly during fieldwork (Jorgensen, 1989; Denzin, 1989a). This hermeneutic process of discovery continues through the presentation of findings (see Agar, 1986; Becker, 1986; Geertz, 1988; Van Maanen, 1988). The ultimate goals of participant observational inquiry are to provide theoretical interpretations and understandings of human existence fully grounded in the experiences and meanings of societal members (see Glazer and Strauss, 1967; Douglas and Johnson, 1977).

At the outset of this inquiry I was incredibly naive about what I only much later learned to identify as "esoteric culture" and the "cultic milieu" (see Jorgensen, 1979). My original aim was to join a cult, but efforts to locate such a group resulted in a series of perceivedly unsuccessful starts. Eventually, other participants in this cultic environment defined me as a "**seeker**" (see Straus, 1976). Spontaneous performance of this nominal membership role enabled me to observe and casually ask questions without being too obtrusive. As a seeker, in other words, I was able to observe the cultic milieu, casually question people, and participate like other members without announcing my identity as a researcher. My use of this covert research strategy was an attempt to avoid disrupting the ordinary course of members' activities. In this way I encountered a bewildering array of beliefs, practices, practitioners, and cultic groups. Perplexed by this diversity, I began focusing attention on how these phenomena were related and organized socially. This initially practical fieldwork problem eventually was defined as a major theoretical issue worthy of systematic investigation.

During early explorations of the cultic milieu I was introduced to the occult tarot, and the divinatory use of these unique, pictorial cards. I received several readings of the tarot, leading members to define me as a "**client**." Performance of this membership role empowered me to observe and participate in members' activities more extensively and intensively. It opened up and enabled me to see portions of the insiders' world theretofore obscured from the standpoint of a seeker. Becoming more deeply involved, I decided to become an apprenticed "**student**" of the tarot so as to gain even more direct experiential access to the activities of practitioners and groups in what insiders' called the "esoteric community." Through these participant observational activities the occult tarot and its divinatory use become another basic axis of study.

Initiation to the occult tarot entitled me to become a "**professional practitioner**" of tarot divination in the community. This membership role provided a unique vantage point for experiencing and observing the insiders' world of meaning and interaction. I thereby was able to observe and experience the members' reality as a fully participating member. Performance of this role resulted in existential and self conflicts. I "became the phenomenon" of scholarly interest (Mehan and Wood, 1975), but I did not "go native" completely (as described more fully in Chapter Five). In performing the role of tarot card reader I passed as a member of the community, while sustaining a definition of myself as a sociologist, not an occultist.

In 1978 I left the setting of this fieldwork and concentrated on analyzing, interpreting, and writing up the results of this research. I struggled to reconcile the results of my fieldwork with seemingly relevant scholarly literature, and I expanded my previous study of esoteric and occult writings. As I gained greater distance from the fieldwork experience, it became easier to interpret my experiences and observations from a sociological perspective. Yet, sociological interpretation tends to distort and reify what I observed and experienced. I am convinced that the relationship between subject and object, knower and known, methods and findings, experiences and interpretations are linked in highly complex and inextricable ways. A literal account of these connections is impossible; but I will attempt to display, analyze, and interpret them so that you will be in a better position to evaluate my reading of esoteric culture, the cultic milieu, and the occult tarot.

EXPLORING THE CULTIC MILIEU

It is not insignificant that my intellectual interest in extraordinary claims to knowledge and socially marginal religious movements self-consciously derives in part from personal, biographical experiences (see Mills, 1959; Douglas and Johnson, 1977; Higgins and Johnson, 1988; Denzin, 1989a, 1989b). My ancestors were among the earliest converts to the new American religion formally instituted by Joseph Smith, Jr., in 1830.They participated in the Mormon experience on the American frontier, enduring hardships, trials, and persecution. Some of them succumbed to disease and the difficulties of frontier life, while others were murdered by intolerant American neighbors. With the assassination of their Prophet, they followed Brigham Young only to become bitterly divided by schismatic differences within this new religious movement (see Jorgensen, 1989, 1990a,1990b, 1990c, 1991).

As a participant in a variant of Mormonism I not infrequently experienced and observed "gifts of the spirit," such as "prophecies" and "healings" by ministerial laying on of hands. I sustained a cardinal identity as a "Josephite," at least until I converted to sociology in college.[2] Even today, this biographical identity as a Josephite Mormon intrudes into my consciousness, influences my thoughts, feelings, and existence. Inexorably it is part of my social history and who I am (see Jorgensen, 1990a).

At the outset of this inquiry my previous experiences were generalized as an interest in what I thought of as "extraordinary knowledge." What I had in mind was a study of some group in which people employed unconventional practices to claim knowledge of an extraordinary, non-empirical reality. I hoped to join such a group, participate in and observe the activities of its members. In this way I expected to focus attention on their accomplishment of extraordinary knowledge. Like other members of American culture I held stereotypical images of occultists based on movies, television, media reports, folklore, and exposure to scholarly literatures. Popular cultural images suggested irrational and mysterious beliefs, bizarre magical practices and rites, as well as odd and even deranged enthusiasts organized by way of highly secretive and sometimes criminal cults (see Shupe, 1981; Melton and Moore, 1982; Beckford, 1985). I suspected that these images distorted insiders' views of their activities, and I endeavored to suspend preconceptions about contemporary American occultists. I intended to experience and observe these beliefs, practices, and adherents' activities without hazardous prejudice about what I might find.

My interest in extraordinary knowledge claims was kindled during the summer of 1975 by a friend, Lin, who played an audio tape recording for me of a "channeling session." This session involved a small collection of people who met on an irregular basis to receive messages from a "spirit," or "multi-dimensional personality," through a trance medium. The "medium," I discovered, goes into a hypnotic trance and assents to a "spirit" who is presumed to communicate a message through her. Trance mediumship, I learned from scholarly writings, is common in many cultures, and readily observable in American spiritualism as well as other social contexts (see Bourguignon, 1973; Evans-Pritchard, 1973; Zaretsky, 1974). It has become popular in recent years within small cultic groups throughout the United States, partly by way of the writings of Jane Roberts (1970) who has attributed several books to Seth, the spirit who communicates through her.

With Lin's assistance I attempted to contact the informal leader of the spirit group, the chairperson of an academic department at the university. I had an opportunity to talk with the medium, a doctoral candidate at the university, later the next summer, but I was unable to arrange attendance at a channeling session as originally planned. While this group was not entirely covert, they were suspicious of outsiders. Not just anyone was invited to attend their activities. These experiences were informative. I was surprised that such well-educated people would be involved so deeply in something as seemingly "weird" as conversing with what they

ILLUSTRATION ONE: Star, *Gareth Knight Tarot Deck*. Reproduced by permission of U.S. Games Systems, Inc., Stamford, CT 06902 USA / Copyright © 1985 U.S. Games Systems, Inc. Further reproduction prohibited.

believed were spirits. My failure to gain entrée to the spirit group, however, demonstrated that this was a false start.

In December of 1975, I made a more solemn commitment to investigating the seemingly strange and obscure world of psychic phenomena, spirit entities, mysterious forces, magical practices, and hidden wisdoms. I was living in a large municipality in the northcentral United States and attending the University where I was a doctoral student in sociology. Since I had nearly completed my course work and planned on taking doctoral examinations during the summer, I was in search of a dissertation project. I therefore began looking for a group to study.

I had little idea about where to find individuals or collectivities involved in these seemingly strange beliefs and practices. I started by searching public sources of information, particularly directories in newspapers, telephone books, and magazines, but I found little useful information. I also began making contacts with people who I thought might be knowledgeable in such matters by raising the topic whenever the occasion permitted and sometimes when it did not. This led to some interesting encounters with people who shared personal experiences with me. Many of the people I met expressed more than casual interest in extraordinary phenomenon; some of them told me fantastic stories about such experiences; and several of them devoted substantial portions of their free time to seeking enlightenment or developing "psychic" powers. None of them, however, practiced with an organized group.

Since everyone knows that sociologists study "groups" rather than individuals, I labored under the idea that I needed to find an organized collection of people to study. During the 1970's there was a general, popular cultural perception that esoteric beliefs and groups abounded. I therefore found it more than a little disconcerting to be unable to locate even one cultic association suitable for study. Early in the spring of 1976 I began searching more actively for such an organization. Through Lin I learned of a study fellowship that held weekly meetings referred to as "Fireside E.S.P." Literature provided by the group listed three different sets of activities: evening meetings, self-help (training) workshops, and a full-time clinic service. It seemed to be exactly what I had been hoping to find.

During the next two months, I attended two evening meetings, talked with members, and collected literature about the group. The ESP fellowship consisted of four core members and an untold number of regular and semi-regular participants. The leaders, a married couple, supported themselves in part through group revenue, which included a two dollars per person "love offering" at weekly meetings, sixty-five dollars for a clinic treatment, and from forty to sixty dollars for special workshops. The predominant focus of all activities was summarized by the motto "making the able—more able." They subscribed to a baffling variety of esoteric doctrines concerning "vital energies, forces, and powers" to gain control of one's person. ESP was an obscure cult that no one had studied before, and it therefore met one of my consummate requirements for a study phenomenon.

I was disappointed, however, with what I observed. The ESP fellowship was not involved with anything that seemed to me especially out of the ordinary, including several demonstrations identified by members as "extra-sensory powers, gifts, or abilities." One evening, for instance, we joined hands in a circle and concentrated on generating a "psychic or spiritual force field" around the group. Later the leader rubbed his hands together, claimed to draw on psychic energies, and placed them on the bodies of willing members. They alleged feelings of physical relief, spiritual renewal, and psychic invigoration. His hands felt warm to me, but otherwise I did not even get a mild tingling sensation.

On another occasion, we employed a prism for occult purposes. Members were told to focus their attention on this translucent crystal, concentrate deeply until they envisioned unusual sensations, particularly colors. They were instructed to merge with this heightened state of consciousness, close their eyes, and enjoy an unusual adventure. Members found this psychic exercise exhilarating, and talked about it endlessly. I saw a few strange colors, but nothing more. Subsequently I realized that these indeed were actual demonstrations of extraordinary experience, even though they seemed pretty ordinary to me. At the time I was unable to envision them as especially exceptional.

On-going participation with the fellowship, it became clear, would require a considerable economic commitment. I also found this very disenchanting. My previous experiences suggested that spiritual enlightenment should not depend on dollars. I knew, of course, that more traditional religious organizations depended on the regular offerings of the membership. This situation, however, somehow seemed different. In the past, nobody ever charged me money for a prophecy, or a laying on of the hands, although I did tithe. In any case, I was not prepared to make the initial commitment of about one hundred dollars. I was planning on leaving this area within a few months anyway. Thinking I might go back sometime, I discontinued attending Fireside ESP.

Almost unknowingly I had observed several significant features of the esoteric scene. My experiences with the group were summarized in a field report and filed for later reference. Afterward, during my research in the Valley, I came to recognize features of the ESP group as significant and persistent dimensions of the larger esoteric scene in America. At the time, however, I regarded this portion of fieldwork as a false start and mostly worthless. And I hoped to do better in another field setting. The process whereby I gradually became a participant in the esoteric scene and learned employ occult ideas and practices for making sense of my experiences is described by Luhrmann (1989: Chapter 21) as "interpretative drift."

UNCOVERING NETWORKS OF OCCULTISTS

In August 1976 I moved to the Valley, a large metropolitan center in the southwestern United States. I had accepted a part-time lectureship at the University, and planned on working on my doctoral dissertation. More importantly, this move afforded me the opportunity to be with Lin, the friend with whom I had become involved romantically. I therefore did not select the Valley as a setting for study. I selected Lin and she happened to live in the Valley where I also was able to find meaningful employment.

Since the Valley contained an astounding and baffling variety of nonconventional beliefs, practices, believers, and groups, it turned out to be a good setting for this study. As a center of unconventional beliefs, practices, and groups in the United States, the Valley clearly is overshadowed by the West Coast, but it is not too dissimilar from several other regions of the country, such as the Southeast and East Coast. Insofar as there is greater esoteric and occult activity in the Valley than in other regions of the United States, it may not be typical or representative of the country as a whole. It was the wealth of esoteric and occult activities in this area, however, that made it an exceptionally good field setting for sociological study. In any case, I was primarily interested in the social meanings of esoteric culture, how it was organized socially, and how it was used by believers, not by how much of it existed or was distributed throughout the United States. Whether or not this setting somehow represented the entire country, I reasoned, simply could not be addressed until sometime later.

Almost immediately I began searching the Valley for individuals and groups to serve as the basis for study. I again started by examining telephone books and other sources of public information. I was not interested, however, in studying groups like Scientology or other well known (and well researched) groups that were identifiable in this way. I eventually learned some of the categories of practitioners and practices necessary for making this a useful strategy, but at the time these public sources of information largely were unproductive. I also began making personal contacts with Valley residents.

During the early phase of fieldwork in the Valley I entertained the possibility of focusing on mediumship and spirit communication. Several spiritualist meetings were listed in the telephone book. I attended spiritualist church meetings, undertook a preliminary analysis of spirit communication, and drafted a related proposal for my dissertation project. Once I read Zaretsky's (1974) excellent ethnography of spiritualism, however, I decided that I could contribute little new to this subject. The possibility of studying spiritualism, then, seemed to be another false start. It was, more or less, although I did encounter in this way some of the people and groups I would later recognize as part of the esoteric community.

My search for informants yielded several people knowledgeable about esotericism, including one of my students, Dee, who identified herself as a "witch." I subsequently learned to recognize many people like Dee as part of the larger cultic milieu, and occasional participants but not members of the esoteric community in the Valley. Dee was a thirty-five year old undergraduate student when I met her. She supported herself and two teenaged children with grants, loans, assistance from her family, and irregular child support from an ex-husband, earning about five thousand dollars in 1977. She owned a home, secured through her divorce, in a working to middle class neighborhood near the university. Dee was raised by her mother and stepfathers, and she had lived in the Valley her entire life. She claimed to have learned witchcraft at an early age from an aunt. Her mother reportedly possessed "psychic" abilities, but since her mother was a practicing Mormon she denied that these abilities were in any way related to occultism. Dee viewed witchcraft as her religion, and she regarded herself as very religious, very strong in her convictions, and devout. She claimed to meet occasionally with other witches in an isolated rural area of the Valley, but I was never able to confirm this contention.

Dee regarded herself as politically liberal; she was reasonably well informed about social and political issues; and while she was not especially active in particular political causes, Dee frequently voiced extremely liberal opinions on marriage, gender, sexuality, family, and economics. She used tobacco, marijuana, "downs," and expressed a willingness to ingest most any substance for the purpose of getting high. Dee dated casually; she reported being sexually involved with several men; and during the period I knew her she had a sexual affair with one of her daughter's boyfriends. This initially created considerable conflict and tension between them, but Dee eventually convinced her daughter that there was nothing improper about both of them being sexually involved with the same man. By the standards of many Americans Dee's life style was radically nonconformist and deviant, even for the 1970's.

Dee and her daughter both used witchcraft, including spells, incantations, potions, and various other forms of magic, to realize personal goals especially their romantic interests in men. They commonly attributed misfortunes and failures to fulfill personal goals to the evil deeds of others, their failure to employ witchcraft properly, or to assorted invisible forces and powers. In my discussions with Dee she frequently interpreted peoples' personalities and actions by reference to a folk astrology. She owned a few standard occult works on magic and witchcraft as well as several decks of tarot cards. Dee claimed to have learned tarot divination from her aunt. She used the tarot almost daily for making personal decisions; performed tarot divinations for family, friends, and acquaintances; and although she claimed to do tarot card readings for pay, I never observed her collecting money for these services.

Another person who provided useful information during the early stages of my fieldwork in the Valley was Kitty. She was a friend of Lin'; they met at the pre-school attended by their daughters. Kitty was twenty-eight years old, divorced, a high school graduate, and a long-time seeker of esoteric enlightenment who worked at low paying jobs while attending the university part-time. She was raised in an upper middle class home in an affluent section of the Valley, and reported being sexually abused and tramatized by her father as a child. Kitty used tobacco, drank alcohol mostly moderately, and occasionally smoked marijuana but otherwise avoided illegal drugs. She saw herself as politically liberal, regularly expressed feminist opinions, and lived a mostly conventional life style. During the period I knew her, Kitty had several casual boyfriends and she eventually became involved in a long-term relationship but declined a proposal of marriage.

While in high school Kitty embraced the hippie culture of the 1960's, and she eventually became interested in alternative forms of spirituality. She reported exploring various cultic groups in the Valley, and joined a local Hindu group as a casual participant for several years. She was knowledgeable about many of the central doctrines of Eastern religion, and she was especially cognizant about health, diet, and esoteric healing techniques. Several friends introduced her to Scientology, and she underwent auditing which eventuated in a conversion experience. After completing about a year of auditing she became an auditor and then enlisted in Scientology's Sea Organization. Kitty reportedly was assigned to L. Ron Hubbard's flag ship and briefly served as one of his personal attendants. In the Sea Organization, according to Kitty's account, she resented the lack of personal freedom, and she was punished several times for infractions of the rules. Terribly unhappy, she secretly left the ship and returned to the Valley by airplane with money wired from her mother. After several months, however, Scientologists convinced her to return. She moved to Los Angeles where she was employed full-time by Scientology. Shortly thereafter she became pregnant, but declined to name or marry the baby's father; and once again she experienced disillusionment with Scientology. When she attempted to leave Kitty claimed that the Scientologists prohibited it and locked her in a room for several days until she agreed to stay. By her account, she covertly escaped, returned to the Valley, and had her baby.

When I interacted with Kitty she had completely disassociated herself from Scientology, although she still maintained a strong belief in many of its basic teachings and practices. She casually participated in the cultic milieu, frequented occult book and supply stores, read esoteric literature, maintained contact with close friends who were members of Eastern religious groups, and sometimes went to a medical clinic which was part of the esoteric community. Lin and Kitty sometimes used the occult tarot for divining the future and making decisions.

Dee, Kitty, and other people like them provided me with extensive information about their personal experiences as well as the activities of friends, associates, and acquaintances. Though interesting, this information was too anecdotal and unreliable for my purposes. My effort to follow up leads on groups and practitioners frequently produced wild chases and dead ends. Through these exploratory activities I learned of several esoteric and occult bookstores in the Valley. This turned out to be a major breakthrough in my early fieldwork.

My "discovery" of these specialty shops provided the initial key to generating substantial information about esoteric practitioners and groups. Book titles and other objects for sale provided a preliminary indication of the diffuse array and range of topics included in this cultural domain, as well as some of the connections among them. What I did not see also provided an indication of what was not included. In book and supply stores I found bulletin boards and business cards advertising meetings, gatherings, special events, and the services of occult experts. I collected this information and asked store personnel about other activities. I began recording this intelligence in the form of a card index of people and groups encountered in this way. Consequently, I deliberately began to develop a sense of the nature and extent of esoteric and occult activities in the Valley. At the time my purpose in collecting this information was to find a particular group to study. It was not until later that I started to realize that the cultic milieu itself might be a worthy topic of research and reporting.

In a relatively short period of time I found that my knowledge had increased to the extent that previous informants were unable to supply useful information about this concrete scene. I continued to use them as a source of communication, and to verify intelligence, including checking their reliability as informants; but it increasingly became apparent that I was able to generate more and better details through my own resources. I also had begun to identify several people, including a bookstore owner, as potential new informants. Retrospectively, I regarded this as a turning point in my fieldwork, a point of replacing previous informants with new and better ones, and becoming increasingly independent.

My most important "discovery" in Valley bookstores was a "spiritual" and a "psychic" directory of individuals and groups. The psychic directory was especially useful since it was published along with articles and other sources of information in a community bulletin, *Psychic Magazine*. Distributed locally, this periodical contained a host of titillating and worthwhile material. It incorporated brief articles on topics like astrology, numerology, psychic personalities, happenings on the national and local scene, and predictions about the future. There were advertisements for a wide variety of books, supplies, and services ranging from international travel, places of special esoteric interest, and study groups to quaint healing preparations, lessons in the occult arts and sciences, and even esoteric birth control devices.

More significantly, *Psychic Magazine* published a directory to about seventy groups in the Valley ranging from unorthodox religions, quasi-religious cults and study groups to esoteric medical clinics and an occult university. It listed future events and activities in the local area, a well as people offering "professional services" ranging from astrology, life, clairvoyant, psychic, and tarot readings to consciousness auditing, dream analysis, healing, hypnosis, and yoga. These lists of groups and practitioners were extremely consequential for my apprehension of this scene generally. They also provided addresses, telephone numbers, and identifying labels helpful for making subsequent contacts and indicating categories of meaning used by insiders. The idea of studying the cultic milieu and related networks of participants and groups more systematically thereby became increasingly attractive.

BECOMING A MEMBER OF THE ESOTERIC COMMUNITY

The apparent renaissance of esotericism and occultism during the late 1960's and 1970's aroused an enormous response on the part of journalists, scholars, and various other experts. Shocked that modern Americans would be attracted to such antiquated and alien beliefs and practices, studies and reports of these phenomena proliferated. My efforts to grasp the insiders' worlds of meaning more fully led to an examination of frequently mentioned texts, literature in related specialty book stores, and successively the writings of journalists, historians, sociologists, and a host of other exoteric experts and scholars (as discussed below).

As I examined this literature casually while conducting fieldwork, I found that very few experts took Americans' esotericism and occultism seriously. They exhibited little sensitivity to adherents' convictions, and generally avoided researching the cultic milieu in depth. With rare exceptions the responses of experts remained ignorant of the considerable history of esotericism and occultism in Western culture generally, and American culture in particular. Experts' explanations of this revival frequently dismissed societal members' claims to knowledge and related activities, out of hand, as too ridiculous for serious study or examination. Efforts to examine them more seriously commonly explained members' claims and activities away from particular scientific standpoints. Popular images and the contentions of experts served as questions to be studied and ways of analyzing emergent fieldwork products. I was not attempting to confirm or refute their arguments and views; yet I thought it would be useful to examine them critically. My principal aim and preoccupation was to experience the insiders' world of meaning directly.

In *Psychic Magazine* I found an announcement for an upcoming "psychic fair." In late October 1976 I attended the first of many such fairs. This proved to be an excellent opportunity to observe a wide variety of Valley practitioners doing everything from metaphysical healing, astral travel, and psychic art to reading palms, the tarot, and tea leaves. At fairs I had opportunities to observe first hand and talk casually with many of the practitioners. These experiences, more than anything else, destroyed many of the stereotypical images I previously held about these people from watching movies and TV, listening to news reports of strange cults, and reading social scientific literature about socially deprived and psychically depraved members of socially marginal movements.

By November 1976 I had accumulated considerable information about collectivities in the Valley. The information I previously recorded on cards was supplemented by data from the directories. In this manner I constructed an extensive list of collectivities and practitioners. This knowledge, in turn, served as a starting point for my subsequent investigation of specific activities. In the course of assembling these lists I began to develop a sense of who was involved, their connections with particular collectivities, the activities of these groups, people performing leadership roles, and interconnections among groups. I eventually realized that part of what I had uncovered was what members called the "esoteric community." At the time, finding out exactly what members' meant by reference to the "esoteric community" became a basic study problem.

Before my participation in fairs, I unintentionally performed a participant observational role as a "**seeker**." The seeker role, I later learned, is familiar to insiders and many outsiders (see Straus, 1976; Balch and Taylor, 1977a). To be a seeker one need only appear at esoteric gatherings, ask questions, engage in discussion, and most importantly demonstrate a serious and sincere interest in what is happening. Like the potential convert to exoteric religion, the seeker is welcome at most esoteric events, and a variety of special activities are designed especially for seekers. In salient ways, seeking is a generic feature of this scene. It is not unusual for someone to be labeled and identified as an adept by other members, if they are able to sustain such an identity socially. But it is considered pretentious from the standpoint of the ethos of esoteric culture to claim adepthood for oneself. Mastery of esoteric bodies of knowledge generally is accompanied by the realization of one's limitations. To claim adepthood is to risk the ridicule of the community, unless such a powerful knowledge can be demonstrated dramatically. Most scene participants are labeled and regarded as seekers of esoteric knowledge.

My entrée into the community and performance of the seeker role constituted a **covert** research strategy; that is, I deliberately did not tell people I was doing research. Although the ethics of covert participant observation sometimes are questioned (Gold, 1958), I strongly believe that it is a defensible approach under many circumstances (also see Douglas, 1976). None of the people or groups with whom I interacted were treated as "subjects" in the ordinary, social scientific sense

ILLUSTRATION TWO: Knight of Swords, *New Tarot Deck*. Reproduced by permission of Taroco, Sausalito, CA 94965 USA. Copyright © 1974 William J. Hurley and J.A. Horler. Further reproduction prohibited.

of this word. I was sincerely interested in esoteric beliefs and activities, even though I also was gathering information for sociological purposes.

Much of my observation and data collection occurred in public settings, like psychic fairs, and I conformed to the interactional rules established by participants in these situations. I, for example, paid for all of the tarot readings collected in the course of this inquiry. I did not manipulate the people with whom I interacted beyond the sort of manipulative exchanges that otherwise are a normal feature of everyday life and these situations. Indeed, many of the fronts presented and used by members were far more deceptive than any of the strategies I employed to penetrate them.

There was no reason for me to suspect that any possible harm, including reputational damage, might come to the people or groups with whom I interacted. Even today it would be extremely difficult for anyone except for the core members of the community to concretely identify the specific people and groups reported herein. I was gradually and naturally accepted and identified by members of the community as a seeker. Unless social researchers are free to employ covert strategies, at least during preliminary stages of fieldwork in relatively unfamiliar territory, meaningful inquiry will be impossible. Its products, moreover, will hopelessly risk confusing private, backstage realities of social existence with public fronts and scenes (Douglas, 1976).

Ultimately, the ethics of covert fieldwork simply cannot be legislated beforehand by self-appointed individuals or bureaucratic committees of the academy or government. These decisions are too complex, too situational, and entirely dependent on the honesty, good will, and responsibility of people doing research (see Jorgensen, 1989). In short, then, the ethics of fieldwork are and must be an ongoing problem. Ethics, in other words, are part of the task and conduct of participant observational inquiry. Ethics necessarily depend on the ethos of the community of fieldwork practitioners (see Johnson and Altheide, 1990b).

My participant observational role as a seeker in the community progressively was transformed. As a regular participant in the community who frequented particular practitioners and groups I came to be regarded by insiders as a particular kind of seeker: as a **client** and **student** of the tarot. These differences in my membership roles, the movement from seeker to client and from client to student, were subtle in many ways. Yet this transition involved noticeable changes in terms of how I was regarded and treated by natives. As a native seeker I was one of many different faces that come and go in the community. As a client and student people recognized and greeted me with familiarity. I thereby was able to develop emergent and ongoing interpersonal relationships with them. They no longer treated me as someone to whom even the most basic aspects of esoteric culture had to be explained. And, even more crucially, they came to see me and treat me as **socially located** in the context of familiar networks of relationship within the community.

Participant observer roles of client and student afforded me a more penetrating look at the community. Yet they also limited the nature and kind of questions I could raise. Questions I asked as a seeker pertinent to sociological research could be justified, easily, as naive. As a client and student I was supposed to know more and consequently raising research issues sometimes provoked suspicion about my motives. As my relationships with members of the community became more intimate and in situations where I needed to ask pertinent research questions, I began, very selectively, to acknowledge and explain my investigation to them.

Initially I feared that revealing myself in this way might led to a widespread knowledge of this study, thereby limiting what I could observe and who would talk candidly with me. This apprehension, interestingly, was unjustified. People talked about me, especially with reference to the activities in which I was engaged as a member. To the best of my knowledge, however, there was little discussion of this research project in the community. I see this as a reflection of my having established trusting relationships. Insofar as the people whom I selectively told of my research discussed it with other members, they apparently also did so discriminatingly and under conditions of trusting those whom were told. The importance of trust in fieldwork, as has been articulated so eloquently by Johnson (1975), seems to be a condition that commonly is passed from one relationship to subsequent relationships and interactions.

During the early stages of this study of esotericism in the Valley I encountered the occult tarot for the first time. Lin became interested in these picturesque cards and purchased a pack in an occult bookstore. She located several manuals describing how to use tarot cards, particularly for divinatory purposes, and she began learning their arcane wisdom. Though highly skeptical of claims to portending the future, I was enamored with the symbolism and artistic renderings of the cards. Within a short period of time we added several more tarot packs to what would become a fattened collection.

In February 1977 I began seriously to consider following Lin's lead, and partly by reference to her experiences, making the tarot a focus of my research. In spite of Lin's encouragement and cogent arguments in favor of this, I was hesitant. To do an adequate study of the occult tarot appeared to involve an overwhelming task of learning its esoteric teachings, as well as techniques for interpreting the wisdom of the cards. Tarot divination usually is not a group activity, and I still labored under the belief that sociological research should concentrate on some form of an organized group.

I eventually resolved this dilemma, though not without conflict and doubt, by convincing myself that the occult tarot was a worthy topic and a useful focal point for my study. Just because tarot activity did not conform to my expectations and original study plan—to become a member of a cult—did not seem sufficient to avoid it. Reflecting on the esoteric activities I had observed in the Valley, I realized that the tarot, a particular body of occult wisdom used for the purposes of divination, meditation, and study, was thoroughly characteristic of this scene.

Edward Tiryakian (1974:18) observed that the occult tarot commonly has been viewed as a key to all arcane wisdom, "perhaps *the* synthesis of esoteric culture." Robert Ellwood and Harry Partin (1988), following Mircea Eliade (1964), argued that "shamanism," a more general label under which divinatory uses of the tarot might be grouped, is a principal feature of esoteric culture. As magic, the tarot might have been part of Max Weber's (1963) highly influential analysis of the role of charisma in religion. In short, then, the occult tarot gradually, doubtfully, and conflictually but defensibly became a focus of my inquiry.

During the winter of 1977, as will be discussed more fully in Chapter Five, I began learning the arcane wisdom of the occult tarot. I started by studying classic, and not so classic, literature on the topic. I practiced reading the cards or using them in a divinatory fashion. Eventually, I received instructions from tarot card readers whom I had observed using the cards for prognosticating. Learning the tarot placed me directly and intensively in contact with key figures in the esoteric community. Most importantly, it provided members with a means for accounting for my presence, and an indication that I was a sincere seeker of esoteric knowledge. Eventually, my use of the tarot lead me to participate in psychic fairs where I read the tarot for pay. Members of the esoteric community thereby defined and identified me as a diviner of the tarot, and a fully participating member of the community.

In addition to participant observation, my fieldwork included a systematic survey of individuals and groups in the Valley. The largest portion of this inquiry was conducted by telephone. I attempted to contact all of the groups and individuals not otherwise known to me when I had intelligence about names, addresses, and phone numbers. Through these interviews I requested a brief description of beliefs and activities, as well as asked whether or not I was welcome at group functions. This information was recorded and filed, along with any other data I had collected on the group, such as advertisements, mailings, or literature. Appendix A illustrates the basic form of this survey of community groups.

By the end of the study I was able to collect some information on approximately 100 groups or collectivities involving an estimated 5,000 to 15,000 people, as well as 125 practitioners (also see Jorgensen, 1982; Jorgensen and Jorgensen, 1982). Interestingly, less than one-half of these groups are included in the national directories used by Stark, Bainbridge, and Doyle (1979) in their **quantitative** study of cults. The reason for this is fairly simple. While most of groups missed by Stark, Bainbridge, and Doyle are public and visible locally, they are not readily discernible to outsiders without information about where to look for them. They generally are not listed under cults or other headings, in the yellow pages, and they generally are not included in national directories of psychic, occult, esoteric, or pagan organizations.

Telephone interviews, like most survey research strategies, are of limited value unless accompanied by previous or subsequent relationships. They generally provide potentially significant but very superficial knowledge. My phone conversations provided important data. In this way I was able to determine where the group was located (when this was previously unknown); if the group even existed (some groups spring up and disappear almost overnight); who the key leaders and members were; basic beliefs and practices, as well as other details, such as interpersonal networks of relationship and related professional practitioners, about the group. In most cases people were very willing to talk with me by phone, and even though they usually were told of my research interests, they frequently treated me as a potential recruit. Their willingness to talk with me commonly derived in part from my familiarity with membership activities in the community, including mutual friends and acquaintances. In many instances people volunteered information about relationships with other individuals and groups in the community, sometimes candidly expressing prejudices and politics.

I endeavored to follow up telephone interviews at psychic fairs where I met and talked with the leaders and members of these groups. In some cases I listened to formal presentations by these people. Over the course of fieldwork in the Valley I attended the activities of more than twenty groups, not counting the bookstores which I frequented regularly. Supplementary knowledge about groups and individuals in the community was acquired through secondhand reports by students, friends, and members of the community. I was able to rely extensively on key informants, including several who were key figures in the community, such as the publisher of *Psychic Magazine*, for information about these people and activities.

Collecting reliable and valid information from key informants was made possible by having previously established trusting relations with them. Lin and I, moreover, had become socially located and identified as tarot diviners. Even after my research interests were known, people in the community generally introduced and referred to us as tarot card readers, not sociological researchers. During the later portion of this investigation, we were married by a female minister in a group within the community. The importance of establishing social location and identity within the natural routine of the field setting cannot be overestimated.

In addition to collecting details about groups and organizations in the community, I constructed a card index of people known as "professional practitioners." Many of the approximately 125 people in this category were not regular participants in the community, and it consequently proved impossible to gather data systematically on all of them. I was able to gather bits and pieces of information pertinent to about half of them. About 50 of these people used the tarot at some time as a service to other people, usually for pay. Lin and I talked informally with them or gathered information about all of them during our fieldwork. Formal, indepth interviews, several of which ran almost four hours, were conducted mostly by Lin with twenty tarot card readers (see Appendix B). The remaining readers were unreachable, unwilling to be interviewed formally, in transition from this area to other parts of the country, temporarily involved with other activities, or changing from tarot readings to another type of practice.

From the fall of 1977 throughout the next year I continuously sustained close friendships with several leaders of the esoteric community. We frequently interacted in one anothers' homes. Social evenings provided excellent, largely unobtrusive situations for building further upon these relationships and collecting a detailed knowledge of the community. In time friendship with some of these people became primary to research. Since most of these informants were highly supportive of this research I rarely experienced conflict over these dual purposes. During this period of fieldwork, the internal dynamics of the community were examined intensely.

Differences between Lin's entrée, roles, and experience of self and mine provide important insights into fieldwork and reflect on the materials collected. Although Lin, too, initially was a seeker, she quickly became a student and reader of the occult tarot. In acquiring the reader identity, she received the assistance of other tarot card readers. They served as teachers, people to whom she could refer in other interactions, and ultimately as sponsors of her community membership. My acceptance in the community was facilitated greatly by Lin's identity and membership. Many of my contacts were impersonal and businesslike, while Lin's were more intimate and personal. While insiders viewed me as a potential member in a variety of different settings, Lin was identified and accepted as a tarot practitioner in specific interactional situations and settings.

These different routes into the community involved substantially different experiences of selfhood. Lin's experience was highly authentic, and it resulted in little role or identity strain. My experience of an occult identity was conflictual, strained and less than unequivocal. I commonly was caught, existentially, between a dual commitment to becoming a member of the community and doing fieldwork. I also came to detest the diviner role. By most indications I capably managed the **performance** of these roles. I also learned to manage the resulting tension, but it was a recurrent problem from the standpoint of my **identity**. This problem, though present, was much less pronounced for Lin, and she was more able to make a sincere commitment to learning the arcane wisdom of the tarot, and using it seriously. In turn, differences in these self commitments were reflected in conversations and interactions with members of the community. Part of my success in gaining access to the insiders' world of meaning was due to Lin's highly authentic commitment, and members' identification of us as a couple.

In the course of fieldwork in the community I vaguely was aware of gender roles and their consequences. Seekers are more likely to be females than males. Unlike the exoteric society, women in the esoteric community tend to be regarded, more consensually and completely, as fully equal participants. Women are esteemed as among the very best professional practitioners, and they commonly perform critical leadership roles as ministers and leaders of particular groups. Partly because men are less likely to be seekers as well as clients and students, I suspect that my participation was perceived to be valuable by members of the community.

We did not deliberately cultivate gender differences as strategies for conducting research. There were, however, at least several advantages to this team research method. Being socially identified as a couple meant that members were less likely to attach sexual implications to our interactions. Clearly, this simplified my interactions with female diviners and other male and female members of the community. Participating and observing as a couple also supplied us with important, but not uncommonly subtle differences in perspective, thereby providing a more balanced knowledge. At the time we did not focus or dwell on these gender differences specifically, but retrospectively I have come to see them as significant.

The information the researcher is able to gather in the field depends on where she or he is located with respect to the phenomenon of interest (see Jorgensen, 1989). In some settings an investigator may be able to gain access to the insiders' world by being identified as a researcher. It may be possible to observe and even directly experience the phenomenon of interest from this standpoint (see Berger, 1981). In other settings, however, access to the insiders' world of meaning cannot be accomplished without direct experiential access to this world. And in these settings direct access may be denied to the researcher by self or others without a total commitment to membership (see Rambo, 1989). Membership in the esoteric community clearly enhanced my ability to observe and experience the insiders' world of meaning and action.

My capability of sustaining friendly relations with some people in the community became more problematic as Lin and I were identified as tarot card readers and thereby linked to particular people, segments, networks, and politics. Discussions with a spokesperson of a particular constellation of groups—their beliefs, practices, activities, and goals—on one occasion were followed by similar discussions with the leader of a rival segment of the community. I compounded this inherent problem by playing sources of information against one another. Though invaluable as a strategy of reliability checking, in so doing I risked revealing friendships with factional leaders and members, and alienating potential informants. As Lin and I became more and more intimately located within a particular segment of the community, it became increasingly difficult to sustain relations with rival factions and leaders. Ultimately, I was forced to choose between two rival segments in the community.

The incident provoking this choice emerged when we were asked to read the tarot, on a voluntary, as opposed to a paid, basis for a minifair sponsored by a coalition of groups constituting a particular confederation in the community. The paramount issue separating these factions was the commercial aspects of the esoteric scene in the Valley. The affiliated networks of practitioners we were asked to read for opposed commercialism, believing the tarot to be a tool for spiritual and self enlightenment. Readers were supposed to be responsible for serving the needs of others without regard for financial arrangements. We agreed to read the tarot for free, and assumed the minister in charge would contact us with final arrangements, such as the time, place, hours, and so on.

In the confusion of a busy weekend we did not remember our agreement until the event was almost over. Talking over the situation we decided that something must have come up and the church sponsoring the minifair had not required our services, since no one had contacted us. We forgot the matter until a week later when the minister called. Upon answering the phone I immediately sensed something was wrong. The minister proceeded to demand hostilely why we had not showed up as expected at the minifair. I explained that we had assumed that we were not needed. Lin also attempted to discuss the problem with him. With anger and resentment, the minister questioned our commitments and sense of responsibility.

Prior to this incident the minister had visited our home several times and a period of growing friendship had followed. Even under the circumstance his behavior seemed out of the ordinary. Only later did we discover that he interpreted our behavior in the context of our participating in fairs for pay. He had come to identify us with the rival alliances in the community and assumed we missed his fair because we could not gain financially from it. This occurred toward the end of my fieldwork and it had little effect on subsequent data collection. It, however, did prevent me from directly collecting subsequent information from this assembly of groups and practitioners in the community. More importantly, it resulted in some emotional trauma, estrangement, and a loss of friendship.

ANALYZING AND INTERPRETING FIELDWORK PRODUCTS

In the spring of 1978 I accepted an academic position at a large state university in the southeastern United States. My fieldwork in the Valley, consequently, was drawn to a close. For a few years I maintained periodic contact with several of my best friends in the esoteric community. I missed them and our friendship. Although I found fieldwork exciting, challenging, and generally rewarding, I welcomed relief from the day to day stress and strain of conducting research.

I had little difficulty in relinquishing my fieldwork identity as a diviner of the occult tarot. As will be discussed more fully in Chapter Five, I rarely enjoyed the tarot card reading role. It was for me an arduous, formidable, and anxiety producing situation. While I did not find reading the tarot as such to be unduly demanding, divining for someone in particular was vexatious and onerous for me. I worried constantly that people might take me too seriously, or worse yet actually make important existential decisions after consulting with me.

After 1978 I casually inquired into the esoteric scene in the Southeast, and I was interested to find that in many ways it closely resembled what I had observed in the Valley. As part of university courses I teach on the esoteric scene, new religious movements, and the sociology of religion my students have conducted participant observational studies of multifarious beliefs, practices, and groups in the local area.[3] Some of these investigations inform this book. Although my direct participation in the esoteric scene did not continue, I have sustained an interest in esoteric and occult thought. Parts of this book therefore reflect this subsequent research, particularly my use of the archival materials of the Institute for the Study of American Religion in Chicago during 1985.

As I gained greater distance from the field, I found it easier and easier to bring an analytic, sociological perspective to what I had observed. While I was immersed in the members' world it was difficult to see clearly many of the issues which I subsequently identified as sociologically important. Fieldwork involved flipping in and out of observing, participating, describing, analyzing, and interpreting. During fieldwork my primary commitment was to observing, participating and describing. Analysis and interpretation were undertaken principally as a way of gaining sufficient clarity, sociologically, to engage in further observation, participation, and description. Analysis and interpretation are facilitated greatly by having co-workers to talk with, and especially by discussions with outsiders who are able to raise provocative sociological questions. Leaving the field, however, freed me from the primary tasks of fieldwork, and permitted me to concentrate on analyzing and interpreting. In my experience, gaining greater existential distance from the field enabled me to focus and concentrate on sociological issues and discern their relevancy to one another and some larger picture. Writing up findings fundamentally involves further analysis and interpretation, and it therefore greatly accelerates this process.

The analyses and interpretations presented by writing also contain inherent dangers. Through this process the experiences and activities of insiders' are translated into matters of sociological concern, and these concerns are sometimes confused with what they describe. My treatment of categories of membership in the esoteric community, for instance (see Chapter Three), ultimately depends on highly rationalistic, conceptual devices. Although grounded in members' words and meanings, it reflects a sociological interest in these phenomena, not necessarily the interests of insiders, and consequently it reifies them. Members might write a book about the esoteric community, but it probably would not be a sociology, and certainly it would not be this book. The categories and meanings derived from my fieldwork are observable. The appropriateness of my distinctions was checked with members repeatedly, as well as by listening to their talk and observing their activities. Whenever possible I employ words and expressions used by insiders in the ways that they use them, but these people commonly use a variety of expressions to describe their experiences and activities, sometimes inconsistently. In some cases I use vocabulary rarely if ever used by members to convey distinctions they make. The point is that the experiences, symbolizations, and interactions of insiders transpire in an exceptionally complex, conceptually messy, oftentimes unclear and even confusing everyday life world. This world of lived experience and activity should not be confused with my efforts to present it, clearly, distinctly, and precisely as a matter of sociological interest.

The theoretical framework underlying the presentation of these materials, as developed in the next chapter, is a sociology of culture and knowledge (see, especially, Berger, 1967; Berger and Luckmann, 1966; Blumer, 1969, 1990; Cicourel, 1973; Denzin, 1989a; Douglas and Johnson, 1977; Garfinkel, 1967; Geertz, 1973; Goffman, 1959, 1974; McCall and Becker, 1990; Schutz, 1967). It takes as the fundamental reality to be described, analyzed, and interpreted whatever it is that people experience and define as reality and, thereby, claim to know. In this view, every description of reality is an interpretation of it from some perspective. There are no facts or objective realities apart from human interpretation of them. All interpretations, in this sense, are equally real, and they possess real human consequences. Interpretations are unique to and dependent on particular social, cultural, and historical perspectives and circumstances. This is not to say that all interpretations and perspectives are equally plausible or adequate.

Sociological interpretations, like those of other human studies, are pertinent to a distinctive order of reality: They are interpretations of the interpretations of societal members; or, in other words, they are second order interpretations of first order interpretations (Schutz, 1967). The plausibility and adequacy of sociological interpretations therefore are evaluated in terms of how well they describe and display the members' interpretations of reality. While this is by no means a simple matter, there are several bases for these judgments. Descriptions based on direct experience with, participation in, and firsthand observation of societal members' beliefs, practices, and activities are better than ones derived in other ways. Descriptions expressed in the language of natives and displaying their voice are better than descriptions expressed in other ways. Richly detailed, thick descriptions are better than less detailed, thin descriptions. Descriptions that are recognizable to members as reflections of what they think, feel, and do generally are better than descriptions that members are unable to acknowledge in this way. Descriptions that enable an outsider to act like and pass as a member further suggest considerable plausibility and adequacy.

Sociological interpretations, however, generally aim to do more than describe reality as it is experienced and enacted by societal members. That is, they aim to present the members' reality in terms of some abstract, general model, perspective, or theory related to sociological traditions and communities. Theorizing, in turn, is expected to illuminate some portion of the human condition to enhance sociological understanding of it. Interpretative adequacy and plausibility therefore are evaluated further in terms of an ability to illuminate human affairs and enhance sociological understanding of existential conditions. Seen in this way, sociological interpretations are not substitutes for, corrective of, or superior to societal members' interpretations (see Garfinkel, 1967).

During my fieldwork, as previously noted, I examined experts' efforts to interpret and explain esotericism and occultism. These writings were helpful; yet I found little agreement among experts, and in many ways their interpretations were as confounding as what they endeavored to explain. I found, for instance, little scholarly agreement over inclusive phenomena, similarities and differences among them, definitions, fundamental study problems, or relevant theoretical perspectives. Scholarly views, not uncommonly, grossly contradicted or otherwise failed to describe what I had experienced and observed in the cultic milieu.

Prior to the late 1960's, scholarly study of unconventional beliefs, practices, activities, and groups in contemporary Western societies was highly sporadic and it rarely was defined as a fundamental intellectual interest by more than a few people. Earlier philosophical, historical, and anthropological studies tended rigidly and sharply to distinguish the beliefs and practices of primitive, premodern peoples from those found in modern cultures. Social studies of beliefs overwhelmingly focused on socially conventional bodies of knowledge, such as religion as defined by orthodox churches. While new, nontraditional religions attracted attention it was because they were perceived as anomalies, and they generally were regarded as less than socially and culturally significant as anything else. Sociological investigations tended to treat unconventional religious or scientific beliefs of contemporary peoples in Western societies as extreme oddities and forms of deviance.

The perception of a massive revival of esoteric and occult beliefs in Western societies during the late 1960's attracted attention precisely because it seemed so strange to scholarly experts. A powerful underlying theme of pertinent scholarship was amazement, surprise, and incredulity that contemporary Americans would subscribe seriously in apparently large numbers to what were regarded as highly unconventional, deviant, archaic, irrational, anti-scientific, nonsensical, or outright stupid beliefs and practices. This theme reflects the widespread assumption of scholars that through modernization American culture and society, including traditional religions, had become increasingly rational, secular, and scientific. Scholarly study of esotericism and occultism was motivated implicitly by an almost compulsive concern for explaining these phenomena away, and thereby defending vested interests in modernism, especially a scientific worldview.

Scientists and other scholarly experts formed associations aimed at debunking esoteric and occult claims to knowledge (see, for instance, Grim, 1982). Psychiatrists and other experts frequently were among the leaders of the subsequent anti-cult movement (see Bromley and Shupe, 1981; Shupe, 1981; Melton and Moore, 1982;

Beckford, 1985; Bromley and Hammon, 1987). Although these activities generally did not reflect serious efforts to study esotericism and occultism in a scholarly way, they reflected experts' views of these phenomena, and they reinforced and were reinforced by serious research. A considerable body of scholarly literature exhibited a scientific preoccupation with the validity of members' claims to knowledge. These claims were dismissed on many different grounds, as gullible, faddish, archaic, anti-scientific, invalid scientifically, lacking collective support, or as instances of con artistry and trickery (see, for example, Bainbridge and Stark, 1979; Benassi et al., 1980; Felson and Gmelch, 1979; Fischler, 1974; Hyman, 1977; Stachnik and Stachnik, 1980; Stark and Bainbridge, 1979, 1980; Tatro, 1974; Truzzi, 1972a, 1974, 1975, 1978; Weiman, 1982). The central points of this perspective on esotericism and occultism were that members' claims to knowledge are not grounded in any material reality known to science, much of it is not socially supported, and many of these claims are self-consciously fraudulent. Members' claims and activities thereby could be dismissed or easily explained away.

There are fundamental problems with this general perspective as a sociological interpretation of esotericism and occultism. It fails to consider adequately the sometimes important role of popular culture and collective behavior in mass movements, their reflection of larger sociocultural processes, and their potential for sociocultural change. To reject unconventional beliefs and practices as non-scientific or unscientific is not very informative. Such an approach fails to consider that even if mistaken, these beliefs and practices hold important consequences for adherents, their activities, and possibly for the larger culture and society (see Blumer, 1969; Berger and Luckmann, 1966; Schutz, 1967; Thomas and Thomas, 1928). It also reflects an unjustified scientific arrogance regarding the superiority of scientific rationality and ontologies over and against other ways of knowing and other views of reality (see Altheide and Johnson, 1979; Cicourel, 1973; Douglas and Johnson, 1977; Garfinkel, 1967; Garfinkel et al., 1981; Livingston, 1982; Mehan and Wood, 1975; Pickering, 1984; Pinch, 1982a, 1982b; Winch, 1958, 1964; Wittgenstein, 1968).

A closely related, distinctively sociological perspective focused specific attention on social functional and structural conditions related to the emergence and development of unconventional beliefs and marginal movements, as well as social psychological processes whereby people are attracted to these beliefs and join groups or movements. This perspective generally leads to the conclusion that socially unconventional beliefs, movements, and their adherents are a reflection of deviance, alienation, deprivation, or mental illness (see Adorno, 1974; Benyon, 1938; Catton, 1957; Dohrman, 1958; Eister, 1972; Festinger et al., 1956; Foranaro, 1973; Harder and Richardson, 1972; Johnson, 1963; Jones, 1981; Lofland and Stark, 1965; Lofland, 1966; Mauss and Petersen, 1973; Petersen and Mauss, 1973; Prince, 1974; Quarantelli and Wenger, 1973; Robbins, 1969, 1973; Shepherd, 1972; Staude, 1970; Wilson, 1970; Wuthnow, 1978). Recent efforts to synthesize deprivation and social exchange (or rational choice) into a theory of religion (Stark and Bainbridge, 1980, 1985, 1987) also falls within this general line of thought (see Chapter Three).

This general theoretical perspective also is defective as an adequate sociological interpretation of esotericism. Most of these theoretical contentions are incorrigible propositions (Mehan and Wood, 1975). Social structural stress and change, social deprivation, social exchanges, and the rest, are defined and manipulated in such a way as always to be discoverable. These supposedly scientific contentions therefore rarely are falsifiable. They simply label phenomena in a highly tautological fashion. The model of the human actor underlying these perspectives reduce societal members to judgmental dopes (Garfinkel, 1967), and it fails to relate human actions adequately to social structural conditions. Whatever social actors do is mediated by largely a priori concepts of scientists about what it really means. What scientists see is not social meaning from the actors' perspective, but their own reflections.

Along with popular cultural images, these theoretical perspectives generally are alien to the sociocultural world they attempt to explain. They consequently distort the beliefs and activities of practitioners in identifiable ways. In so doing, these perceptions serve the ambitions of publics, experts, and interest groups. Since popular and scholarly images are useful for these purposes, efforts to correct them are pointless and futile. They commonly are uninteresting as sociological interpretations of insiders' beliefs and activities, but these cultural images are highly consequential, sociologically, as the reactions of outsiders. They sometimes are discussed in this way here. Some of these specific contentions also are discussed in subsequent chapters for the purpose of clearly distinguishing my arguments from other viewpoints and perspectives.

Still another general theoretical perspective is evident in the writings of sociologists. It tends to exhibit greater sensitivity for members' beliefs and practices, as sociohistorical products, seeing them as efforts to make sense out of human existence. Members' activities, in this view, tend to be seen and interpreted as countercultural reactions to modern society, critiques or rejections of rationalization and secularization, sometimes leading to new social forms (see Collins, 1977; Eglin, 1974; Glock and Bellah, 1976; Greeley, 1975; Greeley and McCready, 1974; Nelson, 1975; O'Keefe, 1982; Scott, 1980; Tiryakian, 1974; Wedow, 1976; Whitehead, 1974). The specific content or meaning of these beliefs and practices is left open, however, to actual study. From a general theoretical standpoint, these views provide a more adequate bases for sociological interpretation.

These sociological formulations provide a meaningful context for serious scholarly discussion. Within such a context it is possible to have earnest differences and debate. While I draw on these discussions, I also think that they raise certain problems and difficulties. Nelson's (1974) model, for instance, deals with the "psychic," thereby limiting its applicability and generality. Greeley's (1974) tendency to equate unconventional beliefs with the sacred is suspect empirically, and his presupposition that ultimate beliefs derive from a basic human need is reductionistic, dubious, and difficult to examine empirically. Tiryakian (1973) overestimates the role and importance of secrecy, confuses distinctions between belief and practice as well as the esoteric and occult, ascribes too much coherence to knowledge and culture, and draws mostly unsupported conclusions about the influence of countercultural sentiments and innovations (see O'Keefe, 1982). Like these thinkers, O'Keefe (1982) examines the consequences of magic from societal members' standpoints, but consistent with Durkheimian realism, he is certain that its underlying reality is an illusion. Though stimulating, his general theory of magic is overly formalistic and while attending to history, it is only quasi-historical.

In short, then, it seems to me that all sociological interpretations (including explanatory ones) must begin with deliberate, sensitive, and careful efforts to describe human meanings from the existential standpoint of their creators. To do otherwise, as is suggested by versions of sociological realism and positivism in the name of science, is fundamentally and hopelessly to confuse social reality with interpretations of it. Popular images of esoteric culture are interesting as interpretations of this scene by outsiders. The realist images created by sociologists and other exoteric experts should be accorded similar status.

No interpretation fully represents or captures social reality. Or, to put the matter differently, all interpretations, inevitably, reify and otherwise distort the lived experience of human existence and its social meanings (realities) to some extent, including my interpretation. This is not to say, however, that all interpretations are equal, as is being argued by contemporary versions of post-structuralist and premodernist thought. This contention commonly leads social analysts to concoct in a highly speculative fashion, interpretations that have little, if any, relationship with social reality as it is experienced and enacted by societal members. In this way it is a form of solipsism. There is no absolute or definitive solution to this interpretative dilemma. I treat it reflexively by constantly displaying and examining the procedures employed to produce the interpretations presented. The theory of esoteric culture developed and delineated in the next chapter is a product of my efforts to generate an interpretative perspective on the products of my fieldwork and related research.

Notes

[1] Throughout this book I have endeavored to use the terminologies employed by members. In some instances I have substituted labels consistent with their meanings. Except when it is not otherwise clear or as a matter of emphasis, I generally have not placed members' terminologies in quotation.

[2] This group avoids use of the label Mormon. They are known officially as the Reorganized Church of Jesus Christ of Latter Day Saints.

[3] I routinely assign student to attend the activities of cultic groups and new religions in this area.

Chapter 2

The Esoteric Scene in America

My fieldwork in the cultic milieu involved constant exposure to a perplexing diversity of beliefs and practices as well as terminologies, definitions, and meanings describing them. Observing everyday life practices it was difficult to discern coherent usages, patterns, and meanings. Members' meanings seemed to derive from a vast cultural reservoir, freely borrowed, arranged, and rearranged in complex and confounding ways. Although it was possible to determine the meanings attached to these symbols, particularly as they were used by some set of practitioners in concrete situations and settings, their use and meaning varied widely across situations, settings, and among adherents such that there was little consensus or preference for a particular idiom. For many of these people what mattered most was some application of knowledge to the mundane conditions of their existence, thereby acting toward themselves, other people, and the world of everyday life in a meaningful fashion. Some of them were concerned with arranging meanings systematically and abstractly; and they would refer to various authorities, texts, traditions, and bodies of knowledge.

Scholarly efforts to resolve this problem, in the interest of conceptual clarity and precision, either by appropriating words and meanings, such as occult, magic, mysticism, metaphysical, and the like, or contributing notions like new religions (new religious movements), nonconventional beliefs, extraordinary groups, human potential movements, magical therapy cults, alternative realities, and so on, has resulted in little consensus (see, for instance, Eliade, 1976; Ellwood and Partin, 1988; Galbreath, 1972, 1983; Jorgensen and Jorgensen, 1982; Judah, 1967; Marty, 1970; Melton, 1978, 1986; O'Keefe, 1982; Tiryakian, 1974; Truzzi, 1972b). The diversity of potentially inclusive phenomena, differences as well as similarities among them, and the eclectic, synthetic, and highly fluid character of beliefs, practices, and groups defy any easy or simple solution to this conceptual obstacle. In a sense there is no definitive solution to it. The lived realities of societal members always are richer and more complex than the capacity to contain them in abstract concepts and formulations. This acknowledgement, however, provides little relief to one of the central dilemmas of sociological theorizing.

Based on a sociology of culture and knowledge, I develop and present a theory of **esoteric culture**. It provides an interpretative framework and perspective for describing and analyzing multifarious beliefs, practices, and activities of contemporary Americans. It specifically focuses attention on: the social meanings of American esotericism as it is experienced and enacted by believers; the manner in which practitioners organize their beliefs and activities socially; and the procedures they employ to accomplish occult knowledge. Esoteric culture includes elaborate bodies of abstract and practical knowledge which characteristically are "theosophical" or "religiophilosophic," related rituals and practices, as well as collective activities. It is distinguished, historically, by a lack of legitimacy in Western societies. This culture is sustained and organized in the form of a "**cultic milieu**." It contains publics and collective behavioral audiences, as well as elaborate networks of seekers, practitioners, cults, sects, and collective movements.

Sources of esoteric knowledge derive from ancient, premodern philosophies, religions, and folklores. Contemporary meanings and sources of esoteric knowledge are a product of the Renaissance Humanists' appropriation and syncretization of these ideas as Hermetic-Kabalistic occultism. Occult traditions periodically have been revived and revitalized, and subsequent generations of occultists have added new sources of esoteric belief and practice. Esoteric folklores and traditions have influenced American culture since the colonial period. Americans have drawn on successive European revivals, and they have innovatively contributed to esoteric culture. These innovations have produced significant collective and religious movements, many of which have been exported throughout the world. During the late 1960's, I argue, esoteric culture and the cultic milieu formed an **esoteric scene** in the United States. The highly fluid esoteric scene in American has undergone constant change. It waned during the 1980's, but esoteric culture remains visible in American metropolises today.

A THEORY OF ESOTERIC CULTURE

The theory of esoteric culture I develop and present is indebted to the groundbreaking work of Tiryakian (1973, 1974). His formulation draws on a structural-functional perspective on culture, society and personality, as well as a related evolutionary theory of sociocultural change. Culture, in this view, consists of cognitive maps defining reality which provide a cognitive and moral paradigm used by people to interpret their experiences and generate social action. In the case of Western societies, Tiryakian argues, there are several cultural paradigms, one of which is institutionally dominant while the other is latent or covert. He (1974:264) refers to the socially dominant paradigm that is manifest in public institutions as "exoteric culture," and defines it as: "a set of cognitive and evaluative orientations publicly recognized and legitimated in the network of social institutions." He objects to the idea that modernization reflects a unitary line in the historical development of Western societies resulting in exoteric culture. Modernization, especially the rationalization of society by way of science, he contends, also produced a countercultural paradigm through the systematic exclusion of particular cultural elements (claims to and bodies of knowledge) from exoteric culture.

Tiryakian (1974:264-265) calls this socially latent, marginal, underground paradigm "esoteric culture." It is composed of beliefs and doctrines, empirically oriented practices, and social organizations. Esoteric culture, more specifically, refers to religiophilosophic belief systems: "the more comprehensive cognitive mappings of nature and the cosmos, the epistemological and ontological reflections of ultimate reality, which mappings constitute a stock of knowledge" (Tiryakian, 1974:265). Esoteric knowledge is based on mystical and intuitive epistemologies. It constitutes theosophies concerning a knowledge of reality that is mysterious, secret, internal, subjective, participatory, hidden, and concealed from the uninitiated. Esoteric knowledge, according to Tiryakian (1974:265) is enacted by way of "occult" practices. These intentional techniques or procedures draft hidden, concealed, nonempirical forces thought to reside in nature or the cosmos in order to achieve empirical results, such as a knowledge of events or altering the course of events through this intervention. Esoteric culture, in this view, is organized by way of hierarchically structured secret societies. Esoteric knowledge is acquired by way of an initiation to secrecy and apprenticeship to a master. It is a source of power since a very few, select people are initiated into its mysteries. Although esoteric culture represents a socially marginal, underground current in Western societies, Tiryakian (1974:268-275) argues that it periodically has influenced the socially dominant, exoteric culture, especially its artistic expressions.

Tiryakian's perspective on esoteric culture is insightful and helpful, but the general theoretical framework in which this formulation is located suffers from serious defects. His Parsonian structural-functional evolutionism provides a sociologically inadequate model of culture, society, human interaction, and self-hood, the processes of sociocultural change and stability, as well as methodology. I see culture and society as much more fluid, dynamic, conflictual, precarious, emergent, historically situated, and dependent on human activity. Insofar as culture provides a cognitive and moral map, it is diffusely distributed and generally only partly available to the people who sustain and enact it. Culture and society, it seems to me, are continuous and discontinuous in human experience and activity, and they are not governed by universal laws, regularities, or properties. Since culture always is pregnant with possibilities, there is no need to talk about latency.

There also are several problems with Tiryakian's specific formulation of esoteric culture. This culture, as he recognizes, has a lengthy history in Western societies. It therefore is more appropriately characterized as a current or tributary which has been neglected and excluded from the sociocultural mainstream than as a separate, underground stream. To equate the occult with the practical accomplishment of esoteric knowledge is entirely artificial and not at all useful analytically; it is inconsistent with the historical meanings of this word; and it unnecessarily excludes from sociological consideration an entire range of esoteric claims to knowledge (also see O'Keefe, 1982). Historically, esoteric culture is supported by secretive orders, and while certain characteristics of secrecy are important, Tiryakian overemphasizes the contemporary significance of secret societies.

My view of esotericism derives from a sociology of culture and knowledge (see, especially, Berger, 1967; Berger and Luckmann, 1966; Blumer, 1969, 1990; Cicourel, 1973; Denzin, 1989a; Douglas and Johnson, 1977; Garfinkel, 1967; Geertz, 1973; Goffman, 1959, 1974; McCall and Becker, 1990; Schutz, 1967).[1] From this standpoint, "culture" is defined as the totality of human activity, including so-called "material" and "nonmaterial" products. It is created, reproduced, and enacted by human beings through an emergent, historically continuous process of symbolic interaction. It is externalized and objectified symbolically through language, and it is internalized and re-appropriated as subjectively meaningful by way of socialization. People use language to produce bodies of knowledge constituting claims, beliefs, and doctrines defining "reality" in humanly meaningful ways. They formulate and use procedures, practices, and rituals to enact and accomplish these visions of reality. They produce tools and artifacts to construct, manipulate, and symbolize what they hold to be real. People formulate designs and procedures whereby their knowledge of reality and related human activities are distributed, structured, connected, and organized socially. Through culture, human beings define and identify themselves, thereby creating and enacting social selves.

Through social interaction people continuously sustain and enact more or less standardized solutions to human existence which may be seen as constituting social institutions. These institutions structure and organize, socially, the human plausibility of culture. Recurrent, customary support of these arrangements historically results in certain traditions. By way of social power, cultural traditions and institutions are sanctioned and legitimated. In this way, particular versions and images of reality constitute traditions supported by communities of believers which become socially dominant historically. Rival images and versions of reality commonly are defined as illegitimate. They may be preserved as traditions, symbolically through artifacts and documents, and sometimes sustained by minority communities. Ideological minorities, however, are subject to more or less serious sanctions, repression, and even extermination by the more powerful ideological majority.

This view of social reality is non-dualistic: Culture is ideal and material, subjective and objective, mentalistic and embodied, determined and determining (intentional and coercive), as well as nominalistic and realistic (see Douglas and Johnson, 1977). Put differently, these classic, dualistic concepts do not provide a sociologically adequate description of social reality. Sociocultural reality is all of them and none of them at the same time (see Murphy, 1989). Insofar as it is possible to talk about the "causes" of culture, its only cause is humanity itself. Human beings create it, enact it, and thereby sustain it through symbolic interaction (see Blumer, 1969; 1990). It does not exist except through human interaction in historically concrete social situations and settings. Since human beings interact creatively with one another in specific historical situations, culture is not regulated by any set of absolute, universal laws. Culture is dispersed and distributed differentially. While it may provide a cognitive map when viewed abstractly, its enactment commonly is based on vague designs and incomplete knowledge. The societal component of culture, like culture itself, is inherently precarious and unstable. Social cooperation, coordination, and organization, thereby, require ongoing human interaction to sustain them. Through human definition and interaction social power and its use may be re-configured constantly.

In the history of Western societies particular claims to knowledge have been defined and sanctioned by people in positions of power as legitimate over and against rival claims to knowledge. Since the Renaissance socially dominant claims to knowledge increasingly have been characterized by rationalism. The driving force, so to speak, behind this process of modernization has been a scientific worldview, but this spirit of rationality also has infected orthodox Western religions to a large extent. Orthodox Science and Religion are predominant components of the exoteric culture of Western societies.[2] Esoteric culture is composed of claims to and bodies of knowledge which have been excluded from the dominant, exoteric culture of Western societies, particularly from the domains of Religion and Science.

There are important differences among esoteric bodies of knowledge as well as inclusive beliefs, practices, and supporting collectivities. What they all share in common is a lack of legitimacy from the standpoint of the human constituencies which sustain exoteric culture. This theoretical perspective on esoteric culture provides a way of conceptualizing similarities and differences among a seemingly disparate range of phenomena. It, consequently, provides a solution to the persistent difficulties scholars have encountered in dealing with matters which are described by labels like mystical, metaphysical, new age, occult, magic, paganism, witchcraft, theosophical, psychic, nonconventional religion, medicine, science, and so on. It recommends that these ideas and inclusive bodies of knowledge, belief, practice, traditions, and communities be examined concretely in their social, cultural, and historical contexts.

The word "esoteric," according to the *Oxford English Dictionary*, derives from the Greek. It occurs first in Lucian (c. 160 A.D.) who attributed to Aristotle a classification of his works into **esoteric** and **exoteric**. The "esoteric" refers to an internal, intuitive, participatory, invisible, nonmaterial, subjective reality as opposed to an exoteric world that is outer, external, detached, visible, material, or objective. Esoteric knowledge is divine, pure, sacred, and True, while exoteric knowledge is vulgar, impure, profane, and false. From an esoteric standpoint the modern distinction between sacred (theology, religion) and secular (philosophy, science) knowledge and truth is nonsense. Esoteric knowledge rejects the sacred/secular dualism, and it seeks to restore the premodern unity of True and Sacred Knowledge. It rests on mystical, intuitive, participatory insights and it is judged by aesthetic and spiritual values. Esoteric knowledge stands opposed to the modern doctrines of materialism, realism, empiricism, and positivism (see Faivre, 1989b).

"Esoteric" was used by later writers, according to the *Oxford English Dictionary*, with reference to secret doctrines taught by Pythagoras to a few select disciples. It thereby came to refer to "philosophical doctrines, treatises, modes of speech, etc.," communicated by a master to a few chosen students. The acquisition of these secret, mysterious, sacred teachings required lengthy periods of study and special training available only from very exceptional, extraordinary masters. Esoteric knowledge was communicated orally, by way of handcopied texts, and it was not available to the uninitiated. This knowledge was thought to be powerful and, consequently, dangerous. Its use by the uninitiated was regarded as vulgar and profane, and inappropriate or unskilled use of this knowledge was held to possess potentially injurious consequences. Being restricted to a privileged few disciples, esoteric knowledge was highly exclusive, and partly as a result it was seen as a source of tremendous personal power (see Tiryakian, 1973, 1974). To be initiated into and become adept in these secret, sacred, and powerful teachings resulted in a radical, personal transformation from vulgarity, profanity, and ignorance, to enlightenment, knowledge, truth, and perhaps divinity.

Esoteric knowledge is composed of "theosophies" or "religiophilosophical" theories and doctrines. Theosophies define and specify connections between perceivedly different orders of reality. These realms include: physical, material, natural, biological realities; worlds of human, social, cultural, and historical existence; and some ethereal, spiritual, divine, godly, supernatural, cosmic realm. Human existence thereby is defined comprehensively and ultimately in absolutely meaningful ways. Esoteric knowledge includes rituals, practices, and procedures. They may be manifest as incantations, magic, sorcery, prophesy, divination, meditation, possession, and trance, among other possibilities. Esoteric practices enable their users to achieve esoteric knowledge and enact these visions of reality in concrete ways. The occult, as discussed below, is a particular aspect of esoteric culture. It constitutes distinctive bodies of knowledge with an extensive history in Western culture. Practices whereby occult knowledge is acquired and enacted, such as divination, are highly consequential; but, contrary to Tiryakian's contention, it is not useful analytically or otherwise to single them out as **the** way in which esoteric knowledge is obtained and performed.

Historically, there is an affinity between esoteric culture and secret societies. Since esoteric knowledge is sacred, powerful and dangerous it was deemed to require special, respectful care and protection from the uninitiated. Disciplines whose training and activities transpired in exclusive organizations therefore commonly took oaths of secrecy. Some of these collectivities, as Tiryakian (1973) observed, became hierarchically structured, characteristically in formal organizations. Yet, knowledge which is intuitive, mystical, and enigmatic, orally transmitted, and used creatively by a few adepts and masters, tends to be highly resistant to rationalization and formalization. It generally lacks a high degree of orthodoxy, and it tends to be characterized by an extreme "epistemological individualism" (Wallis, 1977). A master and other adepts consequently may use this knowledge without ever forming stable associations. When they do interact with one another it commonly is through loosely connected social networks, and by way of small, loosely structured, inherently unstable, and highly transitory collectivities. Groups of this sort characteristically are "cults."

With the invention of printing, esoteric knowledge, historically, was no longer limited to oral traditions, a few handcopied texts, elite masters, or a few select students. It was easily spread by way of printed documents, and, eventually, through other forms of mass communication. Esoteric knowledge thereby became available in some sense to a much larger audience. It became possible for eager publics to consume, spread, and even innovatively generate new forms of esoteric knowledge. Popular consumption of esoteric knowledge generally is disdained by those who have been initiated into secretive cults. Partly it is because this knowledge, or at least particular forms of it, no longer are the exclusive possession of these elites. Esoteric knowledge thereby may become a part of popular, mass culture.

Contemporary esoteric culture sometimes is organized in the form of secret societies. Secretive groups occasionally are able to persist over lengthy periods of time and remain socially isolated. These groups, however, tend to be part of a larger "cultic milieu." This social environment includes publics and audiences which consume esoteric culture, people seeking esoteric knowledge, students, practitioners, loosely connected networks of believers, and cultic groups, all of which may be interconnected to some extent. The cultic milieu provides potential recruits for particular groups. It serves as the basis for the development of common interests and activities. And it provides bases for sustaining and mutually supporting common interests and activities of individuals, as well as the activities and practices of collectivities. Cults sometimes develop into more stable, characteristically sectarian, social organizations. When this happens, however, they also become increasingly independent of the larger milieu. As a consequence, sectarian organizations tend to move out of the immediate nexus of the cultic milieu. When there is sufficient popular, mass interest in esoteric culture to raise it to an unusually high level of visibility within the larger society, it may emerge as a social scene (see Irwin, 1977).

MEANINGS AND SOURCES OF ESOTERICISM

Contemporary esoteric culture derives from an odd assortment of beliefs and practices. It includes a variety of premodern bodies of knowledge: the religions of the ancient world, especially Egypt, Mesopotamia and Persia (such as Zorastarianism); Hebrew cults, lore, and biblical traditions (like the Essenes, and Cabalistic mysticism); Greek philosophies and religions; Roman paganisms, mythologies and philosophies; and Christian gnosticism, cults, and heresies (Nestorianism, Catharism). It also includes: Eastern beliefs, practices, cults, and especially religions such as Buddhism, Confucianism, Taoism, and Hinduism; non-Western folklore, religions, and notably beliefs in magic, ghosts, spirits, witchcraft, trance and possession; and a host of Western paganisms, folklores, magics, witchcrafts, medicines, and healings (such as Celtic, Norse, and Arthurian elements, especially stories of the Holy Grail). A principal source of esoteric knowledge is derived from the occultism of the Renaissance. Older sources of esoteric culture were combined and new bodies of knowledge added from the 17th through the 20th centuries by successive European and American revivals (see Sullivan, 1989).[3]

These sources of esoteric knowledge, seen simply as ideas, are more dissimilar than they are similar. They derive from drastically and substantially different social, cultural, and historical contexts, and in many instances they constituted (or constitute) socially legitimate and even socially dominant traditions and worldviews within their native cultures. These bodies of knowledge, belief, and practice become esoteric by reference to modernism, its thought categories, and a predominant exoteric culture. Efforts to identify substantive similarities among disparate bodies of esoteric knowledge generally demand the imposition of alien concepts, as well as cultural and historical decontextualization.

O'Keefe's (1982:523-581) ability to discern similarities among some of these ideas, for instance, hinges on a distinction between rationality and irrationality, a peculiarly modern dichotomy. His talk about "the occult siege of the ancient world" (referring to Greek thought), and "Hinduism as a permanent occult revolution," depends entirely on a modernist viewpoint. Greek irrationalism becomes occult with its appropriation by Renaissance Occultism, while Hinduism becomes esoteric and perhaps occult when it is removed from its native context and relocated within modern Western thought.[4] O'Keefe's theorizing reflects an unwarranted ethnocentricism, universalism, and absolutism, and it results in conceptual confusion. Greek philosophy and religion, as well as Hinduism may be irrational from a modernist viewpoint, but they are esoteric within a Western cultural context because of a lack of social legitimacy, not because they are irrational.

Contemporary meanings and sources of esoteric culture are indebted greatly to the Renaissance Hermeticists (Yates, 1964; Faivre, 1989c). Unlike the socially dominant modernist worldview with its ideology of progress, these Renaissance scholars romantically looked backward, not forward for inspiration and truth. This knowledge, they thought, was contained in the form of secret and mysterious writings of the Ancients (Yates, 1964). A collection of Gnostic writings from about the 2nd or 3rd century A.D. were translated and synthesized with Greek philosophies (particularly Neo-Platonicism). This literature, particularly in the form of the *Asclepius* and the *Corpus Hermeticum*, took the figure of Hermes Trismegistus (who was identified as the Egyptian god Thoth and the Roman god Mercury) as its central authority and source. To this mix Jewish mysticism (Cabala) was added, forming the Hermetic-Kabalistic tradition (Yates, 1964; also see O'Keefe, 1982; Faivre, 1989c). As O'Keefe (1982:551) concisely observes: "The Renaissance outburst, basically, consists in the gradual recovery of much of the cosmopolitan occult knowledge assembled during the Graeco-Roman period—Hellenic, Roman, Persian, Chaldean, Egyptian, Hebraic magics then syncretized into occult sciences."

Eliade (1976:48) has noticed that: "According to the *Oxford Dictionary*, the term 'occult was first used in 1545, meaning that which is not apprehended, or apprehensible by mind; beyond the range of understanding or of ordinary knowledge.'" In a later context, 1633, he (1976:48) continued: "the word received a supplementary significance, namely, 'the subject of those reputed sciences held to involve the knowledge or use of agencies of secret and mysterious nature (as magic, alchemy, astrology, theosophy).'" In contemporary usage the occult refers to bodies of knowledge and practice held to be secret, mysterious, hidden, or concealed from the uninitiated; outside the domain of ordinary knowledge and understanding; beyond apprehension by mind alone; the subject of arts and sciences, such as alchemy, astrology, magic, theosophy, divination, and so on (see Truzzi, 1972a; Galbreath, 1983; Faivre, 1989a).

It sometimes is appropriate in describing an interest in secret, mysterious, or hidden truths or realities to refer to them as occult. Use of this word as an adjective should not be confused, as it is in O'Keefe's (1982) case, with its use as a noun to describe the emergence of occult knowledge, **the Occult**, as a historically situated tradition. I will use the term "**occult**" specifically as a reference to particular esoteric traditions, bodies of knowledge, practices, and related phenomena. This use of the word is consistent with how it is used by members of the cultic milieu in the Valley, historical interpretations, and conventional definitions.

The Hermetic-Kabalistic tradition flourished throughout Europe during the 15th and 16th centuries. It constituted a massive literature and authorities such as Trithemius, Paracelsus, Cornelius Agrippa, Ramon Lull (Raymond Lully), John Dee, Robert Fludd, and many others. It was entertained as a serious, scholarly philosophy, sometimes influencing leading figures of science. As a prominent philosophy it exerted influence with the Church and may have influenced the emergence of science (see Yates, 1964; Faivre, 1989c). The Hermetic-Kabalistic tradition, however, ran counter to the central ideas of what would become the socially dominant religions and sciences of Western culture. These occult traditions consequently were influenced by subsequent struggles for power to control definitions of "knowledge." They eventually are seen as rivals of Religion and Enlightenment rationality and science. The occult thereby came to be used as a reference to subjects and procedures excluded from the domain of exoteric culture, particularly Religion and Science.

Astrology before the seventeenth century was periodically embraced and tolerated by the Church. Even so, the relationship between the all-powerful Church and beliefs and practices that eventually would be perceived as "heresy" was at best uneasy. Leading Church authorities, such as Augustine, St. Thomas, and other lesser-known figures were sometimes used to support esoteric or occult philosophies; but they also were used against magic, astrology, divination, and many of the ideas that would later serve as the basis for sciences like astronomy. Witchcraft, perhaps the most publicly obvious occultism, clearly was a product of heresy. It no doubt existed throughout Europe in the form of folk and sometimes pagan practices, but the "witch" phenomenon was created by the Catholic response to heretics, like Reformists, Catharists, Amalricians, among other individuals and collectivities (Russel, 1974). The Protestant Reformation provided a sociointellectual context in which both Catholics (with the Counter-Reformation and its Inquisition) and Protestants sought to purge beliefs and practices thought to be superstitious, magical, and heretical.

Occultism not only persisted but it attracted widespread support, especially among intellectuals and social elites, during the 17th century. The "Rosicrucian Enlightenment," as this intellectual movement is referred to by Yates (1972), is seen as an intermediate cultural stage between the Renaissance and a revolution producing science. It reflects continuity with the Hermetic-Kabalistic tradition featuring alchemy, as well as critiques of philosophies and theologies serving as the basis for Religion and Science. Paradoxically, many of these ideas were entertained by the creators of science. In a later context, namely the 18th century, this occult literature and lore (the mysterious pamphlets, *Fama* and *Confessions*, relating the story of a German Knight, Christian Rosencreutz), partly would inspire the organization of lodges of Rosicrucians, Freemasons, and Theosophists.[5]

By the late 17th and the 18th centuries, however, doctrines and practices, such as astrology, numerology, palmistry, alchemy, telepathy, clairvoyance, divination, magic, demons, spirits, and gods, increasingly were perceived as an offense to both the Church and the new-found spirit of scientific rationality—the Enlightenment.

Fischler (1974:284), notices for instance that: "Stripped of legitimacy, astrology in the eighteenth and nineteenth centuries (along with alchemy, palmistry, clairvoyance, and telepathy) encountered both legal and socio-cultural repression." By the Enlightenment, the occult arts and sciences were being forged into a socially marginal and perceivedly illegitimate current of Western culture through the systematic exclusion of these ideas and their adherents from both religious and scientific claims to knowledge and supporting communities.

It sometimes has been assumed that occult disciplines represent the origins and primitive beginnings of science. Alchemy, for example, sometimes is seen as the predecessor of chemistry. Some of the men who became leaders of science also practiced the occult arts and sciences (see Kearney, 1971; O'Keefe, 1982). The relationships between Hermetic philosophy and the ideas stimulating science, as noted above, remain in need of further research and interpretation. None of this, however, supports the tremendous leap that is necessary for arguing that occult disciplines were protosciences. This contention, as Eglin (1974:331) observed, easily is discredited: "When chemical phenomena ceased to be regarded alchemically, it was because a new intellectual/scientific ethos had appeared and banished its predecessor, not that, for example, Newton and Boyle had succeeded in their attempts to transform Alchemy into chemistry." The contention that the occult is protoscientific—reflecting a cumulative, evolutionary view of science—fails as a sociological and historical explanation (see Kuhn, 1970; O'Keefe, 1982).

Since about the 18th century, subjects and procedures excluded from Religion and Science commonly have been labeled and treated as esoteric or occult. Interpretations of ancient and folk beliefs survived in the popular imagination, texts and literature, folk practices, and more formally by way of semi-secret and secretive societies and cults. From time to time esoteric and occult beliefs and rituals have re-emerged and been the subject of popular cultural revival and revitalization. The ideas of Emmanuel Swedenborg (1688-1772), Comte de Saint-Germain (about 1710-1785), and Franz Aton Mesmer (1733-1815) stimulated popular interest, sometimes by exoteric scholars, but they eventually were defined as esoteric, and served as sources of subsequent esoteric cultural innovations. Significant revivals of esotericism and occultism in France and England during the late 18th century and again in the 19th century greatly contributed to the revitalization of this culture. French and English occultism influenced one another, carried over into the 20th century, exerted influence on exoteric culture, and spread throughout the world. Each of these revivals added new sources of esoteric thought, new groups and movements, and contributed to combining and synthesizing old traditions into new systems of belief and practice.

Contemporary esoteric culture tends to be highly eclectic and syncretic. Participants in these cultures mix and match esoteric and exoteric ideas in complex and confounding ways. Many of them are more interested in the uses of esoteric knowledge than with elaborating internally consistent, abstract bodies of thought. While many of the ideas prevalent within the contemporary esoteric milieu run counter to dominant, exoteric traditions in Western thought (as noted by Tiryakian, 1973), the extent to which they represent countercultural movements should not be overblown. Revolts against modernism, for instance, clearly are evident in socially legitimate and even dominant artistic cultures and movements, reflecting the rarely examined influence of esotericism on exoteric culture. Similarly, exoteric critiques of modernism and especially positivism, which do not seem to be influenced by esoteric traditions directly, have emerged in recent years as broad-based intellectual movements (see, for instance, Loyotard, 1984; Murphy, 1989; Boyne, 1990; Brown, 1989; Kroker and Cook, 1987).

EARLY AMERICAN MAGICS AND OCCULTISMS

The early American colonists brought with them pervasive traditions of English folk magic and occultism (Butler, 1979). Belief in witchcraft and the use of magical and occult means for treating illness were products of or co-existed with a socially and culturally dominant Christianity. Although Americans nominally were Christians, as Butler (1979:317) observes: "After 1650 even in New England only about one-third of all adults ever belonged to a church." Magic coexisted with and supplemented Christianity, serving as part of a "popular religion" of the masses, as is illustrated by the prominence of almanacs containing occult ideas (Butler, 1979; also see Quinn, 1987). Before the Revolution, American elites and intellectuals read occult literature and practiced astrology, alchemy, palmistry, and forms of magic (Butler, 1979; Kerr and Crow, 1983). German immigrants imported non-English varieties of esotericism and occultism (Hermeticism, Rosicrucianism, mysticism, magic), constituted separate traditions, and influenced other Americans (Butler, 1979; also see Kerr and Crow, 1983). Quaker mysticism, for instance, illustrates such influences.

After about 1720, American intellectuals and other elites, under the sway of Enlightenment philosophy and science, gradually abandoned and became increasingly critical of magic and the occult, especially in the form of astrology and alchemy (Butler, 1979, 1983). These ideas persisted, however, in the general population and even among elites, throughout the 18th century (Leventhal, 1976). Belief in witchcraft remained popular, although American courts stopped convicting people of this crime after 1692 (Butler, 1979). During the early 18th century American religion experienced significant transformation by way of the Great Awakening. Evangelical Christianity, as Butler (1979:341-342) aptly notices, "paralleled" or transformed magic. The magic/client relationship resembled the clergyman/layperson relationship whereby everyday life apprehensions and predicaments were redefined as the need for **salvation**. Even so, esoteric beliefs and practices persisted; older ideas were defined as esoteric; new, imported ideas were added; and new religious movements, several of which reflected the influence of esotericism or came to be regarded as esoteric, emerged.

Freemasonary (involving Rosicrucian occultism) was imported from Europe and became popular among the middle and upper classes. While the American variety was more a social club and less occult than its European relative, Freemasonary was an important source of occult symbolism, social structure, and ritual for Americans (Ellwood and Partin, 1988:48-50). Swedenborgianism and Mesmerism, both of them new contributions to American esotericism, resulted in cultic organizations, subsequently influenced spiritualism, and in turn, harmonialism in the forms of Spiritualism, Christian Science, and New Thought. Magical and religious imports from Africa were intermingled with Christianity among American slaves after about 1760 (Butler, 1983). Occult in an American context, these ideas and practices exerted little influence on American esotericism, except perhaps in particular regional subcultures, but they provide a rich, if under utilized, source of socially marginal belief and practice. German immigrants of the 19th century reinforced previously transplanted occultisms, particularly medical remedies, mysticism, Rosicrucianism, as well as the use of divining rods and seer-stones (Butler, 1983; Taylor, 1986).

NEW RELIGIOUS MOVEMENTS

The Second Great Awakening resulted in the emergence and proliferation of unorthodox spiritual movements in America during the early 19th century. Evangelicals, seekers, restorationists, holiness and perfectionists, pentecostals, millennialists, adventists, communitarians, transcendentalists and new thought, and a host of other groups and movements were reacting to socially dominant religions and philosophies, and their responses generally were envisioned as religion. Their innovations, however, commonly drew on and/or contributed to esoteric traditions. Though in some sense Christian, many of these movements stressed ecstatic gifts and manifestations of the spirit: speaking in tongues, healing, visions, dreams, prophecies, visitations of angels and Deity, and miracles. Once again, these phenomena paralleled magic, and many of them may be seen as religious transformation of what otherwise would have been (and sometimes were) regarded as occultism. Many Americans, including those who viewed themselves somehow as Christians, subscribed to popular beliefs in magic, astrology, divination, as well as witchcraft, and they employed related practices to manipulate human affairs and nature. Mormonism and Spiritualism provide exceptionally noteworthy examples of new and unorthodox religious movements stimulated by the spiritual awakening of the early to mid-19th century in the United States.

Mormonism is an eminently provocative example of interconnections between American esotericism and new religions of the early 19th century. During his early teens, Joseph Smith, Jr., the founder of Mormonism, used popular occult tools, a divining rod and seer stones, to search for buried treasure near his home, a district of New York State repeatedly "burned over" by revival fever (Taylor, 1986; Quinn, 1987; also see Cross, 1944). Members of the Smith family apparently practiced folk magic, astrology, and more formal ritual or ceremonial magic (Quinn, 1987). Expressing confusion over rival sectarian claims, Joseph Smith reportedly prayed for guidance. Accounts of his subsequent experiences and activities vary (see Quinn, 1987). They also are interpretations based on later events, specifically that Smith would claim to be a modern-day Prophet of God, establish a church organization in 1830, and lead this much publicized and controversial new religious movement until his martyrdom in 1844.

Particularly interesting is Joseph Smith's repeated use of describably occult means in the creation and development of what he and his followers saw as the restoration of the Christian Church. His reported visions or dreams of visitations by angels and deities, and the use of a seer stone to recover and translate the golden plates that became the *Book of Mormon*, as Quinn (1987) carefully documents, contained significant magical and occult elements. Similarly, his fascination with the ancient world and languages (Egypt, Hebrew), and subsequent efforts to translate seemingly ancient documents and artifacts, reflect esoteric elements (Egyptology, Cabalism), as well as popular Christian themes. His most radical religious innovation, Temple Mormonism, with its secretive gestures, code names, endowments, rituals, and hierarchical orders of priesthood, while containing many significant Biblical articles also suggest the powerful influence of an occult Freemasonary (a topic in need of further study, but see Flanders, 1965).

In short, then, the origins and major innovations of Mormonism were directly influenced by esoteric and occult ideas. Even so, Mormonism was closely related to restorationism, among other themes of the Second Great Awakening (see Wood, 1980). Though unorthodox, its adherents past and present see themselves as Christian. Significantly, Mormonism is the most successful new religion in American history, a socially legitimated, influential and even dominant religion in parts of the western United States, and one of the fastest growing religions in the world today. O'Keefe's (1982:523-570) insistence that esoteric knowledge only has a limited potential for effecting exoteric culture apparently neglects the case of Mormonism. Unlike Spiritualism, the organizational success of Mormonism has enabled it to sustain social bases apart from the esoteric and cultic milieu.

Spiritualism, an innovation of the mid-19th century, also emerged as an unconventional Christianity, but unlike Mormonism it became a persistent and influential feature of American esotericism and occultism. Beliefs in spirits and efforts to communicate with them by various means, through trance and mediumship, are widespread historically and crossculturally. Mediumship was hardly unknown in the United States, and Shakers of New York had engaged in efforts to communicate with spirits by making a rapping sound (Ellwood and Partin, 1987:57). Transcendentalism, Mesmerism, and Swedenborgianism contributed to a sociocultural environment in which a spiritualist movement could flourish. Mesmerism, for instance, popularized mentalistic healing, homeopathy, phrenology and phalanstery. Swedenborgian congregations had been established in all major American cities by the 1780's (Butler, 1983). Even so, the emergence of American spiritualism is connected directly with the 1848 activities of the young Fox sisters, Margaret and Kate (see Kerr, 1972; Isaacs, 1983; Melton, 1986).

Margaret and Kate Fox, and later their sister Leah, claimed to communicate with spirits by making tapping sounds. These phenomena were interpreted as occult and by tradition the girls were labeled "mediums" (Isaac, 1983). They embarked on lifelong careers as mediums, reinforced by public demonstrations and investigations attesting to their occult abilities, thereby stimulating an extensive spiritualist movement (see Isaac, 1983). Andrew Jackson Davis, one of the most important mediums and leaders of this movement developed Spiritualism into a system of thought based on an unorthodox Christianity centered around mediumship and spirit communication (Melton, 1986:82). The widespread popularity of Spiritualism attracted debunkers, leading to reports of fraudulent practices in the late 1850's, and an exposé by Margaret Fox in the late 1880's. In spite of this, and ongoing difficulties in developing a strong organizational base for this diffuse movement, Spiritualism experienced slow and steady growth, developed several national organizations; and it has exerted considerable influence on esoteric and occult thought in the United States.

Several other esoteric movements of the late 19th century, Christian Science, New Thought, and Theosophy, were connected loosely to Spiritualism, and the emergent esoteric and cultic milieu it stimulated. Mary Baker Eddy, the founder of Christian Science was a student of Phineas Parkhurst Quimby, a mental healer (Melton, 1986). Claiming to have healed herself through Biblical Truth, Eddy embarked on a career as a teacher and writer. Dismissed from the Congregational Church, she formed the Christian Science Association in 1876, followed by the Church of Christ, Scientist in 1881. Christian Scientists see themselves as Christians, but their emphasis on physical healing by spiritual means and nonconformity to other points of orthodoxy are sources of contention from the standpoint of exoteric Christianity (Melton, 1986:25-28). Christian Science healing practices led to conflict with organized medicine, government and the courts. Friction within the movement contributed to the development of New Thought. In spite of these difficulties, Christian Science became a highly successful, fairly stable, and more or less respectable new American religion. Melton (1986:26) maintains that although there has been a slight decline in Christian Science membership and congregations in recent years, there are more than 400,000 members in over 3,000 branches, about two-thirds of which are located in the United States. Like Mormonism, Christian Science has been able to sustain itself apart from the esoteric, cultic milieu, although its reading centers contribute to this subcultural environment.

The New Thought movement reflects the influence of American esoteric and occult traditions from Mesmerism, Swedenborgianism, and Spiritualism to Warren Felt Evans, Phineas P. Quimby, and Christian Science, among other "metaphysical" groups, thinkers, writers, and teachers (see Judah, 1967). It also has been linked with Hegel, German idealism, Emerson, transcendentalism, and William James. These seemingly related teachings were dubbed "harmonalism" by Ahlstrom (1972) to denote a collection of beliefs that focus on spiritual, physical, and economic well-being (positive thinking) as interrelated by one's personal affinity with the supernatural or cosmos (also see Gottschalk, 1988). More a set of teachings than a particular organization, New Thought served as a basis for an untold number of cultic groups as well as more stable organizations, such as the Church of Religious Science, Church of Divine Science, and the Unity School of Christianity. Since the 1880's New Thought has been a synthesis and repository of many strains of esotericism (see Melton, 1978: 59-73).

Theosophy, one of the most visible and influential esoteric movements of the late 19th century emerged from a cultic milieu prepared and dominated by spiritualism. Helen P. Blavatsky, Henry S. Olcott and William Q. Judge, the 1875 founders of the Theosophical Society in New York, all were interested in spiritualism (see Melton, 1986:87ff). Under the dominant influence of the mysterious and charismatic

Madame Blavatsky, the theosophists, including a Bohemian following, studied a full range of esoteric and occult ideas (see Ellwood and Partin, 1988:60-64). *Isis Unveiled*, Blavatsky's first book, published in 1877, was an impressive summary of Western occultism. In 1878 Blavatsky moved to India and over the next ten years combined Western esotericism and occultism with Eastern religions (Hinduism and Buddhism) and esotericism into a theosophical system. Before Blavatsky's death in 1891 the Theosophy Society, with principal chapters in India, the United States, and Britain, was plagued with organizational discord and the inability to sustain a stable, growing membership. Following her death, Theosophy continued to splinter. In addition to the numerous organizations using this name, there are a variety of cultic and occult groups constituting diffuse movements, such as the Arcane School, the I AM Religious Activity, the Liberal Catholic Church and the Rosicrucian Fellowship (Max Heindel)—all of which have produced additional schisms, that are based on Theosophy (Melton, 1978:135-176, 1986:92). The influence of Theosophy on American esotericism and occultism has been far greater than its ability to sustain equally powerful, cohesive movement organizations.

ORIENTAL LIGHTS, THE GOLDEN DAWN AND SCIENTIFIC ANOMALIES

In the United States Eastern religions generally have not been accorded social legitimacy. Yet, ancient and Eastern religious ideas and practices have fascinated Westerners, produced endless theories and speculations, and influenced esoteric and occult traditions. Transcendentalism, according to Melton (1986:108) "was the first substantial religious movement in North America with a prominent Asian component." Transcendentalisms' mysticism influenced American esotericism, as reflected in Spiritualism, New Thought, Christian Science, and Theosophy. Through Theosophy formulations of Eastern ideas became part of Western esotericism and familiar to many Americans. The 1893 meeting of the World Parliament of Religions in Chicago generally is credited with introducing "oriental religion in explicit institutional form" (Ellwood and Partin, 1988: 65; also see Galbreath, 1983). Several conference speakers, Soyen Shaku (a Japanese Zen monk), Anagarika Dharmapala (a Buddhist from Ceylon), and especially a disciple of the Hindu saint, Ramakrishna, Swami Vivekananda, were able to stimulate consequential interest in Eastern religions in America (Ellwood and Partin, 1988:65-66). Vedanta Societies were established in the United States as a result of Vivekananda's efforts, while several of Soyen Shaku's students, notably D.T. Suzuki, later came to America and popularized Zen Buddhism. During the 1920's Paramahansa Yogananda founded the Self-Realization Fellowship in the United States (Ellwood and Partin, 1988: 66). After WWI, Krishnamutri, Rudolf Steiner, and G.I. Gurdjieff further popularized oriental religious ideas, and sparked organizations or subsequent movements (see Melton, 1978: 355-444).

Since the Enlightenment esoteric and occult claims to knowledge periodically have been seen as scientific or pertinent to science as well as religion. There is a socially recurrent pattern to the confrontation between esoteric/occult claims and those of orthodox science (see McClenon, 1984). Unconventional phenomena, sympathetically or critically, are entertained ontologically by science and subjected to its epistemologies and methodologies. Phenomena or procedures that met scientific criteria for truth are integrated into or subsumed by scientific theories or paradigms; those that do not are examined further or rejected, partly depending on the nature of the claims and accumulated evidence. Rejected claims and procedures tend to be regarded as esoteric or occult, and therefore are subject to the ridicule of scientists.

Persistent esoteric or occult claims sometimes lead to the formation of organizations aimed at debunking. Such a pattern is evident with respect to astrology and alchemy in the United States after about 1720 (see Butler, 1979, 1983), as well as the claims of Mesmerism, Spiritualism, and Christian Science during later periods. The resiliency of esoteric and occult claims, partly by way of reformulation, synthesis, revitalization, and innovation, along with the phenomena and claims introduced by science, constantly produces additional claims and phenomena—werewolves, fairies, mermaids, dragons, ghosts, meteorites and thunderstones, X and N rays, continental drift, behavioral bioassay, ball lightning, unidentified flying objects (UFO's), hypnosis, extrasensory perception (ESP) and psi, auras, pyramid energy, lost continents—and scientific responses (Truzzi, 1977; McClenon, 1984).

In the United States since about the 1880's this situation has resulted in the formation of science-like communities and societies devoted to the study of extraordinary claims and phenomena. These organizations sometimes include exoteric scientists and skeptics, but unlike debunking organizations they commonly include believers and people dedicated to the verification of extraordinary knowledge. The Society for Psychical Research (SPR) was founded in 1882; the American Society for Psychical Research was established in 1884; and during the 1930's J.B. Rhine instituted a research program in the Psychology Department at Duke defining "parapsychology" as a field (McClenon, 1984). By 1973 there were 15, mostly American, parapsychology organizations (most of which exist today), and 10 related periodicals, comprising what McClenon (1984) calls "deviant science" (also see White, 1973).

The first half of the 20th century generally is not noted for esoteric or occult innovations or activities. Rather, it is seen as a period of renewed commitment to traditional religion, as reflected in the growth of the exoteric churches in the United States during the 1940's, 50's and early 60's. Such a view, it seems to me, is at least partly mistaken. Many of the esoteric and occult traditions of previous centuries persisted among the general population and within cultic milieus, even if they did not attract widespread public attention.

The British occult revival and revitalization of the late 19th and early 20th centuries built on the French revival as well as earlier traditions, contributed to Theosophy (and was influenced by it), produced several important secretive societies, writers, literature, and charismatic leaders, and stimulated followers and groups world-wide. One of these groups, the Hermetic Order of the Golden Dawn remains the preeminent occult secret society. The Golden Dawn was founded in London around 1887 as a Masonic organization. Many of its founding members belonged to the Societas Rosicruciana in Anglia (or Soc. Ros.), a "fringe-masonic" group established in 1866 (Cavendish, 1975:33-39). Officially, it was founded by Rev. A.F.A. Woodford, Dr. Woodman, and Dr. Wynn Westcott, but a charismatic Scottish Freemason, Samuel Liddell Mathers (better known as MacGregor Mathers, and later as Le Comte de Glenstrae) was the "visible" head of the Golden Dawn at its zenith around 1890. Besides Mathers, who was the brother-in-law of the French philosopher Henri Bergson, its more prominent members included William Butler Yates, fiction writers Algernon Blackwood and Arthur Machen, Annie Horniman, the founder of Abbey Theatre, Dublin, the founder of the British Buddhist Society, Allan Bennett, and Charles Williams (see Cavendish, 1975). In addition to Mathers, Order members Aleister Crowley, Israel Regardie, and Alfred Edward Waite became highly influential disseminators of Golden Dawn occultism. The theosophy of the Golden Dawn represented a grand synthesis of all manner of esotericism and occultism (see Chapter 6).

About 1890 the original Golden Dawn schismed producing several organizations that remain influential to the present-day. The Great Beast, Aleister Crowley, founded the Argentinum Astrum (A.A., the Order of the Silver Star), and later headed the German Ordo Templarum (OTO). He transplanted several occult organizations, including the OTO, to the United States where additional groups, based on or heavily influenced by Crowley's teachings—including sex magik—have been established (see Melton, 1978:256-257). Paul Case, an initiate of the Order of the Golden Dawn in New York, founded the Builders of the Adytum (BOTA) in 1920 (Melton, 1978:258-259).

A host of other magical and occult groups were formed during the 1920's and 1930's, including the Brotherhood of the White Temple, Philosophical Research Society, Soulcraft, Inc. (or Silver Shirts), the Church of Light, the Lemurian Fellowship, and the Sabian Assembly (Melton, 1978:183-196). Rosicrucian fellowships established earlier (Fraternitas Rosae Crucis, 1858, Societas Rosicruciana in Civitatibus Foederatis or S.R.I.C.F., 1880) continued to function, and new organizations were added: the Societas Rosicruciana in America in 1907; and The Ancient and Mystical Order Rosae Crucis (A.M.O.R.C.) during the early 1900's (Melton, 1986:68-75). Witches commonly claim descent from ancient and family traditions, and related organizations traditionally have been secret or semi-secret. Yet, discernable organizations of witches, pagans, and neo-pagans seem to be recent (see Adler, 1986). The Long Island Church of Aphrodite, founded in 1938, is one of the first known neo-pagan groups in the United States (Adler, 1986:233). Though unrelated to witchcraft, Our Lady of Endor Coven, the Ophite Cultus Satanas, the oldest contemporary Satanist group in the United States, was established in 1948. By the 1930's astrology and related occultisms were entrenched in newspapers, as well as represented by assorted specialty magazines, and popular books (see Marty, 1970; Galbreath, 1983).

Spiritualism, New Thought, and Christian Science experienced steady growth in the United Sates during most of this century (Melton, 1986). Theosophy produced new splinters: The Arcane School in New York was founded by Alice Baily in 1923; and Rudolf Steiner founded the Anthroposophical Society in 1912. The I AM of the Ballard family developed during the late 1930's. The Summit Lighthouse was instituted in 1958 by Mark L. Prophet, and the subsequent organization of the Church Universal and Triumphant, led by his widow, Elizabeth Clare Prophet, has attracted considerable recent attention. Many, many other groups derived from these traditions of esotericism emerged during the first half of this century (see Melton, 1978:59-117).

Most of the Eastern religious groups that became established early in the United States primarily served immigrant populations (see Melton, 1978: 355-444). Among the general population, previous interest in oriental religion continued and attracted followings, especially the Beats of the 1940's and 1950's. Vedanta Societies were stable. Beginning in 1920, Yogananda spent thirty years establishing Self-Realization Fellowship Centers in the United States (Ellwood and Partin, 1988:189). The related, Self Revelation Church of Absolute Monism was established in 1927 (Melton, 1978:362). The Divine Life Society, based on the teachings of Sivananda, was founded in 1936. The Gedatsu Church of America, an eclectic Shinto Buddhist, Christian mixture, was incorporated in 1951 (Melton, 1978:406). Soka Gakkai arrived in America following WWII by way of men who had been stationed in Japan and their Japanese wives and girlfriends (Ellwood and Partin, 1988:246).

The Association for Research and Enlightenment (ARE) was founded by the influential Edgar Cayce in 1932. Parapsychology also emerged and became established during the 1930's. UFO reports began during the late 1940's. Additional reports during the 1950's and 60's spawned numerous flying saucer clubs, a related literature, and assorted cults (Jacobs, 1983; Festinger, et al., 1956; Melton, 1978:198-211). Related interest in scientific anomalies and science fiction constituted an elaborate milieu by at least the late 1940's. This is the milieu in which L. Ron Hubbard developed *Dianetics* and from which Scientology eventually would emerge (Wallis, 1977; also see Adler, 1979: 266-267). Hence, although esotericism and occultism did not enjoy highly visible, extensive public support, attract massive media exposure, provoke controversy or produce dramatic innovations during the first half of the 20th century, there was considerable subcultural activity. These traditions, related networks as well as establishments facilitated subsequent events.

THE CONTEMPORARY ESOTERIC SCENE

It is my contention that the esoteric, occult, and cultic milieu in the United States today constitutes what Irwin (1977) calls a **social scene**. It consists of common themes (esoteric and occult knowledge) and means (social networks, study groups, cults, sects, movement organizations, confederations, published literature) whereby participants structure and organize their experiences and activities. It provides bases for collective involvement and participation, opportunities for making interpersonal contacts and developing intimate relationships, sources of physical, sensual, and intellectual stimulation, and an element of reputational risk vis-a-vis the stigma sometimes attached to esoteric and occult belief. Through the esoteric scene people define and identify themselves socially, and they make sense out of their existence.

Like other social scenes (Irwin, 1977), the recent esoteric scene in the United States may be read in terms of a natural history. During the late 1960's and early 1970's the esoteric scene emerged. Drawing on existing, underground esoteric and occult traditions, it became visible and popular as an interest in unconventional beliefs and practices, and attracted a core of additional devotees. As the esoteric scene became more visible it elicited significant media attention and expanded. Exploitation by the media and mass involvement in this scene during the late 1970's led to "corruption" of its original meanings through their reinterpretation and use by new members. During the early 1980's the central activities of the esoteric scene increasingly came to be seen as routine and taken for granted. Particular ideas and groups also became less innovative and more accommodative to the larger society. Spontaneous public excitement about esotericism began to subside. The media labeled esoteric groups as **cults**, defined them as destructive, and an anti-cult movement developed. As the media became less attentive, the popularity of the esoteric scene waned, and it became less visible and increasingly stagnant. Although esotericism as a highly visible, public scene has paled, it has not disappeared, and its demise seems unlike in the near future. The overall level of participation by Americans in esotericism probably is as high as, if not higher than in the period prior to its recent revival. As in earlier periods of American history, it seems likely that esotericism will continue to comprise a sociocultural underground, and it most likely will be the source of subsequent revival and revitalization.

Significant journalistic and scholarly attention to esotericism and occultism, beginning in the late 1960's, commonly was justified by citing evidence of massive public interest and revival. These reports noted that in the United States 1,200 of 1,750 daily newspapers publish horoscope columns, the zodiac business was a $200 million a year enterprise involving an estimated 40 million Americans, and 5 million people reportedly planned their lives according to astrological predictions (Freeland, 1972; Heenan, 1973). Furthermore, astrological and tarot readings were available by telephone in most American urban areas, and advertisements for the services of magicians, palmists, card readers, and other seers were visible in most cities as well as many smaller towns.

Popular books, magazines, television programs, movies and songs dealing with topics ranging from mysterious creatures from outer space, lost continents, astrology, divination, magic, and Eastern religions to psychic healing, hypnotic regression, spirit communication, demonology, witchcraft, psychic powers, healing, and a host of related matters abounded. Many colleges and universities offered courses on meditation, yoga, Eastern religions and thought, psychic phenomena, as well as the occult arts and sciences. In most areas of the country paraphernalia ranging from toys, games, oils, and cards to posters, jewelry, incense, and even bank checks were readily available (see Marty, 1970; Staude, 1970; Shepherd, 1972; Truzzi, 1972a, 1972b, 1974, 1975; Heenan, 1973; Quarantelli and Wenger, 1973; Tiryakian, 1974; Stupple, 1975).

Public opinion surveys indicated that large numbers of Americans and other Western peoples accepted and subscribed to seemingly strange and irrational beliefs. Greeley (1975) reported that between 24 and 59 percent of the American population claimed to have had "psychic" experiences ranging from deja vu to clairvoyance, 35 percent claimed to have had "mystical" experiences, and 27 percent claimed some feeling of contact with the dead. A Gallup poll (1978) maintained that 57 percent of the people aware of UFO's believed in their existence, 54 percent of the population believed in angels, 51 percent believed in ESP, 39 percent believed in devils, 29 percent believed in astrology, 11 percent believed in ghosts, and 10 percent believed in witches. Based on a French national sample Fischler (1974) reported that 30 percent of the population believed in astrology, and 12.5 percent consulted at least one fortune-teller, seer, or someone who predicted the future. Nelson (1975) observed that 10 percent of the population of English towns claimed some experience of "psychic" phenomena. Gallup (1978) maintained that 27 percent of his British sample believed in flying saucers, 20 percent believed in ghosts, and 7 percent said they had seen a ghost!

Rowley (1970) estimated the combined population of the new religions (Indian and Eastern religions, native cults, and "avant garde" Christianity) at 2.5 million Americans. Melton (1978) identified over 1200 active, mostly unconventional religious groups in the United States. Wuthnow (1987) estimated that by the middle 1970's about 10 percent of the north American population had participated in a new religious movement. Stark and Bainbridge (1985) claimed that there were 2.3 cults per million people in the United States, and 3.2 cults per million inhabitants in Great Britain (but see Hervieu-Leger, 1986; Campiche, 1987; Wallis, 1984, 1986, 1987; Wallis and Bruce, 1986).

Enormous media attention was devoted to unorthodox movements like Jesus people, Scientology, Hare Krishna, the Unification Church, the Children of God, witches, and satanists. The tragic death of more than 900 members of the Peoples' Temple at Jonestown, Guyana, in 1978 was transformed into a media event and contributed greatly to the definition of an American cult problem (Jorgensen, 1980). The emergence of an anticult movement during the mid 1970's attracted extensive media coverage, thereby contributing to the perception that large numbers of brainwashed Americans are involved with cults (see Beckford and Cole, 1987; Shupe and Bromley, 1980; Harper, 1982; Shupe, 1985; Bromley and Shupe, 1987).

Public interest in esoteric teachings, practices, and groups, according to some indicators, waned and declined during the 1980's. Wuthnow (1987) maintained that by about 1975 the growth of new cults and sects had stabilized and begun to decline. Memberships in several of the more controversial movements, like the Unification Church, Hare Krishna, Scientology, and the Divine Light Mission, apparently declined significantly (Appel, 1983; Rochford, 1985). This ostensible decline, however, may be in part an artifact of earlier perceptions and indicators of the revival.

In many instances the number of people involved with unconventional beliefs and groups was grossly exaggerated (see, for instance, Balch, 1980). Beliefs and groups that looked to be new and bizarre during the earlier period seem much less so today (Robbins, 1988). Though well established, extraordinary religions did not radically transform American life (Marty, 1985). Strange beliefs and groups still are news, but media attention to them is less extensive and sensational (see Beckford, 1985; Harper, 1982; Kilbourne and Richardson, 1984; Robbins, 1988; Robbins et al., 1985; Shupe and Bromley, 1980, 1985). Declining interest in popular beliefs, practices, and products of the 1970's seems to be most pronounced among those people for whom these matters were mostly entertainment and a casual diversion. The cultic milieu, even during the 1970's, was composed of large numbers of casual devotees, seekers and clients.

Public interest in esotericism is less visible and less intense today. It is noteworthy, however, that many of the beliefs and groups coming to public attention during the 1970's were not at all new (Melton, 1978). Interest in esotericism, as I have shown, has a long history in Western cultures, and it has been a persistent, recurrent, and periodically influential feature of American life. Americans' interest in esotericism did not emerge overnight, and when renewed interest was stimulated, pre-existing traditions, establishments, networks, groups, and organizations greatly facilitated its growth and expansion. Many of the smaller groups of the 1970's went unnoticed and uncounted (Jorgensen, 1982; Appel, 1983). Greeley (1989) reporting a repeat of the 1972 survey (mentioned above) again in 1985 found that Americans reporting ecstatic experiences had risen to 40 percent, with 7 percent reporting them often. Significantly, people reporting a feeling of being in contact with someone who had died went from 25 percent in 1972 to 42 percent in 1984, a 17 point increase (Greeley, 1989: 59).

Many different factors contributed to the emergence, expansion, and decline of the esoteric scene in America. Post WWII economic prosperity afforded more Americans, particularly a growing middle class, with increased leisure time to pursue entertainment and serious avocations, like esotericism. The sociocultural conflict, dissent, turmoil, critiques, and countercultures of the latter 1950's and especially the 60's (civil rights, youth movements, anti-war sentiments, riots, political demonstrations, women's and gay liberation movements) contributed to an environment in which esotericism might flourish. The role of youth movements, however, should not be overestimated. Contrary to O'Keefe's (1982:564) exaggerated pronouncements, the emergence of the esoteric scene necessarily depended on existing traditions, establishments, and social networks involving older, long-time believers. While American youth were over-represented in some portions of this scene (Jesus movements, oriental religions, and some cults), contributing greatly to its vitality and visibility, it also involved countless numbers of older publics and extensive networks of groups and practitioners who were not describably young.

Developments in mass communication, television, advertising, and publishing, contributed significantly to the visibility of the esoteric scene, images, and definitions of it, and the availability of esoteric entertainment, goods and services, including both exoteric and esoteric periodicals and books. Clearly, scholarly attention contributed to expansion of this scene and definitions of it. The role of publishing, once again contrary to O'Keefe's (1982:564) simplistic exaggerations and distortions of it, must be appreciated contextually. An occult publishing establishment (Marty, 1970) predated, even if it later facilitated, the emergence of this scene. Similarly, scholarly interest in magic, seemingly strange beliefs and practices, esotericism, occultism, nonconventionality, mass movements, and so on were well established long before the 1960's. Scholarly attention past and present surely contributed to the esoteric scene, yet the contention that recent scholarship was itself part of the occult revival distorts and otherwise neglects important features of this situation. As noted above, scholarly appraisals of the significance and magnitude of the esoteric scene both over- and under-estimated it. Much of the research conducted before the early 1980's failed to connect the esoteric scene with historical traditions, particularly in the United States. While some scholarship was sympathetic to esoteric culture (Yates, Tiryakian), much of what was written, as discussed above, was highly critical, explained esotericism away, and exoteric experts actively were involved in the debunking and anti-cult movements. Other scholarship, such as Butler's, clearly demands a reinterpretation of American religious history, based it seems to me on sound arguments, and I do not detect in this work any romanticism.

Insofar as the esoteric scene has paled, and I think it has, this seems to be partly a reflection of diminished media attention and redefinition. Experts looking for hot topics and quick publications have moved into other areas, and scholarship on this topic seems to have entered a more careful, deliberate, systematic, historically grounded phase. Coincidentally, the entertainment value of esotericism, like many fads and fashions, has diminished by way of over exposure, exploitation, and the limited attention span of publics. The media and general publics have been convinced that cults are dangerous, and people consequently are less inclined to find certain discredited movements, at least, attractive.

The sociocultural climate has shifted in other ways. For a variety of complex reasons, Americans have become more politically moderate to conservative, more preoccupied with economic success, and more religiously conservative, as is vividly illustrated by popular support of evangelical and fundamentalist movements, not to mention media attention to them. Even so, Americans' interest in esotericism and occultism continues, and while the public scene may be diminished, it is unlikely to disappear. Many of the larger movement organizations seem to be stable. Some beliefs, such as witchcraft, paganism, neo-paganism, seem to be experiencing growth (see Lloyd, 1978; Scott, 1980; Adler, 1986; Luhrmann, 1989). And various refocused human potential and therapy movements continue to emerge and attract significant followings. The core of the esoteric community, as described in the Chapter Three, still exists.

Notes

1 These writings sometimes are referred to as social constructionism, symbolic interactionism, cognitive sociology, ethnomethodology, interpretative interactionism, existential sociology and interactionism, interpretative anthropology, dramaturgy, cultural studies, and phenomenology. My use of them supports the contention that they form a coherent sociology of culture and knowledge, but this claim will not be explicated further since it would detract unnecessarily from the specific problematics of this book.

2 Capitalization of such terms throughout this work serves as a way of emphasizing that certain bodies of knowledge have been socially defined, sanctioned, and legitimated over and against potentially rival claims to knowledge. Hence religion (Christianity) becomes Religion (Protestantism), science (empiricism or biology) becomes Science (Experimentalism or Evolutionism), and knowledge (what everyone knows) becomes Knowledge (the claims of Religion and Science).

3 This is at best a very rough, crude sketch of meanings and sources of esoteric knowledge. In spite of the publication of impressive historical studies of esoteric knowledge and its relationship with exoteric culture over about the last twenty years, the literature on this topic is far from definitive. Even within restricted areas, such as occult traditions, much work remains to be done. My purpose in this section is merely to introduce and arrange in a hintful way meanings and sources of esoteric culture to be examined later in this book.

4 O'Keefe's (1982:552) assertion that the works of Yates (1969, 1972), Walker (1975), and French (1972), were "perhaps part of the twentieth century occult upsurge!" is even more bizarre and absurd. This literature may be sympathetic to the occultism, and occult thinkers may have used it, but it was produced by exoteric scholars and exoteric science, not occultism

5 The *Fama* is a reference to the *Fama Fraternitaitis* or *The Fame of the Fraternity of the Meritorious Order of the Rosy Cross Addressed to the Learned in General and the Governors of Europe*. The *Confessions* refers to a pamphlet entitled *Confessions of the Rosicrucian Fraternity*. These documents were claimed by subsequent generations of occultists as the basis for the organization of secret orders which were otherwise indebted to the Hermetic-Kabalistic tradition.

CHAPTER 3

The Esoteric Community in the Valley

The "esoteric community" is a loose confederation of individuals and associations, geographically dispersed throughout the metropolitan Valley, which is organized by way of overlapping networks of social relationship. Its members include assorted leaders, seekers, students, and practitioners, as well as business enterprises, cultic groups, and cultic associations. The members of the esoteric community believe in and practice a full range of esoteric teachings. In spite of tremendous diversity in what they believe and practice, members more or less share in common an ethos of esotericism, channels of communication, definitions and images of themselves as well as their relationships with the exoteric society. They construct and enforce codes of ethical practice defining relations with clientele, and they define and enforce community boundaries.

The esoteric community is part of the larger cultic milieu and esoteric scene in the Valley. This esoteric scene interfaces with exoteric culture by way of literature, other mass communications, and commercial products which express and convey popular cultural images of esoteric culture. Although the beliefs, practices, and activities of some minority groups and many of the new religious movements of the 19th century commonly are seen as esoteric from the standpoint of the exoteric culture, most of them are not connected socially with this scene in the Valley. Like many of the larger, more visible, recent new religions, they comprise socially separate spheres of activity. Some of the recent new religious movements are part of this esoteric scene. They depend on the supportive cultic milieu for recruits, and some of them are related in very limited ways to the esoteric community. A few of these groups overlap with the cultic milieu and the esoteric community within the larger esoteric scene in the Valley. The esoteric scene includes a host of seekers, clients, students, practitioners, and sometimes cultic groups that socially exist within the cultic environment but do not sustain persistent, stable connections with other participants or groups.

This description, analysis, and interpretation of the esoteric scene and community in the Valley contributes to sociological theorizing about cults, sects, and the cultic milieu. Although the idea of a cultic milieu has been discussed extensively within the scholarly literature, it very rarely has been concretely described and analyzed. This discussion provides a fairly detailed image of the cultic milieu as it existed in the Valley during the middle to late 1970's. While the character of esoteric knowledge encourages extreme individualism and mediates against the formation of stable, enduring groups and movement organizations, the cultic milieu serves to support socially the persistence of esoteric culture in America.

THEORIZING ABOUT CULTS, SECTS, AND THE CULTIC MILIEU

One of the central sociological problems that emerged during my fieldwork in the Valley was to observe connections and relationships among beliefs, practices, and groups that seemed to share in common a lack of social legitimacy in the exoteric society. This problem generally has been treated theoretically, as something to be solved by conceptualizing types of unconventional beliefs or groups whereby similarities and differences among them are identified (see, for example, Glock and Bellah, 1976; Ellwood and Partin, 1988; Needleman, 1970; Zaretsky and Leone, 1974). Research has tended to focus on a specific type or types of nonconventional beliefs, practices, adherents, and groups, particularly in the form of cults and sects, sometimes with reference to larger but proximate historical, cultural, or social contexts. Much less research has concentrated on systematically observing and analyzing possible relationships among these phenomena.

Campbell's (1972) notion of the "cultic milieu" rarely has been examined systematically and concretely. The idea of a cultic milieu (subculture, social world, social networks or related formulations) generally has been used as the largely unexamined context in which the activities of a particular cult or sect take place. In spite of this neglect, certain features of cultic milieus had been described more exactly by the late 1970's. Truzzi (1972, 1974) sketched the multidimensionality of American occultism, emphasizing its popular cultural attributes. Other studies (Balch and Taylor, 1977a; Lynch, 1977, 1980; Wallis, 1977) observed more serious levels of participation and identified social networks of believers. Balch and Taylor (1977b; also see Balch, 1980) as well as Lynch (1977, 1980) described the importance of networks within the cultic milieu for the conversion process. Studies of witches, pagans, astrologers, mystics, and assorted other practitioners of nonconventional doctrines provided further evidence of informal and formal networks, some of them crossing local, regional, and even national boundaries (Hartman, 1976; Adler, 1979; Scott, 1980). And I had reported on the esoteric community in the Valley (see Jorgensen and Jorgensen, 1977; Jorgensen, 1978, 1978, 1980).

In a proposed synthesis of deprivation and social networks' models of recruitment to religious groups, Stark and Bainbridge (1980; also see Bainbridge and Stark, 1979, 1980) disputed the idea that American occultism was supported by social networks. The cultic milieu, they (1980:1392) argued, "resembles a mass audience more than a real subcultural phenomenon." I (1981:427-429) commented by noting that this assertion was not supported by a growing body of evidence, including my own research. Problems with their contention derived from the use of a questionnaire, a preoccupation with quantification, a peculiarly narrow operational definition of the occult, and a sample of college students, the very people who are more likely to dabble in the occult than participate in social networks. Ironically, even Bainbridge's (1978) earlier study of a satanic cult contradicted their hypothesis about the lack of networks of occultists.

In reply to my comment, Stark and Bainbridge (1981:430-433) referred to their previous distinction among "audience cults," "client cults," and "cult movements" (see Stark and Bainbridge, 1979; also see Bainbridge and Stark, 1979, 1980a, 1980b, 1981; Stark, Bainbridge and Doyle, 1979). Yet, as I have argued elsewhere (see Jorgensen, 1982; Jorgensen and Jorgensen, 1982), this distinction begs the issue of networks and results in further confusion. Neither audiences or practitioner/client relations are "cults" in any ordinary sense. Stark's and Bainbridge's view of cults and sects, as Wallis' (1977) earlier work showed, empirically fails to distinguish between them and thereby limits observation and analysis of organizational transformations. Wallis' (1977) view of cults and sects, on the other hand, contributes to a theory of cult development and sectarianization, and it is invaluable for examining the cultic milieu.

My observations in the midwestern, southwestern, and southeastern United States strongly suggests that "cults" are the most common form of organization within the contemporary milieu of esotericism (also see Scott, 1980). Viewed sociologically, **cults** characteristically are fairly small (most commonly involving less than 100 participants), loosely organized, nonexclusive collections of seekers, clients and devoutly believing members (see Campbell, 1972; Nelson, 1968; Buckner, 1965; Wallis, 1977). Cult beliefs characteristically are unconventional, but flexible, nonsectarian, eclectic, synthetic, and informal thereby lacking standardization, formalization, orthodoxy, or dogma (see Scott, 1980). Cult leadership may be centered around authoritative, charismatic personalities, but cult participation commonly is democratic, and not hierarchical to any large extent. Cult beliefs and participation tend to be highly individualistic, a condition Wallis (1977:14) calls "**epistemological individualism**." Membership in cults, consequently, fluctuates and these groups are precarious, short lived and highly transitory (Wallis, 1977).

Cultic milieus reflect the proliferation of these precarious, transitory groups, and sometimes constellations of related activity. Publics, audiences, and masses support this environment, and make it seem even more robust. Within such milieus seekers and clients move from group to group and, along with other cult members and assorted practitioners, forming multiple overlapping networks of social relationship. A charismatic leader (such as Joseph Smith, Mary Eddy Baker, L. Ron Hubbard) or unique circumstances (UFO's, tapping and rappings) may provide a catalyst for sustaining a mass movement, more stable organizations, or the persistence of some loose aggregation of publics and cultic groups, as illustrated by Spiritualism, New Thought, and Theosophy in the 19th century. Those relatively rare instances in which cults become more cohesively linked by networks or form more stable organizations led some thinkers (see Nelson, 1968, 1969; Yinger, 1970) to speak of established cults or cultic movements.

Cults sometimes undergo ideological and organizational transformation, although these are not necessary conditions, nor is such a sequence unidimensional (Wallis, 1977:13). There may be several avenues whereby cults are transformed into less precarious, more enduring, stable organizations. A crucial dimension, however, is some transition from epistemological individualism toward greater "**epistemological authoritarianism**" (Wallis, 1977:17). Truth and knowledge, in other words, are defined more specifically, and concretely located in more centralized authorities, such as particular texts, documents, writings, or leaders. In the process, cults become more characteristically "sectarian" (see Wallis, 1975; Wilson, 1970). Sectarianization, then, is defined by greater doctrinal orthodoxy, definitions of and requirements for inclusive membership (and exclusivity), more exacting definitions and standards of conduct within the group, the specification of more standardized roles and functions, mechanisms for controlling collective life, organizational specialization and differentiation, hierarchy, and centralization (Wallis, 1977).

Sects, unlike cults, consequently are more cohesive and stable organizations. Greater stability makes the group less dependent on the cultic milieu as well as more self-sufficient, and greater doctrinal orthodoxy leads it to reject cult-like beliefs. If sects are successful in attracting members, they of course grow and become increasingly powerful movement organizations. As they become larger and more powerful, sects are likely to be perceived as threatening to the exoteric society. Sectarian beliefs and organizations therefore are likely to be defined socially as not merely unconventional but deviant and even dangerous, leading to hostility and conflict between the group and the exoteric society. In order to grow, flourish, and perhaps even survive, sects must find ways of dealing with social conflict.

Sects may emerge in other ways too, such as by way of schism within existing sects or denominations. For a variety of reasons (see, for instance, Johnson, 1957, 1971; Yinger, 1970; Wilson, 1961), sects over time tend to become more denominational in character, reflecting in part accommodation to the larger society and less conflict, tension and hostility between the group and the exoteric society. It is ironic that many of the groups disparagingly referred to as "cults" in America today are **sects**, sociologically, and some of these groups increasingly have become denominational in character in spite of the lingering stigma of their former, more pronounced sectarianism. Mormons and Christian Scientists, from the 19th century, and Scientologists in this century, seemed to have moved in these directions.

ESOTERIC CULTURE AND THE CULTIC MILIEU

The Valley is a culturally pluralistic, urban social environment containing a perplexing variety of nonconventional, unorthodox, esoteric, and occult beliefs, practices, believers, and groups. This includes elements of exoteric culture, such as scholarly literature, journalism, movies, television programs, publics, audiences, as well as consumer goods and services reflecting popular cultural interests, nonwhite cultures and ethic subcultures, new religious movements of the 19th century, like Mormons, Christian Scientists, and Spiritualists; more recent new religions, such as Transcendental Meditation, Scientology, and Vedanta Societies; a cultic milieu supporting an esoteric scene; and networks of seekers, clients, practitioners, and group comprising an esoteric community. In spite of similarities among these phenomena, some of them are not connected socially to the esoteric scene in the Valley; and while others contribute to a supportive climate of opinion, they are not directly part of it socially. The phenomena connected socially by the esoteric scene in the Valley constitute different centers and networks of human interaction (see Figure One, page 56).

During my fieldwork in the Valley, as briefly discussed in Chapter One, I began assembling card indexes of practitioners and groups. Along with observation, participation, and informal interviewing, I eventually developed an extensive body of information about social connections and relationships among a host of nonconventional beliefs, practices, people, and groups. Once I developed a sense of what was included in the esoteric community, as discussed in detail below, it became possible to generate analytically a fairly detailed picture or map of the community, its connection to the larger esoteric scene, and thereby other inclusive or exclusive phenomena. Of about a million inhabitants of the Valley in 1975, I crudely estimate that around 25,000 people may have been involved in the esoteric scene, not counting untold numbers of the general public who are entertained by esotericism or dabble individualistically in it. I collected information on 100 groups involving anywhere from 5,000 to 15,000 participants. Figure One (see page 56) depicts the esoteric scene in the Valley, and phenomena related and unrelated socially to it, within the context of the exoteric society in which it is located. This figure serves to illustrate the following discussion.

Scholarly discussions of unconventional groups commonly include and even focus on new religious movements of the 19th century, such as the Mormons, Christian Scientists, Jehovah's Witnesses, and Seventh-day Adventists. In the Valley, participants in the cultic milieu sometimes mention these religions favorably, but none of them is part of this scene as envisioned by insiders. Neither did I get any indication that these religions see themselves as part of the esoteric scene. Unlike the cults forming this milieu, most of the new religions of the 19th century have undergone a sectarianization process. Insofar as they were at one time part of a cultic milieu, they have long since moved out of this environment, except perhaps in the mind of some publics, such as Christian fundamentalists. Some of these groups, such as Christian Science and Mormonism, developed more denominational organizations. The case of the Mormons is unique in that in this region of the United States they comprise a powerful minority, and in certain Valley municipalities, a politically dominant majority group. Mormons and Christian Scientists are shown in Figure One as autonomous religious organizations in the exoteric society.

More recent new American religious movements, such as Scientology, the Children of God, and transplanted Eastern religious organizations (14 of which exist in the Valley) like the Vedanta Society (see Damrell, 1977), Hare Krishna (see Rochford, 1985) and Transcendental Meditation seemed to be undergoing a sectarianization process. Scientology, for instance, has been transformed dramatically by this process (see Wallis, 1977). Some of these groups advertise in the esoteric community, and depend on the cultic milieu of the esoteric scene for recruits, but they rarely participate directly in this scene or the community. Several of these

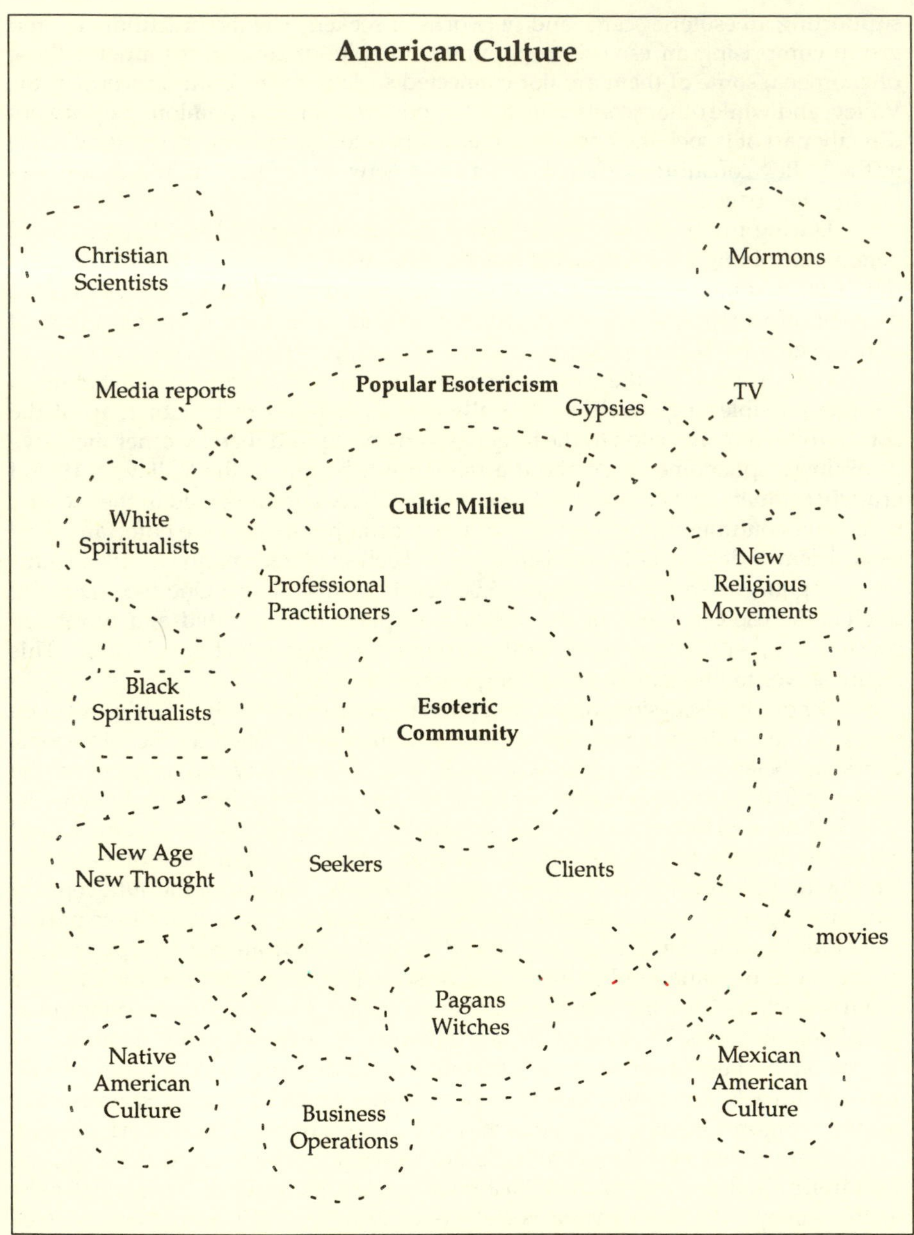

Figure 1: The Esoteric Scene in the Valley

groups (Scientology, Eastern Religions) are shown in Figure One to illustrate these relationships. Though not part of the scene, their boundaries touch the scene and overlap with a sphere (represented by the circle around the scene in the Valley) in which the exoteric society and esoteric scene intermesh or intermingle. These sect-like groups advertise in the esoteric community, and recruit from the related cultic milieu.

I found, as a general principle, that the more a group had been transformed by sectarianization, the less likely it was to be identified, by the group or scene participants, as part of this scene or the community in the Valley. Conversely, organizations or movements that had not undergone sectarianization were more likely to be identified and/or participate to some extent in this scene and the community. The six New Age Christian churches in the Valley are linked socially by way of a local New Thought Alliance (as shown in Figure One). They identify with the esoteric scene, advertise in the community, and recruit from this cultic milieu, but they do not participate directly in the community. In Figure One they therefore are shown as a distinctive set of groups that overlap with the esoteric scene. The New Age churches and their members also sustain social relationships, apart from this scene, in the exoteric society, and consequently they are depicted as extending beyond the boundaries of the esoteric scene in the Valley.

There are twenty or more spiritualist churches in the Valley, including several predominantly Black congregations. Many of these groups, including two Black churches, identify with and advertise in the community, as shown in Figure One. Some of the white spiritualists actively participate in this scene, and several of them are viewed by insiders as part of the community. Since the spiritualists also draw directly and even extensively from the larger population (people who are otherwise not connected to this scene), they are presented in Figure One as extending into the exoteric society. The spiritualist churches are shown as connected by belief (touching) but represented by separate constellations of organizations.

Business organizations, based elsewhere, which marketed esoteric beliefs and practices periodically were visible as part of the local scene. Their sponsors manifest considerable knowledge of the local scene and community, recruit from the cultic milieu, and advertise in the community. Seekers and members of local groups sometimes purchase these goods and services, but none of these organizations are otherwise directly involved with the esoteric community. Since these business also aim to recruit from unconnected populations in the larger society, as shown in Figure One, they overlap the vague zone between the esoteric scene and the exoteric society. Gypsy fortunetellers (see Tatro, 1974), as presented in Figure One, also occupy this zone. These people, who engage in palmistry and card reading for pay, are highly visible in the Valley. They are perceived by outsiders as part of this scene and the community, but (as will be discussed in detail below), they are deliberately excluded by members from involvement in the esoteric community.[1]

The esoteric scene and community in the Valley included people who identify themselves as witches, magicians, and pagans. During my fieldwork in the Valley I earnestly attempted to locate groups organized on these bases. In all cases, however, members were unable to identify concretely specific groups of practitioners. Some of the cultic groups composing this scene and participating in the community are not open to outsiders and see themselves as secret or secretive organizations. Persistent rumors of groups of witches and pagans suggest that they may exist, but I was unable to locate them. Pagans and witches, along with other secretive cults, are depicted in Figure One within the esoteric scene to reflect this possibility. More recent events suggest that witchcraft and paganism have become a part of the esoteric scene, but they seem to reflect a distinctive and largely autonomous sphere of activity within this sociocultural arena (see Lloyd, 1978; Scott, 1980; Adler, 1986). In this respect the American scene differs considerably from the much more open, dense networks of British occultists, magicians, witches, and pagans described by Luhrmann (1989).

Media reports, scholarly literature, exoteric bookstores and businesses selling esoteric goods, movies, TV programs, as well as publics and audiences consuming esoteric goods and services are located by Figure One in the zone between the esoteric scene and exoteric society. Although these phenomena generally are viewed with disdain by serious scene participants and members of the community, they contribute significantly to it (as described in Chapter Two). Popular images of esotericism are sustained by and transmitted through popular, mass culture. Even those people who eventually become devout insiders to the esoteric scene generally dabble in popular esotericism. Unlike sects which commonly insulate and isolate their members from the exoteric society, cult participants constantly interact with the larger society.

The cultic milieu of the esoteric scene in the Valley during the mid-1970's, as presented in Figure One, involved a diverse and diffuse array of beliefs, adherents, practices, and cults. The esoteric community was one center of this activity (as shown in Figure One), but overlapping networks of social relationship suggest the possibility of other centers of activity, ones that I did not study in detail. In addition to beliefs and practices already mentioned, the esoteric scene included: **occultism**, alchemy, astrology, numerology, palmistry, magic, divination, the tarot, and other teachings and techniques associated with the Hermetic-Kabalistic tradition; **psychic** phenomena and research, psychic, psychical, or parapsychological research and phenomena referred to as psi, clairvoyance, telepathy, and the like; **folk and esoteric medical practices**, such as the use of herbs, tonics, potions, and other unconventional preparations, mentalistic or faith healing, reflexology, and so on; and an eclectic host of other, commonly syncretic beliefs, practices, and groups. Interestingly, there was little mention of satanism in the Valley during this period. This cultic milieu includes people who move from group to group in search of "enlightenment, friends, good health, or any number of equally elusive goals" (Balch and Taylor, 1977a:31); private practitioners who occasionally meet with groups, perform demonstrations, or do readings; small cultic study groups; business enterprises (clinics, book stores, publishers, educational or therapeutic institutes); quasi-religious (or spiritual) groups; and associations of psychic practitioners, astrologers, and researchers. Groups and individuals within this cultic milieu are loosely connected and interrelated. Interaction among and between groups is bounded by social networks.

THE ESOTERIC COMMUNITY

The **esoteric community** is a very loose collection and network of seekers, clients, practitioners, groups, businesses, confederations of practitioners and groups, and a few central activities, such as psychic fairs, all of which are dispersed geographically throughout the Valley.[2] It exists in the imagination (ideation) of its members, their symbolizations and talk, and their activities. In spite of tremendous diversity, it is sustained by their sense of community (mutual belonging), differences with the exoteric world, similar values, ethical and normative principles and worldviews, as well as their collective symbolizations, interactions, relationships, and other involvements.

There is no comprehensive list of individuals or groups belonging to what insiders called the esoteric community. When I asked participants to identify inclusive individuals and groups they oftentimes referred me to lists of practitioners and groups contained in local publications. Yet, I knew that many of these people and groups had little, if any, connection to the activities in which I had participated and observed. **Epistemological individualism**, I found, was characteristic of the entire community. No one wanted to define membership, particularly if this meant excluding other people, their beliefs, or groups.

The ethos of the esoteric community in the Valley very much resembled the "core beliefs" described by Scott (1980:Chapter Two) on the basis of a participant observational study of two esoteric groups in the San Francisco Bay area. She identifies the basic premises of esoteric beliefs as including: a unity of spiritual and material realities which include humanity, reflecting the Hermetic principle of "as above, so below"; some divine origin of all reality; multiple levels or planes of reality, and multiple paths to knowledge of reality; the possibility of communication with alternative, sometimes invisible realities, spirits, and forces; positive and negative, or good and evil powers, spirits, and forces; order, harmony, and balance in a purposeful universe; the possibility of human perfection by way of training and evolution; interaction with cosmic realities through ritual and practices involving magical procedures; and a respect for the power and danger of esoteric knowledge. All of these basic principles are manifest in some way as part of the ethos of the esoteric community in the Valley.

Members of the esoteric community exhibit an openness and toleration for nearly every possible claim to knowledge and truth. Members eclectically mix esoteric teachings and intermingle them with borrowed exoteric elements. While exoteric thought tends to be interpreted esoterically, members live in and are part of the exoteric society. Cultic existence, unlike sectarian life, does not insulate and isolate members from the larger society. Their esotericism, consequently, sometimes is expressed in an idiom inconsistently and blaringly reflecting incomplete synthesis. Jay, the Editor of *Psychic Magazine*, speaking as a community leader, expresses the spirit of epistemological individualism partly in the language (objectivity) of exotericism:

> [In] the areas of communication, education, and research, every idea and theory, religious and otherwise, is considered objectively. This is not a missionary endeavor whereby we are to convert *anyone* into believing contrary to their natural instincts. We just happen to believe that there is much on this earth that is not dreamed of in our sciences and philosophies.

It is considered a serious breach of community ethics for members to criticize one another's beliefs or practices, at least publicly. Refusal to acknowledge many paths to truth and enlightenment is perceived as dogmatic and intolerant.

The epistemological individualism of the esoteric community is evident is cultic organizations and it is reflected in activities such as research, counseling, education, and particularly practitioner/client relationships. These activities reflect a preponderance of dyadic relationships, although some of the more spiritually oriented cults engage in collective ritual. Esotericism is concerned with the collective human condition, even though this commonly is expressed individualistically. Esoteric practitioners sincerely believe that they are on the vanguard of a spiritual revolution, the dawn of a new age of human awareness and understanding whereby the universe will be rediscovered through esoteric knowledge and related practices. Esotericism is for members an abiding preoccupation, and sometimes a full-time activity. In either case it is a way of life. The esoteric community, in this respect, is composed of like-minded people.

My questions about the composition of the community not uncommonly provoked responses (blank stares, vagueness, flip answers, change of topics) suggesting that this knowledge (who did and did not belong) was part of the members' common stock of knowledge (Schutz, 1967; Garfinkel, 1967). Members knew who they were, recognized other members (and nonmembers), and took the matter for granted. Clearly, my questions reflected a sociological research problem, not an issue of concern to members.

Using the card indexes I was constructing, I began noting and mapping observable connections in the form of friendships, mutual awareness or recognition, overlapping group memberships, and business relations. Once I was able to ask for specific information (Were Bill and John friends? Was Mary a member of this group?) informants were able to supply additional intelligence concerning these matters. The best indicator of inclusion in the community was, however, whether or not people and groups were involved in psychic fairs (as discussed in Chapter Four). In this way I was able to construct a tentative picture of the community. As I participated, observed, and talked with participants I was able to check and verify this emergent picture. This strategy enabled me to sort the card indexes into different categories: individuals and groups repeatedly observed as part of the community; others thought to be involved but not yet verified; individuals and groups about which I was uncertain; and still others which were not in any discernable way included. This process was repeated throughout my fieldwork. In this way it became easier and easier to eliminate individuals and groups on my card indexes as not part of the esoteric community in the Valley, while having subsequent opportunities to verify these interpretations. I eventually identified about 300 people and 35 groups as parts of what members called the esoteric community.

Most members of the community are white. They predominantly are lower-middle to upper-middle class: their incomes ranged from $5,000 to $30,000 a year per person; their dwellings generally reflect the upper ranges of these income levels (lower level income people commonly reside with a husband, wife, or other family members), as do the neighborhoods in which they are located; and their social status is confirmed by demeanor, talk, and dress. Community members tend to be middle-aged. They range in age from 20 to 80 years, excepting members' children. A majority of them are between 35 and 55 years of age. They are about equally divided by gender, but there are many more females in positions of leadership and authority proportionately than in the exoteric society. Most of these people are high school graduates; many of them have college training; some of them have college degrees; and a few have graduate training or degrees. Members are employed in a wide variety of jobs and occupations, but they are over-represented in human services fields, such as social work, counseling, teaching, and health care. Politically, they tend to be moderate to liberal on most issues, although most of them are not active in political causes. These findings generally are collaborated by Scott's (1980) and Luhrmann's (1989) studies of substantially different settings.

Peter, for example, is a twenty-two year old college graduate who regularly uses the occult tarot for meditation and scholarly-like studies. He earned about ten thousand dollars in 1977 while attending school. He has no religious preference and never attends church, but maintains he is religious minded. Politically he describes himself as very liberal. He uses tobacco, alcohol, caffeine, and occasionally marijuana. He was raised by both parents; he has never been married; and he has resided in the Valley for about eight years. Peter reportedly became involved with esotericism in the late 1960's through a girlfriend who claimed to be a witch. He subsequently read a great deal of occult literature and began experimenting with numerology, astrology, and water scrying, in addition to tarot cards. He uses the tarot seriously to make personal decisions and foresee the future. Peter uses the tarot and other occultisms as a topic of general conversation; he performs divinatory readings of the tarot for friends; and he reports that the tarot is especially useful for dealing with women. Peter frequents psychic fairs; sometimes attends public lectures; and periodically participates in a small, informal, cultic study group in the esoteric community.

Cathy is a regular participant in a small cultic spiritual group in the community. She is fifty, widowed, and lives in a very nice home in an upperclass section of the Valley. All three of her children are grown, but one still lives at home and the others visit frequently. She has sustained a serious interest in occultism for more than twenty years; possesses an extensive knowledge of esoteric literature; and participated for several years in Scientology. She became interested in the tarot about 1972 through a friend; attended classes on the tarot offer by the minister of a spiritual group; and eventually became a regular participate in this cultic circle. Although she sometimes conducts divinatory readings of the tarot for herself, Cathy's principal interest in the tarot is as a form of meditation and study. Cathy regards herself as politically moderate, and does not admit to using any illegal drugs.

Della is a twenty-three year old female. She moved to the Valley in 1975, after completing high school in the East, to live with a girlfriend. Della has worked on several different, low paying jobs to earn sufficient money to support herself. She would like to attend college, but does not have sufficient funds to do so without also working full-time. Della expresses little interest in politics or public affairs, and little experience with or interest in exoteric religion. She became seriously interested in tarot divination after visiting an occult book and supply store; she eventually enrolled in formal classes at the store; and she hopes to eventually read the cards for pay in the esoteric community. Della has visited four or five cultic groups in the community, but reports that none of them seemed interesting enough to motivate her to join.

Mark is the forty-nine year old minister of a spiritual group in the esoteric community. He was raised on the West Coast, completed high school, and attended college for several years while working in a department store. His parents were not religious, but he periodically attended a Unitarian Church. He married, started a family, and found a better paying job in sales. After eight years of marriage he was divorced. During this period of his life Mark reports changing jobs and moving several times. He embarking on a quest for spiritual meaning in his life. He drifted in and out of many different esoteric groups on the Coast, and eventually participated for several years with an occult order. As a member of the order he became familiar with the Hermetic-Kabalistic tradition, learned astrology, and studied mysticism. According to Mark conflicts within the order involving leadership and authority forced him to leave. A former member of the group introduced him to the leaders of another, more religious minded spiritual organization. After a brief period of intense participation with the local chapter, he reportedly was invited to the national organization for special training. Within about a year he became an ordained minister of the group, and shortly thereafter agreed to serve as the leader of the affiliated church in the Valley. As minister he earns little more than is necessary to support himself without other employment.

Though impressionistic, these data are consistent with long term patterns of cult participation in the United States. Members of the community predominantly are middle-class, white, adult, urbanites. Their activities are adult, not child oriented, and reflect greater gender equality than is characteristic of the larger society. My materials do not support the frequent contention that cult participants and those attracted to esotericism during the 1970's predominantly were disillusioned American youth. As Stark and Bainbridge's (1979) data show, college age youth dabble in the occult, but they generally do not participate in its supporting cultic milieu. American youth are more likely to join more cohesive organizations of Eastern religion, nonconventional new American religions, and more sectarian organizations, such as Scientology, or the Children of God.

I asked people how they became involved in esotericism, although I did not survey members of the community systematically. I heard a variety of different responses to this question. They expressed dissatisfaction with the solutions offered by orthodox religion or science, but rarely reported that this involved a particular life crisis. They talked about extraordinary experiences (clairvoyance, telepathy, astral projection, mentalistic healing, spirit communication) to explain why they believed in esoteric teachings. Many of these people were relative newcomers to the esoteric scene, yet at least half of the members I talked with had been involved with esotericism for more than ten years. In most cases their involvements reportedly were stimulated by direct contact with a particular group, dynamic leader, or an extraordinary belief, practice, or experience during a seeking process. For many members of the community sincere interest in esoteric teachings was reinforced by receiving money for psychic readings or some other practice.

The esoteric community is defined in part by relations with the exoteric society. Recognition that esoteric beliefs, practices, and groups lack social legitimacy in the exoteric society is a powerful source of solidarity and identity for members. They resent the perceived intolerance of the larger society toward them, and their social marginality. Forced to endure public incredulity and even hostility, community members transform their marginality into a badge of distinction to be worn pridefully. They disdain the perceived dogmaticism and orthodoxy of exoteric religion and science. Here too, social marginality is pridefully understood as a mark of superiority. The official, legal status of esoteric practices in the Valley, as will be discussed below, reinforces and underscores these feelings.

Membership Roles

By observing and participating within the community I gradually learned to see several seemingly basic categories of membership or roles performed by participants. These membership categories are presented in Table One.

Table 1
Categories of Membership in the Esoteric Community

<table>
<tr><td colspan="3">Leaders</td></tr>
<tr><td rowspan="2">Practitioners</td><td colspan="2">Professionals</td></tr>
<tr><td colspan="2">Non-Professionals</td></tr>
<tr><td rowspan="3">Seekers</td><td colspan="2">Students</td></tr>
<tr><td rowspan="2">Clients</td><td>Belivers</td></tr>
<tr><td>Non-Believers</td></tr>
</table>

They include: **leaders**, people who organize activities and direct the affairs of particular groups (see Chapter Four); **practitioners**, those who engage in particular esoteric or occult practices; and **seekers**, people who move from group to group or practitioner to practitioner looking for wisdom, enlightenment, and self-knowledge and thereby consume esoteric or occult goods and services. Practitioners are distinguished as: "professionals," people who engage in practice for pay, in public settings, and as a full-time activity or as a result of special expertise; and nonprofessionals, people who practice in private without receiving pay. Among seekers there are: students, people who engage in scholarly study; and clients, people consuming goods and services of practitioners or groups. Clients are distinguished further as:

believers, those people who are receptive to esoteric or occult teachings; and nonbelievers, people who resist esoteric or occult teachings, even though they sometimes consume goods and services. These categories cross-cut participation or membership in particular cultic groups in the community. A particular person may perform the role of nonprofessional reader as the member of a certain cult in some situations and also may be seen as a seeker in another context. Another person may be a client of a certain professional practitioner and also a member of one or more cultic study groups.

In many ways activities, relationships, and social networks within the esoteric community revolve around the practitioner membership role. People perform these roles for pay and for free, as part of private practices, and within the contexts of cultic groups. Practitioners engage in a variety of esoteric and occult practices, including akashic life readings, astrology, biorhythms, psychic (clairvoyant) counseling, dream analysis, yoga, healing, numerology, palmistry, past-future life regressions-progressions, psychic art, and hypnosis. Most of the people I observed and interviewed in the community, including many seekers, employ some kind of esoteric or occult practice from time to time. Many of these people, for instance, own a tarot and use it for amusement. Some of them occasionally read it for self-understanding, periodically draw on the occult wisdom of the cards for making important life decisions, or read the cards three times a day.

Less than 125 members of the community engage in esoteric or occult practices for pay and claim special expertise. Nearly anyone may begin an occult practice and claim expertise. Many of these claims, however, go unacknowledged. To be accepted as a professional practitioner by the community, and to be successful, one must be listed in the various directories, gain access to community publications for advertising, develop a reputation, and be invited to participate at public events, especially psychic fairs.

The length of time one has been involved in serious practice, as well as the character and quality of the performance (particularly if it seems very extraordinary) are signs of expertise, and they contribute to one's reputation. Such claims to expertise sometimes are advanced quite militantly, as in the case of a tarot card reader we interviewed.

> See, I'm kind-of a snob. 'Cause I hate these people who in 1965 all of a sudden decided to get involved in the occult. And, I had this experience last night where I really wanted to physically beat up on this girl. I happen to consider myself a professional, number one. Number two, she was batting out of her league. I just can't deal with these people that get into the tarot and they think they're in. I'm just above all that.

Within the community claims to lengthy involvement are made by about one-half of the practitioners. About a third of these people, however, are relative newcomers to the scene.

Newcomers to the community may attempt to gain recognition as a practitioner in several ways. If one moves to the Valley after establishing a reputation in another area of the country, a claim to expertise may be made on the basis of longstanding commitment and practice. Claims of this sort are tested by gatekeepers (leaders) through observation and by discussion: Does the reader exhibit recognizable skills? Is the person able to give verifiable references? Newcomers who pass these preliminary tests generally are given an opportunity to practice (at a fair or to advertise) for a probationary period. Further observation is needed in most cases before the practitioner is granted full privileges of membership in the community as a practitioner. A novice practitioner faces greater obstacles. A beginner might attempt to become adept through self-study and then seek membership. More often, novices complete a period of study from a reputable group or member of the community, and if they are successful, they become sponsored. To become successful the novice must establish a reputation thereby passing further testing in the community.

Professional practitioners see themselves as sincere and legitimate, and they borrow from exoteric counseling and ministry as models. They sustain identities as sincere and legitimate **professionals** by reference to "gypsies," people regarded as insincere and illegitimate. In esoteric lore, gypsies also are regarded as an ethic group from Eastern Europe who periodically have been carriers of these traditions. The Editor of the *Spiritual Directory* explicitly addresses this issue:

> The real question is: Who is a good reader? The [Valley] police department has warned us that 50 to 60 "gypsy" families have moved into the city and have opened up numerous fortune-telling enterprises in the last few years.
>
> Being of gypsy origin does not automatically make one a crook, but these "gypsies" are not legitimate nor ethical in their operations—they may not even be real gypsies! They will lie and defraud their clients, cheating them of a lifetime's savings.
>
> The gypsy systems of fraud are too many to enumerate here, but be cautious of anyone not listed with the [*Spiritual Directory*].

Partly because of the commercial nature of readings for pay, practitioners are especially sensitive to being compared with gypsies. Members of the community appropriately observe that there are differences between themselves and people called "gypsies."

Gypsies tend to advertise in exoteric publications, such as newspapers and telephone books, exclusively. They commonly perform a variety of divinatory services generally referred to as "fortunetelling," and make highly exaggerated, extraordinary claims. They are predominantly female and use titles like Sister, Madame, or Mrs. And, according to Tatro (1974), they hold a "deviant" self-image. Advertisements from a local newspaper are instructive.

> Mrs. Silva. Psychic Tarot Card Reader. I have with God's miraculous power, healed people from evil spirits that have done damage to you and your loved one. I guarantee that once you contact Mrs. Silva, psychic spiritualist, beyond any doubt, who will put you on God's road to happiness, money, restore your nature, remove the pain from your mind and body of bad luck, and evil influences surrounding you. Names, dates, facts, lucky hands and lucky days. All readings $5 (with this coupon). 7 days a week [address and phone number deleted].
>
> Sister Annette. Palm and Card Reader. Tells past, present, and future. Helps you with all problems: love, marriage, business, health, names, dates, facts. If you have any of these problems come and see her today. Special: $5 reading with this ad [phone and address deleted]
>
> Madame Walker. Fortune Teller. Card Reader. Palm Reader. Past-Present-Future. Are you worried, troubled or in doubt? Do you want happiness, success and peace of mind? I can help you to overcome your obstacles, see me. I can and will help you. One-half Price Reading with this Coupon [phone number deleted].

Practitioners in the esoteric community rarely advertise in exoteric publications, generally refrain from making explicit promises, and rarely advertise expertise in more than one area. They are nearly as likely to be male as female. They use titles like Dr. and Rev., sometimes list esoteric or exoteric degrees, and sometimes refer to associations, like the National Association of Psychic Practitioners. They generally are ministers of groups in the community (as described below). And, they construct and enforce codes of ethics, as well as sustain nondeviant self-images. Several advertisements from *Psychic Magazine* are illustrative of practitioners in the community.

> Tarot Readings by Dawn. Appointment Only. [phone number deleted].
>
> Tarot-Astrology. Will 1978 be your year? I can't promise that it will be, but why don't we get together and find out? [name deleted]. [phone number deleted]. Member: National Association of Psychic Practitioners. Horoscopes make nice Christmas gifts!
>
> [The Cosmic Star Church of Spiritual Development] (non-denominational). Private Counseling and readings. Call Rev. [name deleted]. Check on classes starting soon—call [phone number deleted] and [address deleted].

What is most important, sociologically, about the gypsy stereotype is that it serves to distinguish absolutely the moral order of the esoteric community from practices thought to involve trickery, fraud, and con artistry.

Occult practices are legally regulated in three cities in the Valley. In these locations laws require practitioners to pay a license fee. The amount of these fees varies. City ordinance in one town requires anyone engaged in "magic arts," defined as "palmistry, phrenology, astrology, fortunetelling, mind reading, clairvoyance, or any similar calling," for profit to obtain a license. The required fee of forty dollars a year is seen as reasonable by esoteric community members. This situation even is deemed beneficial since from the members' perspective it discourages gypsies. Members who reside and practice in this area fondly point out that in comparison with areas of the Valley perceived to have a lot of gypsy practitioners, their city is relative free of these undesirables.

In another municipality, "Every palmist, astrologer, fortune-teller, or soothsayer shall obtain a license from the finance director or his authorized representative before carrying on such activity within the City." Town code requires a $150 nonrefundable fee for the license application, and upon acceptance an additional $100 a year. Practitioners are accessed another fifty dollars if they transfer this license to a different address. Esoteric community members see this fee as unreasonable and interpret it as an effort to discourage or eliminate their practices.

A third municipality regulating occult practices clearly aims to eliminate them. By city ordinance:

> Every clairvoyant, astrologer, seer, palmist, soothsayer, fortune teller, spiritualist or spirit medium charging or receiving fees, rewards or anything of value, shall pay a license fee of seven hundred fifty dollars ($750.00) in advance, and the license shall be obtained at least thirty (30) days prior to its effective date. Such license may be revoked at any time for cause, by the Clerk, on the demand of the Chief of Police.

Violation of the ordinance is defined as a misdemeanor, and punishable by a fine "not to exceed $300.00 or by imprisonment in the City Jail for a period not to exceed three (3) months, or both a fine and imprisonment" (Ordinance Number 1017). It seems to me more than coincidental that this municipality is controlled politically by Mormons.

City ordinances pertinent to members' practices are almost never enforced. I know of several instances of community members practicing without a license. These laws seem to be designed primarily to discourage occult practices and to provide exoteric legal authorities with a means of dealing with undesirables, should this become necessary. Licensing requirements do define particular areas of the Valley as more or less desirable places to practice from the standpoint of community members.

Members employ a rather simple mechanism they believe protects them from local ordinances. They define themselves and their businesses as nonprofit religious organizations and become ministers. Emergent cults commonly define themselves as churches by purchasing a charter from a national, mail order organization, and individuals obtain ministerial certificates in this same way. I purchased a minister's license for five dollars from a mail order address-organization located in the southeastern United States during my fieldwork in the Valley. By getting two additional people to purchase a license, I became a "bishop." To the best of my knowledge, nothing else is required, and the mail order organization expects no further relationship with its ministers. Community members believe that by being ministers they are exempt from local ordinances, and almost without exception they are "ordained ministers." As clergy they do not charge for services, but offer them for a recommended or required donation. Likewise, churches in the community do not charge a fee for anything, but they do expect a donation. In this sense, then, virtually all of the cults and practitioners in the community are "religious."

Although I observed few differences between readings performed for or without pay, the commercial (pay) reading creates a variety of special problems for practitioners. In the pay situation the practitioner feels constantly on trial. Unknowledgeable clients require instructions on where to sit, how to ask questions, what to expect, how to interpret information, and the theosophy of the practice (see Jorgensen and Jorgensen, 1977). Strangers may be skeptical, distrustful, or absolute nonbelievers. In the words of one practitioner in the community, reading for pay is "a whole different trip."

> I refuse to tell a client what they want to hear. I tell them what I see. I used to, when I first started. When I first started reading as a professional reader—accepting money. But, the money thing—'cause the money thing is a whole different trip.

Practitioners in the community, unlike exoteric experts, do not have an elaborate professional culture (or training) to draw from in dealing with clientele. Even so, they construct and enact norms of what they regard as professionalism. Esoteric knowledge derived from readings is seen by practitioners as awesome and even dangerous, thereby requiring skill, judgment, and responsibility. A tarot card reader, for instance, observed that: "When you're going into people's lives with the cards you become one with the person." This danger demands responsibility to self and clientele: "Sometimes I think people really get drunk with this power. It is a powerful thing, and it's a responsibility." Other practitioners in the community told us:

> A little bit of other people's garbage goes a hell of a long way. We all have a certain number of negative things in our own lives and problems we have to contend with. If you can help somebody else, great ... but if you can't, you overload yourself. It's a tremendous responsibility and I didn't know if I wanted it. I think that the fact that people wanted it done and needed it done, was the thing that made the difference for me.

Altruism, as a norm of professionalism, is exhibited by some practitioners in the community:

> I do try to go out and help people if I can. Because I think I should. Because if you have anything or try to do anything, if you don't help people, then you lose it. You really do. A lot of people lose a lot of their inner good because they clutch it.

Like exoteric service personnel, practitioners in the community have rationale for treating the potential conflict between professional altruism and accepting money.

> It's on an energy exchange basis, whatever the other person offers, usually between ten and twenty dollars. I just make it clear that it's an energy exchange, however we work it out. I believe that I was born with so many readings to give. I don't know how many I've got left and I don't know how many I've given. But, every time I do a reading there has to be a purpose behind it. I will never deny anyone a reading. I've read for people who not only could they afford it, but they didn't need it. Which, of course, came out through the reading. But I will never deny a person a reading. I will not take less. Like, let's say, I've had someone say they couldn't afford to pay me thirty dollars for a reading; and, I say, then you don't have to pay me anything.

Practitioners commonly predict or foretell events. Predicting transverses the fine line between what members see as their divinatory (or reading) activities and gypsy fortune-telling. Practitioners have several ways of dealing with this situation.

> I deal with games that are going on in a person's life, and patterns. So it's not really predicting the future. But the patterns will repeat unless there's some intervention. So in that sense it's forecasting.

> It's a con, sure, but it's better to con them that way [by letting them believe what they may about the magic of the cards] than to do what the gypsies do and say, "Hey! Somebody put a curse on your mother when you were two years old. I'll sell you $600 worth of candles to remove it." I probably predict, through the use of the tarot, in less than one out of fifteen readings. Sometimes I predict as a grabber. When I hear myself predicting a definite happening within a certain time frame, all right, it's so that it will hit them with the validity of what I'm saying in the entire reading. That's the only purpose that it's used for.

Practitioners describe difficulties with getting clients to take responsibility for themselves. Most of these people subscribe to beliefs in freedom of human will, and they attempt to educate clientele to exercise their volition.

> I think a lot of people feel that if they believe in the tarot cards, it's going to happen no matter what. And they don't take into account the free will that they have. And the possibility that they might be able to change what is there. [The tarot] must be used with integrity toward the client. By that I mean that I don't think it's right to predict, to encourage the person to not take responsibility for being at cause in their life. My whole trip is to get people to begin taking more and more responsibility for what they're doing, rather than encouraging any kind of dependency. If I do my job right, you're going to learn you don't need me. That's what it's all about. Not fostering this dependency. That doesn't mean that I don't have continuing clientele, because I do.

Practitioners feel that to get clients to reveal themselves may destroy the magical quality of a reading for the uninitiated. Yet they believe that it is important for the client to open up so they may be of greater assistance. Closed querents uniformly are regarded as the worse type, not because the reader will not be able to offer suggestions, but since successful divination depends on interaction (see Chapter Eight). A tarot card reader, for instance, told Lin:

> If you know a little bit about your client, it certainly helps you to know how the interpretation should go. Because we all run into things that are rather defiant in terms of being able to say this belongs with this or it has to do with this situation. And if you know a little bit about your client one way or another, sometimes I feel the reading is much more meaningful because you can tie it in properly.

Practitioners rarely attempt to get clients to reveal themselves before a reading; they prefer people who actively participate. Esoteric practices are not seen as mechanical magic. Rather, the magic (self-discovery) results from a complex interaction among a sacred text or stimulus, an expert in the use of esoteric knowledge and its practice, and a seeker.

Application of a model of professionalism to esoteric practice is especially evident in the several codes of ethics published in the community.[3] The Spiritual Code, for example, reads:

> I will approach counseling with respect, reverence, and responsibility.
> I will seek higher guidance.
> I will keep the welfare of my client uppermost at all times.
> I will respect the trust of my client.
> I will strive for greater competence.
> My advertising will reflect my integrity.
> I will strive to give full value.
> I will respect all who adhere to this code.

Practitioners in the esoteric community express meaningful concern for the ethics of what they do, and they employ and enforce codes of conduct in presenting an image of professionalism to clientele and publics. Their strategies are not unlike those of other socially marginal occupational groups.

Membership Associations

Group-like organizations in the community overwhelmingly are cultic in character. Analytically, several basic types of cultic groups, as shown in Table Two, are identifiable. This includes cultic organizations, cultic groups, and businesses.

TABLE 2
FORMS OF COLLECTIVITIES IN THE ESOTERIC COMMUNITY

Cultic Organizations	churches
	institutes
	associations
	clinics
	study groups
	professional practitioners
	students
Cultic Groups	churches
	study groups
	institutes
Business Esterprises	book and supply stores
	clinics
	institutes
	professional practitioners

Cultic organizations generally are medium sized groups (with from twenty to one hundred or more members), with fairly strong, identifiable leaders and sometimes other more specialized roles (including acknowledged professional practitioners), more or less permanent locations (buildings), regular meetings (typically once, twice, or three times a week), and some general range of interests (psychic phenomena, healing, occultisms). A variety of smaller cultic groups may be directly derived from these organizations or loosely associated with them. Cultic organizations may be referred to as churches, institutes, associations, or not-for-profit groups. One or more cultic organizations may serve to anchor segmented networks of people within the community.

Cultic groups, as shown in Table Two, are characteristically smaller than cult organizations (with perhaps as few as three core members). They generally lack clearly identifiable leaders, more specialized roles, or regular, public meetings. Cultic groups sometimes have permanent locations, but they more commonly use the facilities of a cult organization, or move from location to location, such as by alternatively meeting in members' homes. These groups tend to form around members' specific interests (in astral travel, mediumship, anomalies, or an esoteric text), and their continued existence depends on that interest. Commonly they arise and disappear within weeks or months. They rarely persist for years, and in many of the cases where they seem to exist for more extended periods of time it commonly is by way of a constantly fluctuating membership. Cultic groups not uncommonly emerge, and they also tend to reproduce additional cults.

Business enterprises, as shown in Table Two, typically are bookstores or groups selling books and assorted other goods and services. Some businesses primarily or exclusively offer healing or particular esoteric procedures. Businesses commonly are operated by a single proprietor or partnership. They sometimes encourage the development of related cultic study groups. In some cases a business may be operated as part of a cultic organization or it may be linked to cultic organizations by formal or informal networks and social arrangements.

ASSESSING THE CULTIC MILIEU

Popular cultural images of what are called "cults" convey a stereotypical impression of coercive, authoritarian organizations, powerful deranged leaders, and mindless, youthful followings. These images no doubt serve the interests of certain publics, such as Christian Fundamentalists, deprogramming enterprises, and other portions of the anti-cult movement in America, but they fail to describe the people and activities I observed in the esoteric community. Insofar as such organizations exist, they characteristically are what sociologists define as "sects." Unlike sectarian organizations, cults are loosely organized, precarious, notoriously short-lived, more or less democratic collectivities based on flexible, eclectic, non-dogmatic beliefs and practices. Although cult leaders may be charismatic, they generally are not particularly authoritarian. Most of the members of cults in the esoteric community characteristically are middle-aged Americans.

Stark's and Bainbridge's contention that American occultism is not supported by social networks is refuted by my description and analysis of the esoteric community in the Valley. The studies of Hartman (1973, 1976), Lloyd (1978), Scott (1980), Adler (1979, 1986), and Luhrmann (1989) reinforce these findings and further discredit Stark's and Bainbridge's claims. Though geographically dispersed throughout this urban center, the community includes leaders, seekers, students, and practitioners, as well as business organizations, cults, and associations of occult practitioners, all of which are interrelated and linked in complex ways through social networks of relationship. These collectivities and individuals share an ethos, forms of communication, collective images of themselves and the exoteric society, ethics, and a sense of community. In spite of factionalism within the community, as will be described in the next chapter, members participate in collective activities, especially psychic fairs.

The esoteric community was described and analyzed here as part of the cultic milieu and the larger esoteric scene in the Valley. The notion of a cultic milieu frequently has been discussed but it rarely has been described by sociologists. In addition to the esoteric community, the cultic milieu supporting the esoteric scene in the Valley includes multifarious seekers, students, practitioners, cults, businesses, and assorted collective organizations. By way of this esoteric scene and the cultic milieu, esoteric and exoteric cultures interface. While this milieu includes what Stark and Bainbridge call audience and client cults, neither audiences nor cults constitute "cults" in any sociologically meaningful sense of the term. In focusing on highly visible, larger movement organizations, Stark and his associates have missed much of the activity that is central to the cultic milieu and the esoteric scene in America today. Most of these organizations, including older and newer sectarian groups, sustain themselves independently of the cultic milieu. While some of them depend on this environment as a source of recruits, most of them maintain few other social relationships with the cultic milieu or the esoteric community.

The cultic milieu is terribly important, sociologically, for the persistence of esoteric culture. Esoteric knowledge, fundamentally, is individualistic. When believers and practitioners form collectivities, their activities are most likely to be organized in a cultic fashion. Cults provide an exceptionally precarious social basis for esoteric culture. If esoteric culture were dependent entirely on particular cults, even a few successful ones, it generally would cease to exist with each generation or require reproduction constantly. This is unnecessary since the cultic milieu, quite unintentionally, facilitates the constant reproduction of small, loosely organized groups and, thereby, provides more or less continuous support for esoteric culture Notesin America.

Notes

[1] Native American and Mexican-American folk beliefs and practices sometimes are seen, mostly from an outsider's perspective, as related to this scene. Participants in this scene mention such beliefs and practices favorably, and sometimes draw on pertinent published literature, but I did not observe members of these cultures participating in the local scene or community.

[2] My use of the term "esoteric" to describe this community is consistent with members' usage; however, they also describe it as "occult," "new age," "metaphysical," "psychic," and so on.

[3] A very similar code is published in *Psychic Magazine.*

Chapter 4

Confederated Networks of Occultists

The esoteric community in the Valley is composed of loosely interconnected networks of practitioners and collectivities which constitute particular factions, segments, or alliances. The people form what they define as a "community." In other words, they organize their activities socially by developing bonds of acquaintanceship, friendship, mutually satisfying and practical interests, as well as commercial and organizational relations. Their interactions with one another sometimes are organized socially by way of collectivities which generally are discernable as businesses, cultic groups, and cultic associations. Seekers, students, practitioners, and group members are linked by way of networks of relationships, and they circulate among the collectivities in the community. These individuals and collectivities, furthermore, relate with one another through the formation of more encompassing assemblies, alliances, affiliations, or confederations within what they envision as the community.

Within the esoteric community in the Valley three principal confederated networks of individuals and collectivities are connected socially in this way. These factions or segments of the community are presented in Figure Two. Esoteric culture is defined and enacted socially by community members within these specialized spheres or domains of interaction. Each of these segments of the community is defined by somewhat unique, distinctive definitions and images of esotericism.

One faction of the esoteric community in the Valley, which I call the **hermetic assembly**, exhibits a special interest in esoteric study and physical well-being, healing, or medicine. Another faction of the community, I labeled the **augur alliance**, is distinguished by a preoccupation with psychic powers, extrasensory perception (esp), anomalies, or what may be described as a more secular concern for esoteric and occult science. The third faction within the esoteric community, which I define as the **metaphysic affiliation**, is a loose association of "ministers" and "churches" which see themselves as fundamentally committed to spiritual concerns or esoteric religion.[1]

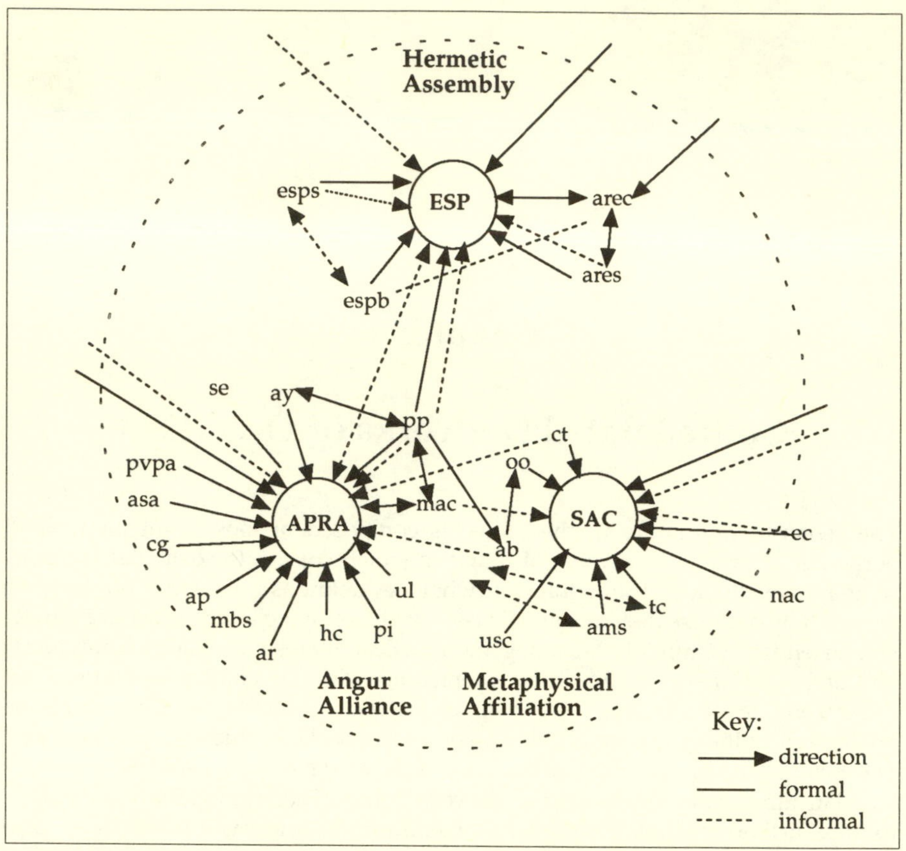

Figure 2: The Esoteric Community Networks of Social Relations

These distinctive orientations to esoteric culture, organized in terms of factions of the community, serve to differentiate among members and their activities. While these differences generally are not visible to outsiders, among the core participants in the community these variations serve as bases for powerful sentiments, tensions, conflicts, and politics. Publicly, leaders and members of particular factions generally sustain seemingly friendly, cordial, and cooperative relations with one another. Privately, among close friends and within particular cults, they sometimes express their differences openly and vigorously, defaming one another. Conflicts sometimes erupt publicly as quarrels among individuals and groups in the community, but these occasionally bitter disputes are more likely to be enacted out of the direct view of other members. Part of the culture of the community includes a common, more or less shared knowledge of the history of these confrontations, clashes, feuds, and skirmishes among competing individuals, collectivities, and factions.

In spite of these sociocultural and personal differences members sustain a powerful sense of "community." Their sense of community is accomplished, in part, by way of the more or less shared ethos, ethics, values, and meanings described in Chapter Three. This culture of the community is created and enacted through social interaction. It is reinforced and re-created powerfully through common activities known as "psychic fairs." During my observation and participation, large community-wide fairs were held twice annually. Several smaller psychic fairs periodically were sponsored by multiple groups and factions in the community. Many other mini-fairs were organized by particular cults, usually churches, or confederations of practitioners and groups comprising factions of the community. These events, viewed sociologically, serve as critical bases for social solidarity among otherwise loosely organized networks and factions of the esoteric community in the Valley.

THE HERMETIC ASSEMBLY

One set of social networks in the esoteric community, described as hermetic, reflects a scholarly-like concern for nonconventional teachings and knowledge, with an emphasis on physical well-being, healing, or esoteric medicine.[2] The people composing this specific network of social relationships tend to be among the best educated. They usually work at exoteric occupations, are successful at them, and exhibit middle-class life styles. They devote non-work time to esotericism, and they are more inclined to engage other members of the community in discussions, than to join a particular cult.

Sallie, for instance, is sixty-three year old, retired, widow. She and her husband, a department store manager, moved to the Valley around 1965 from Michigan, and purchased a home in an upper middle class neighborhood. They raised two children, and Sallie had worked periodically as a nurse's aid. While their children were at home they infrequently attended the Methodist Church. Sallie's husband was an avid reader of science fiction, and they both sustained an interest in UFO reports and psychic phenomena. After her children were grown, Sallie began going to a Christian Science reading center where she became interested in mentalistic healing. Her studies eventually included the works of Edgar Cayce and Jane Roberts.

Friends from Michigan introduced them to the ESP organization (described below) shortly after they arrived in the Valley. They subscribed to the ESP newsletter and casually attended study group meetings of special interest. After her husband's death in 1975, Sallie began serving as a volunteer in the ESP bookstore. To the best of my knowledge, she is not a regular participant in any of the related cultic study groups; she reported attending one of the largest Spiritualist churches in the Valley occasionally. She seemed to live an entirely ordinary lifestyle. Several of her best friends also are volunteers with ESP, and this organization seemed to serve as the center of Sallie's social life. Her principal form of participation in the community is through volunteer activities, reading esoteric literature, and practicing esoteric health and healing.

Categories of membership in the hermetic healing segment of the community are shown in Table Three. They include: **coordinators**, or leaders who organize collective activities; **volunteers** who assist the leadership; **practitioners**, people who provide esoteric goods and services; and **seekers**, people who are in search of enlightenment, including ritual healing. Practitioners are distinguished further as professional or nonprofessional. Professional practitioners include: **readers**, people performing services like past life regressions, tarot divination, palmistry, and astrology, typically in terms of a practitioner/client relationship; **teachers** who direct classes or provide instruction on esoteric topics; and, **medical practitioners**, people who do healing or provide other esoteric medical services. There are two categories of seekers: **students** who attend classes or otherwise engage in scholarly-like studies; and **clients** who seek services from practitioners.

TABLE 3
MEMBERSHIP CATEGORIES IN THE HERMETIC ASSEMBLY

<table>
<tr><td colspan="3">Coordinators</td></tr>
<tr><td rowspan="4">Practitioners</td><td colspan="2">Non-Professional</td></tr>
<tr><td rowspan="3">Professional</td><td>Readers</td></tr>
<tr><td>Teachers</td></tr>
<tr><td>Medical</td></tr>
<tr><td rowspan="2">Seekers</td><td colspan="2">Students</td></tr>
<tr><td colspan="2">Clients</td></tr>
</table>

Within the hermetic healing faction of the community, networks of social relationship and activities tend to revolve around a cultic organization called ESP, as shown in Figure Two. Several study groups (ARES, ESPS), a book and supply store (ESP-B), and a medical clinic (AREC) are connected socially through ESP. A variety of other cultic study groups and practitioners are casually and loosely associated with ESP. This cultic organization, operated by a core of six members and an untold number of volunteers, functions as a clearing house for information. They maintain a suite of businesslike offices in a predominantly middle-class section of the Valley. For a fee of twenty dollars a year members are entitled to a regular monthly mailing of organizational activities, as well as miscellaneous benefits, such as discounts on items purchased in the affiliated book and supply store. The ESP bookstore, located in a small strip shopping center several miles from the main offices, is staffed by volunteers. It offers a wide range of esoteric books and supplies, with a better selection of medical, health, and healing materials than other similar stores in the Valley. Classes sponsored by ESP commonly are held in the back room of the bookstore. ESP is a legally non-profit organization that claims a paid membership of about 1,700 people. Over 3,000 people receive the monthly mailing without charge.

The ESP calendar of events includes activities for every day of the month. These range from speakers, some of who have national reputations, films, and demonstrations, to classes in astrology, tarot, numerology, palmistry, and hypnosis. Unlike many of the cultic organizations in the community, ESP is not expected to support the people who run it. Speakers and teachers generally are hired from outside the organization, typically from among practitioners in the community. These arrangements solidify ESP's relationship to the larger community.

ESP sponsors an untold number of cultic study groups that typically meet once a month to discuss esoteric topics. Once a study group is established, ESP may lose track of it unless participants continue to advertise in the organization's bulletin or otherwise maintain contact with coordinators. Since this cultic organization makes no serious attempt to exert control over study groups, even the organizers tend to be unaware of exactly how many groups are functioning at any given time.

I, for instance, attended an ESP sponsored meeting on the topic of spirit communication. A guest speaker from the west coast, a student of Jane Roberts, was brought in to lead discussion. During the preliminary meeting of thirty-five to forty people, members explored the idea of forming a regular study group. It became clear during the meeting, however, that people's interests were widely divergent. A second meeting attracted about half as many people. At least two, or perhaps three, study groups were formed. One study group continued on the general topic of spirit communication and channeling but discontinued advertising in the ESP bulletin. Another study group formed around the guest speaker and focused on a highly stylized form of past life regression called "rebirthing," and they continued to advertise with ESP. I suspect that a third group of four or five people formed around a married couple without the knowledge of other members.

ESP is closely related through overlapping friends and members with a full-time medical clinic, AREC. It is operated by two physicians (M.D.'s), a married couple, with the assistance of a small staff of medical and "psychic" practitioners. From the standpoint of the exoteric society, this clinic, perhaps obviously, is one of the most culturally legitimate organizations in the esoteric community. With the important exception of the use of esoteric techniques along with exoteric medicine, the clinic resembles its exoteric counterparts. AREC hosts an annual conference of national accolade, and it supports an untold number of cultic study groups specializing in hermetic medicine and healing.

The hermetic assembly, then, serves to define a distinctive faction of individuals and groups in the esoteric community. These people and collectivities exhibit a special concern for hermetic study and esoteric medicine. Their activities are coordinated through a particular organization, ESP, that thereby links otherwise discrete individuals and groups. ESP, its members, and other individuals and groups linked together in this way sustain a variety of complex connections with other individuals, groups, and factions in the esoteric community.

THE AUGUR ALLIANCE

Social networks composing the augur faction of the esoteric community predominantly involve people and groups with a more secular focus on exploring the human mind, particularly hidden or concealed senses whereby occult knowledge is viewed as a path to personal power and success. Many of these people are devout occultists. They rarely use this word, however, especially when talking with outsiders, because of the less than favorable image it presumably projects to publics. Members of this psychic segment sometimes earn all or part of their income from the sale of esoteric goods and services. They come from working to middle class backgrounds; some of them have college educations; most of them had or have middle income occupations in social services, health care, education, business, and the like; and they tend to espouse moderate to liberal social and political values. Most of the cultic groups involved are officially non-profit, religious organizations, but their official status reflects legal relations with the exoteric society, not whether or not they engage in commerce or see themselves as particularly religious.

Liz, for example, is a thirty-eight year old "psychic practitioner" who specialized in past-life regressions, a form of hypnosis through which the client is asked to recall what is regarded as a previous existence. Her parents moved to the Valley when she was a young girl; she graduated from a local high school; completed a college degree in psychology on the West Coast; married and had two children before being divorced. During college Liz became especially interested in psychic phenomena and studied related literatures on parapsychology. She worked as a case worker and counselor in a public welfare office until about four years before I met her. After about six years of marriage, Liz reported, she and her husband developed divergent interests and gradually drifted apart. About this time she became increasingly interested in esoteric studies and began interacting with members of the local community. A cousin was the leader of a therapeutic cult in the community; he eventually became a successful writer and lecturer; and before my arrival he developed a national reputation marketing esoteric training courses and therapy. Liz worked part-time for her cousin and quickly gained a local reputation as a psychic practitioner and counselor.

Shortly after her divorce, Liz quit her welfare job and started a psychic counseling service with a partner, a man she knew from the therapeutic cult. They married a short time later. Liz and her husband successfully recruited a collection of about ten to twelve professional practitioners representing a variety of specialities as affiliates of their organization. It quickly became one of the more prestigious associations of this type within the community and both partners eventually were able to support themselves exclusively by way of group activities. They reside in an upper middle class section of the Valley, and they are among the most respected leaders in the esoteric community.

Stella is another professional practitioner connected with the augur alliance. An accountant for an insurance company, she was thirty-four years old, the mother of a nine year old daughter, and divorced. Stella was born and raised on the East Coast by both parents; she was educated at Catholic schools, and still considers herself to be at least nominally Catholic. She was married shortly after graduating from college. Stella claimed to be a moderate to liberal Democrat, but I saw no indication that she was especially active politically. She uses tobacco and alcohol, but denied any involvement with illegal drugs. Outspoken almost to a fault, Stella seemed to live a commonplace professional lifestyle with the exception of her occultism.

Stella reported that she frequently had unusual dreams and psychic experiences as a young girl, but failed to recognize them as extraordinary until she was a teenager. During high school, according to her account, Stella and several girlfriends began reading popular occult literature and experimenting with magic and astrology. She claimed to meet a psychic who became a mentor while in college. He taught her to read tarot cards, construct astrological charts, and instructed her in the use of various other forms of magic. According to Stella, she began providing these services to friends and acquaintances for free, and eventually started charging money for them, although the circumstances whereby she began collecting fees is unclear. She owned a modest occult library and was better informed about classic occult traditions than most of the professional practitioners I knew.

Stella moved to the Valley after being divorced around 1970, and receiving a reportedly attractive job offer. She talked about a boyfriend, but I am very unclear about most of the details of her private life. In the esoteric community Stella practiced astrology, palmistry, and tarot. She conducted readings from her home, at psychic fairs, and in conjunction with several cultic groups. Stella also taught classes through groups in the augur alliance, and occasionally lectured publicly.

Membership categories in the augur alliance of the community are represented in Table Four. They include: people who organize psychic fairs or otherwise provide leadership for collective activities; practitioners providing services; and seekers. **Psychic practitioners** tend to be specialized. In addition to the previously discussed distinctions between professionals and nonprofessionals, these categories encompass people with extensive expertise versus people without acknowledged specialized expertise. Professional practitioners, as shown in Table Four, also include: **teachers** who offer classes or direct studies of the esoteric and occult; researchers who engage in scientific-like studies of psychic, esoteric, or occult phenomena; and **readers** who provide services like astrological charts, numerology, palmistry, and tarot divination to clientele. **Clients** and **students** as seen by members are types of **seekers**. Clients are distinguished further as believers versus nonbelievers.

While professional practitioners operate in all segments of the community, they are highly visible and the most active in this psychic segment. Their services include akashic life readings, astrology, biorhythm charts, psychic (clairvoyant) counseling and readings, dream analysis, yoga, healing, numerology, palmistry, past-future life regression-progression, psychic art, hypnosis, and tarot readings. Most practitioners engage in private practices, but they sustain some affiliation with a cult or cultic organization. They actively compete for clientele and affiliation with community groups. Within the community professional practitioners are evaluated by reputation based on perceived competency. Of over 100 people engaged in esoteric or occult practice in the community, less than twenty are thought to be truly

TABLE 4
MEMBERSHIP CATEGORIES IN THE AUGUR ALLIANCE

Organizers			
Practitioners	Non-Professional	Experts	
		Non-Experts	
	Professional	Teachers	
		Writers	
		Researchers	
		Readers	
Seekers	Students		
	Clients	Disbelievers	
		Believers	Regulars
			Non-Regulars

outstanding, and there probably are no more than thirty or forty who are widely regarded and acknowledged as highly reputable and competent.

These networks of practitioners exhibit a similar ideological orientation to esoteric or occult knowledge. They see it as useful for self-understanding and as a way of producing practical results. Such an orientation sometimes has been labeled "magic" and juxtaposed with "religion." Unfortunately such a distinction oversimplifies the complex view of reality in which occult practices are embedded. The tarot, for instance, from a psychic perspective is viewed as a tool for self-understanding and enlightenment: "I see the cards," one reader told us, "as triggers to intuition, rather than having specific meanings each time. I see them as a system we can use to dope out the future, as a fantastic tool for self-understanding." In this sense occultists are interested in attaining practical, instrumental, or magical results. Another reader, for instance, observed that:

> I'm finding out that so much of it works if we can bring it down to earth. I don't like to keep things super esoteric and way out. If metaphysics works, we ought to be able to bring it right down to earth, right now, and program the goodies on an everyday basis. I do think there is something magical about the cards. Mainly because they've been around for a long time and people have cranked a lot of energy into them.

Magical interests sometimes derive from emphasizing the scientific pretensions (prediction, control) of occult knowledge, not from differences between magic and religion. Occultists, of course, recognize tensions between esoteric and exoteric science. A practitioner who uses the tarot as a therapeutic tool remarked that: "My intention with all of the occult studies is to make the intuition—the right side of the brain—as respectable as the left. I have professional credentials and background [an M.Ed.]. Hopefully that will bridge the gap someday." Later she told us that:

> My Gestalt trainer would get really pissed: "Why are you doing this reading shit?" You know? He said, "it's all projecting anyway. It's the ultimate projection trip," he kept saying. And it really bothered me because I wanted to know the difference between projecting and coming up with information that I couldn't possibly have known about this person.

Hence, the psychic orientation acknowledges the mysterious character of occult knowledge.

The augur alliance, as pictured in Figure Two, is the largest, most complex, and most active faction of relationships in the esoteric community. APRA, an association of psychic practitioners, anchors these relations and activities, and it is the most central cultic organization in the community. Its founders, a married couple, devote themselves full-time to APRA, the related publication of *Psychic Magazine*, production of psychic fairs, promotion of two-day and week-long seminars (focusing on hypnosis) held throughout the country, and private practice. The membership of APRA consists of about forty professional practitioners. Like ESP, they host some kind of activity for every day of the month. This includes private counseling or readings (palmistry, astrology, tarot, clairvoyance, hypnosis, and especially past-life regressions); classes on these topics; lectures and demonstrations; and psychic research projects. Unlike ESP, APRA is expected to make a profit. This cultic organization leases a large suite of offices in an upper-middle class section of the Valley.

APRA, as shown in Figure Two, is connected socially to other commercial enterprises (MBS, SE, CG), several bookstores (AY, AB, PA), research associations (PVPA, AR), and various religious cults (UL, MAC, TC, HC, CCT, CHSC). They are linked to APRA through advertising and other contributions to *Psychic Magazine*, participation in psychic fairs, business relations, and a very complex array of overlapping social (friendship) relations. Commercial cults, presumably, are what Stark and Bainbridge (1980a) call "client cults," and some of the activities of cultic organizations, like APRA, are what is meant by "audience cults." Neither clients or audiences are cults, however, unless these people become members of related groups. Clients and audiences, alone, do not constitute cults. The commercial cults described here do have small memberships, including leaders who organize activities, core memberships supporting these activities, and affiliated professional practitioners. These cults, furthermore, are linked by complex networks of social relationship with other groups and organizations within the cultic milieu of the esoteric community and its various factions.

Esoteric bookstores sustain business relations with many of the cultic groups in the psychically oriented segment of the community. Besides providing books and supplies, they serve as centers of information, a place where interested parties meet unceremoniously in public, and as the sponsors of classes on tarot, astrology, hypnosis, numerology, and palmistry that appeal to the public. Store owners sometimes serve as instructors (teachers), but bookstores more commonly hire teachers from among professional practitioners in the esoteric community. Owners and practitioners split fees for classes with approximately ten to twenty-five percent of the fee remaining in the store.

Commercial cults operate in much the same fashion. They tend to emphasize some aspect of mental and / or physical well-being with some groups specializing in **service-therapy** and other groups in **education-instruction**. Basic types of service are: private readings or counseling; special workshops, usually offered on a week-end; and extensive therapy or education, typically involving weekly meetings for 6 months. The cost of these services varies among cultic businesses, and by the reputation of the professional practitioners, the type of training or therapy, and where the service is performed. For instance, palmistry is less expensive than hypnosis, while private readings are more expensive than public readings at fairs. In spite of efforts to standardize fee structures, prices generally are fixed (and adjusted) on the basis of professionals' perception of the market. Private readings cost from five to fifty dollars, short-term workshops run from thirty to sixty dollars, and a full course of study or therapy varies from $200 to $400. Extensive programs of study or therapy generally are divided into beginning and advanced sessions. Completion of a full course of study in hypnosis or mind and body science might run as high as $3,000 or $5,000.

Commercially oriented groups employ similar methods for recruiting clien-tele. They advertise in esoteric and sometimes exoteric publications. One business, for instance, periodically runs a local TV advertisement. The favored way of attracting clients and members is through mailing lists. Every commercial cult has a list of potential students obtained by registration of people at psychic fairs as well as having members name friends. Some of these groups have existed for more than 10 years (a very long time for cults), and consequently rather extensive and tested mailing lists exist.

The publisher of *Psychic Magazine*, for example, maintains a mailing list of more than thirteen thousand people. A subdivision of this list includes the names of approximately five thousand people known to have consumed community goods or services at some time. Mailing lists are exchanged among friends and sometimes sold to other people or cults. They, however, are not available to just anyone. A bitter conflict ensued when the leader of the psychic segment refused to sell one of his lists to an organization judged to be fraudulent.

The augur alliance, in short, is the largest faction in the esoteric community. It members specialize in psychic, esoteric, and occult practices viewed as in some sense "scientific." Their practices and activities are intended to produce money. Their commercialism is disdained by other community members, particularly those composing the metaphysic faction. Psychic practitioners see their money making activities as a form of professionalism. They thereby define themselves as being like exoteric professional experts and specialists. By way of its activities, APRA, is one of the central organizations within the esoteric community. Through it multifarious individuals, groups, and factions within the community are tied together socially.

METAPHYSIC AFFILIATION

The metaphysic (spiritual) faction of the esoteric community primarily consists of religious (or quasi-religious) cults. The word "spiritual" denotes an emphasis on the religious and moral condition of humanity. Members composing these segmented networks tend to be concerned with salvation, liberation, and enlightenment. They see their mission as service to humanity, and they stand opposed to the perceived "materialism" of people in the psychic (augur) segment of the community. Members of the metaphysic faction of the community generally are from lower to working class backgrounds; few of them are college educated; most of them work at low to moderate income jobs; they frequently have been seekers for lengthy periods of time, and commonly have been involved in many different esoteric groups.

Harold, for instance, is a forty-four year old minister of a cultic group and the operator of a book and supply store. He grew up in the Valley, graduated from a local high school, and had a lengthy and highly varied career in the esoteric community. His mother and aunt were regular attenders of a Spiritualist church which provided Harold with an introduction to esotericism at an early age. By his early teenaged years he was conversant with much of the classic literature on occultism and a practitioner of many forms of magic. He apparently took little interest in exoteric education, although he reported graduating from high school, and I strongly suspect that he was perceived as somewhat strange by his teachers and peers. Harold, according to others' accounts, had been married numerous times. His current spouse reportedly was a eighteen year old women whom he met when she joined his cult.

Community lore indicated that Harold had been involved with numerous cultic groups over the years. He apparently participated in the formation of several groups which later dissolved as a result of disputes among the members as well as conflicts over leadership and authority. It is unclear to me as to whether he owned the book store (or the occult section of it), or if he simply operated it as partnership with someone else. As the operator of the book store he sustained contact with many of the other groups in the community. As minister of a cultic group he also energetically participated with other ministers composing the metaphysic faction of the esoteric community. I was unable to collect any kind of direct information about his cultic group. It was rumored to be a secretive occult order patterned after the Golden Dawn, and community members insinuated to me that Harold was a devotee of Crowley and, perhaps, thereby sex magic and witchcraft.

He tended to be aloof and somewhat arrogant regarding his own expertise and activities. My questions about these matters sometimes were treated with the disdain of a master for an ignorant outsider who asked stupid questions. Even so, Harold very freely offered information about the community, its members, and activities with which he was familiar. Although the book store regularly offered classes in various occult arts and sciences, to the best of my knowledge Harold never taught them, nor did I ever know him to engage in any form of professional practice as a service to the general public. Unlike Harold, many of the other ministers in the metaphysic faction of the community do engage in professional practices.

Sara, a professional practitioner in her early fifties, provides a contrasting example to Harold. She is a warm, friendly, quiet, soft-spoken woman who people seem to trust almost immediately. She teaches part-time in a private school, but it seems likely that she has other sources of income. A widow, she lives with her elderly mother in a middle class neighborhood, and they are very devout Catholics. Sara became interested in astrology, tarot, and related occultisms as a mature adult through a friend who is a member of a spiritual group in the community. She is not a member of any of the nontraditional spiritual groups in the metaphysic segment of the community, but she sometimes teaches classes and frequently provides tarot card readings through one of the spiritual churches. Sara's occultism serves as a supplement to an otherwise conventional religiosity. By all indications she lives a rather conservative life-style.

Spiritually (or metaphysically) oriented tarot card readers see this occult text as a sacred body of knowledge and its divinatory application as a means of revealing relationships between humankind and the cosmos. Divination thereby differs from "fortunetelling." One spiritual reader, for instance, remarked that:

> Every time I would get into an oral reading, I would get into these esoteric things. My tarot reading is a very esoteric type of reading, a very spiritual reading. But I found that that's the kind of people that come to me. If they want to know about the tall dark handsome man they're going to meet next Tuesday, they go see the gypsy down the street.

Even metaphysically oriented occultists recognize that their "spirituality" oftentimes is incomprehensible to outsiders. Referring to her mother, a tarot reader in her fifties noted that:

> I think that the psychic things really bother her. More in the sense that she can't make the connection that I make between the psychic and spiritual. I have no problem in working my spiritual life and my occult life and astrological work together in a nice blend for me.

In some cases occult spirituality is integrated with even more orthodox ideas about the supernatural. One devotee observed that: "Tarot readings, astrology, or anything, if you put it in the hands of the Father, it comes." And another spiritually oriented occultist explained that:

> To me the occult in true essence is trying to understand God in that which is not usually taught and given. It is hidden because you don't understand; you can't relate to where there's more answers. And, if you search for them, you're really doing occult searching.

The occult, in this way, may be reconciled with more traditional religiosity.

Membership categories in the spiritually oriented segment of the community (pictured in Table Five), though similar to other factions, take on a distinctive character. These roles include: **ministers**, usually people who are associated full or part time as ordained officials of a cultic group; **members** who are recognized by others as active participants in particular cults; and **seekers**. Three ministerial roles are identifiable: the principal **leaders** of groups; **teachers** who perform this special function; and **counselors**, ministers who offer services like tarot card readings, astrology, palmistry, and hypnosis. Members may be identified further as the **staff** of a cult who assist in group work (most of whom are wives, husbands or close friends of the minister), and **regulars**, people who can be depended upon to attend group functions and support its activities. **Seekers** are distinguished as **clients**, **students**, and **visitors**. Clients and visitors may be identified further as believers and disbelievers.

TABLE 5
MEMBERSHIP CATEGORIES IN THE METAPHYSICAL AFFILIATION

Ministers	Leaders	
	Teachers	
	Counselors	
Members	Staff	
	Regulars	
Seekers	Students	
	Clients	Disbelievers
		Believers
	Visitors	Believers
		Disbelievers

Membership in cultic, spiritual groups is relatively small, generally ranging from five to fifty people per group, transitory, and lower-middle class. Cults commonly are organized around a charismatic leader or several dynamic personalities. Female leadership is very common. The continued existence of these groups depends on regular contributions from members, and visitors (seekers) who move from cult to cult. Ministers not uncommonly are indebted to an anonymous wealthy backer. They sometimes receive economic support from a parent or charter organization, typically located on the west coast of the United States. Ministers and members sometimes offer a variety of professional services, like tarot readings, for a fee or recommended donation. Cult ministers regularly participate in psychic fairs. During the 1970's a popular money making strategy was to sponsor a mini-fair. Two or three cults in the spiritual segment of the community sometimes jointly produce a fair for one group, and later exchange the favor.

Spiritual, metaphysical networks in the community in some ways are the most loosely organized, and yet social ties among groups and members tend to be very strong. The principal coordinating organization is SAC. A number of cults, as shown in Figure Two, are linked together by SAC. This organization is composed of minister-leaders from each cultic group who meet and discuss matters of mutual interest once a month. Through a local bookstore owner, who leads a spiritual group, SAC publishes the *Spiritual Directory*. Otherwise SAC is not especially active. This metaphysic affiliation was intended to solidify the spiritual faction of the community and provide a basis for intergroup activities outside the domain of the augur alliance. Its members, however, found it difficult to agree on goals and joint activities.

The metaphysic affiliation, though the smallest faction of the esoteric community, is based on strong social bonds among participants. These people exhibit a spiritual or religious orientation to esoteric culture. Their images of esotericism stand opposed to the commercial, professional emphasis of the augur alliance. Unable to organize a viable alternative to this powerful psychic faction of the community, these spiritually oriented occultists are dependent on the augur alliance and its members. While the beliefs and practices of these people are esoteric and thereby culturally marginal, otherwise they very much resemble more conventional religious groups in the exoteric society.

PSYCHIC FAIRS

In the Valley **psychic fairs** are organized by members of the esoteric community around professional practices such as readings or treatments (see Jorgensen, 1979, 1983). Ostensibly, fairs are designed to make money in support of practitioners, organizers, or cultic groups. More importantly, psychic fairs provide the esoteric scene and community in the Valley with focal activities. They provide a setting for direct contact between this scene and the exoteric society. Through fairs community members meet publics, seekers, clients, and fellow members, make money, as well as present and manage public images of esotericism.

Fairs provide a setting and situations for interaction among disparate practitioners and members of particular cultic churches, study groups, associations, organizations, business enterprises, and bookstores. In this setting members create, negotiate, and sustain a sense of community, linking overlapping but segmented networks within the cultic milieu. These activities and social relationships mitigate against the anonymity and casual, secondary group characteristic of urban existence, and serve as bases for intimacy, identity, and social solidarity. During my fieldwork in the Valley large psychic fairs were held twice a year, once in the spring and again in the fall or early winter. Many smaller fairs were held throughout the year.

Producing A Fair

Larger psychic fairs are elaborate productions that attract consequential (1,000 to 3,000 or more people), heterogeneous audiences to a public site (commonly a motel convention center) where community members and groups selling esoteric goods and services are assembled. Small fairs are less elaborate productions that attract smaller (one hundred to maybe three or four hundred people), more homogeneous audiences to an affair sponsored by a cultic group or groups in the community, most often at the facilities of one of these group. Large or small, a principal objective of psychic fairs is to generate money in support of community members and cults.

Small fairs are designed to generate economic support for a particular group or groups in some segment of the esoteric community. Overhead expenses are minimized by using facilities owned or rented by a cultic group and employing the services of practitioner-members or unpaid volunteers. Visitors to a mini-fair typically pay a two to three dollar cover charge which sometimes includes several readings or other services. In some cases visitors may buy a ticket for around three to five dollars to cover several readings or services. Even with extensive advertising, an unlikely possibility due to the expense, mini-fairs generally attract modest audiences, mostly composed of friends, seekers, regular clientele of guest readers, and a sprinkling of students, explorers, and perhaps a few denouncers. Audiences tend to resemble cult members in terms of such characteristics as age, education, employment, income, beliefs, and general social backgrounds. Insofar as members of these cultic groups are middle-aged, somewhat disproportionately female, and working to lower-middle class folks, for instance, they tend to attract audiences resembling themselves. Mini-fairs oftentimes do not fulfill sponsors' expectations as revenue generating enterprises. Yet, if they attract a few potential cult recruits, and they usually do, they are defined as successful.

Larger psychic fairs are expected to produce sizable profits for the organizer or cultic sponsor, as well as the professional practitioners and groups who participate. Unlike mini-fairs, they incur considerable overhead expenses. The fair producer may find the facilities of a cultic organization an adequate setting, but it is commonplace to rent convention accommodations of a resort motel complex. It is expensive to advertise and promote a large fair. The sponsor generally advertises in community publications, including the several magazines and assorted newsletters, depends on mailing lists, and uses exoteric outlets such as shopping guides, radio, and sometimes television. While exoteric newspaper advertisements are used in many regions of the United States for this purpose, they are almost never used in the Valley. The major Valley newspaper declines to accept advertising from the esoteric community, especially psychic fair advertising. The official reason given for this is the paper's inability to ensure the ethics of esoteric practitioners. Community members see this as a pretense, since the paper accepts advertisements of highly dubious exoteric businesses, and they take it as a reflection of tensions with the exoteric society.

A psychic fair must mobilize a wide variety of professional practitioners and experts, readers, lecturers, demonstrators, cultic groups, so as to appeal to the widest possible audience. To sell esoteric goods and services, fair participants are required to purchase a booth from the sponsor. Booth fees vary from $15 to $50 per person (or per booth) a day, depending in part on the anticipated size of the audience. Potential fair participants express concern about their ability to make money based on these circumstances, carefully calculate costs and benefits, and they demand assurances about profits from the sponsor.

The sponsor commonly determines participants' booth fees by figuring basic expenses, facilities, advertising, and any other overhead. Booth fees are expected to

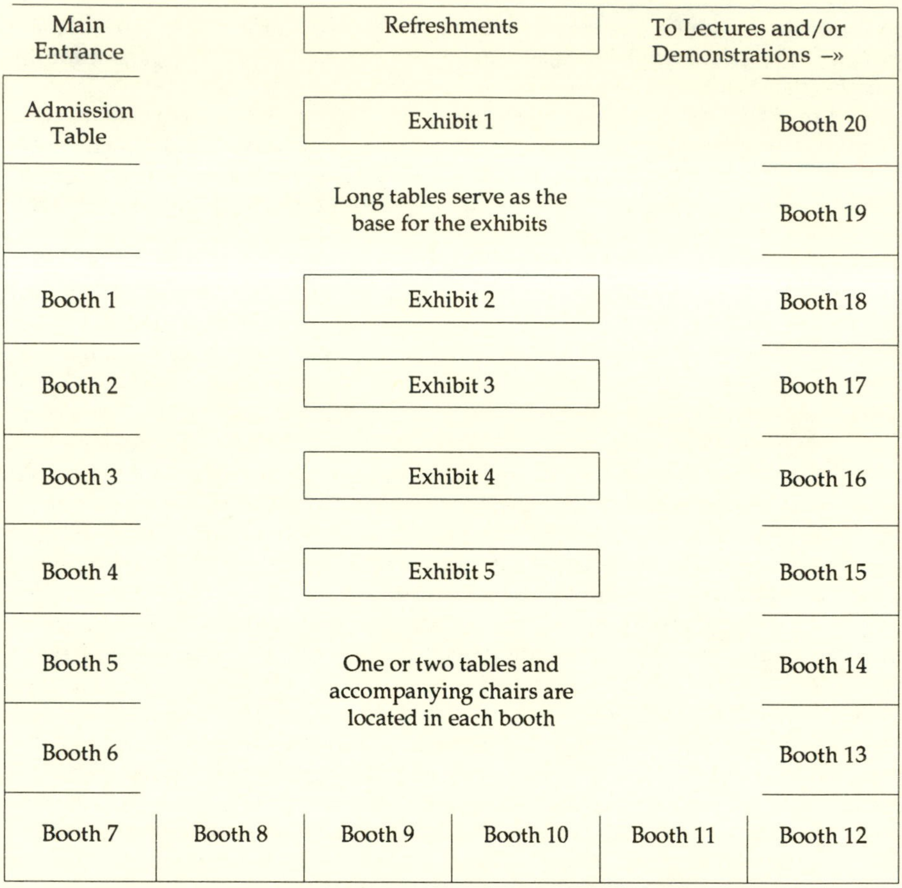

Main Entrance		Refreshments			To Lectures and/or Demonstrations –»
Admission Table		Exhibit 1			Booth 20
		Long tables serve as the base for the exhibits			Booth 19
Booth 1		Exhibit 2			Booth 18
Booth 2		Exhibit 3			Booth 17
Booth 3		Exhibit 4			Booth 16
Booth 4		Exhibit 5			Booth 15
Booth 5		One or two tables and accompanying chairs are located in each booth			Booth 14
Booth 6					Booth 13
Booth 7	Booth 8	Booth 9	Booth 10	Booth 11	Booth 12

Figure 3: The Physical Arrangement of a Psychic Fair

cover these expenses with the sponsor's profit deriving from an admission fee, usually two to three dollars per person (or the reverse). Visitors know or discover that there are additional charges for the various goods on display and a variety of readings or treatments. The sponsor checks with selected professionals, particularly the ones with prestigious reputations in the community, regularly throughout the fair in order to gauge profits. If the most reputable professional practitioners are not making money, in most instances portions of the booth fees are refunded to all of the participants at the close of the fair. Under these circumstances it is not uncommon for less eminent professionals to lose money or earn modest profits, while the more acclaimed practitioners earn sizable sums of money. The organizer of a psychic fair sometimes observes booth traffic systematically to gauge how well practitioners are doing, or bases these judgments on more impressionistic observation. It is taken for granted by the sponsor and participants that self-reports of revenue always err conservatively.

The physical layout of a psychic fair partly depends on the particular facilities, but most fairs share certain features in common, as illustrated by Figure Three. Large and small, fairs generally are located in a room where partitions are used to divide the spaces along the perimeter into semi-private booths. Space permitting, exhibits of books and supplies usually occupy the center of the room. Smaller rooms off of the central meeting place sometimes are used for private readings, and such rooms are used for any lectures or demonstrations held at the fair. Lectures and demonstrations frequently are included in the price of admission, and they are used strategically to attract a large audience. Lecturers and demonstrators sometimes are paid by the organizer for their services.

Most psychic fairs, particularly larger fairs, have a refreshment booth operated by the producer where soft drinks and snacks may be purchased. Refreshments are provided as a convenience to the public and as a source of additional revenue. Unlike many public events, alcoholic beverages are not sold at psychic fairs in deference to the feelings of some community members. A producer who attempted to sell alcohol on one occasion faced a rebellion from the spiritually oriented faction of the community as well many of the people devoted to physical health.

The potential profit from sponsorship of fairs, particularly large psychic fairs, might be expected to attract competitive organizers. This is not the case. During my fieldwork only one person, the leader of APRA (and publisher of *Psychic Magazine*), was able to organize and produce a successful large fair. In conjunction with his leadership of the psychic faction of the community, his ability to produce large fairs makes him one of the most powerful members of the esoteric community. The less than successful effort on the part of the local university to produce a psychic fair illustrates this situation.

The APRA leader offered to organize the university fair, but the student government declined the offer in hopes of making a larger profit. Student government leaders did not have contacts inside the community and they were unable to attract an extensive variety of reputable professionals. They mistakenly presumed that occult practitioners were motivated by a desire to help, not by money. And they misunderstood the target populations and the need for advertising. Student leaders assumed the topic of occultism was of interest among students generally. It was not, but instead attracted mostly older students (many of whom were not on campus during the psychic fair), and university staff. They failed to advertise beyond the university community. Consequently, the fair was a financial failure, and student leaders ended up refunding most of the booth fees to the few angry professionals who did participate. The leader of APRA strategically used this situation to point out his skill in organizing successful fairs, and community members agreed.

There are important differences between large psychic fairs and mini-fairs; size and nature of the audience, types and range of professionals, fee and economic structure. Generally speaking, however, these are differences of degree, not kind. Large fairs are a highly public form of presenting the occult. Since professional participants are engaged in money-making before general audiences, their public performances are more polished, less intimate, and involve more show than the same activities performed in less formal settings. My discussion of fairs is most pertinent to large productions, but it also applies within the parameters noted to mini-fairs as well as related activities in other settings.

Fair Participants

Participants at psychic fairs, as illustrated by Table Six, principally are insiders or outsiders to the esoteric community. Outsiders include exoteric publics or visitors as well as seekers and clients, many of whom are drawn from the larger cultic milieu of the esoteric scene. Community members recognize several types of visitors. Some of them are viewed as students who engage in casual study of esotericism. Other visitors are viewed as explorers (seekers) who move from group to group and teaching to teaching investigating and seeking personal truths and identity. Every psychic fair produces a few denouncers recognizable by their extreme skepticism and passion for debunking members' beliefs and practices.

TABLE 6
CATEGORIES OF PARTICIPANTS AT PSYCHIC FAIRS

<table>
<tr><td rowspan="6">Insiders</td><td colspan="4">Organizers</td></tr>
<tr><td colspan="4">Organizational Staff</td></tr>
<tr><td rowspan="4">Professional Practitioners</td><td colspan="3">Readers</td></tr>
<tr><td colspan="3">Lecturers</td></tr>
<tr><td rowspan="2">Groups</td><td colspan="2">Commercial</td></tr>
<tr><td colspan="2">Non-Commercial</td></tr>
<tr><td rowspan="6">Outsiders</td><td rowspan="6">Seekers</td><td rowspan="3">Clients</td><td rowspan="2">Believers</td><td>Regulars</td></tr>
<tr><td>Non-Regulars</td></tr>
<tr><td colspan="2">Non-Believers</td></tr>
<tr><td rowspan="3">Visitors</td><td colspan="2">Students</td></tr>
<tr><td colspan="2">Explorers</td></tr>
<tr><td colspan="2">Denouncers</td></tr>
</table>

The public setting of fairs and the heterogeneity of audiences blurs community members' ability to distinguish among visitors and seekers. While many seekers are recognizable as scene participants, in the case of believing regular clientele, many of them are not. Many people who resemble clientele are not recognizable as regulars; some of them are seen as nonbelievers. Students as well as explorers may or may not be people who otherwise frequent the esoteric scene or community.

I did not formally gather information from seekers or visitors at psychic fairs, but I did have many opportunities to observe them. Indicators such as style and mode of dress and speech, conversations about their backgrounds, and information gleaned from reading for clients and discussing clients with other readers enable me to describe these people, if only impressionistically. The location of semiannual psychic fairs at a resort motel in an upper-middle class suburban area of the Valley and the fair fees tend to exclude people from the lower socioeconomic strata of the population, except perhaps for a few regular clientele of particular readers or groups. Seekers and visitors otherwise tend to be middle to upper-middle class, as indicated by occupation, education, and income. People of retirement age are disproportionately attracted to this area of the Valley, especially during the winter, and show up in large numbers at psychic fairs. People who attend large psychic fairs only rarely are under thirty years of age, and most of them are between thirty-five and sixty-five years old. Women outnumber men by about three to one, especially in terms of people who purchase goods and services. Visitors and seekers come to fairs with particular problems: love, marriage, family, life changes, physical problems, and so on; but I did not observe anything more than a usual range or degree of life's troubles. I never encountered, in other words, a person who might be regarded as seriously mentally ill. These people tend to be at least nominally religious in a traditional sense, and moderate to conservative politically. In most respects, then, they reflect the general characteristic of the larger population of this suburban area of the southwestern United States.

Participants at psychic fairs who are insiders to the esoteric scene and community, as shown in Table Six, include the organizer (producer) and his staff, as well as cult representatives and professional practitioners (some of whom generally do represent cultic groups or organizations as well). The sponsor's staff arrange booth and exhibit facilities, collect admissions, sell refreshments, organize lectures and demonstrations, trouble-shoot, gather information for the producer, and listen to complaints from visitors and professional participants. The basic activities at a psychic fair, as pictured in Table Seven, include lectures or demonstrations, readings, treatments, exhibits, and a dinner party.

Lecturers and demonstrators are local experts or people of national prominence in the esoteric scene. They discuss and sometimes demonstrate magic, astrology, hypnosis, as well as a host of other esoteric topics, such as pyramids, Atlantis, astral projection, reincarnation, and UFO's. Lectures and demonstrations generally aim to win believers, and sometimes gain converts to a cult.

Representatives of cultic groups recruit members, and they serve as readers and professional practitioners. Many of these cultic groups demonstrate occult practices, display and exhibit esoteric knowledge, and offer particular goods, such as art works, books, jewelry, oils, incense, and the like, for sale. Exhibits sometimes are primarily or even exclusively commercial operations, as in the case of some bookstores, and occasionally the maker of esoteric charms and jewelry.

Professional practitioners engage in divinatory activity of some sort, and/or provide treatments to the public for a fee. Divinatory readings offered for sale, as shown in Table Seven, include tarot, playing cards, astrology, numerology, palmistry, sand paintings, runestones, I Ching, tea leaves, hand-writing, psychic art,

TABLE 7
CATEGORIES OF ACTIVITY AT PSYCHIC FAIRS

Readings	Tarot Playing Cards Astrology Numerology Palmistry Sand Rune Stones I Ching Tea Leaf Handwriting Psychic Art Psychic (clairvoyant) Psychometric Pendulums Scrying Auras Hypnosis	
Treatments	Psychic Healing Chiropractic Yoga Reflexology Biorhythms	
Lectures/Demonstrations	Pyramids Atlantis Astral Projections Reincarnation UFO's Magic	
Exhibits	Commercial	Art Books Supplies (trinkets) Educational Therapeutic
	Noncommercial	Research Religious (spiritual) Professional Associations
Dinner/Party		

clairvoyance-telepathy, psychometrics, pendulums, scrying, auras, and hypnosis. Treatments are a somewhat different kind of activity. Unlike divinatory readings which tend to resemble counseling, treatments tend to emphasize physical well-being. Treatments, as depicted in Table Seven, take a number of specific forms. Psychic healing attempts to remedy a client's physical problems either by requesting the client to concentrate on them and/or by the psychic practitioner mentally concentrating on these physical ills. Esoteric chiropractic treatments resemble their exoteric counterparts, but they sometimes incorporate mentalistic or psychic healing practices. Yoga, reflexology, and biorhythms also deal with various aspects of a client's bodily existence. Professional practitioners generally are identified by the primary activity in which they are engaged, even though many of them perform more than one activity or service. Hence, they are known as tarot card readers, psychics, astrologers, and so on.

A dinner party for insiders usually is held on the first or last evening of the psychic fair. It specifically aims to provide an occasion for insiders to make new friends, renew old friendships, exchange ideas, and engage in shop talk. Parties held at the opening of a fair result in discussions of what practitioners will be doing, new techniques, recent events in their lives, speculation about the success of the fair, and perhaps agreements as to prices to be charged for particular services. Parties held toward the end of a fair produce talk about successes and failures, problematic clientele, and future events in the community. Fair parties are greatly anticipated by members and sometimes viewed as of sufficient importance as to off-set the lack of financial success at a fair.

Doing Fairs

The culture of the esoteric community includes principles and understandings about the definition and organization of activities at psychic fairs. Participation at a fair in principle is open to all insiders. In practice, however, the inclusion of professional participants and cultic groups is selective. Initially, the fair producer contacts prospective participants in the community, oftentimes previous performers, prior to any public announcement of the fair. Potential participants not in regular contact with the producer thereby are excluded from the beginning. The selection of participants is guided by several criteria. Organizers attempt to attract the widest possible variety of topics, readings, treatments, and exhibits, and to seek out people with established reputations and experience.

In addition to reputational prestige ratings informally acknowledged within the community, a hierarchy of specialities is discernable. During the 1970's past-life regressions and future life progressions, highly stylized forms of hypnosis increasingly attracted large followings and gained in prestige. Astrology is highly attractive while card readings are less prestigious, even though there is a regular market for these services. Psychic readings, especially when performed by esteemed practitioners are highly valued. Less honored, but still attractive are numerology, sand readings, hand-writing analysis, psychic art, aura reading, and other practices commonly performed by a very few experts. Divination by playing cards, palmistry, tea leaves, and scrying are less highly valued. Highly prestigious practices, like hypnosis, commonly are incorporated into elaborate professional performances and demonstrations designed especially for the public at a psychic fair. Professional reputation cross-cuts this fluid hierarchy of practices, such that an accomplished tarot card reader is valued over a hypnotist of questionable competency and reputation.

Fair organizers are expected to gatekeep. Community members presume that gypsies, anyone using gypsy-like practices, and professionals without established reputations will be excluded from fair participation. Novice practitioners attempting to break into fairs encounter serious difficulties. They typically are told that all booths have been sold. This rarely is the case, since organizers almost always can make room for one or two additional booths, and they do when famed practitioners apply late. Organizers have been known to set up a new booth on the day of the fair, even after turning half-a-dozen applicants away. Producers of psychic fairs occasionally take a chance on an unknown expert or novice. This usually requires sponsorship. A sponsor commonly is a former teacher, a reader with whom one has developed a trusting relationship, or someone in another community known to the gatekeepers.

Fair participation is a special case of professional practice and it is judged in much the same way as previously described (see Chapter 3). There usually is a period of probation. If the reader exhibits recognizable skills, attracts clients, and does not get negative reviews from clients or other readers, they generally are accepted. However, if new professional practitioners are perceived to behave in a gypsy-like fashion, or if negative reports about them circulate, they are excluded from psychic fairs and from the esoteric community. During my field research several readers were excluded from fairs and otherwise stigmatized in the community because of perceptions of illegitimate practices or unethical conduct.

Booth assignments also depend on reputation and relations with fair producers. Experts with national reputations and established locals receive the best locations. "Best" is determined by high visibility and accessibility to clientele. Practitioners with lesser reputations, fewer inside contacts, or newcomers receive less desirable booths, such as next to the refreshment stand, near busy intersections, or in more out-of-the-way places.

As insiders prepare for the opening of a fair they hang signs over their booths advertising services to be offered. They set up and dress tables, arrange props, such as decks of cards, crystal balls, candles, and all manner of esoteric paraphernalia, and otherwise prepare to meet the public. In casual conversation, they check out other displays, evaluate other practitioners' booths, engage in shop talk, and discuss esoteric teachings. Since making money is crucial, this matter is widely discussed. In some cases practitioners have been shunned by other experts when perceived to have outdone themselves. Professional practices tend to be highly competitive.

The time for setting up also is used to determine the going rate for goods and services at the psychic fair. Practitioners poll one another about anticipated fees. Eventually a base fee for particular services, especially readings and treatments, is established. Prices for readings during my fieldwork were fixed at between $10 and $30 depending on perceptions of the market, oftentimes defined by the social class of clientele. Should the fixed rate turn out to be too high, as measured by practitioners' perceptions of the number of people asking for readings, fees may be renegotiated. Once minimal rates have been established, everyone is expected to conform. It is permissible to charge more, but rate cutting is a severe breach of community norms and strongly sanctioned. I know of several readers who were excluded from subsequent psychic fairs because other fair participants believed they were undercutting the going rate for service.

Professionals perform readings for one another. This is usually done on an exchange basis, such that a tarot card reader, for instance, trades such a reading for a psychic reading. Since readings are evaluated unequally (past-life regression is worth more than tarot divination) trades may be difficult to negotiate without one party becoming indebted to the other. This situation, however, tends to generate further relations and bonds among community members.

Other rules of conduct are observed and enacted by professionals and clientele at psychic fairs. Unless close friendships are well established it is not appropriate to ask readers how much they have earned. Professional participants do exchange this information, but it generally is manipulated for specific purposes. Profit estimates, as noted earlier, almost always err conservatively. In doing this practitioners aim to leave organizers with the impression that booth fees were too high. If the psychic fair generally is seen as successful, professional practitioners rarely admit to losing money: An admission of losses while others presumably were making a profit would reflect badly on one's competency and reputation in the community. At the same time, fair-wise professionals do not brag about profits. This is especially important if one is a newcomer since it leads to professional jealousy and a tarnished reputation.

Once a psychic fair is underway, conversations among practitioners generally are limited to neutral territory, such as vacant booths, aisleways, and hallways. It is a severe breach of fair norms to converse with another reader in that person's booth unless one is invited to do so explicitly, as in the case of breaks or slack periods. An occupied booth discourages clientele. Readers therefore attempt to make their public availability visible to prospective clients.

Readers are especially careful to demonstrate respect for one another's clients. Popular readers sometimes have several clients waiting for readings while other readers are unoccupied. It is unethical, however, for another practitioner to offer services under these circumstances, since it is perceived as stealing. In some cases a reader may suggest to clients that they seek out other services, particularly if they are exceptionally busy, and they generally will direct a client to a particular reader. A previously negative experience with a client also will lead to the person being sent elsewhere.

Publicly, professionals expect to exhibit respect for one another. To disparage other readers, especially to clientele, is considered unethical and it is strongly sanctioned. This rule applies even when there is general consensus that another reader is incompetent. It applies only generally to interactions among readers, largely depending on the nature of their relations with one another. There are occasions when a collection of readers, particularly if they are very close friends, will gossip about the competency or reputation of other practitioners. This norm also is enforced on clientele. Readers rarely listen to clients' complaints about other readers, and almost never comment on or reinforce such behaviors.

Since psychic fairs are public and booths provide little privacy, psychic fair participants are expected to observe a reasonable distance around the territory of readers. Readings are expected to be private affairs. Practitioners sometimes will decline to read in the presence of others, even a relative or friend. Anyone detected to be encroaching on a professional's private territory may be asked to move away or leave. Since professionals encounter this problem routinely, they sometimes have a standardized comment. One psychic reader tells unwanted bystanders that being too close messes up the "vibes" and results in an inaccurate reading.

NETWORKS OF OCCULTISTS IN PERSPECTIVE

Interaction within the esoteric community in the Valley is organized socially by way of loosely interconnected networks of practitioners and collectivities. These networks of occultists and cults constitute particular social factions and orientations to esoteric culture. Three principal confederations are discernable within the community. These rather special purviews on esoteric culture differentiate among members and their activities, as well as among groups composing the community.

The hermetic assembly, organized around a group that coordinates manifold activities of study groups, is composed of people engaged in esoteric scholarship and healing. Members of this faction generally are well-educated, successful at exoteric occupations, and middle-class. Their leisure time is occupied by a devotion to esotericism. The focal group in this coalition, ESP, coordinates study groups, sponsors other regular, monthly activities, operates a bookstore, and sustains close relations with a full-time exoteric-like medical clinic. This assembly of individuals and groups are linked with the augur alliance by channels of communication, and through overlapping members.

Distinguishing characteristics of the augur alliance are a preoccupation with psychic science and occult practices, the offering of professional services to the public, publication of a community magazine, and sponsorship of large psychic fairs. A multitude of therapy cults and professional practitioners compose this faction. It is the largest and most powerful segment of the esoteric community.

The metaphysic affiliation is composed of ministers and cultic churches. Characteristically lower to working class, these people exhibit a distinctively spiritual or religious orientation to esotericism. Though opposed to the perceived materialism and commercialism of the augur alliance, the participants in this confederation are dependent on the social support of the larger community.

In spite of these consequential differences, these people sustain a sense of community by way of more or less shared values and meanings. This culture of the community is enacted by way of social networks and common activities, particularly psychic fairs. The many psychic fairs held in the community provide members with opportunities to engage the public and audiences, make converts, serve clients, and advance images of themselves. Through psychic fairs disparate practitioners, cult members, and collectivities interact. These activities serve as bases for developing intimate friendships, defining one's self, and generating a spirit of social solidarity. In these ways the esoteric community serves its members by mitigating against the anonymous, casual, touch and go character of urban life.

NOTES

[1] The labels used to identify these factions of the community are mine and they are defined and applied here analytically. My selection of these terms is fully grounded in members' meanings and usage, even though these particular labels are not necessarily used by members or consistently and uniformly employed by them. The word, "hermetic" is used by members but participants in this faction of the community are more likely to define their activities as "esoteric," "psychic," "healing," "medicine," and the like. My term, "augur," refers to what members fairly consistently define as "psychic," but they also use words like "esoteric," "occult," "metaphysical," "philosophical," "scientific," and so on. Members of what I call the "metaphysic" faction use this label, but they more commonly define themselves as "spiritual" or "religious," and they sometimes use terms like "esoteric" and "new age."

[2] For a more recent study of "ritual healing" in the United States that includes a diversity of healing groups see McGuire (1988).

Chapter 5

Becoming a Tarot Diviner

During my fieldwork in the Valley, as briefly discussed in Chapter Two, I encountered the occult tarot, learned to read the cards, and thereby became a participating insider in the esoteric community. My movement from outsider to insider, and my performance of different membership roles: seeker, client, student, and eventually tarot card reader, provided different perspectives on the esoteric scene and community. In becoming the phenomenon (Mehan and Wood, 1975) of interest I gained direct experiential access to a world of meaning and interaction that is largely hidden from outsiders, seekers, and many other participants in this scene. The role of tarot card reader, however, was stressful and I periodically experienced intense, existential conflict while performing it. In spite of an ability to pass as a member in the community, I was unable to see myself as a fully committed occult practitioner, to assume and internalize an occult identity, to go native completely. Throughout the fieldwork experience I remained fundamentally and existentially a sociologist doing research while opportunistically, though not insincerely participating as an insider to the esoteric community (see Adler and Adler, 1987; Jorgensen, 1989).

It is not possible to reconstruct literally the process whereby I became a tarot card reader. My fieldnotes did not systematically focus on this process, partly because it emerged as a problem during the course of fieldwork. Concern for membership roles was one of a variety of issues that came to occupy my attention. At the time, these experiences seemed partly personal, less relevant, and less observable than many of the seemingly more visible aspects of the members' world. My previous description and interpretation of becoming a member of the community was based on fieldnotes and related impressions of this experience, and it was constructed at the time or shortly thereafter (Jorgensen, 1979). It therefore is the most comprehensive discussion of this problem available to me. I have re-analyzed and re-interpreted my fieldwork experiences with an aim of drawing out their significance for this work, and I have edited the earlier description to avoid confusion and misunderstanding as well as to communicate more succinctly. But I also have preserved to the largest extent possible the narrative voice of the earlier description to circumvent too great a distortion and reification of it, and for the purpose of displaying some reflection of the lived experience, although I now find parts of this to be naive, vague, poorly written, and somewhat embarrassing.

BECOMING THE PHENOMENON

The traditional wisdom and lore of fieldwork warns the researcher against becoming overly or intimately involved with insiders, identifying with them, taking on and internalizing membership roles, or "going native" (see Gold, 1958, 1969; Junker, 1960; Wax, 1971). Complete participation, Gold (1958, 1969) argues, conflicts with the principal research aim of observation. Too great a rapport with insiders and assuming their worldview is thought to result in conceptual confusion, blurred vision, and thereby a loss of **objectivity**. Even if going native is seen as a beneficial fieldwork strategy, Wax (1971,1979) notices, it ultimately is impossible for fieldworkers to internalize completely an alien culture and experience the world as a native.

A distinctive advantage of participating while observing, however, is the possibility of experiencing the insiders' world of interaction and meaning, directly and existentially (Jorgensen, 1989). Adler and Adler (1987) observe that the performance of membership roles in field research was nonreflectively part of the many classic studies of the early Chicago sociologists who implicitly drew on their insider roles to describe social meanings and interactions. Against the idea that the members' thoughts, feelings, and activities are somehow epiphenomenal, subsequent schools of thought have argued cogently that these phenomena constitute the basic human realities to be described, analyzed, and interpreted (see Berger and Luckmann, 1967; Blumer, 1969; Bruyn, 1966; Schutz, 1967; Garfinkel, 1967; Douglas and Johnson, 1977). There are several outstanding examples of the tremendous value of "becoming the phenomenon" as a fieldwork strategy (see Mehan and Wood, 1975).

While conducting fieldwork in Africa, Jules-Rosette (1975) became a member of a native fundamentalist-Christian sect. Concerned that she did not understand insiders' religious practices and rituals, Jules-Rosette experienced conversion to the group and participated as a member. Through this experience she reports feeling and seeing a world of meaning theretofore obscured from the standpoint of an outsider and even less intimately involved participating observer. Similarly, Damrell's (1977, 1978) studies of two religious groups as a member strongly suggest that he thereby gained a unique and illuminating picture of the religious experience and life of its native members. Neither of these cases, or several other examples that might be cited (see Jorgensen, 1989) provide any indication that the researchers lost their ability to describe, analyze, or interpret human existence sociologically (also see Krieger, 1985).

Earlier critiques of realism, positivism, and related strains of Enlightenment rationality more recently have culminated in a diffuse, broad-based intellectual movement, commonly referred to as postmodernism (see Murphy, 1989; Boyne, 1990; Featherstone, 1988). Epistemology is relativized radically and methodology is rejected by postmodernism (see Gadamer, 1975; Feyerabend, 1978). Ethnography and participant observation have been viewed as part of the modernist preoccupation with methodology and thereby a privileged scientific epistemology (see Clifford and Marcus, 1986; Lakoff and Turner, 1989; Marcus and Fisher, 1986; Van Maanen, 1988). Denzin (1986, 1989a, 1989b, 1989c, 1991), for instance, argues that a concern for methods or procedures for collecting qualitative materials by way of participant observation or related strategies derives from a modernist infatuation with objectivity and scientific truth. Postmodern ethnography, in Denzin's view, sees theory and method joined in an interpretative process, and it concentrates on thickly describing (Geertz, 1967, 1988) experiences and activities of societal members, thereby displaying the voices, emotions, and actions of natives so that lived experience is accessible, directly, to the reader. Methodology, consequently, is an unnecessary preoccupation that leads to unwarranted claims to truth (or Truth). From a postmodern perspective truth is relative, a part of its interpretation.

I agree, substantially, with Denzin and the so-called postmodernist critique of modernism, especially its realist and positivist reflections. I disagree, however, with his conclusion that rejecting the subject/object dualism, methodological positivism, and explanatory theorizing also requires us to forsake a concern for a methodology of participant observation. I also reject existing formulations of epistemological relativism. All interpretations of reality are not equal. Positivistic methodologies and realist explanations are inadequate because they largely ignore the experiences and meanings of societal members. The epistemological status of my interpretations of esotericism is debatable. The experiences and meanings of members, however, constitute their realities. This is what I seek to describe, analyze, and interpret; and the ways in which I have done this, by a methodology of participating and observing from the standpoint of membership roles, are crucial. Since theory, findings (my interpretation), and method (becoming the phenomenon) are linked inexorably, some discussion of how this was accomplished is of the utmost importance.

ENCOUNTERING THE TAROT

At the outset of my inquiry into extraordinary experience I remained ignorant of the tarot and its divinatory use. My initial encounter with the cards came through Dee, a student who claimed to be a "witch," during my earliest explorations of the cultic milieu in the Valley. She invited Lin, me, and our children to her home one evening for the purpose of discussing occultism. Dee had previously mentioned her divinatory use of the tarot, and in anticipation of this meeting we decided to ask her for a reading. Shortly after our arrival Dee brought out several tarot packs. As she explained the cards and how they worked we looked them over carefully. Though quite young, our children exhibited special interest in the packs. Like the children, I was fascinated with the pictures as art and as symbolic images.

Later that evening Dee eventually spread the cards for me and talked about past, present, and future events in my life with a strange certainty. My notes on the evening (recorded the next day) indicate that I was not exactly impressed with the reading. Discussing the matter, Lin and I agreed that the tarot was something of

ILLUSTRATION THREE: Temperance, ***Salvador Dali's Tarot.*** Reproduced by permission of Naipes y Especialidades Garficas, S.A., Barelona, Spain. Copyright © Naipes y Especialidades Garficas, S.A. Further reproduction prohibited.

special interest to us. It was one of the first occult practices I had observed and experienced first-hand.

We continued to interact with Dee and her children socially, and from time to time we got together to discuss matters of mutual interest, commonly the occult, a dominant theme in Dee's life. On one of these occasions Dee again read the tarot for us. My reading was especially unusual since after spreading the cards and making a few comments, Dee refused to continue on the pretense that she could not tell me what the cards said at this time. I noticed that Dee's readings tended to dwell on the relationship between Lin and myself. Her references to one or both of us having a sexual affair with someone else became a recurrent feature of these readings. Lin and I were not married and we deliberately refrained from revealing the nature of our relationship to most people, although our living arrangements and interaction left little doubt that we were a couple. I suspected, however, that Dee's readings were a not so subtle attempt to get us to reveal more about our relationship.

Shortly thereafter I became convinced that Dee's references to Lin's prospective affair was an effort to manipulate us. Her comments included a detailed description of a particular male, with blonde hair. I initially passed it off as ludicrous, but it aggravated me and I gradually came to entertain these suggestions seriously. Almost unwittingly I found myself looking for the blonde-haired male among our friends, associates, acquaintances, and other people with whom Lin interacted. Rationally I regarded this response as rather stupid, but it was a compelling matter emotionally. Lin felt my reaction was silly, but since these prophecies bothered me, they also bothered her. Lin's fieldnotes, pertinent to this situation (recorded a month after the first meeting with Dee) are instructive.

> [Dee] has read the cards for herself, her family, and friends for years and has a collection of decks, several of which I found exceptionally pleasing in an aesthetic sense. She read the cards for Danny and me, but her interpretations were, on the whole, vague and at this point I can remember only a couple of items from my reading which were specific. One prediction she made was rather noteworthy, more because of our reaction to it than because of its possible accuracy: she stated that I was going to have an affair with a blonde man. My first response was, "Oh, how silly!," and Danny and I reasoned that since we both had noticed a romantic attraction by [Dee] toward Danny, she was in a roundabout manner attempting to either create discord between us or to question our attitudes about an open relationship. Even though we verbally negated the idea of my having an affair, I began to notice in Danny's behavior what was, in my opinion, an irrational jealousy directed toward all the blonde men with whom I interacted. To me this was a real revelation: my Danny, the most sane, most rational, most skeptic of men—being affected by a prediction made by a tarot card reader!

It is difficult, retrospectively, to convey the social context in which this situation arose, but I admit that this forecast really agitated me. I responded by distancing myself from Dee.

Stimulated by Dee's use of the tarot, Lin became interested in getting a deck of her own. We began visiting occult bookstores in search of a tarot. Since it was Lin who was especially interested in the tarot at this point of our fieldwork, her notes (recorded months later) about this situation are informative.

> I was fascinated and intrigued by the power (or suggestion?) inherent in the tarot and decided to obtain a deck of my own. We were researching several occult groups in the area at the time, and I also felt that my interest in and knowledge of the tarot could serve as an entreé, a ticket for acceptance by the participants in these activities. Having legitimized my desire to own a tarot deck, we began a search for purchase that extended from [the Valley] to [the West Coast] and finally ended when Danny bought me the *Aquarian* tarot deck (illustrated by David Palladini) and the accompanying *Symbolic Key to the Ancient Mysteries* by F. Graves.

Using the book's instructions Lin began learning the symbolic meanings of the seventy-eight cards and other information necessary for doing divinatory readings, such as shuffling and spreading the cards, as well as particular techniques for interpreting the order of the cards, and so on. By early 1977 she was doing readings for herself, the rest of the family, and a few close friends.

The occult theosophy of the tarot, as discussed in Chapter Seven, is rather complex, and divinatory readings require memorization of meanings as well as an ability to integrate these ideas in such a way as to make them available for immediate recall. Although tarot divination looks simple, it requires an elaborate knowledge and specific skills. On this point Lin's fieldnotes are instructive.

> I practiced many layouts for myself, family, and friends, gradually discerning what I had to learn in order to become an accomplished Tarot reader. This in itself was a discovery since I had initially thought that I had only to learn the meanings of each card in order to execute a reading. However, I soon realized that my first task was to acquire an understanding of the spread, or layout, I used—the Celtic method in which eleven cards are positioned more or less in the shape of a double cross. I designed a diagram of this spread and memorized the explanations of each of the positions, for I had realized that the position in which an individual card is placed affects its meaning in the spread. With this came my first comprehension of what an intuitive process the Tarot is.

Lin's early readings, consequently, were performed in a very uneasy and sometimes tedious fashion. As part of her plan of study, Lin used the book accompanying her deck as a workbook, writing in different interpretations of the cards and additional

ILLUSTRATION FOUR: Queen of Pentacles, *Yeager Meditation Tarot Deck.*

information in the corresponding sections of the text. Her early divinatory efforts depended on extensive consultation with these notes and the text. She also "obtained several more books on the Tarot which offered alternative meanings for each card." She reported that these additional materials "allowed me more freedom in my interpretation" (fieldnotes).

Lin enrolled in a class on tarot offered by a "professional" tarot card reader, a man who also was the minister and leader of a religious cult in the Valley. In attending these classes we were surprised and disappointed that the instructor seemed to be simply reading divinatory meanings of the tarot to the class from standard reference works. Lin recorded that:

> I began to take lessons from a professional Tarot reader with the hope that we could garner more information about how the reading of the cards was accomplished and about what the Tarot meant, and to what extent it was used, in the lives of members of the class. This turned out to be a failure, however, since the classes consisted primarily of the teacher reading from his favorite book on the Tarot and the students dutifully copying the interpretations for each card mentioned.

As a nonparticipant observer I was interested to see that Lin commonly knew as much about the cards, from her previous study of standard sources, as the instructor. As is her style of learning, the first several class meetings were characterized by a constant dialogue between Lin and her teacher. I found these sessions an excellent opportunity to collect information about tarot card readers and the theosophy of the cards, but Lin quickly became disenchanted with the classes. She observed that:

> There was little interaction among the group and the only "discussion" on a personal level was short and direct answers to questions I raised. Finances also being a pervasive influence on our decisions about how our time was taken, we decided to abandon the classes and obtain our data from other sources.

Thinking that she could accomplish as much by individualized study, Lin stopped taking lessons. She negotiated withdrawal from this class with the minister, and we maintained trusting and friendly relations with him until the end of our fieldwork (as discussed in Chapter One).

In February 1977 I started seriously considering the possibility of following Lin's lead and making the tarot the focal point of my fieldwork. In early March I attended another psychic fair. This time I decided to request several tarot readings to learn more about its operation. At the fair I paid for and received two tarot readings from different professionals in the Valley. The first reading was very general and it did not impress me as especially interesting or unusual. The second reading was more interesting, largely due to the obviously polished and accomplished performance of the reader. Over the next few days, weeks, and months I periodically reconsidered the advice of the tarot reader and made a conscious effort to seek verification of the more specific predictions. After several months I arrived at the conclusion that some of the predictions had indeed happened, but not in ways that seemed especially out of the ordinary. By a year later, however, a different assessment had begun to emerge. Several interim events, coupled with an emergent friendship with the second reader, left me uncertain about the accuracy of his predictions. I was beginning to formulate some of the ideas that later became part of my interpretation of tarot divination (see Chapter Eight).

As a tarot card reader, Lin's experience and interpretation of the psychic fair differed from mine. She observed that:

> Upon listening to and transcribing the tapes several factors became apparent to which I had formerly given little attention. One aspect—the experienced vs. inexperienced querent and/or the silent vs. verbal querent—enabled me to see just how important the interaction between the "client" and the reader is to a successful reading. Prior to that time I had concentrated my thoughts only on my performance as a reader. Another observation concerned the degree to which we agreed that a reader was "good," or "successful," or "professional." This brought to me certain criteria for judging a reader, and raised the question: "How does one known when he/she is an accomplished reader?" We also noticed certain idiosyncrasies and/or common conventions of the readers that made me more aware of my own practices during a reading.

Lin's observations eventually resulted in our more formal concern with the process whereby we were "becoming the phenomenon," the evaluation of a reader's competency, and what constituted a successful divinatory accomplishment (Jorgensen and Jorgensen, 1977; Jorgensen, 1984).

Over the following year I began an involved process of becoming a tarot card reader. While I started using the cards in a divinatory fashion, my abiding preoccupation with the tarot tended away from divination and toward a study of different schools of occult thought based on the tarot. I commonly used it for meditation, and even more commonly spent my time with different texts on the occult tarot. This investigation led me deeper and deeper into the literature on esotericism and occultism. In these ways my encounter with the tarot served as a concrete point of departure into the world of contemporary esotericism, and the focus of subsequent observation and participation. It justified some of my activities as a seeker, provided reasons for being a client, and led me to become a student in the esoteric community.

LEARNING DIVINATION

I was reading occult literature on the tarot, extensively and intensively, receiving tarot cards readings in the esoteric community, and observing Lin's divinatory use of the cards. It therefore was not extremely difficult for me to begin using the cards for divinatory purposes. The transition from an observer of divination and querent was eased by personal difficulties. I began using the cards to talk with myself and divine possible alternative courses of action. It was reassuring to be able to generate information from the cards about personal problems and decisions I was facing. In consulting the cards I learned that upcoming events would result in satisfactory outcomes for me, and they did. Yet, taking occult divination seriously was conflictual for me.

I constantly asked myself why anyone would take such nonsense seriously, and almost without exception I was able to dismiss and explain away seemingly extraordinary events rationally and sociologically. Entering into an occult frame of reference became possible for fairly brief periods of time and under particular circumstances, like when I faced existential dilemmas. There was a game-like quality to this in my experience. Unavoidably, I found myself constantly snapping back into a more rational, sociological perspective. Having made a sincere commitment to directly experiencing an occult reality and being unable to sustain an occult interpretation of events only intensified this conflict.

Another factor easing my transition from tarot observer to participant and reader was the frequency with which Lin was conducting divinatory readings. The people who came to our home in search of a tarot reader provided opportunities for me to begin reading the cards for friends and strangers. After about a dozen rather clumsy attempts at divination I became increasingly confident of my ability to read the tarot. Within several months I was reading the cards with a degree of success and self-confidence that surprised even me. I found this ability to deliver a seemingly successful performance rewarding, and it appeared that I might be able to verstehen the members' reality in this way.

Throughout 1977 I continued to collect esoteric literature pertinent to the tarot and decks of cards. Study of this literature provided me with a enhanced sense of the occult meanings of the cards and an underlying theosophy. My study of tarot literature reflected a growing commitment to this occultism and, like many students, I started to interpretatively integrate the occult lore of the tarot into a personal meaning system. My powerful commitment to a rationalistic, scientific worldview still made it difficult many times to accept occult teachings or take them at face value. Gradually I learned to suspend belief in science sufficiently so as to be able to enjoy occult experiences and teachings. I found it possible to slip in and out of interpretative frames, perspectives, and worldviews, even though this commonly required a huge leap of faith. It became easier to interpretatively manipulate an understanding of the occult such that it did not appear so ridiculous and conflictual from a scientific viewpoint.

My growing interest in and commitment to the occult tarot led to widening my literature search, and the inclusion of more academically legitimate sources of information. Study of the history, philosophy, theosophy, and uses of the tarot gave rise to a series of related questions about the history of esotericism in Western cultures. I increasingly came to the conclusion, reflected in Chapter Two, that esotericism essentially constituted a distinctive cultural tradition. Though perhaps naive, I felt that to appreciate esotericism adequately, the entire history of Western culture would need to be rewritten. These conclusions, then, reflected the manner in which I was able to synthesize a commitment to exoteric science with an interest in esoteric arts and sciences, like the occult tarot. While sustaining my commitments to rationalist and empiricist epistemologies and related ontologies, I also felt a growing appreciation for the limits of such knowledge. Esotericism and occultism added dimensions lacking in scientific worldviews, for me, especially an acknowledgement of emotional and intuitive aspects of human experience. I was not willing to relinquish a scientific worldview, but I was willing to call it into question, radically, and modify it in terms of occult claims to knowledge and conceptions of reality.

Our apartment became a common meeting place for a diverse collection of people interested in esotericism and occultism during 1977-78. The tarot frequently was the focus of discussion, and Lin regularly was requested to provide divinatory readings for visitors. She recorded that:

> In an effort to gain more experience as a reader of the cards, I began to orally advertise my skills to friends, students, and neighbors. Their response was gratifying; not only did they request readings, they also brought their friends and relatives to me.

Having gained considerable confidence in my own ability to read the cards, I too began reading the tarot for friends and other visitors. As the news of our divinatory activities circulated among our friends and acquaintances, people began requesting this service with greater frequency. Evenings commonly were spent with friends and recent acquaintances reading the tarot and discussing its arcane wisdom.

Applying readings of Goffman (1959, 1974), I found the ability actually to read the cards less important than the ability to manage and sustain the impression that one is able to divine past, present, and future events. The art of impression management is developed and honed in the process of reading the cards, not necessarily by any amount of study or intellectual preparation. I developed divinatory skills by a combination of reading the tarot and referring to esoteric literature on the topic. Knowledge of esoteric and occult literature enhanced my repertoire of meanings associated with the symbolic cards, while performing tarot divination provided occasions to apply my arcane knowledge and cultivate my performance in concrete situations.

I disliked being in the position of counselor for strangers and listening to their problems. I was a sociologist, after all, not a psychologist or counselor. Yet, the tarot provided a series of structural procedures and solutions for dealing with people's problems, as well as a routinized format for talking about them, about issues I otherwise found too intimate to raise. I generally did not feel comfortable, in other words, informing people that they had problems with relationships, family, careers, and the like, not to mention giving them advice about these matters. After considerable practice with tarot divination I gradually became increasingly confident that I could read the cards **in a manner much like people who provided this service for pay**. Perhaps I wasn't a tarot card reader, but I thought I could deliver a fairly convincing performance. Divination, after all, seemed pretty artful. Who was to say that my insights were not psychic or occult?

Many of the people I interacted with, however, were novices to the occult. Since my primary research interests were in people who engaged in esotericism as a way of life, I began exploring the possibility of taking a course in tarot from a professional reader in the esoteric community. In the summer of 1977 I attended an organizational meeting of a formal class on the tarot in the community. The instructors, a couple who read the cards as part of full-time involvement with esotericism in the Valley, were people with whom I had interacted before and respected. Lin and I previously had received readings from Ham, and we knew from participation in the community that he widely was regarded as a leading tarot adept, perhaps the best reader of the tarot in the Valley. During the meeting and for over an hour afterwards I talked with Ham about my interest in the tarot. He knew I had been reading the cards on my own and questioned my need to enroll in the course. I explained that I felt it necessary to receive more formal instruction from someone with expertise in tarot divination. I was pleased that Ham did not seem to be interested in me simply as a source of tuition, and I convinced him that I would profit from formal instruction.

The following weekend we met the instructors at a local occult bookstore for the purpose of taking the first of two half-day lessons. Out of about 20 people who had attended the organizational meeting, we were the only ones to show up for the classes. Ham decided to cancel the class, but he agreed to take us on, informally and without pay, as students. After about an hour of discussion during which time we asked Ham and his spouse Sue many questions about the tarot and its divinatory use, Ham suggested that we practice doing readings for one another. Reading the tarot, he asserted, was the best way to learn it. Furthermore, he noted, the tarot was like a complex book of knowledge. Like many books the more one read it the more one learned and gained insight. Divination was one way of applying this knowledge and gaining further insight. I was asked to provide a reading for Sue, and Lin and Ham paired off to do a second reading.

It would be impossible to overstate my anxiety and discomfort with this situation. Theretofore I had done readings for many different people, well over a hundred readings, but never before I had read the tarot for an accomplished reader, let alone my instructor. Amidst indescribable apprehension, perhaps even terror, I asked Sue to shuffle the cards and cut them. I then spread the cards in a very simple past, present, future format and began offering divinatory information. To my surprise words came easily, as before in my attempts at divination. For me reading the tarot was like telling a story. There always seemed to be a story in the cards, and my job was to find it in the symbolic images, bring it alive, weave these meanings together, and relate them to someone's life, hopefully in a way they found meaningful. As I continued reading, patterns of meaningful people and events began to emerge from the cards, and I arranged these meanings into a set of instructions and advice that I hoped would seem significant to Sue. Still ill-at-ease, however, I hurried quickly through the reading, bringing it to an abrupt close, no doubt prematurely. A sense of failed performance, if not incompetency, pervaded my consciousness.

I nevertheless posed the standard closing to a reading, something I learned from observing and receiving readings. "Do you have any questions about anything?," I asked. Sue asked a few questions about my divinatory advice, carefully and gracefully managing the situation so as to indicate her appreciation. She almost convinced me that I had been helpful. She told me that I had done an adequate job. We then reversed the roles, and she provided me with a reading. Sue finished the reading and we discussed it before turning to find out how Ham and Lin were doing. Ham had just finished reading the cards for Lin and they were wrapping up the discussion of his advice. It now was Lin's turn to read the tarot.

With her usual poise and polish Lin began reading the cards for Ham while we watched and listened. I experienced a tremendous sense of relief that my turn was over, and I became absorbed with the event. As Lin began reading the cards for Ham I noticed that her usual intuitive capabilities were operating. Occasional comments by Ham and Sue suggested that Lin was "hitting" on people, places, and events that they recognized as significant. As the reading progressed, Lin became more and more confident about what she was saying to Ham. At several points I became uncomfortable with the directness and candor of Lin's commentary, particularly as she touched on aspects of Ham's personality and life style. I wondered about how this information would be received. Toward the close of the reading Lin became very specific and personal about Ham's self. Almost breathlessly I awaited his reaction.

To my relief he immediately indicated that he was impressed with Lin's reading as well as the boldness of her extrapolations. Yet, he seemed resistant to confirm what Lin had said. Sue promptly entered the conversation and slowly, almost point by point, confirmed Lin's assessments, while checking to be sure that such a degree of self disclosure was not objectionable to Ham. With Sue's input, Ham became more open and he seemed to confirm his spouse's disclosures. Having concluded our readings I checked the time and discovered to my surprise that we had been working with the tarot for more than two hours. As it was late, we drew closure on our meeting. Before leaving, however, Ham and Sue encouraged us to try reading the cards for pay either at a psychic fair or in connection with one of the occult bookstores. Clearly it had been a worthwhile experience for all. In parting we planned to get together again in the near future.

This meeting marked the beginning of a growing friendship. Although we did not even informally receive additional lessons on the tarot as such from Ham or Sue, it was a common focus of informal conversation. On many of these occasions Ham, in particular, assumed the role of instructor and proceeded to educate us about the tarot, its divinatory use, the ethics of occult practice, the mores of the community, and related matters. Although it never was acknowledged explicitly by any of us, our relationship had come to resemble the classic form of occult education, namely one involving a master or adept and his/her apprentices. Comments by other members of the community as well as our corresponding treatment by them left little doubt but that we were regarded within the community as Ham's students. Being identified in this way also meant that we were seen as part of the psychic segment of the community. As our teachers and sponsors, Ham and Sue were to prove invaluable in facilitating our acceptance in the community as tarot card readers. Ham's extensive involvement with the occult and detailed knowledge of the local scene and community also made him an outstanding informant. Throughout the remainder of my fieldwork Ham regularly was consulted about the particulars of

Alliance Alleanza

Alliance

Bündnis Alianza

Deux des Bâtons Due di Bastoni

Two of Wands

Zwei-Stäbe Dos de Bastos

ILLUSTRATION FIVE: Two of Wands, *Barbara Walker Tarot Deck.* Reproduced permission of U.S. Games Systems, Inc., Stamford, CT 06902 USA. Copyright © 1986 U.S. Games Syster Inc. Further reproduction prohibited.

the community, and occult practices. By the conclusion of my fieldwork he was not only my teacher, sponsor, and most valued informant, but a trusted and trusting friend.

READING THE CARDS

In the early fall of 1977 Lin and I were asked to read the tarot for a fund raising event at the local Unitarian Church to which several of our friends belonged. In spite of my apprehension about doing tarot divination in public, for pay, before complete strangers, we agreed. This was a ground-breaking experience for me. Lin had done many readings for complete strangers in alien settings, but I had never before read for complete strangers outside of our home. My consternation about this was increased by the knowledge that many, if not all, of the potential querents would not be familiar in the least with the occult, and they therefore would be unprepared for an actual demonstration of it. Next to the hostile, disbelieving client, the novice, as discussed in Chapter Eight, is regarded by readers as the most difficult type of person to serve. Put simply, the novice querent generally lacks the background necessary to understand and acknowledge an occult performance.

My first reading confirmed all of these fears. Arriving at the Church after Lin had been reading for several hours, I found a long list of people signed up for readings. So as to give anyone an opportunity to receive a tarot reading I quickly organized a table in the room with Lin. My first querent was a woman about 45 to 50 years of age who had been quite anxious to receive a reading. Unbeknownst to me, she had expected a completely **private** reading; that is, a reading in a setting without other people present. I briefly explained the tarot and provided instructions about shuffling and cutting the cards. I then proceeded to spread and read the tarot. She met every comment I made with absolute, total, and complete rejection, almost before the words were out of my mouth, it seemed. Nothing I could say fit her experience. After about ten minutes of this horror, I stopped and indicated that all I could do was to read the cards. What they signified with respect to her life required her participation. I suggested further that if she was unhappy about the reading, I would refund her money. We agreed to continue, and she was less combative. She even occasionally acknowledged the gist and propriety of the comments. I hurried to finish the reading, but she insisted that I spread and read the cards again so she might really get her money's worth. I agreed, only for the purpose of being rid of her without further argument.

Once the reading was over I was ready to leave, and I did not care if I ever read the tarot again. The minister came by and explained to me that the woman had been upset that the reading was not private. Slowly, what had happened fell into place. I hurriedly arranged to relocate my table in another room and continued reading the cards for other querents. Much to my relief, the rest of the readings were very routine. I even counted two of the readings as successful. This enabled me to salvage some sense of accomplishment at reading the tarot in public. Having survived this experience I found it difficult to imagine that anything in the future could shake my faith in an ability to read the tarot.

From January to the middle of April 1978 was our most intensive period of participation involving the tarot in the esoteric community. We (mostly Lin) conducted interviews with all of the key people who read the tarot for pay, and other key informants with whom trusting relations had been established. We also socialized with many of these people, some of whom were among the core membership of the community. Social evenings in the homes of practitioners or at our place provided an excellent and unobtrusive setting in which information about the tarot and the community could be gathered. In important ways our participation with these people came to be defined as friendship, to which the collection of research materials was secondary. Lin also conducted a class in tarot divination during this period. Once a week our home became the headquarters for a small group of people learning to interpret the tarot for divinatory purposes. It also was a frequent gathering place for people interested in the occult, and a place where people (many of them friends) came for tarot readings.

From my standpoint frequent requests for divinatory readings had become a problem. I many times simply was not in the mood to do a reading. To do a satisfactory reading I found it necessary to mentally prepare and concentrate intensely. It was not something I could easily turn on and off. Most of my tarot readings took an hour to complete, and I not infrequently spent up to an additional hour talking with the querent. I decided to stop reading the tarot for just anyone unless I collected a fee, although I did relent occasionally and read for friends without compensation.

Drawing on a previous relationship with Jay, the leader of APRA, we hinted about being interested in reading the tarot at a psychic fair. He did not pick up on the allusion immediately. Although I knew that not just anyone was accepted as a fair participant, I still did not fully realize how the gatekeeping process operated. Accidently, but fortunately, I mentioned in a subsequent conversation with Jay that Ham and Sue had stimulated our interest in reading the tarot at a psychic fair. Talking with Ham later on I found out that Jay had discussed our fair participation with him. Ham told me that he assured Jay of our competency and legitimacy, thereby becoming a sponsor after a fashion. Clearly implicit in Ham's remarks was the idea that if we screwed up it would reflect badly on him.

In February we accepted an offer from Jay to purchase a booth and read professionally. We received further support and encouragement in this decision from Ham and Sue. Reading the tarot for pay at a psychic fair radically reoriented my perception and understanding of the esoteric community, practitioners, and professional practice. As a professional reader I assumed a perspective on the occult from which I theretofore had been excluded. In attending previous fairs as a seeker, I arrived after the fair was in full operation, after all of the front work had been done, and practitioners were prepared to meet outsiders. As a professional practitioner I was privy to this mostly backstage work, and I experienced giving professional performances directly in the community context.

Since we were just beginning professional practice in the community, we purchased one rather than two booths. The idea was for one of us to read for a while and then trade off. In this way we both would have an opportunity to read for pay without incurring the expense of an additional booth. This strategy provided us with much needed rest periods, as well as opportunities to circulate among insiders and conduct research.

We arrived at the psychic fair around eleven-thirty, half an hour before it opened to the pubic. Our booth was off in a corner of the room. I was more or less aware that the best locations were reserved for regular fair participants, prestigious specialities, and practitioners of reputation, although I had not given the matter serious thought before. Jay apologized for locating us in the corner, drawing my attention to the matter, but he did not offer to relocate us to a more centralized position. Subsequent conversations with readers at the fair reinforced the importance of booth location for making money and as a reflection of one's prestige. I determined to study this matter further. Jay's apology did seem strange to me. As a novice practitioner in the community I had few expectations. I certainly did not expect to be treated with deference. Besides, my primary interests were in doing research, not reading the tarot, even though these interests had become interrelated. I sensed that since Jay was dependent economically on practitioners who purchased booths, he was making a concerted effort to keep us happy. Later I learned that community members easily are offended by where they are located. Bad feelings and long standing disputes among people derive from these situations, ones which may seem trivial to an outsider.

We proceeded to set up the booth. Lin brought a fringed shawl to use as a table covering. A friend made us a large poster advertising tarot readings. With the sign in place over the booth and the table arranged to our liking, complete with tarot packs, we were ready for business. Even though it was not my first time, I was nervous about reading for pay. Only one of us would be able to read at a time, so I retired to the car to brush up on my divinatory skills. Lin came out in about an hour. Business was slow and she was anxious to share some new information with me. Just before the public arrived, she reported, several professional practitioners went from booth to booth casually asking what people planned to charge for a reading. A fee of ten dollars a reading was defined as the going rate at this fair. No one said that undercutting the ten dollar rate would be regarded as a breach of the emergent order, but this was clear to us with little reading between the lines. Ham later explained the ethics of this to me in detail.

As the fair progressed we became concerned about covering the expense of the booth, a forty dollar a day investment. Lin had done only two readings and we therefore needed two additional customers just to break even for the day. Our concerns were intensified by the frequency with which this was a predominant topic of conversations among other professionals. Everyone's primary concern, it seemed to me, was with whether or not they would make expenses and show a profit for the time invested. The better known psychics were doing a good business, but we were not alone in having only a few customers. The lack of activity throughout the day provided plenty of opportunity simply to sit and talk with other professionals. This was a fortunate situation from my standpoint as these conversations contained ample insight into the actual work-a-day world of professional practitioners.

By the end of the day we had conducted 4 readings for pay. We would not have done even this many except that Ham and Sue sent several clients to us as they were too busy to handle everyone. This experience and subsequent observation led me to the realization that many of the clients were regulars at fairs. They knew the readers by reputation, and were more likely to request service from experienced practitioners of note. The following day was not much better for us. We did six readings and thereby covered our fair overhead. We, however, also spent nearly sixteen hours in the booth over two days!

Lin did several more readings in the afternoon. Even so, when I arrived in the late afternoon she was somewhat discouraged by the lack of business. I was excited, however, by the wealth of information she had collected from casual conversations with practitioners during the day. Lin left shortly after I arrived as we had a dinner engagement that evening. I planned to read as long as there was business and then to join her at our friends' house. Just as I was ready to leave several querents sat down at my booth. I had no sooner finished two readings than another client arrived. I finished this reading and prepared to leave when Ham sent another client to me. Though already late for dinner, I felt more obligated to Ham, and I provided the querent with a reading.

As I reflected on fair participation I realized that reading the tarot for pay was not an enjoyable experience for me. It was extremely demanding emotionally, and even nerve-racking. It consumed valuable time and provided little reward beyond the collection of research materials. The clients I seemed to attract most frequently, women between fifty and sixty years of age, were the very people I experienced the greatest difficult in reading for. All of my readings had gone well. I felt greater and greater confidence in reading. My performance and professional demeanor were greatly improved. But, I did not enjoy the experience in the least.

Reading at the fair had provided invaluable experience and insight about professional practices in the esoteric community. In the fair setting the reader has no choice of clientele. The service is provided on demand. Except under the most exceptional circumstances it is considered unethical to refuse service to a client, even a difficult one. Even under the best of circumstances, I found tarot divination to be a very risky business. In the more confined, private setting of a home I had the opportunity to prepare mentally for a divinatory performance. I was able to draw up knowledge of divinatory meanings of the cards and mentally anticipate each step of the reading. In the private setting I usually had an opportunity to become acquainted with the querent before reading the cards. In doing the reading I found time to explain what was happening to the client, and prepare them for what to expect. It was possible, in other words, to negotiate with and convey to them my understanding of the occult tarot. Once the cards were spread I felt little pressure to immediately demonstrate deep, extraordinary insight into the querent's life. If I felt unsuccessful in the private setting, there was plenty of time to spread the cards and try again, without revealing professional incompetence.

The more casual, private setting of a reading is radically transformed in the highly public context of a psychic fair. Divinatory readings are requested by complete strangers. I never knew when someone would come by and request a reading. I either had to be prepared constantly, or get ready quickly. Since I did not know the querent, unless I asked directly (and readers sometimes do this), there was no way of knowing if I was dealing with a novice or a more experienced client. Beyond agreeing to a price, readers at fairs rarely converse with clients before beginning a reading. I eventually learned, however, to do this as part of the reading during the very early stages. In the fair setting, I experienced a subtle but immediate concern for revealing some deep insight into the querent's life. If an account based on the cards was not forthcoming or if the querent did not recognize and participate in the construction of meaning, there was a temptation to read the querent; that is, employ even the slightest verbal and especially nonverbal signs and cues to render meanings. Every reader is conscious that such information is available, and that it may be useful in the event that one is unable to "get anything" from the cards. Unlike casual readings, public readings at fairs created great anxiety about the possibility of failure or showing incompetence. Querents have paid for and expect a demonstration of the occult. Other practitioners expect you to deliver. Your reputation and identity in the community literally depends on an ability to deliver a successful performance of divination on demand.

Most of the time I experienced little difficultly in finding sufficient material in the cards to perform divination. The symbols and patterns of significance commonly seemed to jump out at me, words flowed easily, and querents provided sufficient feedback to confirm that what I was saying was meaningful. If this does not happen professional practitioners have a remedy, namely "cold reading" (see Hyman, 1977). By way of this technique readers check out the querent's style of dress, age, gender, rings, and any other visible or verbal cues that might be potentially useful. On this basis the reader attempts to demonstrate quickly a deep insight into the querent's life. If lucky, the reader hits on something to which the querent responds. Once a dialogue is established it then becomes possible to return to the cards and develop this theme: health, sex, marriage, money, career, and so on, based on an attribution of the cards.

Lin's fieldnotes provide a concrete examples of how tarot card readers feel about cold reading. She observed that:

> There is another element involved in Tarot situations, that of "reading the querent." I've discovered that, especially when spreading the cards for people I don't know, I rely on a variety of cues to help me with the reading: i.e. sex, age, marital status, and apparent socioeconomic status (e.g., dress, speech), to mention the most obvious. I approach a reading for a middle-aged female with a different "mind-set" than a reading for a youthful unmarried male. Events suggested by a certain card are put into a perspective presented by the above-mentioned cues and are given directional assistance.

Professional readers attempt to do straight readings, ones based exclusively on the cards or related techniques for their interpretation, whenever possible. But most of them also resort to cold reading techniques when all else fails. This is especially important for the reader attempting to establish a reputation. Once a considerable reputation has been established, it then may be possible occasionally to admit that for whatever reasons, one's psychic abilities simply are not working.

I have heard readers make such comments, but such an admission is potentially disastrous for the psychic fair newcomer.

Tarot card readers also express concern for difficulties deriving from dependence on cold readings of a client. Lin, for instance, recorded in her notes that:

> There is a danger, however (especially when reading for friends), in allowing these cues and other known information to interfere with, or even take precedence over the observations of the cards. On the one hand, attention must be given to visual and verbal cues; on the other, meaning must be derived from the cards themselves. Too frequently there's a temptation to read what I believe should be, rather than what is, available in an interpretation; to offer my own advice rather than that of the cards.

Hence, while tarot card readers do not deny being influenced by visible and verbal information about a client, they generally feel that these resources must be integrated with an interpretation of the tarot cards. Like Lin, tarot card readers in the esoteric community commonly bestow a certain reality on the tarot itself, apart from their interpretation of it.

It is no secret among insiders to the community that readers sometimes use cold reading techniques. The service-for-pay situation itself is viewed by many members as a form of professional prostitution. Readers uniformly distinguish between serious readings, performed for self, friends and other members, as different from readings performed for pay. This is not to say that readings for pay are discernably different from other readings. The fundamental difference resides in the way in which readers' experience and regard them, not in the results. At the aforementioned psychic fair insiders joked about particular clients ("what a dope") and the reading for pay situation. Toward the end of the fair, after the early afternoon tension subsided and readers were more relaxed and tired, a reader broke up the insiders present with the behind the scene remark that: "Well, here comes another mark, oops, I mean client."

In the spring of 1978 we again read the tarot at a psychic fair in the esoteric community. Having been through this experience before I was much more relaxed, and the fair seemed more routine. I still did not find reading the tarot for pay to be a pleasant experience, but at least it was not painful. We clearly were treated at this fair as members of the community. There were many signs of this. That we were invited to participate again in a psychic fair was a very positive indication that we had passed the most severe test of membership. Our booth was located in a central meeting area, widely regarded as one of the better areas. Community members and leaders congregated in and around our booth during slack and break periods, engaging in casual conversation, gossip, and fair talk. We were greeted with familiarity, and conversations not uncommonly involved discussions of participants' personal lives, as well as all varieties of esotericism. I was invited to deliver a special lecture on a topic of my choosing. I understood this to be an honor and took it as a significant sign of being accepted as a fully participating member of the community.

As summer approached I gradually discontinued participating actively in community affairs. My attention focused on describing findings, analyzing them, and writing a dissertation. Movement away from intensive participation in the community was facilitated by less activity in the community during the hottest summer months. I continued to interact with close friends in the community as I prepared them for my eventual disengagement. I also used this period of fieldwork to test out preliminary formulations of findings with trusted informants and friends, like Ham and Jay. Since I had been applying for academic positions elsewhere I was not completely unprepared for an eventual departure from the Valley. I liked the area, however, and hoped to remain somewhere in the state. Our move from the Valley across the United States in September 1978 happened too quickly for me. Leaving the field was a rather abrupt experience. Except for a few close friends and informants, I was unable to negotiate satisfactory closure on relationships with members of the esoteric community.

MEMBERSHIP IN PERSPECTIVE

My initial exploration of the cultic milieu was conducted from the standpoint of a sociology graduate student looking for a dissertation topic. At the outset what I knew about the occult was based on popular cultural images and a very casual reading of pertinent scholarly literature. This knowledge about the occult was not inaccurate, it fairly faithfully reflected popular and scholarly views of the occult, but it had little to do with the esoteric scene as it is experienced and lived by members of this American milieu. I was unprepared for demonstrations of occult practice, and consequently when I observed them, I failed to see anything particularly extraordinary. Although most of the beliefs, practices, people, and groups constituting the esoteric scene and community in the Valley are visible, I did not know where to look to find them, and I was unable, initially, to distinguish readily observable patterns of belief, cults, practitioners, or networks of social relationship among them.

Once I encountered information about where to find practitioners and groups I found it easy to attend public meetings, lectures, and psychic fairs. In frequenting these activities I hoped to locate a group to join and study, but I was not aware until much later that insiders would see me as a nominal member of this scene and define me as a seeker. Although I moved deeper and deeper into the esoteric scene and community in a relatively brief period of time, what this meant to members and how my perspective on their affairs changed just as rapidly, was only gradually realized in my experience. The decision to become a client of practitioners in the community was a more deliberate decision. I was vaguely aware that as a client people treated me differently than as simply a seeker. I recognized that it was becoming easier for me to distinguish among insiders, including particular bodies of knowledge, practices, practitioners, groups, and patterns of social relationship, and that insiders increasingly acknowledged me with greater familiarity. Yet, I only gradually learned what this meant from the standpoint of the esoteric community.

To be an insider to the esoteric community is to possess a knowledge of esotericism and occultism, categories of membership, types of practitioners and groups, as well as patterns and networks of relationship constituting distinctive worlds of meaning. Before attending the first psychic fair I was completely unaware of the esoteric community, not to mention the different factions I learned to distinguish. Differences among tarot card readers and psychic practitioners seems obvious and even taken-for-granted to me now, but it had no meaning to me before I became involved in community affairs. Through my use of the tarot I learned to see specific theosophical orientations to the cards, styles of interpretation, and particular procedures. None of these meanings existed for me before. Whatever I thought about gypsies as an outsider was significantly different from the type of person I learned about as a member of the community. For members this label serves to identify an illegitimate practitioner and it clearly reflects the moral order of the community over and against fakes and frauds. As a matter of routine, members recognize different esoteric doctrines, related practices, and types of people associated with these practices. Tarot card readers never use the term "fortune-telling" to identify what they do. "Fortune-telling" is what gypsies do.

To become a devotee of the occult is to learn new and different ways of interpreting the mundane affairs of everyday life. Divinatory performances, as discussed in Chapter Eight, require a shift of consciousness so that parties to these procedures are prepared to appropriate occult knowledge. These realities differ from the cognitive style of the natural attitude as ordinary everyday life realities are described by Schutz (1973) and Berger and Luckmann (1966). As a finite province of meaning, occult realities transform wide-awake consciousness, suspension of doubt, practicality, self awareness, intersubjectivity, and a sense of time in remarkable ways. In occult practice wide-awake consciousness is greatly expanded, not in the unconscious or inattentive style of dreaming or the seemingly disorganized style of insanity, but in the sense of a heightened awareness of things unavailable to mundane consciousness. Occult thought, in this regard, is similar to scientific ideas about objects like the id, superego, atoms, germs, black holes, anomie, and deprivation, most of which are also unavailable through ordinary experience. Like scientific knowledge, occult realities require more or less extensive training and socialization whereby the adept learns to see what is otherwise unavailable (see Tiryakian, 1973). Normal consciousness of time, self, and sociability also are expanded. Esoteric realities include souls, spirits, and entities without ordinary historical limitations. Occult time is cosmic, and it may include a belief in extra-terrestrial ancestors of earthly humankind (see Scott, 1980).

The process of becoming an occultist is a gradual experience. It generally is not marked by a single dramatic moment after which the world is suddenly different. Luhrmann (1989:Chapter 21) accurately describes this process as "interpretative drift." Like Luhrmann, Lin and I drifted into occult beliefs as a way of interpreting the world of everyday life. Unlike Luhrmann, Lin, and myself, people generally experience interpretative drift more or less unreflectively. Once a person has begun to accept the plausibility of occult interpretations, however, the use of an occult frame of reference sometimes becomes intoxicating.

Occult knowledge becomes a way for people to make ordinary life decisions in non-ordinary ways. After her introduction to the tarot, Leah, one of Lin's students, changed her name and thereby her social identity to correspond to an esoteric understanding of reality. She regularly used the tarot to envision present situations and anticipate the future. It became a means of making sense out of virtually every aspect of her life. Not incidentally, she was otherwise a fairly ordinary woman from a respectable middle-class background. When I first met Leah she was 28 years old, divorced from her first husband, teaching public school, raising her daughter, casually dating, and doing art.

By her account, to illustrate further, a girlfriend invited her to a local bar where they were to meet other friends and play a few games of backgammon. After several visits to the bar, Leah decided one evening to take her tarot cards. In retrospect she maintained that she had a **feeling** that she should do a reading for a man they had met. At the bar that evening she mentioned the tarot to this man and another person near them immediately became attentive and requested a reading. Although they had not met before, Leah had previously seen this man in the bar and she agreed to read the tarot for him. This meeting, she felt esoterically, must have been preordained. Through the tarot reading they became friends and later began dating. When I first met her friend, a lawyer, at Leah's home one evening, they both talked about the tarot and how significant Leah's reading had been for them. We were playing a regular card game that evening and Leah's date began talking about psychic powers and seeking Leah's cooperation in meditating upon receiving a good playing hand. They would join hands across the table and concentrate on particular cards. Several outstanding hands merely reinforced this attempt to call upon psychic powers. Though perhaps frivolous, their beliefs were not insincere.

Several days later Leah came to our house. Since meeting the lawyer they had become almost constant companions and the esotericism of the tarot had become an important source of solidarity between them. He had invited her to go with him on a business trip to Hawaii. Leah was anxious to go but a previous boyfriend lived in Hawaii, a guy about whom she still cared and wanted to see. To complicate the situation further, Leah was aware that since she and the Hawaiian boyfriend had been apart, he had become involved in a romantic relationship with another woman. Although she wanted to go to Hawaii, in thinking about the trip, Leah began to realize that the lawyer was not the person she wanted to be with. By Leah's account she attempted to resolve this very complex situation by tarot divination.

In consulting the cards she had the feeling, attributed to divination, that the man in Hawaii was about to call her. Sure enough, by her account, he did call within several days to report that he had just broken up with the woman he was seeing, and he wanted Leah to come for a visit (thereby confirming her divinatory intuition). In relating this story it became clear that Leah was using the tarot and related occultisms to interpret present circumstances and make decisions about what course of action to follow. The evening she related the story we were asked to read the tarot for her. Neither of the readings we provided pointed directly to a particular course of action. Indeed, I deliberately used the tarot as a way to explore Leah's feelings about the situation, and raise questions she might want to consider in choosing among alternatives. She used my comments, however, to justify making a **particular** decision. I encountered an untold number of situations like this during my fieldwork. Like many other people, Leah learned to use esoteric knowledge to make sense of her existence and to make complex decisions.

Leah's experience stands in stark contrast with the experiences of people who do not subscribe to occult teachings. To interpret events esoterically requires that one at least accept the plausibility of these doctrines and practices. Once this assumption is made esoteric interpretations become real. If this assumption does not hold, practices like tarot divination are impossible. This was demonstrated vividly to me in an attempt to explain the operation of the tarot to a friend, a graduate student from a large midwestern university. Unable to accept the plausibility of tarot divination, my friend found it absurd and laughed almost uncontrollably at my efforts to provide a demonstration for him.

My divinatory use of the tarot at psychic fairs made accessible to me the backstage activities of professional practitioners. It would have been difficult by any other means to uncover the informal rules and implicit understandings in the community defining ethical practices, practitioners and relationships among them, techniques for producing a divinatory performance, ways of establishing fees, perspectives on clientele, and a host of related matters. In reading the tarot I gained first-hand experience with this occult practice and its social accomplishment. My membership in the community, in all relevant ways, facilitated rather than inhibited efforts to describe this social world sociologically.

Unlike Rambo (1987; also see Rambo-Roni and Ellis, 1990) who experienced serious difficulty in separating her role as a member (exotic dancer) from her role as sociologist, I constantly fought to keep my sociological consciousness from controlling my membership experiences. Although I was able to perform the role of tarot card reader and pass as such in the community, to think, feel, and act as an occultist for more than brief periods of time was exceptionally difficult for me. My experience of occult realities always was game-like. My ability to experience an occult reality was greatest when I used the tarot for study and meditation, rather than in a divinatory fashion. In reading the tarot for clients I constantly feared that something I said would become the basis for important, consequential actions. Though not inconsistent with discussions I found in occult literature, particularly the writings of Crowley, my experiences and accounting for them only vaguely resembled the more ordinary abilities of community members to suspend doubt about nonempirical realities. My interpretations of these experiences ultimately were more philosophical and sociological than occult, as I understood them.

Unlike the most committed members of the community, my occult identity was temporary. I was fully aware that it was something that could be shed once the research was finished. While I temporarily became the phenomenon, I did not go native, if going native requires that one abandon self and surrender completely to the occult. This is extremely important since it reflects, perhaps negatively, on my interpretation of the members' world of experience and meaning.

Lin's experiences with becoming a tarot card reader were quite different. Unlike me, she much more fully incorporated an occult identity as part of her "self." In part this process was facilitated by testing occult claims to knowledge. Shortly after she began reading the tarot for other people, Lin recorded that:

> I decided to attempt an experiment with this influx of new "clients," most of whom I did not know well: I asked each querent to write out a specific question for the Tarot to answer, without allowing me to see it. The results were frequently rather astounding to me: e.g., the cards for the querents who asked about their love life showed a majority in the suit of cups [the suit associated with love]; students requesting information about their studies had a majority of cards in the suit of swords [the suit pertinent to intellectual matters].

Lin, like many tarot card readers in the community, also reported having experiences, typically ones perceived as somehow anomalous, which confirmed the extraordinary quality of divinatory knowledge. She observed:

> One reading was especially significant to me, for I had preconceived notions about the question I thought the querent would ask. My neighbor, Debi, requested a Tarot reading shortly after a conversation we had in which she informed me that the disease with which she is afflicted, Muscular Dystrophy, was worsening, and that she would have to wear a leg brace. I was certain that the question she would ask would be directed in some fashion towards her physical condition. However, the cards in the spread I read for her were concerned with her vocation, more precisely with an artistic endeavor in which she was about to engage. Her question: Will I fulfill my desire to become a photographer?

Her experiences with reading the tarot thereby served to reinforce the idea that something extraordinary indeed was happening, and these experiences supported her emergent identity as an occultist.

Lin, like other readers in the esoteric community, construed assorted experiences with the occult as indicative of "professional" competency. She noted that:

> I started this "journal" of my experiences with the Tarot almost a year ago, and have had many varied experiences and involvements since that time. I have read the cards, as a professional, at a Church fund raising event; I have read the cards for local professional readers who put their seal of approval on my competency; I have taught classes on reading the cards; I have even accepted money for my Tarot services.

Reflectively questioning further whether or not she truly had become a professional tarot card reader, Lin reasoned that:

> First, I have been accepted by acknowledged professional readers as worthy of their esteem—my readings were perceived by them to be accurate, and my advice to the point. Second, and perhaps most

> importantly, I am aware of my abilities; I know, by comparing my performance with that of other readers, that I am as capable, and as knowledgeable, as some of the best readers with whom I have come in contact. Because of this I have arrived at a place with friends and acquaintances where I sometimes feel like the physician who is cornered at a party and expected to provide free medical advice. How should I let my friends know that I am now less willing to spend several hours of my time on a reading if there is no return for it? Perhaps I would feel differently if it were a more occasional activity, but lately I have had three or four request a week for my "professional services" with the assumption made that it will be free.

Lin's experiences consequently served as a basis for comparison and contrast with mine. My frequent inability to take occultism seriously except as an interesting fieldwork exercise was balanced through our conversations by Lin's genuine, existential reflection of an insider's viewpoint.

Chapter 6

The Occult Tarot

Tarot cards most likely were a 15th century Italian invention mainly used for playing games. Toward the end of the 18th century these unique cards were attributed to the Ancients and defined as a body of esoteric knowledge. The seemingly mysterious origin of the tarot cards fueled further speculations and hermetic interpretations. With the successive occult revivals in France during the 19th century the tarot was defined in terms of Hermetic-Kabalistic traditions as a principal occultism. These esoteric interpretations of the tarot climaxed in the late 19th century British occult revival when it was fully integrated with Hermetic-Kabalistic occultisms as the **symbolic key** to all arcane wisdom. Through this interpretative, historical process the tarot became an elaborate occult theosophy and an enduring part of esoteric culture.

TAROT CARDS

The tarot I encountered in the Valley ostensibly is a unique pack of 78 pictorial cards. Fifty-six of these emblems, the **lesser** (smaller, minor) cards, are equally divided among four suits, similar to standard playing cards. The names of the tarot suit signs, except for spades, differ from the clubs, hearts, and diamonds of ordinary playing cards.[1] In spite of some variation from deck to deck, the tarot suits commonly are called **swords** (spades), **wands** (sceptres, batons), **cups** (chalices, goblets), and **pentacles** (coins, circles) when expressed in English.[2] The minor portion of a tarot deck contains: sixteen **court** (coate, costume, figure) cards, ordinarily referred to in English as **king**, **queen**, **knight**, and **page** within each suit; as well as 40 small cards, called **pips**, illustrated by markers of each suit numbered from **ace** (one) through **ten** (see Douglas, 1972; Kaplan, 1972, 1978, 1986).

The twenty-two **greater** (larger, major) tarot cards, **the special trumps**, have no counterpart in a deck of playing cards, except perhaps for the joker. These trumps consequently are the tarot's most distinguishing feature. Although titles, numbers, and sequences vary from deck to deck, the twenty-two tarot trumps commonly are labeled in English: the **Fool** (Vagabond); the **Magician** (Juggler); the **High Priestess** (Popess, Junon); the **Empress** (Isis, Queen); the **Emperor** (Osiris, King); the **Hierophant** (Pope, Jupiter); the **Lovers** (Marriage, Eros); the **Chariot** (Tirumphal Car, Wagon); **Justice** (Scales); the **Hermit** (Wise Man, Sage); the **Wheel of Fortune** (Fate, Chance, Rota); **Strength** (Force, Fortitude); the **Hanged Man** (Traitor, Thief); **Death** (Skelton); **Temperance**; the **Devil** (Satan, Typhon); the **Tower** (House of God); the **Star**; the **Moon**; the **Sun**; **Judgment**; and, the **World** (Universe). Kaplan (1978, 1986) identifies and illustrates about 400 tarot packs, some of which reflect radically different designs. Several dozen or more tarot decks are available in contemporary editions.

By way of largely familiar emblems and icons, the tarot trumps and sometimes the lesser cards, graphically portray culturally recurrent patterns of human experience and existence. Some of the trumps represent human selves, identities, characters, statuses, roles, and personages: buffoons, tricksters, charismatics, politicians, bureaucrats, clerics, ascetics, recluses, and derelicts. Other tarots depict human values, states and qualities, and situations, such as virtues and vices, emotions, attachments, departures, changes, submission and domination, bounty, chance, sobriety, restraint, catastrophe, and beauty. Some of the tarots reflect human interactions, relationships, groups, associations, and institutions, as well as other human products and artifacts: friendships, kinships, cliques, polities, economies, asylums, unions, foundations, theaters, merchandise, vehicles, dwellings, and edifices. And still other tarot cards portray would-be human connections to an elusive, extra-human domain: natures, macrocosms, creations, nirvanas, hells, deities, ecstasy, rapture, enlightenment, and the cosmos.

The illustrative symbolism of the tarot provides a means whereby streams of human experience and existence may be represented, conceptually categorized, interpreted, evaluated, and expressed meaningfully. Its abiding allure unfolds in large part from the elegant, pictorial images and aesthetic symbols depicted artistically in the cards, particularly the major trumps, and human proficiencies for abducting from them an infinite array of meanings. The sociological importance of this cannot be overstated. Like all symbolic schemes, the tarot provides a language through which subjective, personal experience can be represented and expressed intersubjectively, publicly, and socially (see Berger and Luckmann, 1966). And, as with religious systems of symbolism and meaning, the tarot shares in common the capacity for defining, interpreting, legitimating, and sanctioning the mundane world of everyday human life existence in terms of ultimately realistic, cosmic forces and conditions (see Berger, 1967; Geertz, 1973).

The precise origin of the tarot is unknown, and this historical uncertainty contributed immensely and significantly to its mystique. The Italian, "trionfi," was used during the 15th century with reference to the twenty-two tarot trumps. In the 16th century, "triontif," was replaced by the word "tarocchi" (or "tarocco" in the singular), which eventually included all of the 78 cards (Kaplan, 1978:1). More or less standard editions of tarot cards developed between the 15th and late 18th centuries in western Europe. The French denouement, "tarot" eventually was adopted and popularized in English as the standard label for this pack of cards (Kaplan, 1978:1).

The tarot consequently was a product of a historical process, the course of which came to be seen as a problem to be explained.

The tarot has been the subject of interminable speculation, and monumental efforts to decode its illustrative mysteries allegorically. Since the late 18th century it has been interpreted as an esoteric body of knowledge attributed to the Ancients. Succeeding generations of occultists zealously endeavored to correct, replenish, restore, rectify, and purify the profane and degenerate tarot they initially encountered. In the tarot they discovered a sacred, occult text and two athenaeums of Truth: The **Major Arcana**, represented by the secret and hidden wisdoms of the twenty-two trumps; and, the **Minor Arcana**, an occult knowledge embodied in the lesser tarots. Culturally defined as an occult text, the tarot became a fertile subject for subsequent elaboration and interpretation.

Occult interpretations of the tarot climaxed during the late 19th and early 20th centuries when it was fully integrated with the Hermetic-Kabalistic tradition. Occult interpreters of the arcane text sometimes innovated radically on existing traditions, establishing tarot correspondences with ancient (Egyptian, Persian, Greco-Roman) philosophies, mythologies, and mystery cults, Cabalism (numerology, the Hebrew alphabet, the Tree of Life), alchemy, astrology, numerology, magic, witchcraft, paganisms (Celtic, Arthurian), as well as other symbolic infrastructures (plants, animals, colors) and assorted esotericisms. This **occult tarot** is a body of knowledge, a socially, culturally and historically constructed human text. It is embodied as a dynamic esoteric language, representing vocabularies and grammars of symbolic meaning that may be applied for the purposes of scholarly-like, hermetic inquiries, self-study and meditation, as well as portending and divination.

Members of the esoteric community in the Valley who use the tarot share unevenly in an occult knowledge of this vibrant text. What they know is an eclectic folklore, constituted as oral traditions, more or less supported by more formal occult traditions and literature. They subscribe to many variations of occult theories of the tarot, intermingled with their understanding of Religion, Science, and other exoteric ideas, and they commonly innovate on these themes in applying occult knowledge. Some of them know little and hardly could care less about esoteric literature and traditions. Other members of the community take formal traditions of occultism seriously and possess an impressive knowledge and understanding of them. In any case, it serves members of the community as a body of knowledge useful for making sense of human existence.

A HERMENEUTICS OF THE TAROT

In leaning to become a tarot card reader I surveyed the published literature on the cards.[3] This search was consistent with my apprenticeship. I was encouraged to read and consult occult guides to the tarot, but I was not required to do this systematically or comprehensively. My interest in occult traditions and literature to a larger extent reflected a commitment to exoteric scholarship, not occult practice. I read selectively, only vaguely aware of the relevance of particular works, and I cumulatively began to develop some sense of formal traditions of occult knowledge.

ILLUSTRATION SIX: Eight of Swords, Three of Cups, Nine of Pentacles, Four of Wands, *Royal Fez Moroccan Tarot Deck.* Reproduced by permission of U.S. Games Systems, Inc., Stamford, CT 06902 USA. Copyright ©1975 Stuart R. Kaplan. Further reproduction prohibited.

The materials I examined varied tremendously in quality, focus, orientation, date of publication, style of presentation, perspective, and so on. This literature includes: scholarly works on the origin and history of cards pertinent to the tarot; primary, classic and highly influencial occult texts, some of which deal specifically with the tarot; and, secondary works, representing summaries, syntheses, and scholarly-like studies of classic occult books on the tarot. Much of the published literature on the tarot is presented as compendiums to interpreting and using the cards, especially for divinatory purposes.

Tarot decks usually are accompanied by instructions for their use, and handbooks on the tarot frequently are based on a specific pack of cards. Guides to the tarot oftentimes are rather crude attempts to capitalize on public interest in fortunetelling, and they sometimes synthesize occult traditions, once in a while in innovative ways. Other textbooks eschew or disavow traditions, misrepresent them, and/or aim to establish novel interpretations of the tarot. Some of the primary, occult studies of the tarot are manuals and handbooks. More scholarly examinations of the tarot sometimes are critical and disdainful of particular theories or portions of them. These writers sometimes exhibit exoteric values, norms, interests, and skills in the analysis, interpretation, and presentation of evidence, while affirming some belief in the occult tarot. Very few unbelieving, exoteric scholars have attempted to analyze and interpret this occult body of knowledge and practice.[4]

I have not systematically examined all of the primary and secondary literature on the occult tarot. I have followed exoteric interpretations of Western occultism, as outlined in Chapter Two, and I have depended selectively on what seem to be the best available sources on the occult tarot, as reflected in the works referenced here. I am interested in the tarot, and related literature, as products of human activity: socially constructed bodies of knowledge, texts, that provide social meanings constituted as traditions. These meanings and traditions are grounded in human interpretations of the cards. They are advanced as attributions, theosophies, theories, and claims to knowledge. I am **not** interested in correcting, resolving, or adjudicating these matters. I am interested in providing an interpretation of them.

In developing this interpretation I make no claim to having captured definitively the meanings or histories of the cards, or the occult tarot. Unlike many scholars and occultists I cannot envision a definitive, objective, real History or Explanation of the occult tarot independently of its human interpretation. There are human, social, historical, and cultural products: texts, customs, traditions, bodies of knowledge, belief, and practice; all of which require and only exist by way of human interpretation. This is not to say, however, that all interpretations are equal. On the basis of available evidence, its evaluation, and argument, some interpretations are more plausible and credible than others. My hermeneutics of the occult tarot, perhaps ironically, is in some ways similar to the epistemological stance of some occultists.

Aleister Crowley and Alfred Edward Waite, for instance, in spite of otherwise radically different points of view, distance themselves from implausible theories of the tarot, particularly ones grounded in empirical claims about highly fanciful histories of the tarot's ancient origin. They, moreover, avoid reformulating a history of the occult tarot on empirical grounds, while attempting to sustain an ontology of the tarot based on alternative epistemologies. Crowley [1974 (1944):3-4, 42], for instance, observed that:

> Unimportant to the present purpose are tradition and authority. Einstein's Theory of Relativity does not rest on the fact that, when his theory was put to the test, it was confirmed. The only theory of ultimate interest about the Tarot is that it is an admirable symbolic picture of the Universe, based on the data of the Holy Qabalah.... [T]he Meaningless and Abstract, when understood, has far more meaning than the Intelligible and Concrete.

Waite, in spite of otherwise important differences with Crowley, expressed similar sentiments. In the "Preface to the English Translation" of Papus' 1889 classic, [*The Absolute Key to Occult Science*] *The Tarot of the Bohemians: The Most Ancient Book in the World* [*For the Use of Initiates*], he (1975:vii-viii), declared that:

> The chief point regarding the history of Tarot cards, whether used as pretexts for fortune telling or as symbols for philosophical interpretation, is that such history does not in fact exist. There are tangible symbolical reasons for believing that some part of them is exceedingly old in conception, though not in form, and perhaps, in the last resource, they can be held to rank as the more interesting and curious on this account.

In spite of similarities, there are important differences between my sociological interpretation of the tarot, and its occult interpretation. Occult interpretations of the tarot are claims to an extraordinary knowledge of reality. My interpretation makes no such claims. I claim to provide a sociological interpretation of extraordinary knowledge claims. I cannot say sociologically whether or not occult claims yield an extraordinary knowledge of reality.

In short, then, there is no need to correct or revise occult histories or theories of the tarot. They are what they are, humanly constructed and fashioned products. Theories and histories of the tarot, as social products, are subject to multiple interpretations, some of which are more illuminating than others. I have endeavored to display, selectively and in a limited way, a flavor of the social historical construction of the occult tarot, and related traditions. My interpretation of the occult tarot aims at some greater understanding of it, especially how it is related to the divinatory practices of tarot card readers in the esoteric community.

OCCULT APPROPRIATION OF THE CARDS

Occultists, among other interested parties, have offered many different theories of the tarot's origin. These contentions frequently serve as bases for attributing meaning and offering related theosophies of an occult tarot. The earliest speculations about the origin of the tarot predate the deciphering of the Egyptian hieroglyphics and subsequent exoteric scholarship on ancient civilizations. It occurs within a social and intellectual climate characterized by an overwhelming fascination with the Ancients, mediated commonly by Renaissance Hermeticism, especially an infatuation with the mythical, Thrice-Great, Hermes Trismegistus, the Greek duplicate of the Egyptian god of erudition and charisma, Thoth (see Yates, 1964). A central principle of Hermeticism, as above so below, envisions a unity of macrocosm and microcosm, mediated symbolically by the tarot. These ideas had produced an "Egyptian rite" of Freemasonry, the Knights Templar of the Temple of Solomon, multifarious Rosicrucian orders, brotherhoods of Martinists, and various other artistic, literary, occult, and cultic manifestations throughout Europe (Cavendish, 1975; Kaplan, 1978, 1986; Yates, 1972).

Once these traditions had been established, exoteric scholarship on the Ancients, the rationalization of Religion (with the Protestant Reformation and the Catholic Counter-Reformation), and the advent of Science did little to quell occult speculation about the tarot or related cultures. In this and subsequent sociointellectual and cultural contexts, the tarot is thought, alternately, to be: derived from China, India, or Persia; an Egyptian book of knowledge preserved by wandering gypsies; recovered and returned to Europe by the crusaders; brought into Europe by invading Islamic armies; invented in Europe; a preserved Egyptian religion or the mystery religion of Mithras or part of a pagan Celtic tradition; a product of medieval heretics; the teachings of Cabalists in Morocco; related to the collective unconscious; and/or associated with the symbolism of Dante's *Divine Comedy* (see Cavendish, 1975; Douglas, 1972; Kaplan, 1972, 1978, 1986). Most of these theories of the occult origins of the tarot have been discredited, even within occult circles, yet many contemporary practitioners subscribe sanctimoniously to a particular theory of origins, related theosophies and esoteric traditions.

The origin or origins of the tarot is abstruse and perhaps inexplicit historically. Cards in general were known in Korea and China as early as the 10th century C.E. (Hargrave, 1966; Douglas, 1972). They appeared later in the West, probably around the 13th or 14th centuries. The idea of cards is widely supposed to be an Eastern cultural innovation which eventually was spread by way of East/West trade (see Kaplan, 1978, 1986). Dummett (1980a, 1980b, 1986) is certain that playing cards were introduced into Europe from the Islamic world during the last quarter of the 14th century. It is not difficult to imagine that an Italian merchant recently returned from the middle East or far East directed some craftsman to construct a pack of cards based on a knowledge of Eastern cards (see Kaplan, 1978; Douglas, 1972). Any connection between Eastern and Western cards, however, is indirect (see Douglas, 1972). The earliest known Eastern cards differ considerably in design and structure from what appeared later in the West.

Experts disagree over whether or not the earliest Western card pack was a tarot. Similarities between tarot and other playing cards suggest a common origin. It is possible that the tarot developed from playing cards, by adding the major trumps and a knight to the court cards. It also is possible that playing cards came about by dropping the tarot trumps, except for the knight, and perhaps the fool which may have been retained as a joker. The matter simply is not clear. Playing cards and tarot cards may have originated independently at about the same time.

And several independent ancestries of tarot and/or playing cards are conceivable. Dummett (1980a, 1980b, 1986) is certain that tarot cards were devised first at Milan, Ferrara, or Bologna, Italy, independently of playing cards.

The earliest extant tarot was created for Filippo Maria Visconti, the Duke of Milan, probably between 1415 and 1442 (Dummett, 1986:6; Douglas, 1972:22; Kaplan, 1975b). Young Filippo was a member of the powerful Visconti-Sforza families who dominated an extensive territory around Milan from about the mid-14th to the mid-15th centuries. Heraldic devices, symbolic representations of a dove, the ducal crown, the sun, an eagle, a lion, and interlocking rings, which mark the Visconti-Sforza tarocchi cards, have been used to identify several partial decks (see Kaplan, 1975a, 1978, 1986). In the late 1970's the most nearly complete of all these existing decks, the Pierpont Morgan Bergamo pack, was reproduced and marketed as the Visconti-Sforza Tarocchi deck (see Kaplan, 1975c; Dummett, 1986a).

Early cards in the West were hand painted. They therefore were owned and used primarily by the wealthy. The Visconti pack is a very ornate, hand painted work of art. It probably was commissioned to honor special events, like weddings. Among the literate classes, many different kinds of cards were used to provide instruction in human society, law, logic, the Bible and religion, Greek mythology, history, geography, math, grammar, and astronomy. They also were used to teach technical skills like carving meat and fish (Cavendish, 1975:18-21). Cards, probably including tarots, were used for playing games. Recurrent religious symbolism in early tarot packs suggest that it may have been used for meditation. Whether or not these tarots were used for divination or fortunetelling is unclear. There is little indication that the earliest tarot packs were associated formally with the emergence and development of Renaissance occult traditions (but see O'Neill, 1986).

With the decline of the Byzantine Empire, Italian merchants came to control trade with the East and the Savory passage into Europe. The invention of block printing made card decks available to a larger population. Purveyors spread the tarot from Northern Italy to Flanders, France, and northwest Germany. The tarot eventually was disseminated to England, Scandinavia, Russia, and then the rest of the world (Douglas, 1972:26-38). Tarot cards, like playing cards in general, were used for instruction, education, entertainment, divination, games, and gambling (Hargrave, 1966). Italians used the tarot for playing tarocchi, a game like modern pinochle which probably is derived from tarocchi. In this game the twenty-two special cards serve as a permanent trump suit. Players bet on the number of points or tricks they can take on a given hand (see Douglas, 1972:226-232; Dummett, 1980a, 1980b). The game of tarocchi (or tarock) eventually spread throughout Europe where it still is played today (see Douglas, 1972; Kaplan, 1978, 1986).

The association of cards with gambling as well as related activities, such as drinking and cheating, lead to the disapproval of churchmen and other authorities (see Douglas, 1972). Some people, such as St. Bernardino of Siena, John Northbrooke, John Wesley, and Brother John of Brefeld, believed cards were an invention of the devil. Cards also were thought by some commentators to be related to paganism (Cavendish, 1975). The fortunetelling use of cards at times was seen as contradictory to Church teachings about the nature of God and Divine plans for the future. Cavendish (1975:16) notes that: "All games of chance and all methods of telling

ILLUSTRATION SEVEN: World, Eight of Coins, ***Pierpont Morgan-Bergamo Visconti-Sforza Tarocchi Deck.*** Reproduced by permission of U.S. Games Systems, Inc., Stamford, CT 06902 USA.

fortunes, by card-reading, astrology, palmistry and other popular techniques, imply the existence of a different, impersonal mechanism behind events, much closer to pagan ideas of Fate than to Providence." The use of the tarot, particularly for forecasting the future, was opposed by the Church, religious leaders, and secular authorities (Douglas, 1972). In spite of opposition to them, cards in general and tarots in particular were popular and used widely.

The design and motifs of early tarots varied substantially from one pack to another. The early Italian tarots contained four suits, called spade (swords), bastoni (staves, batons), coppe (cups), and denari (coins), of fourteen cards. Each of these suits incorporated four court cards, presumably depicting a Re, (king), Dama (Regina, queen), Cavallo or Cavaliere (knight) and a Fanti (knave, jack, page), as well as ten pip cards, each one illustrated by from one (ace) to ten suit markers (see Douglas, 1972:13; Kaplan, 1972: 1-6).

The twenty-two special cards, the trumps (triumphi, atutti), pictorially portrayed various personages and scenes, none of which were labeled or numbered (Kaplan, 1978:74). Based on a French pack published in 1557 by Catelin Geofroy containing the earliest known numbering of portions of the major trumps, Kaplan (1978:65-73, 1986:182, 1972:4-5) identifies them in sequence as: the Fool (Il Matto); the Magician (Il Bagatto, Bagattel); the Popess (La Papessa); the Empress (L'Impératrice); the Emperor (L'Empéreur, L'Imperatore); the Pope (Le Pape, Il Papa); the Lovers (L'Amoureux, Gli Amanti); the Chariot (Il Carro); Justice (La Giustizia); the Hermit (L'Eremita); the Wheel of Fortune (Rota di Fortuna, Ruota della Fortuna); Strength (La Forza); the Hanged Man (Il Penduto, L'Appeso); Death (Il Morte, Lo Specchio); Temperance (La Temperanza); the Devil (Il Diavolo); the Falling Tower (La Torre); the Star (La Stelle); the Moon (La Luna); the Sun (Il Sole); Judgment (L'Angelo, Il Giudizio); and, the World (Il Mondo). Compare these titles, however, with those of the Tarot of Marseilles design described below.

Tarot packs, many of them with different designs, labels, numbers, sequences, and suit markers, were produced throughout Europe between the 15th and 18th centuries (see Kaplan, 1986:270-312). A more or less standard pack of tarots, ripe with artistic Renaissance imagery and symbolism, eventually emerged. After 1750 the names of Italian suit signs and labels for the major trumps commonly were expressed in French for tarot decks made and dispersed outside Italy (Douglas, 1972:13-15). By the 19th century the **Tarot of Marseilles** design had become a standard throughout Europe (see Kaplan, 1978:137-167). These designs probably began their development in the late 15th or 16th centuries. The name of this design of the tarot is taken from the French city of this name which housed a large number of card makers (Kaplan, 1986:270). In spite of similarities between these decks and the early Italian packs, differences in artistic renderings and symbolism among them suggest discontinuity, rather than a progressive line of development, as well as the possibility of some as of yet undiscovered antecedent or antecedents.

The names and titles of the Tarot of Mareilles designs were printed in French (or the language of the region) and they used Italian suit markers (spade, bastoni, coppes, denari) expressed in French: epées, batons, coupes, deniers, with variations in spellings of these signs (Kaplan, 1972:6). The court cards presumably were called Roi (king), Reine (queen), Cavalier (knight), and Valet (knave, page). The major trumps (atouts in French) used Roman or Arabic numbers and included card titles written in French. These, according to Kaplan (1978:138-140, 1986:186), were: (unnumbered) Le Mat (the Fool); I) Le Bateleur (the Juggler, and later Le Bataleur—the Magician); II) La Papesse (the Popess); III) L'Impératrice (the Empress); IIII) [IV] L'Empereur (the Emperor); V) Le Pape (the Pope); VI) L'Amoureux (the Lovers); VII) Le Chariot (the Chariot); VIII) La Justice (Justice); VIIII) [IX] L'Hermite (the Hermit); X) La Roue de Fortune (the Wheel of Fortune); XI) La Force (Strength); XII) Le Pendu (the Hanged Man); XIII) La Mort (Death); XIIII) [XIV] La Tempérance (Temperance); XV) Le Diable (the Devil); XVI) La Maison de Dieu (the House of God); XVII) L'Etoile (the Star); XVIII) La Lune (the Moon); XVIIII) [XIX] Le Soleil (the Sun); XX) Le Jugement (Judgment); and, XXI) Le Monde (the World). Later Junon and Jupiter were substituted for La Papesse and Le Pape, respectively, in deference to the Church. Eventually, these titles also were changed to The High Priestess and Hierophant, respectively, as reflected in contemporary tarots. This was the tarot design that became popular among European occultists.

During the late 18th century the tarot was interpreted from the standpoint of a Renaissance worldview as book of sacred knowledge attributed to the Ancients, chiefly Egyptian civilizations. It was imbued and empowered with Renaissance occult significance, thereby requisitioning a central position among the Occult arts, sciences and literature. There is a consensus that the publication of **Antoine Court de Gébelin's** (1725-1784) prodigious 8 (or 9) volume work on civilization, *Le Monde Primitif Analyse et Commpare avec le Monde Moderne,* between 1775 and 1784 initiated occult appropriation of the tarot (see Cavendish, 1975; Douglas, 1972; Kaplan, 1978, 1986). Court de Gébelin was a Protestant clergyman, Freemason, and lay scholar with interests in mathematics, history, language, mythology, and antiquity.

In a section, "Le Jeu des Tarots," of his larger work, Court de Gébelin concluded that the tarot was **Egyptian** in origin (see Douglas, 1972:118). The symbolic pictures of the tarot, he argued, represent the structure of the world and the purest doctrine of ancient Egyptian priests. Anticipating the demise of their civilization, these godly adepts synthesized the totality of their wisdom in the symbolism of the tarot. Evidence for this was found in the symbolism of the cards: the allegories reflect the civil, philosophical, and religious beliefs of Egypt; the ancient symbol of the High Priestess; the horns of Isis icon; a triple cross of the Emperor; Isis represented as the Moon; the Star illustrating Sirius, the Dog-Star; and, the importance attached to the number seven in tarot games and ancient Egypt [see Waite, 1989 (1910):44-47]. The tarot was disguised as a game, however, to prevent its destruction by Christians. Wandering bohemians, gypsies, allegedly preserved the tarot as a game and eventually spread it throughout Europe [but see Waite, 1989 (1910):52].[5] The word "tarot," Court de Gébelin argued, derived from "tar," the Egyptian word meaning road or way, and "ro," meaning king or royal. Hence, he concluded, the French word "tarot" meant the royal road [see Waite, 1989 (1910):46].

Court de Gébelin described and illustrated the tarots but he did not disseminate a deck (see Kaplan, 1978:139). The drawings in "Du Jeu des Tarots" illustrate the suits of swords, staves, cups, and coins, presumably in their usual sequence. The tarot suits, he thought, reflected Egyptian social classes: the sovereigns and military (swords); agriculture (sticks, clubs, or batons); priesthood (cups); and, commerce

ILLUSTRATION EIGHT: Jupiter, La Lune, III of Deniers, IV of Batons, ***Swiss 1JJ Tarot Deck.*** Reproduced by permission of U.S. Games Systems, Inc., Stamford, CT 06902 USA.

(denier). This was confirmed by numerology (Kaplan, 1972:38). The theory of Egyptian origin also explained anomalies, such as the Popess (female pope), and the allegorical meanings of the Star (Isis), the Chariot (Osiris), and other major trumps (Kaplan, 1972:38-40). Hence, it must be the ancient Book of Thoth.

Though less ornate and artistic than many Tarot of Marseilles designs, this tarot seems to retain more or less standard symbols and imagery. The sequence of the major trumps was modified significantly, however, and some of them have been retitled. The sequence and titles of Court de Gébelin tarots, according to Kaplan (1978:137), are: (unnumbered) the Fool; 1) the Thimble-Rigger; 2) the King; 3) the Queen; 4) Chief Hierophant or High Priest; 5) High Priestess; 6) Osiris Triumphant or the Chariot; 7) the Lovers; 8) Force or Strength; 9) Tempérance; 10) Justice; 11) Prudence; 12) the Sage or the Seeker of the Truth; 13) the Sun; 14) the Moon; 15) the Dog Star; 16) Death; 17) Typhon; 18) the House of God or the Palace of Plutus; 19) the Wheel of Fortune; 20) Creation or the Last Judgment; and, 21) Time or the World.

Court de Gébelin's theory was criticized by Singer, who thought the tarot was a Venetain game of Arabian origin, and it subsequently (in 1848) was rejected by Chatto [see Waite, 1989(1910):52-53].[6] It easily is discredited today on many different accounts. There is, of course, no exoteric evidence that tarot cards were related in anyway to Egyptian civilizations. Following earlier critiques, Douglas (1972:20), notices that: "Gypsies did not appear in the West in any numbers until the middle of the 15th century, a full hundred years after the cards were known in every country from Italy to Northern France."[7] Even so, the Egyptian-Gypsy theory, reinforced by successive generations of occult writers, still enjoys a certain popularity among contemporary practitioners. Whether or not it is true, empirically, therefore is not a particularly interesting or relevant issue, sociologically.

THE SYMBOLIC KEY TO ARCANE WISDOM

Court de Gébelin's theory of the tarot was popularized by Alliette, a Parisian barber, wig-maker and fortuneteller, who used the name, **Etteilla**, his given name spelled in reverse (Cavendish, 1975:28-30; Douglas, 1972:119). Etteilla, who claimed to be an alchemist, cabalist, and student of the mysterious magician, Count of Saint-Germain, interpreted dreams, constructed horoscopes and talismans, read palms as well as the tarot, and conducted classes in occult subjects. Kaplan (1978:140) observes that: "Etteilla believed himself a learned professor of cartomancy and an interpreter of the hieroglyphics of the Book of Thoth. He made a detailed study of the ancient sciences and published many volumes dealing with cartomancy, interpretation of dreams and visions, and numerology."[8]

Etteilla added ideas borrowed from the Cabala and Raymond Lull (or the literature attributed to him), along with some of his own innovations, to Court de Gébelin's Egyptian-Gypsy theory, which Etteilla claimed to have anticipated (Cavendish, 1975:29). The tarot, Etteilla argued, was composed 171 years after the Flood, and written 3,953 years ago by the God-like Hermes (Kaplan, 1972:42; McIntosh, 1972:51), a viewpoint he developed in *Maniére de se recréer avec le Jeu de Cartes nommées Tarot*, published in 1783 and 1785. Around 1800, after Etteilla's death, a tarot based on or inspired by his writings and illustrations appeared. Several subsequent tarots—a popular version published by Grimaud, the different *78 Tarots Egyptiens Grand Jeu de L'Oracle des Dames* published by Delarue, a mid-19th century German pack, and various other decks—were attributed to Etteilla (Kaplan, 1986:398).

The Etteilla tarots deviate considerably from other decks, and they seem to be designed primarily for fortunetelling. In some decks divinatory meanings are written on the cards; there sometimes are two titles per card, one for upright and another for reversed meaning; and the cards are numbered from one to seventy-eight sequentially. While the suits and markers of the 56 lesser cards are retained, they also are numbered from 22 to 77. The sequence, titles, and imagery of the greater trumps are modified drastically. Seven cards are used to represent the days of creation. The trumps of the Etteilla tarot and their approximate correspondence to more standard renditions, as described by Kaplan (1978:140), are: 1) Etteilla—Le Questionnant (Le Pape); 2) Eclaircissement (Le Soleil); 3) Propos (La Lune); 4) Depouillement (L'Etoile); 5) Voyage (Le Monde); 6) La Nuit (L'Imperatrice); 7) Appui (L'Empereur); 8) Etteilla—La Questionnante (La Papesse); 9) La Justice (La Justice); 10) La Tempérance (La Tempérance); 11) La Force (La Force); 12) La Prudence (Le Pendu); 13) Mariage (L'Amoreux); 14) Force Majeure (Le Diable); 15) Maladie (Le Bataleur); 16) Jugement (Le Jugement); 17) Mortalité (La Mort); 18) Traitre (L'Ermite); 19) Misére (La Maison de Dieu); 20) Fortune (La Roue de Fortune); 21) Dissension (Le Chariot); 78) Folie (Le Mat). Etteilla is held in contempt and widely ridiculed by subsequent generations of occultists. Yet, he introduced and spread the tarot as a popular occultism. Several Etteilla tarots are available commercially today.

French Occult Revivals and Revitalization

About the mid-19th century Western occultism underwent impressive revitalization in France. Its preeminent figure, Éliphas Lévi Zahed (1810-1875), interpreted the tarot as **central** to the entire tradition. Born Alphonse Louis Constant, he reportedly translated his name into Hebrew, and wrote under **Éliphas Lévi** (Douglas, 1972:120). Constant received a seminary education, trained for the Roman Catholic priesthood, and he was ordained a deacon in 1835. He became preoccupied, however, with occultism and read Postel, Raymond Lull and Cornelius Agrippa. Lévi published *Dogme de la Haute Magie* in 1855 and *Rituel de la Haute Magie* in 1856, works sometimes referred to simply as *Le Dogme et Rituel de la Haute Magie* (see Cavendish, 1975:30; Douglas, 1972:120).[9] Referring to the tarot in this work, Lévi observed that:

> The universal key of magical works is that of all ancient religious dogmas—the key of the Kabalah and the Bible, the Little Key of Solomon. Now, this Clavicle, regarded as lost for centuries, has been recovered by us, and we have been able to open the sepulchres of the ancient world, to make the dead speak, to behold the monuments of the past in all their splendour, to understand the enigmas of every

ILLUSTRATION NINE: Gate of the Sanctuary, Iris-Urania, Cubic Stone, Master of the Arcanes, *Egyptian Tarot Deck*. Reproduced by permission of U.S. Games Systems, Inc., Stamford, CT 06902 USA. Copyright ©1980 U.S. Games Systems, Inc. Further reproduction prohibited.

> sphinx and to penetrate all sanctuaries. Among the ancients the use of this key was permitted to none but the high priests, and even so its secret was confided only to the flower of initiates (quoted from Douglas, 1972:121).

Talking about Lévi's efforts, Cavendish (1975:30) observes that: "This splendidly romantic work, vivid, verbose, vague, sometimes abstruse and sometimes patently absurd, was written with a verve, insight and evocative power which has kept it selling to this day...." It was followed by other influential books: *Historire de la Magie* (1860); *La Clef des Grands Mystéres* (1861; also *La Clef des Grands Mysteres, ou L'Occultisme Devoilé*, 1898); *Le Livre des Splendeurs* (1894); *Clefs Magiques et Clavicules de Salomon* (1895); *Le Grand Arcane ou L'Occultisme Dévoilé* (1898); and, *Les Mystéres de la Kabbale.*[10]

Lévi generally is credited with being the first to **systematically** develop a relationship between the tarot and the Cabala, and fully establish the tarot as part of a Renaissance Hermeticism. Both *dogme* and *rituel* contain twenty-two chapters, corresponding to the major secrets of the cards. The tarot was envisioned as: "the sum of all the sciences," "the inspirer and regulator of all possible conceptions," "an absolute hieroglyphical science and alphabet...convertible into numbers," "one of the finest things bequeathed to us by antiquity, an universal key" (quoted from Cavendish, 1975:30). Lévi believed that the cards were Jewish, although the *Book of Thoth* (of Hermes, The Tarot), he thought, originated in Egypt (Cavendish, 1975:30). The tarot trumps or major secrets (arcana) were linked with the twenty-two letters of the Hebrew alphabet. The other cards, the minor arcana (secrets), were connected in other ways: the four tarot suits were connected with the Tetragrammaton, the name of God, by way of the Hebrew letters, Yod-He-Vau-He, representing YHWH (Yahweh) or JHVH (Jehovah); and, the pips from one to ten were associated with the ten aspects of God (Cavendish, 1975:30; Kaplan, 1986:22).

Éliphas Lévi's version of the major arcana (or greater secrets) conforms to the French standard (Tarot of Marseilles), except that the unnumbered card, the Fool, is placed between Judgment and the World, making it the twenty-first card in the sequence. As Douglas (1972:122) notes: "This was because Lévi attributed The Fool to the Hebrew letter Shin, said to symbolise the fire of the spirit, and Shin is the twenty-first letter of the Hebrew alphabet." The correspondences between the major arcana and the Hebrew letters, as Lévi envisioned them, are: I) the Magician=aleph; II) the High Priestess=beth; III) the Empress=gimel; IV) the Emperor=daleth; V) the High Priest=heh; VI) the Lovers=vau; VII) the Chariot=zain; VIII) Justice=cheth; IX) the Hermit=teth; X) the Wheel of Fortune=yod; XI) Fortitude=kaph; XII) the Hanged Man=lamed; XIII) Death=mem; XIV) Temperance=nun; XV) the Devil=smekh; XVI) the Tower=ayin; XVII) the Star=peh; XVIII) the Moon=tzaddi; XIX) the Sun=qoph; XX) Judgement=resh; The Fool=shin; XXII) the World=tau (Douglas, 1972:122-123; Cavendish, 1975:58).

In this way, Lévi laid a foundation for subsequent occult interpretations of the tarot as **The Key to All Arcane Wisdom.** After reading J.A. Vaillant's work (1857-1863) on the origin of cards, he later endorsed the idea that Gypsies spread the tarot through Europe (Douglas, 1972: 121).[11] He did not publish a tarot, but Kenneth

MacKenzie of the Societas Rosicruciana in Anglia (discussed below), supposedly saw Lévi's drawings of the trumps in 1861 while in Paris (Kaplan, 1986:22). The tarot later developed by Oswald Wirth, as will be discussed, was heavily indebted to Lévi.

Jean Baptist Petois was a student of Lévi's who used the occult pseudonym, Paul Christian. His employment in a Paris library provided access to rare books and occult works (Kaplan, 1978:22). Christian constructed a Kabalistic astrology related to the Tarot, and he argued that evidence for its Egyptian origins were found in a book on Egyptian mysteries attributed to Iamblichus, a 4th century C.E. Neoplatonist (Cavendish, 1975:30-31). He thought Iambliches was an initiate of Osiris, and that the tarot trumps derived from a secret gallery in the Pyramids containing these symbolic pictures. Christian published *L'Homme rouges des Tuileries* in 1863, and *Histore de la Magie* in 1870, among other works, thereby establishing a place for himself among occultists of the period (Kaplan, 1978:22).

From the late 19th century through the early 20th century was a period of intense and abundant occult activity, especially in France and Great Britain. Ely Star, who also was known as Eugene Jacobs, published *Les Mystéres de l'Horoscope* in 1887 based on tarot pictures derived from Court de Gébelin, thereby contributing to a growing body of literature on the occult tarot (Cavendish, 1975:31). Star is described by Cavendish (1975:31) as "a quack doctor and seller of magical amulets, whose wife was a professional fortune-teller." There was an active collection of occultists in Paris during the 1880's, and they built upon earlier traditions, particularly the work of Lévi.

Oswald Wirth, a Swiss participant in this milieu, developed a "rectified" version of the tarot (Cavendish, 1975:31). The 1889 Wirth tarot included twenty-two engraved and hand painted cards, referred to as *Les 22 Arcanes du Tarot Kabbalistique* by the publisher, E. Poirel (Kaplan, 1986:391). Wirth was a Mason and member of the French Theosophical Society, who practiced "curative magnetism," a form of hypnosis. He associated with the Kabalistic Order of the Rose-Cross, founded in 1888 by the Marquis Stanislas de Guaïta, became a discipline of Guaïta and his secretary (Cavendish, 1975:31). A much later, redesigned Wirth tarot, issued along with *Le Tarot: des Images du Moyen Age* in 1927, still is available today (see Kaplan, 1986).

Wirth's design of the tarot was sanctioned by Guaïta, a devotee of Lévi, whose massive *Le Serpent de la Genêse—Livre II* and *La Clef de la Magie Noire* (1902) dealt with the symbolic tarot (Douglas, 1972:121). **Marquis Stanislas de Guaïta** (1861-1897) was a dynamic young French magician who, according to Cavendish (1975:31), had a mysterious and very "curious" stature: "He was said to own a familiar spirit, which he kept locked in a cupboard when not in use, and to be able to volatilize poisons and project both them and his own body through space." He published *Au seuil du Mystere* in 1886. Guaïta adorned his living quarters in scarlet, wore a red grown (not unlike a Cardinal), experimented with drugs, such as morphine, cocaine and hashish, praised Baudelaire, and had ambitions as a poet (Cavendish, 1975:31). A friend of Guaïta's and a fellow member of the Kabalistic Order of the Rose-Cross, Gérard Encausse, who is known best by the pseudonym, Papus, popularized esoteric teachings, thereby becoming a leading proselytizer of magic, and otherwise contributed to the occult atmosphere in France.

ILLUSTRATION TEN: Le Fou, La Papesse, IIII of Deniers, V of Epees, ***Oswald Wirth Tarot Deck.*** Reproduced by permission of U.S. Games Systems, Inc., Stamford, CT 06902 USA

A Spaniard by birth, **Papus** (1865-1916) went to France in his youth where he was trained as a physician (Douglas, 1972:122). In the practice of medicine, he reportedly possessed and employed "clairvoyant diagnostic powers" (Cavendish, 1975:31). Papus joined the Theosophical Society, became disenchanted with its emphasis on oriental religion, and turned his attention to the Cabala and the writings of Lévi. In 1888 he published *Traité Élémentaire de Science Occulte*. It was followed in 1889 by **the first handbook on the tarot**, *Le Tarot des Bohémiens*, wherein Papus (1975:9) asserted that: "[T]he game of cards called the Tarot, which the Gypsies possess, is the Bible of Bibles. It is the book of Thoth Hermes Trismegistus, the book of Adam, the book of the primitive Revelation of ancient civilizations" (also see Douglas, 1972:122). In this work he used Oswald Wirth's "rectified" version of the tarot (see Cavendish, 1975:31; Kaplan, 1986:391). Papus followed Lévi's attributions of the major arcana (the trumps) to the Hebrew alphabet and otherwise reinforced and popularized his occult interpretation of the cards (Douglas, 1972:122).

In 1891 Papus published *Traité Méthodique de Science Occulte*, followed by *Le Tarot Divinatoire* in 1909. His writings summarized existing traditions (Court de Gébelin, Etteilla, and especially Lévi) and reinforced occult belief in the tarot as the absolute key to arcane knowledge: "the most ancient book in the world," which had been passed from the ancients "to the Gnostics, and by way of the Arabs, the Alchemists, the Knights Templar, Raymond Lull and the Rosicrucians to the Masons and Martinists" (Cavendish, 1975:33). He stood opposed to "materialism," "empiricism," and "Caesarism in all its forms," believing that the ancient principles and laws of the occult tarot were consistent with the fundamental truths of the Bible, Homer, Virgil, the Koran, and Hindu scriptures (Papus, 1975[1889]:343-347; Cavendish, 1975:33). Efforts like Wirth's to restore the pictorial tarot reinforced Papus' occult interpretations of it as a sacred, esoteric text.

Papus founded a school, L'Ordre des Silencieux Inconnus, and provided leadership for a Martinist group (see Douglas, 1972:122). He attracted a large following, but his society remained unsanctioned by French Freemasonry (see Cavendish, 1975:31). This group was connected with the Order of the Temple of the Orient (OTO), Aleister Crowley, and sex magic. Traveling to Russia, Papus became a friend of the Tsar, and he served in the French army during WWI.

In 1896 an actor in La Comedie-Francaise, R. Falconnier published a small book on the tarot, *Les XXII Lames Hermétiques du Tarot Divinatoire: Exactement reconstituées d'aprés les textes sacrés et selon la tradition des Mages de l'ancienne Égypte*.[12] The text explained that: "[There are people] who may be surprised that a comedian would pursue such abstract studies, but after all, the theater is a modern tarot, which revives the past and often predicts the future evolution of the human spirit" (as quoted in Kaplan, 1986:391). The accompanied designs of the Major Arcana (trumps), in black and white, by Maurice Otto Wegener, were meant to be cut out, blocked, and colored (Kaplan, 1986:391). This **Falconnier Tarot** aimed to be a hermetic rendition faithful to Egyptian art, following the legacy of Etteilla, Lévi, Papus, Wirth, and Guaïta (Kaplan, 1986:391). Waite [1986 (1910):332] noticed that it "has been hailed by French occultists as presenting the Tarot in its perfection, but the same has been said of the designs of Oswald Wirth, which are quite unlike and not Egyptian at all." Kaplan (1986:391) believes this tarot inspired later Egyptian designs, such as Comte

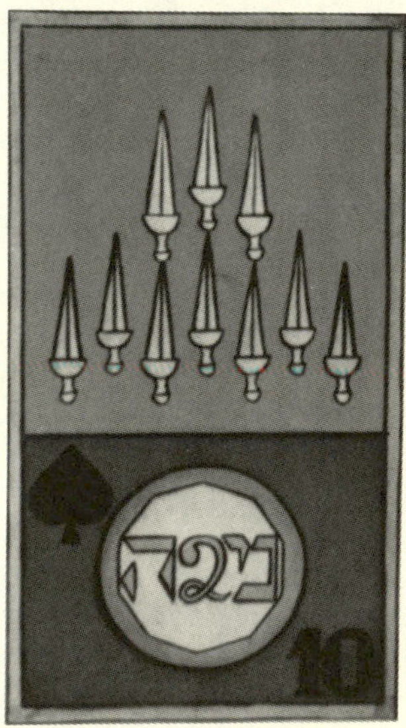

ILLUSTRATION ELEVEN: Emperor, Tower, Tens of Swords, Cups, ***Papus Tarot Deck.*** Reproduced by permission of U.S. Games Systems, Inc., Stamford, CT 06902 USA.

C. Saint-Germain's 1931 deck, and C.C. Zain's 1936 tarot (as discussed below). The Falconnier tarot was reissued in 1976.

Syncretisms of The Golden Dawn

In Great Britain the writings of Lévi also had stimulated interest in the occult tarot. **Kenneth Mackenzie** visited the revered Master, Lévi, in Paris during 1861. Mackenzie was associated with the Societas Rosicruciana in Anglia (also known as Soc. Ros.), founded in 1866, and in 1877 he promulgated *The Royal Masonic Cyclopaedia*. Mackenzie believed in spiritualism, proclaiming himself to be "Baphometus" (a diabolical idol linked to the Knights Templar), Astrologer and Spiritualist (Cavendish, 1975:33). He apparently planned an occult work on the tarot, but it was never published. Along with Lévi, Mackenzie is appropriated as an occult ancestor of the subsequent Golden Dawn.

Members of the Soc. Ros. were instrumental in founding the **Hermetic Order of the Golden Dawn**, as briefly discussed in Chapter Two, around 1887 in London. This secretive masonic, occult organization only existed for a very few years before it schismed. Yet, directly and indirectly, nothing else has exerted greater influence over occult interpretations of the tarot. Attempting to synthesize the totality of esoteric and occult knowledge, the Order innovated on major themes, including the works of Lévi and Papus, producing a highly fertile integration of the tarot with the traditions of Western occultism. Contributors to the Golden Dawn's interpretation of the tarot, like Mathers and Crowley, disseminated their views independently, influentially, and broadly. Waite, like Crowley, published an occult tarot pack and an assessment of it. Schismatic and derivative groups served as conduits for the Golden Dawn interpretation of the occult tarot. Francis Israel Regardie [1989(1937-1940)] revealed in print "the original account of the Teachings, Rites and Ceremonies" of the Order, and much later a tarot (see Wang, 1978). Other subsequent members, like Dion Fortune, became highly influential, and some of them, like Case, published decks and commentaries on them.

Samuel Liddel Mathers, a Scottish Freemason and member of the Soc. Ros., was recruited to head the Golden Dawn. Reflecting his Jocobite affinities, Mathers added McGregor to his name, and later while living in Paris he was known as Le Comte de Glenstrae (see Cavendish, 1975:33; Douglas, 1972:123). **McGregor Mathers** was unable to proselytize his brother-in-law, the famous French philosopher, Henri Bergson, to a magical occultism, but he was a principal architect of Golden Dawn doctrines and rites, including its interpretation of the tarot. In 1888 he published a booklet on the occult tarot, emphasizing its divinatory uses.[13] The grand occult syncretism of the Golden Dawn linked the tarot with the Kabala (the Hebrew alphabet, the Tree of Life), astrology (the zodiac, planets), alchemy (the elements), numerology, ritual magic, and many other Rosicrucian, masonic, gnostic, Graeco-Egyptian, Arthurian, pagan, and hermetic elements and themes (see Cavendish, 1975; Douglas, 1972; Regardie, 1989).

Arthur Edward Waite (1857-1940) joined the Golden Dawn in 1891 after experimenting with Spiritualism and Theosophy (see Cavendish, 1975:34-37; Douglas, 1972). Unlike Mathers and other initiates, he apparently was not a significant

ILLUSTRATION TWELVE: Magician, Chariot, Three of Swords, Nine of Pentacles, *Rider-Waite Tarot Deck*. Reproduced by permission of U.S. Games Systems, Inc., Stamford, CT 06902 USA. Copyright ©1971U.S. Games Systems, Inc. Further reproduction prohibited.

contributor to the Order's formulation of an occult tarot. Waite became adept in this tradition, however, and he emerged as its most widely recognized and effective spokesman. After the Order schismed, Waite gained control of the London temple, and as its leader opposed magick, rewrote some of the doctrines and rituals in a Christian spirit. Soliciting little support for these revisions, he terminated this variation of the Golden Dawn in 1914.

Waite wrote extensively on Western occultism: "like a ponderous ferret he plunged into the rabbit-holes of the Cabala, alchemy, Rosicrucianism, Freemasonry, ceremonial magic and the Grail legends to flush out the secret tradition from its hiding places" (Cavendish, 1975:34). In 1910 he published *The Pictorial Key to the Tarot: Being Fragments of a Secret Tradition under the Veil of Divination*. It was accompanied by a replenished tarot illustrated under his authority by Pamela Colman Smith, another member of the Golden Dawn. This Waite tarot, also known as the Rider deck or Waite-Rider tarot, after its publishing company, became the best known and most popular deck. It established a standard against which tarot motifs and interpretations most commonly are evaluated even today. Since the tarot used by the Golden Dawn was never disseminated publicly, Waite's version generally is regarded as one of the best available representations of this secret tradition.[14]

In writing about the tarot, as in his other works on occultism, Waite endeavored to present arcane traditions in such a fashion as to render them understandable to an average person or general public. These efforts brought him widespread recognition, and even devoted followings; but they also resulted in jealousy, rivalry, and potent contempt, ridicule, and criticism, particularly from occult initiates and adepts who felt that Waite betrayed a sacred trust. Reflecting some of these sentiments, Cavendish (1975:37) remarked that: "The book [*The Pictorial Key to the Tarot*] is impatient and contemptuous in tone, conceals far more than it conveys and on some points is deliberately misleading." Waite's work on the tarot disclaimed any effort to reveal the higher meanings and secrets of the tarot, being intended as little more than a discourse on the tarot's divinatory significance. Noting that Aleister Crowley "satirized him mercilessly as a pompous pedant and humbug," Cavendish (1975:34), on balance, maintained that: "in the Tarot field he [Waite] showed a firmer grasp of reality than his predecessors and many of his successors."

The architects of the Golden Dawn tarot, like their predecessors, found it necessary to "rectify" the symbols, imagery, numbers, and sequences of this arcane text to bring it into conformity with their occult interpretations. The logic of this is clear and its sociological import should not be underestimated: The tarot was believed to be a sacred text containing the secret wisdom of the Ancients, a Truth far greater than our own; through history other sages understood its significance and they have contributed to this sacred text, but it was disguised as a game, profaned, and its True meanings were hidden; the current interpreter (Court de Gébelin, Lévi, Papus, the Golden Dawn) has, at least partially, recaptured its True meanings; it, therefore, has been necessary to redesign the tarot so as to restore the occult text to its original significance. As a revitalized doctrine, the tarot was subject to further interpretation and it would serve as the basis for cultic followings and organizations.

Before the Waite tarot the 56 minor cards contained few **symbolic pictures** or representations beyond the suit signs and the personages depicted by the court cards. The minor arcana of the Waite tarot, and many subsequent packs, are richly illustrated, portray enigmatic scenes, and fully burst with symbolic icongraphy. Waite's modifications of the major arcana greatly influenced subsequent designs. He transposed the order of Justice, making it XI, and Strength, designating it as VIII, and he endeavored to revitalize the symbolism of the twenty-two major secrets. There were theosophical reasons, as will be discussed in Chapter Seven, underlying these changes.

Aleister Crowley (1875-1947), a highly colorful and infamous British occultist, was one of the most original and contentious members of the Golden Dawn. Crowley was raised among the Plymouth Brethren but reacted strongly to this early training in Christianity, even as a child. He joined the Golden Dawn during his early 20's and became a disciple of Mathers. Ambitious, disputatious, and irascible, he separated from the Golden Dawn. After arguing with his pundit, Crowley reportedly: "summoned up the great demon Beelzebub and forty-nine attendant demons, whom he packed off to chastise the erring Mathers in Paris" (Cavendish, 1975:37). Cavendish (1975:38) notes further that: "When Mathers died in the influenza epidemic of 1918, some suspected that Crowley had murdered him by black magic."

In 1905 Crowley founded the Argenteum Astrum (or Silver Star), and later provided leadership for the OTO. The epitome of the Hermetic-Kabalistic Magus, Crowley claimed to be: the reincarnation of Éliphas Lévi; the Great Beast 666 of Revelation whose mission was to destroy Christianity; the oracle of the Age of Horus—a new aeon about to supersede the Christian age; and, Baphomet, "Supreme and Holy King of Ireland, Iona and all the Britains that are in the sanctuary of the Gnosis" (Cavendish, 1975:38; Douglas, 1972:130). The British press called him "the Wickedest Man in the World," and even today Crowley is frequently mentioned in American press coverage of paganism, witchcraft and satanism. That several of his wives went mad and/or committed suicide only added to his reputation as a perverse villain, the High Priest of Occult Magick.[15]

Crowley was known both for his occult writings and other literary works. Eventually, he issued a guide to the tarot, *The Book of Thoth*, in 1944. His rectified version of the cards, artistically executed in a cubist style by Lady Frieda Harris—the spouse of a Liberal politician, Sir Percy Harris—are **strikingly erotic, eccentric, unconventional, tantalizing, and bizarre**. The carnal symbolism of Crowley's tarot reflects the importance of **sex magick** in his occult system. Lady Harris's pictorial images are highly erogenous, yet, as Cavendish (1975:38) observes:

> Crowley was not the first to see the cards in this light. On the contrary, sexual symbolism is seldom far beneath the surface of...the Tarot, including Waite's, which is riddled with innuendo. This does not mean that the earlier authors practised sexual magic, as Crowley did, but it does imply a less austere attitude to sex than is attributed to them.... To take only one example...Justice shows a woman holding a sword in one hand and a pair of scales in the other. The symbol is a traditional one and seems quite obvious and straightforward. But in most Tarot interpretations the sword is a phallus and the scales are

ILLUSTRATION THIRTEEN: Lust, Universe, Ace of Swords, Two of Cups-Love, ***Crowley's Thoth Tarot.*** Reproduced by permission of U.S. Games Systems, Inc., Stamford, CT 06902 USA. Copyright ©1978, 1983 U.S. Games Systems, Inc. Further reproduction prohibited.

> testicles. This explains Papus's otherwise mystifying description of the woman as the Mother, who is "Nature performing the function of Eve." Crowley simply called her the Woman Satisfied.

Many subsequent tarots follow Crowley's lead and some of them graphically depict even more sexually explicit scenes.

The Thoth tarot reflects Crowley's heavy indebtedness to the Golden Dawn. Crowley was, however, immensely sophisticated philosophically; he completely rejected materialisms and empiricisms; and he fully understood the radically metaphorical epistemological implications of esotericism, as illustrated by his assiduously ironic statement quoted above. Crowley's comprehension of symbols and metaphor, as well as his burlesque, satirical manner, is reflected, abundantly, in the Thoth tarots. They are fully packed with imagery drawn from astrology, the Kabalistic Tree of Life, Greco-Roman-Egyptian mythologies, alchemy, Arthurian legends and lore, Celtic paganism, Rosicrucianism, Hermeticism, and gnosticism. In reflecting these and other themes, the Thoth tarot deviates enthusiastically from conventional suit markers and labels as well as the more ordinary names and sequences of the major arcana. Insofar as the Waite and Case tarots generally are taken as more or less faithful renderings of the Golden Dawn tarot, Crowley's designs, while preserving important themes, are passionately innovative.

The minor arcana of the Thoth tarot retains standard suit markers, with very slight modification, which are linked in a Golden Dawn motif with alchemical elements: swords to air; wands (batons) to fire; cups to water; and disks (coins, pentacles) to earth. The court cards are redefined as knight (rather than king), queen, prince (rather than knight), and princess (rather than page or valet), representing the Golden Dawn notion of a Hebrew family of father, mother, son, and daughter. In the Crowley tarot the small (pip) cards of the minor arcana, excepting the aces, are assigned specific names. The swords are labeled: 2) peace; 3) sorrow; 4) truce; 5) defeat; 6) science; 7) futility; 8) interference; 9) cruelty; and 10) ruin. The wards are: 2) dominion; 3) virtue; 4) completion; 5) strife; 6) victory; 7) valor; 8) swiftness; 9) strength; and 10) oppression. The cups are attributed as: 2) love; 3) abundance; 4) luxury; 5) disappointment; 6) pleasure; 7) debauch; 8) indolence; 9) happiness; and 10) satiety. Disks are defined as: 2) change; 3) work; 4) power; 5) worry; 6) success; 7) failure; 8) prudence; 9) gain; and 10) wealth.

In the Crowley tarot, the major arcana are identified as "Atus of Tahuti," representing a hieroglyphics of the universe, and reflecting the Golden Dawn influence of Hermetic astrology as well as the Kabalistic Tree of Life and its ten sephiroth and twenty-two paths, as will be discussed below. The "Atus" redefines four of the major arcana: VIII) Justice becomes Adjustment; XI) Strength is called Lust; XIV) Temperance changes to Art; and, XX) Judgment is attributed as The Aeon. The Crowleyian system, as discussed in Chapter Seven, establishes a full range of correspondences between the Atus of Tahuti and other symbols.

Francis Israel Regardie (1907-1985) joined the Stella Matutina Temple of a subsequent British Order of the Golden Dawn in 1934. He worked with Aleister Crowley, serving as his secretary in the late 1920's; but following a disagreement they went different directions. During the 1930's Israel Regardie published a series

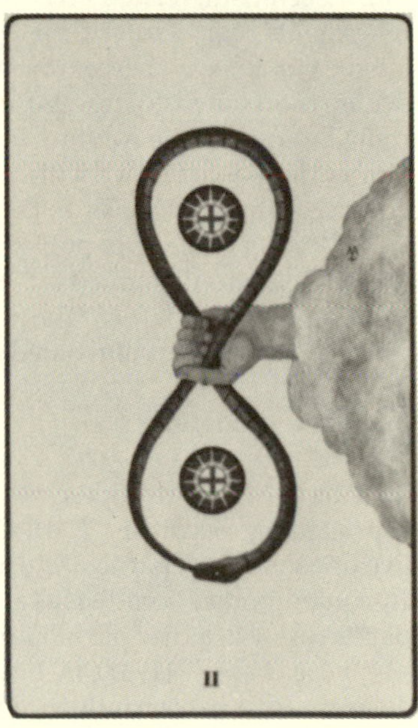

ILLUSTRATION FOURTEEN: Lovers, Judgment, Ace of Wands, II of Pentacles, *Golden Dawn Tarot Deck.*

of occult studies: *A Garden of Pomegrantes; The Tree of Life; The Middle Pillar; The Art of True Healing;* and *My Rosicrucian Adventure.* Regardie came to the United States permanently in 1937 where he worked as a chiropractor, studied psychoanalysis, and continuing writing on Western occultism. Believing that the era of occult secrecy should end, Regardie published "a nearly complete set of rituals and teachings" of the Order in four volumes between 1937 and 1940. Portions of this occult manual discuss the tarot within the larger framework of the Hermetic-Kabalistic system of magic developed by the Golden Dawn. A sixth, revised and expanded edition of the *Golden Dawn,* as this treatise is called, was published in 1989 under the editorship of Carl Llewellyn Weschchke (see Regardie, 1989).

During the late 1970's a tarot painted by Robert Wang under the supervision of Israel Regardie was released. The *Golden Dawn Tarot* is based on a deck that was hand copied by Regardie as a member of the Order. Wang (1978) says it was not a strict copy of this deck, but an "archaeological reconstruction" buttressed by published and unpublished Golden Dawn materials. It claims to be "the only truly esoteric deck ever to be published and the only deck designed for the exclusive use of a powerful secret fraternity to reach the public" (Wang, 1978:159). Like the Case tarot that also derives from this tradition, the minor arcana of this pack is not personified graphically. It differs from the Waite and Crowley tarots in this respect, as well as in a much less ornately stylistic treatment of the major arcana (see Kaplan, 1978:256).

British occultism, related texts and organizations greatly influenced American developments. **Paul Foster Case** (1884-1954), for example, was influenced by Waite and the Golden Dawn (see Cavendish, 1975:38). He claimed to be the head of the Order in the United States and Canada, its Praemonstrator General. Case founded the Builders of the Adytum in the United States. This quasi-secret society modeled after the Golden Dawn with headquarters in Los Angeles still exists today. He wrote three influential books on the tarot, the best known of which is *The Tarot: A Key to the Wisdom of the Ages* published in 1947. A rectified version of the tarot produced by Case and illustrated by Jessie Burns serves as the official deck of the Builders of the Adytum (BOTA). The major arcana of this tarot resembles the Waite design, but the pips are not illustrated in this fashion (see Kaplan, 1978:239)

Subsequent Interpretations

There have been many other interpretations of the tarot, some of them occult or appropriated by occultists. **Carl G. Jung's** (1953, 1963, 1967) theory of the "collective unconscious," particularly his notion of archetypical images, frequently is used by contemporary occultists as an interpretation of the tarot (see Wang, 1978). **P.D. Ouspensky** was a disciple of Gurdjieff, the Russian mystic. Ouspensky's, *A New Model of the Universe* (1931), included a discussion of the tarot (see Cavendish, 1975). He seems to have been influenced by Oswald Wirth's tarot. Elbert Benjamine, better known by the pseudonym, **Z.Z. Zain**, produced a black and white tarot of his own design, distinguished by its Egyptian imagery (see Kaplan, 1978:240-241). He founded a quasi-secret society called the Church of Light in Los Angeles. Another group using the tarot, the Philosophical Research Society of Los Angeles, was founded by **Manly Palmer Hall.** His tarot designs, based on Oswall Wirth's work, were drawn by J.A. Knapp. The Knapp tarot with a discussion by Hall was published in 1929 (see Kaplan, 1978:198). The **Insight Institute** of England published a tarot based on a Tarot of Marseilles design and the Waite-Rider tarot (see Kaplan, 1978:197).

Since the mid-1970's an almost promiscuous variety of tarots, ranging from reprints of portions of the earliest extant decks and traditional occult renditions to highly contemporary, innovative artistic, commercial and conventional portrayals of these picturesque symbolic images, have been marketed. For example,*Tarot Classics*, reprints woodcuts by French craftsman, Claude Burdel, from around 1751, representing a Tarot of Marseilles design (see Kaplan, 1978:242). The lovely *Aquarian Tarot*, illustrated by David Mario Palladini, develops an art deco style of tarot motifs. The *Mountain Dream Tarot* created by Bea Nettles of North Carolina's Penland School of Crafts, though based on a Waite-Rider design, employs photographs to illustrate the cards. Marty Yeager's *Tarot of Meditation* delineates human personages in anatomically explicit ways, and provides an most attractive surrealistic representation of the tarot. The deck created by Morgan Robbins and drawn by Darshan Chorpash is a highly unorthodox, black and white endowment of the cards reflecting the 1960's counterculture, especially an interest in Eastern mysticism (see Kaplan, 1978:257). Peter Balin's *Xultun Tarot* is an intriguing but highly alien painting of the cards in terms of pre-Columbian, Mayan imagery. Provocatively, when the major arcana of this tarot are put together they complete a composite picture (see Kaplan, 1978:289). *Salavdor Dali's Tarot*, a luscious surrealistic interpretation of the cards, as should be expected, may be the only version of the tarot ever created by one of the world's greatest artists (see Pollack, 1985). All of these tarots are readily available today from esoteric and occult cults, speciality shops, exoteric bookstores, as well as manufactures and publishers.

DELIBERATING ON THE OCCULT TAROT

The occult tarot was a product of historical interpretations of a unique pack of seventy-eight cards which probably were invented in Italy around the middle of the 15th century. Beginning in the late 18th century tarot cards were embued with an esoteric significance attributed to ancient Egypt. Subsequent generations of French occultists linked the tarot with Hermetic-Kabalistic occultisms, eventually defining it as the symbolic key to all arcane wisdom. In the Hermetic Order of the Golden Dawn the occult tarot was fully integrated with all manner of esoteric knowledge.

From an exoteric standpoint, occult histories and interpretations of the tarot commonly are discredited as unsubstantiated by other evidence. These observations are not particularly interesting, sociologically, except as rival claims to knowledge. Occultists' belief in claims to knowledge based on the tarot are sufficient, sociologically, for the production of human consequences. These beliefs, as well as related practices and activities of occultists are interesting and important aspects of human existence.

ILLUSTRATION FIFTEEN: Empress, Emperor, One of Disks, Five of Wands, *Brotherhood of Light Tarot.* Reproduced by permission of The Church of Light, Los Angeles, CA 90031 USA. Copyright ©1936, 1964 The Church of Light. Further reproduction prohibited.

ILLUSTRATION SIXTEEN: Sorcerer, *Xultun Tarot Deck*. Reproduced by permission of Lotus Light Publications, Wilmont WI 53192 USA. Copyright ©1976 Lotus Light Publications. Further reproduction prohibited.

The occult tarot I learned to use for divination in the esoteric community is a product of this esoteric culture. This esoteric body of knowledge constitutes an ornate occult theosophy. Tarot theosophy is the subject of the next chapter. Its use for hermetic study, meditation, and divination is discussed in Chapter Eight.

NOTES

1 The suit of spades is an Italian suit sign, spade, expressed as swords in tarots labeled in English.

2 This qualification is necessary, as will become clear in the following, because even today tarot titles and labels not uncommonly are expressed in Italian or French.

3 Fairly comprehensive bibliographies on the tarot and related matters are presented by Kaplan (1978, 1986).

4 Most of the experts cited here on the tarot do not otherwise possess the obvious characteristics of exoteric scholarship. In many instances it is writters seem to be believers in some sense, even thought they exhibit conformity to ordinary scholarly norms. Exoteric scholars who have taken on the tarot, such as Joseph Campbell (see Campbell and Roberts, 1979), and Theodore Roszak (1988), are in some sense believers.

5 Waite seems to think that the Gypsy origins of the tarot was introduced first by a French writer, Bointeau d'Ambly's *Les Cartes a Jouer et al Cartomancie*, published at Paris in 1854.

6 Waite (1986[1910]:322) refers to: Samuel Weller Singer's, *Researches into the History of Playing Cards* (London, 1816). This critique apparently was developed in: William Andrew Chatto, *Facts and Speculations on the Origin and History of Playing Cards* (London, 1848).

7 Waite (1986[1910]:237) thinks this criticism was developed by Romain Merlin, *Origine des Cartes a Jouer* (Paris, 1869).

8 Published between 1783 and 1787, according to Waite (1986[1910]:320-321), these now exceptionally rare works included: *Les Septs Nuances de l'oeuvre philosophique Hermetique; Maniere de se recreer ave le Jeu de Cartes, nommees Tarots; Fragments sur les Hautes Sciences; Philosophie des Hautes Sciences; Jeu des Tarots, ou le Livre de Thoth*; and, *Lecons Theoriques et Pratiques du Livre de Thoth*.

9 This probably is a consequence of their translation and publication in English as a single volume entitled *Transcendental Magic*.

10 In 1896 William W. Westcott, of the Golden Dawn, translated, edited, and published a work on the tarot credited to Levi: *The Magical Ritual of the Sanctum Regnum, interpreted by the Tarot Trumps*. The dates of the later publications clearly indicate the importance attached to Levi's work by later generations of occultists.

[11] Douglas (1972:343) references J.A. Vaillant's works as: *Les Romes, Histoire des vrais Bohemiens* (Paris, 1857); *La Bible des Bohemiens* (Paris, 1860); and, *Clef Magique de la Fiction et du Fait* (Paris, 1863). Vaillant's work became a standard source for subsequent occult writings.

[12] In English: The XXII Hermetic Pages of the Divinatory Tarot: Exactly reconstituted after the sacred texts, and after the tradition of the Magi of ancient Egypt.

[13] Cavendish (1975) cites this work as: *The Tarot* (New York: Occult Research Press, paperback reprint, no date). Also see: Gilbert, R.A. (ed.). 1983. *The Sorcerer and His Apprentice.* Wellingborough, England: Aquarian Press, for hermetic writings of S.L. MacGregor Mathers and J.W. Brodie-Innes with sections on the tarot.

[14] There is little doubt that Waite's tarot reflects what he learned from the Golden Dawn. The "Golden Dawn Tarot" produced by Regardie and Wang very well may faithfully reflect the original designs. Even so, the Waite tarot, independently, carries a certain tradition with it.

[15] It apparently was Crowley's reputation that earned him a central role in sociologist Randall Collin's novel, *The Case of the Philosophers' Ring* (New York: Crown Publishers, 1978). In this mystery attributed to Dr. John H. Watson, Sherlock Holmes is summoned by Bertrand Russell to investigate the theft of Ludwig Wittgenstein's mind. From an all-star cast, including members of the Hermetic Order of the Golden Dawn (Yates), the Theosophical Society (Annie Besant), the Society for Psychic Research, Virgina Woolf and Lytton Strackey of Bloonsbury , and the Cambridge Apostles (Russel, Moore, Keynes), Aleister Crowley, "the high priest of post-Edwardian mysticism," emerges as a likely suspect.

Chapter 7

Occult Theosophies of the Tarot

The occult tarot, I argue, is formed by **theosophies**, or religiophilosophical, mystical, and esoteric infrastructures of human meaning. By way of these conceptual frameworks esoteric and occult significance is attributed to the pictorial tarot cards, and their images and icons, and human meanings are derived from them. Viewed hermeneutically, the occult tarot—this theosophically meaningful human text—is a vigorous, animated, replete esoteric idiom, vernacular, or dialect. It thereby may be analyzed and interpreted, sociologically, as a kind of language.

The **occult language** of the tarot is composed of **vocabularies** and **grammars** of human meanings. Occult theosophies of the tarot provide grammars of human meaning: that is, principles and procedures for attributing, deriving, arranging, and structuring symbolic meanings so as to creatively fashion arcane significance. These occult theosophies of the tarot, consequently, reap a rich harvest of human intelligence: expansive dictionaries and vocabularies of symbolic meanings. Vocabularies and grammars of the occult tarot empower its users to construct intricate, humanly meaningful interpretations of the otherwise senseless and absurd universe around them. Occult interpretations and applications of the tarot may be instituted as hermetic studies, meditation, or divination, as well as used ritually.

Though esoteric, mystical and occult, theosophies of the tarot fundamentally are **cognitive** frameworks. They, in other words, provide principles and methods for specifying types and typifications of a thereby knowable world; ways of conceptually categorizing and arranging ideas in terms of schemes, models, and theories (see Schutz, 1967). The ideas organized and expressed by tarot theosophy and symbolism refer to and objectify human experiences and feelings: the flow of life as a constant stream of pre-typified feeling and experience; the lived realities of human existence in an outer world (see Berger and Luckmann, 1966; Douglas and Johnson, 1977). Occult theosophies of the tarot mediate and connect an inner, subjective world of human feeling with an outer, objectified, collective, symbolic, social world of human existence. Macrocosm and microcosm thereby are joined, hermetically.

The private, public, and divine are linked together in a single, unified, cosmic totality or whole. Occult theosophies of the tarot consequently enable believers to make sense of everything esoterically.

In the previous chapter I sketched the historical context in which the tarot was defined socially as an occult text. This chapter discusses some of the ways in which the tarot has been developed theosophically. Use of the tarot for study, meditation, and divination will be explored in the next chapter.

VOCABULARIES OF OCCULT MEANING

Historically, occult meanings have been attributed to and associated with each of the cards in a tarot deck. The language of tarot may be presented in elementary form as a vocabulary defined by a dictionary of meanings. Tarot meanings, however, are robust and highly fluid. A wide range and variety of meanings have been linked with the cards historically, and there is minimal consensus among authorities as to exactly what each card means or signifies. The vocabulary of tarot, in other words, lacks standardization. Even when more or less standard meanings have been attributed to particular tarot cards, they are subject to multiple interpretations and theosophies whereby a given definition may be modified, elaborated, and amplified. In this sense there are multiple tarot dialects, some of which are so different as to nearly comprise separate languages. Insofar as speakers of tarot share pictorial images and theosophies in common to some extent, they are able to communicate with one another. When they do not, meanings must be negotiated extensively and cross-tarot communications become difficult and sometimes impossible.

Meanings of the Major Arcana

Table 8, A Dictionary of Tarot Meanings for the Major Arcana, selectively illustrates attributions of divinatory meanings to the cards. The significance of the major arcana, as provided in Table 8, are presented in terms of three expert authorities. Waite (1989) is the best known authority on the tarot, and a representative of the Golden Dawn theosophy. Douglas (1972) is a respected tarot scholar without concrete ties to a particular theosophical school. Kaplan (1972) is a contemporary writer and popularizer of the tarot who has endeavored to synthesize divinatory meanings of the tarot by drawing on the writings of the best known authorities.

These authorities represent a widely respected literature on the tarot. They reflect different viewpoints but form some middle ground in an otherwise divergent field of interpretation. This illustrative vocabulary of tarot therefore does not reflect widely disparate views, such as those of Aliester Crowley or many of the cultic groups based on tarot. Table 8 supplies a definition or in most cases a set and range of meanings associated with each card of the tarot.

Divinatory definitions of the tarot are viewed by many occultists as weak meanings; that is, the simplest, most elementary significance of the cards. In some

ILLUSTRATION SEVENTEEN: Fool, Magician, Sun, Rejuvenation, *Tarot of the Cat People Deck.* Reproduced by permission of U.S. Games Systems, Inc., Stamford, CT 06902 USA.

schemas of interpretation a particular card has two meanings, depending on whether it appears up-right or up-side-down in a spread. When meanings are separated by a "/," the description preceding the slash is the dominant or up-right meaning, while the depiction following the slash is the subordinate, lesser, or reversed meaning of the card.

As the simplest, most elementary meanings of the tarot, these definitions clearly distort the full range of rich attributions of tarot significance from the standpoint of many occultists. This feature is especially useful for illustrating tarot meanings to an uninitiated audience. Once these divinatory meanings of the tarot have been presented, I will demonstrate in an illustrative way how the grammar provided by occult theosophies of the tarot may be used to derive even more complex ways of attributing significance. Knowledge of certain dictionary meanings of a language, in other words, is necessary but not adequate in and of itself for the artful production of occult talk about the tarot.

TABLE 8:
A DICTIONARY OF TAROT MEANINGS FOR THE MAJOR ARCANA

The Fool

D: unexpected influence; decisions to be made; a new cycle of destiny/problems from impulsive action.

K: thoughtlessness; irrationality; insecurity; spontaneity; pleasure; lack of discipline; indiscretion; beginning of an adventure; initiative; enthusiasm/ faulty choice; indecision; apathy; lack of confidence.

W: folly; mania; extravagance; intoxication; delirium; frenzy.

The Magician

D: strength of will; initiative leading to success and triumph; adaptability and versatility; diplomacy and self confidence/ weakness of will; failure of nerve; inability to face reality.

K: originality and creativity; utilization of capabilities; imagination; self-reliance; will power; self-confidence; flexibility; slight of hand; bewilderment/ weakness of will; indecision; ineptitude; delay; lack of imagination; willpower applied to evil ends.

W: skill; diplomacy; address; subtlety/ sickness; pain; loss; disaster; enemies.

The High Priestess

D: the revealing of hidden things; bringing strength and hope; intuitive insight; source of creative talent/ difficulties from emotional instability; problems from lack of foresight or reluctance to take sound advice.

K: wisdom; sound judgement; common sense; understanding; serenity; objectivity; ability to teach others; intuition; lack of patience; platonic relationships/ short sightedness; lack of understanding; selfishness; improper judgement; conceit.

W: secrets, mystery; future unrevealed.

The Empress

D: fertility; abundance; fruitfulness; motherhood; domestic stability; honesty; inspiration through nature; sense of security through pleasures of the senses; growth/ domestic upheaval; over-protectiveness; sterility; psychic alienation; poverty.

K: feminine progress; action; development; fertility; attainment; marriage; children; material wealth; evolution; harassment; a leader; practical; intuitive/ vacillation; inaction; lack of interest; delay in progress; anxiety; infertility; loss of material possessions; frittering away of resources.

W: fruitfulness; action; initiative; length of days.

The Emperor

D: willpower; self-control; conquest; authority; ambition; knowledge through experience/ immaturity; weakness; subservience; loss of position; failure of ambition.

K: worldly power; accomplishment; confidence; wealth; stability; authority; leadership; war-making tendencies; paternity; male influences; direct pressure; conviction; combination of intelligence and reason over emotion and passion; strength; attainment; goal directed/ immaturity; ineffectiveness; lack of strength; indecision; inability.

W: stability; power; protection; realization; aid; reason; conviction.

The Hierophant

D: good counsel; advice; imposition; teaching; giver of wisdom; freedom through knowledge; inspirational help; the comfort of religion/ misinformation; distortion of the truth; slander; propaganda; bad advice; misrepresentation.

K: ritualism; ceremonies; mercy; humility; kindness; goodness; forgivingness; inspiration; alliance; compassion; servitude; inactivity; lack of conviction; timidity; conformity; inept in adapting to new circumstances; clinging to former ideals/ over kindness; susceptibility; impotence; vulnerability; fragility; unorthodox.

W: marriage; alliance; captivity; servitude; mercy; goodness; inspiration.

The Lovers

D: time of choice; advised reliance on intuition rather than intellect; a moral choice/ danger of a moral lapse; severe temptation; inability to make choice.

K: love; beauty; perfection; harmony; unanimity; trials overcome; confidence; trust; honor; beginning of a possible romance; infatuation; oblivious to consequences; examining; speculating; yearning/ failure to meet test; unreliability; separation; frustration in love and marriage; interference by others; untrustworthiness.

W: attraction; love; beauty; trials overcome.

The Chariot

D: success; triumph over obstacles; secure progress; victory through personal effort/ one who rides roughshod over others; overbearing forcefulness; inattention to rights of others; egocentricity; ruthlessness.

K: adversity overcome; turmoil; vengeance; success; possible journey; escape; fleeing from reality; perplexity; urgency to gain control of emotions; determination/ unsuccessful; defeat; failure; sudden collapse of plans; conquered; overwhelmed.

W: succor; providence; war; triumph; presumption; vengeance.

Strength/ Fortitude

D: opportunity to put plans into action; defeat of base impulses; reconciliation with an enemy/ defeat; surrender to unworthy impulses; failure of nerve leading to loss of opportunity.

K: strength; courage; fortitude; conviction; energy; determination; resolution; defiance; action; confidence; innate ability; zeal; fervor; accomplishment; conquest; heroism; virility; tireless efforts; liberation/ weakness; pettiness; sickness; tyranny; lack of faith; abuse of power; indifference; succumb to temptation.

W: power, energy, action; courage; magnanimity; success; honors.

The Hermit

D: need to retire from activities to think and plan; help and advice from wise counsellor; need to take things slowly; discretion and silence/ refusal to take sound advice; suspicion of motives of others; fear of innovation; rejection of wisdom and assistance.

K: knowledge; solitude; prudence; discretion; caution; self-denial; withdrawal; regression; desertion; annulment; insincerity; misleading; misguided; failure to face facts/ imprudence; hastiness; prematurity; foolish acts; incorrect advice; immaturity.

W: prudence; circumspection; treason; dissimulation; roguery; corruption.

The Wheel of Fortune

D: commencement of a new cycle; processes of destiny working through time; laws of fortune; suspicious omen/ turn for worse; closing of a cycle of fortune.

K: destiny; fortune; fate; outcome; felicity; special gain or loss; culmination; conclusion; inevitability; unexpected events; advancement; progress/ failure; ill luck; unexpected bad fate; broken sequence; interruption or inconsistency.

W: destiny; fortune; success; elevation; luck; felicity.

Justice

D: act of judgement; arbitration; agreements by negotiation; vindication of truth; integrity/ injustice; lack of fair dealing; bias; prejudice; legal tangles.

K: fairness; reasonableness; justice; proper balance; harmony; equity; righteousness; virtue; honor; virginity; just reward; good intentions; self-satisfac-

tion; equilibrium; impartiality/ bias; false accusations; bigotry; severity in judgement; intolerance; abuse.
W: equity; rightness; probity; executive; triumph of the deserving side of law.

The Hanged Man

D: ability to adapt to changing circumstances; flexibility of mind; wisdom; justice from the unconscious/ materialism; impending psychic disorder; inner struggle ending in defeat.
K: life in suspension; transition; change; reversal of the mind, way of life; boredom; abandonment; renunciation; sacrifice; repentance; readjustment; reorganization; improvement; rebirth; surrender; lack of progress/ lack of sacrifice; failure to give of one's self; false prophecy; useless sacrifice; preoccupation with the ego.
W: wisdom; circumspection; discernment; trials; sacrifice; intuition; divination; prophecy.

Death

D: unexpected major change in circumstances; destruction as a blessing in disguise; removal of outdated or superfluous/ element of chance.
K: clearing of way for new efforts; transformation; unexpected change; loss; failure; alteration; loss of income or financial security; beginning of a new era; illness/ stagnation; immobility; slow changes; partial change; inertia; narrowly missing a serious accident or escaping from death or disaster.
W: end; mortality; destruction; corruption.

Temperance

D: success possible by control of volatile factors; harmonious partnership/ opposition by ineptitude; progress thwarted.
K: moderation; temperance; patience; accommodation; harmony; compatibility; fusion; adjustment; good influence; fortunate omen; consolidation; possibly too moderate to reach goal/ discord; disunion; conflict of interest; hostility; inability to work with others; impatience; sterility; frustration.
W: economy; moderation; frugality; management; accommodation.

The Devil

D: need to sublimate lower self; hidden forces at work/ lust for power; temptation to abuse one's position for personal ends; dangerous; repression of instincts.
K: subordination; ravage; bondage; subservience; downfall; lack of success; weird experience; black magic; unexpected failure; violence; shock; fatality; self-destruction; disaster; unethical/ release from bondage; respite; divorce; enlightenment.
W: ravage; violence; extraordinary efforts; force; fatality.

The Tower

D: suffering of individual by forces of destiny; apparent unfairness of natural disasters which strike all/ unnecessary suffering; self-undoing.

K: sudden, complete change; breaking down of old beliefs; abandonment of past relationships; changing opinion; unexpected events; disruption; adversity; calamity; misery; deception; bankruptcy; termination; havoc; downfall; ruin; divorce; loss of stability; loss of money; loss of security, love; setback; breaking into new areas/ continued oppression; following old ways; living in a rut; entrapped in unhappy situation; imprisoned.

W: misery; distress; indigence; adversity; calamity; disgrace; deception; ruin.

The Star

D: insight into possibilities of future; widening of horizons; new life; vigor/ rigidity of mind; self-doubt; lack of trust.

K: hope; faith; inspiration; bright prospects; mixing of past, present; promising opportunity; optimism; insight; good omen; spiritual love; astrological influence; fulfillment; satisfaction; pleasure/ unfulfilled hopes; disappointment; pessimism; bad luck; lack of opportunity; stubbornness; imbalance.

W: loss; theft; privation; abandonment; hope; bright prospects.

The Moon

D: crisis of faith; need to use intuition; not reason/ failure of nerve; fear of stepping beyond safe boundaries.

K: deception; obscurity; trickery; dishonest; disillusionment; danger; error; bad influence; insincerity; selfishness; deceit; false pretenses/ trifling mistakes; overcoming bad influences; taking advantage of someone.

W: hidden enemies; danger; deception; occult forces; error.

The Sun

D: vindication of daring ideas; success; achievement against all odds; triumph of innovator; safe refuge after peril; acclaim; approval; just reward/ misjudgment ending in failure; fantasies of success replacing real attainment.

K: satisfaction; accomplishment; contentment; success; favorable relationships; love; joy; devotion; engagement; favorable omen; happy marriage; earthly happiness; liberation/ unhappy marriage; loneliness; canceled plans; broken engagement; clouded future; lack of friendship.

W: material happiness; fortunate marriage; contentment.

Judgement

D: joy in accomplishment; new lease on life; return to health; justified pleasure in achievement/ loss; guilt; reproach for wasted opportunities; punishment for failure.

K: atonement; judgement; need to repent, forgive; conduct toward others unfair, unkind; rejuvenation; improvement; promotion; legal judgement in one's favor/ disappointment; delay; failure to face facts; indecision; procrastination.

W: change of position; renewal; outcome; loss through lawsuit.

The World

D: final, successful completion of matters in hand; culmination of events; ending of a cycle of destiny/ stagnation; loss of momentum; failure of will.
K: attainment; completion; perfection; ultimate change; success; assurance; synthesis; fulfillment; triumph; admiration of others/ imperfection; failure to complete task started; lack of vision; failure; disappointment.
W: assured success; recompense; voyage.

Key: D=Douglas (1972); K=Kaplan (1972); W=Waite (1989).

This table illustrates the contention that meanings of tarot are fluid and lack complete standardization, even when widely divergent meanings are excluded. Take, for example, the contents associated with "The Fool" of the major arcana, as shown in Table 8. Waite says it refers to folly, mania, extravagance, intoxication, delirium, and frenzy. Kaplan sees this card as signifying thoughtlessness, irrationality, insecurity, spontaneity, pleasure, lack of discipline, indiscretion, beginning of adventure, initiative, enthusiasm; or reversed, faulty choice, indecision, apathy, and a lack of confidence. Douglas takes this same card to mean unexpected influences, decisions, a new cycle of destiny; or, reversed, problems deriving from impulsiveness. Though these definitions of the Fool generally are not contradictory or even inconsistent with one another, they reveal more than slight ambiguity about the meaning of this card.

"The Lovers" card provides another example from the major arcana of the tarot. Waite says it means attraction, love, beauty, and/or trials overcome. For Kaplan it signifies love, beauty, perfection, harmony, unanimity, trials overcome, confidence, trust, honor, beginning of a possible romance, infatuation, oblivious to consequences, examining, speculating, yearning; or, reversed, failure to meet test, unreliability, separation, frustration in love and marriage, interference by others, and/or untrustworthiness. The card, according to Douglas, refers to time of choice, advised reliance on intuition rather than intellect, a moral choice; or, reversed, danger of a moral lapse, severe temptation, and/or inability to make a choice. While there is considerable agreement between the definitions of the Lovers provided by Kaplan and Waite, Douglas introduces a dramatically different range of implications.

Meanings of the Minor Arcana

Tarot authorities not uncommonly have left the divinatory meanings of the individual cards of the minor arcana specifically undefined. Occultists, however, generally dispute the idea that this situation somehow implies that the minor arcana are less important. Since the Golden Dawn, occult interpretations of the tarot commonly have attempted to remedy previous neglect of the minor arcana. I have selected two experts who do specify meanings for the minor arcana for illustrative

PRINCESS OF SWORDS

PRINCESS OF DISKS

PRINCESS OF CUPS

PRINCESS OF WANDS

ILLUSTRATION EIGHTEEN: Princesses of Swords, Disks, Wands, Cups, *Gareth Knight Tarot Deck.* Reproduced by permission of U.S. Games Systems, Inc., Stamford, CT 06902 USA.

purposes. The definitions of the minor arcana depicted in Tables 8A to 8D reflect the interpretations of Kaplan (1972) and Paul Foster Case (1947). Like Waite, Case is a well known occultist in the tradition of the Golden Dawn, and he reflects the viewpoint of an American cultic group which sees itself in this tradition.

The Suit of Wands

The tarot suit of wands, rods, scepters, batons, or staves, as illustrated in Table 9A, commonly is associated with creativity, intuition, and/or spirituality. Cavendish (1975:159) associates this suit with fire, masculinity, vigorous, creative energy, work business, enterprise, initiative, and pressing things. Kaplan (1972) relates it to enterprise, growth, progress, advancement, animation, invention, energy, modesty, humility, and laborer-worker relations. Douglas (1972:134) attributes the notions of fire, domination, strength, strife, victory, valor, swiftness, strength, and oppression to this tarot suit. These basic themes provide a context of meaning for attributing significance to particular cards in the suit of swords.

TABLE 9A:

A DICTIONARY OF TAROT MEANINGS FOR THE MINOR ARCANA—WANDS

Ace

C: energy; strength; enterprise; principle; beginnings.

K: creation; beginnings; invention; start of undertaking; fortune; enterprise; gain.

Two

C: domination.

K: mature individual; ruler; attainment of goals, needs; boldness; courage; dominant personality.

Three

C: established strength.

K: practical knowledge; business acumen; strength; enterprise; negotiation; trade; commerce; undertakings.

Four

C: perfected work.

K: romance; society; harmony; newly acquired prosperity; peace; tranquility; fruits of labor; rest after peace.

Five

C: strife; competition.

K: unsatisfied desires; struggle; labor; endeavors; violent strife; conflict; obstacles.

Six

C: victory after strife; gain.
K: conquest; triumph; good news; gain; advancement; expectations; desires; result of efforts.

Seven

C: valor; courage in face of difficulties.
K: conquest; success; gain; overcoming obstacles and challenges; surmounting overwhelming odds; advantage; victory.

Eight

C: activity; swiftness; approach to goal.
K: swift activity; sudden progress or movement; speed; hastily made decisions; too rapid advancement.

Nine

C: preparedness; strength in reserve; victory after opposition.
K: expectation of difficulties, changes; awaiting tribulation; anticipation; hidden enemies; deception; discipline; order; a pause in current struggle.

Ten

C: oppression; burden of ill-regulated power.
K: overburdened; excessive pressures; problems soon to be resolved; striving to meet a goal or to maintain a level or position; possibility of power for ends.

Page

C: dark young man; messenger; brilliance; courage.
K: faithful, loyal; envoy; emissary; consistency; important news.

Knight

C: dark, friendly young man; departure; change of residence.
K: departure; journey; advancement into the unknown; alteration; flight; absence; change of residence.

Queen

C: dark woman, magnetic; friendly; business success.
K: a sympathetic, understanding person; friendly; loving; honorable; chaste; practical; full of feminine charm and grace; capable of meaningful expression; love; gracious hostess; sincere interest in others.

King

C: dark man; friendly; ardent; honest; possible inheritance.
K: honest, conscientious; mature; wise; devoted; friendly; sympathetic; educated; gentleman; married; fatherly.

The ace of wands, as presented in Table 9A, is defined by both Kaplan and Case as related to origins. While they do not agree about other qualities and characteristics defining this card, their definitions may be seen as complementary. Slightly different interpretations of other wands are evident. In most instances, the general themes of virtue, integrity, and wholesome spirituality are manifest as characteristics of particular wands.

The Suit of Cups

The tarot suit of cups, as illustrated in Table 9B, commonly is associated with love, marriage, and human emotions. Kaplan (1972:145), for instance, observed that cups "represent love, happiness, gaiety and joy." They, moreover, are seen as a "symbol of pleasure," representations of "passions and deep feelings," and indicative of a "humane person." In Douglas' (1972:134) view, cups are associated with water, love abundance, pleasure, and success. Cavendish (1975:162) referred to cups as lucky, feminine, and intense, positive emotions. These themes provide the general context of meaning for identifying the significance of particular cards in this tarot suit.

TABLE 9B:
A DICTIONARY OF TAROT MEANINGS—CUPS

Ace

C: fertility; productiveness; beauty; pleasure.
K: great abundance; fulfillment; perfection; joy; fertility; opulence; fullness; happiness; productiveness; beauty; pleasure; goodness; overflowing; favorable outlook.

Two

C: reciprocity; reflection.
K: love, friendship beginning or renewed; passion; union; engagement; understanding; cooperation; partnership; marriage.

Three

C: pleasure; liberality; fulfillment; happy issue.
K: resolution of problems; conclusion; solace; healing; satisfactory result; partial fulfillment; compromise.

Four

C: contemplation; dissatisfaction with material success.
K: weariness; aversion; disgust; disappointment; unhappiness; bitter experience; stationary period.

Five

C: loss in pleasure; partial loss; vain regret.

K: partial loss; regret; friendship without meaning; marriage without love; imperfection flaw; delayed inheritance; incomplete union.

Six

C: beginning of steady gain; only beginning; new relations; new environment.

K: memories; past influences vanishing; childhood; nostalgia; faded images; longing.

Seven

C: illusionary success; ideals; designs; resolution.

K: fantasy; unrealistic attitude; imagination; daydreams; foolish whims; wishful thinking; illusionary success.

Eight

C: abandoned success; instability; leaving material success for something higher.

K: discontinuance of effort; disappointment; abandonment of previous plans; shyness; modest; abandoned success.

Nine

C: material success; physical well-being.

K: success; material attainment; advantage; well-being; abundance; good health; victory; difficulties surmounted.

Ten

C: lasting success; happiness to come.

K: home; abode; happiness; joy; pleasure; peace; love; contentment; good family life; honor; esteem; virtue; reputation.

Page

C: fair, studious youth; reflection; news.

K: studious and intent; reflective; meditative; loyal; willing to offer services; helpful; trustworthy worker.

Knight

C: fair man; Venusian; indolent; arrival; approach.

K: opportunity; arrival; approach; advancement; attraction; inducement; appeal; request; challenge; proposal; proposition.

Queen

C: fair woman; imaginative; poetic; gift of vision.

K: warmhearted; fair; poetic; beloved; adored; good friend, mother; devoted wife; practical; honest; possesses loving intelligence; gift of vision.

King

C: fair man; calm exterior; subtle; violent; artistic.

K: responsibility; creativity; learned person; professional; business person; lawyer; religious; scientist; considerate; kindness; reliable; liberal; artist; generous.

The definitions of cups, like wands, as shown in Table 9B, reflect at least slightly different interpretations by these occult experts. For example: while Case interprets the four of cups as contemplation and dissatisfaction with material success; Kaplan sees it as weariness, aversion, disappointment, unhappiness, and/or a static condition. These attributions of meaning to particular cards clearly reflect the overall theme of the suit of cups; that is, a preoccupation with human emotionality, particularly multiple variations on the notion of love and kindness.

The Suit of Swords

The tarot suit of swords commonly is associated with evil, death, disaster, courage, conflict, and intellectual matters. Cavendish (1975:164) observed that swords are unlucky and ominous, suggesting war, bloodshed and death. He also linked this suit with the element of air, intellect, and instability. Douglas (1972:134) connected swords with the alchemical element of air, as well as the characteristics of peace, sorrow, defeat, success, despair, cruelty, and ruin. Kaplan (1972:129) said that swords represent courage, boldness, force, authority, aggression, and ambition. Meanings associated with particular cards in the tarot suit of swords are presented in Table 9C, most of which play out some variation of these basic themes.

TABLE 9C:
A DICTIONARY OF TAROT MEANINGS—SWORDS

Ace

C: invoked force; conquest; activity.
K: great determination; initiative; strength; force; activity; excessiveness; triumph; power; success; fertility; prosperity; deep emotional feelings; love; championship; conquest.

Two

C: balanced force; indecision; friendship.
K: balanced force; harmony; firmness; concord; offsetting factors; stalemate; affection.

Three

C: sorrow; disappointment; tears; delay; absence; separation.
K: absence; disappointment; strife; removal; dispersion; diversion; opposition; separation; delay.

Four

C: rest from strife; relief from anxiety; quietness; rest; not a card of death.

K: respite; rest after illness; repose; replenishment; solitude; exile; retreat; temporary seclusion; abandonment.

Five

C: defeat; loss; failure; slander; dishonor.

K: conquest; defeat; destruction of others; degradation; adversaries; revocation; infamy; dishonor.

Six

C: success after anxiety; passage from difficulties; journey by water.

K: trip, journey; travel; voyage; route; headstrong attempt to overcome difficulties; expedient manner; success after anxiety.

Seven

C: unstable effort; uncertainty; partial success.

K: new plans; wishes; fortitude; perseverance; attempt; endeavor; hope; confidence; fantasy; design.

Eight

C: indecision; waste of energy; crisis.

K: crisis; calamity; conflict; domination; imprisonment; turmoil; bad news; censure; criticism; sickness; calumny.

Nine

C: worry; suffering; despair; misery; loss.

K: misery; concern; unhappiness; miscarriage; anxiety over a loved one; worry; despair; suffering.

Ten

C: ruin; pain; desolation; suffer misfortune; not a card of sudden death; end of delusion in spiritual matters.

K: ruin; pain; affliction; sadness; mental anguish; desolation; tears; misfortune; trouble; disappointment; grief; sorry.

Page

C: vigilant; acute; subtle; active youth.

K: adept in perceiving, uncovering unknown or less obvious; insight; vigilance; agility; spying; discreet; active youth; alert and awake to unknown dangers.

Knight

C: active; clever; subtle; skillful; domineering young man; enmity; wrath; war.

K: bravery; skill; capacity; strength; heroic action; opposition; war; impetuous rush into unknown without fear.

Queen

C: widowhood; mourning; keen, quick; intensely perceptive; subtle woman; unusually fond of dance.

K: sharp; quick-witted; keen; intensely perceptive; subtle; widow or sadness; mourning; privation; absence; loneliness; separation; previous happiness, present misfortune.

King

C: distrustful; suspicious man; full of ideas; thoughts and designs; care; observation; extreme caution.

K: active; determined; experienced; authoritative; controlled; commanding; professional; proficient; analytical; justice; force; superiority; full of ideas and designs.

Consistent with the general meanings associated with the suit of swords, Case and Kaplan, as illustrated in Table 9C, define most of these cards in terms of unlucky, unfortunate, or situations which tend to be evaluated negatively by human beings. As with the meanings they ascribe to wands and cups, the swords tend to reflect some moderate consistency around a core or central quality, but also some variation, especially when extensive meanings are elaborated. Interpretations of swords, it should be observed, tend to associate human intellect with power which commonly is used in dangerous ways.

The Suit of Pentacles

The suit of pentacles, as shown in Table 9D, generally is associated with material success, business, employment, professions, careers, and money. Kaplan (1972:153) envisioned pentacles as the suit of merchants and tradesmen, and linked it with sensitivity and involvement. Douglas (1972:134) related coins (pentacles) to the element of earth, change, power, trouble, success, prudence, and wealth. Cavendish (1975:168) added the characteristics of property, status, influence, and security as attributes of the suit of coins (pentacles). As with the other tarot suits, these characteristics provide a general context of meaning for attributing significance to particular cards.

TABLE 9D:
A DICTIONARY OF TAROT MEANINGS—PENTACLES

Ace

C: material gain; wealth; contentment.

K: perfection; attainment; prosperity; felicity; great wealth; riches; bliss; ecstasy; gold; valuable coins or artifacts; treasures; combination of material and spiritual prosperity.

Two

C: harmony in midst of change.

K: difficulty in launching new projects; difficult situations arising; new troubles; embarrassment; worry; concern.

Three

C: construction; material increase; growth; financial gain.

K: great skill in trade, work; mastery; perfection; artistic ability; dignity; renown; rank; power.

Four

C: earthly power; physical forces; skill in directing forces.

K: love of material wealth; usurer; miser; ungenerous.

Five

C: concordance; affinity; adaptation.

K: material trouble; destitution; loss; failure; error; impoverishment; mistress; lover; mis-affection.

Six

C: material prosperity; philanthropy; presents.

K: generosity; philanthropy; charity; kindness; gratification; gifts; material gain.

Seven

C: success unfulfilled; delay, but growth.

K: ingenuity; growth; hard work; progress; successful dealings; money; wealth; treasure; gain.

Eight

C: skill in material affairs.

K: apprenticeship; craftsmanship; fast to learn; candor; frankness; modesty; handiwork; personal effort.

Nine

C: prudence; material gain; completion.

K: accomplishment; discernment; discretion; foresight; safety; prudence; material well-being; love of nature.

Ten

C: wealth; riches; material prosperity.

K: prosperity; security; safety; family; ancestry; inheritance; home; dwelling.

Page

C: diligent; careful; deliberate youth.

K: keen concentration; application; study; scholarship; reflection; respect; knowledge; desire for learning; ideas; a do-gooder; bearer of news.

Knight

C: laborious; patient; dull young man.

K: mature; responsible; reliable; methodical; patient; persistent; able to conclude task; laborious; organized; capable.

Queen

C: generous; intelligent; charming; moody; married woman.

K: prosperity; well-being; wealth; abundance; luxury; opulence; extreme comfort; generosity; security; liberty; magnificence; grace; dignity; charitable; noble soul.

King

C: friendly; steady; reliable; married man.

K: experienced; successful leader; character, intelligence; business acumen; mathematical ability; loyal friend; reliable in marriage; successful business person; wise investment; ability to acquire money and valuable possessions.

Key: C=Case (1947); K=Kaplan (1972).

The occult meanings of the tarot suits composing the minor arcana and each of the cards within the suits of wands, cups, swords, and pentacles, as shown in Tables 9A through 9D, illustrate a range of divinatory interpretations of this text. Occult attributions of significance to the cards in a particular suit very generally conform to more or less agreed upon characteristics of each of the four tarot suits. Cups, for instance, generally are associated with the alchemical element of water, and refer to such human, cultural features as love, pleasure, and success. The three of cups, as shown in Table 9A, provides a concrete illustration. Kaplan takes it to mean resolution of problems, conclusion, solace, healing, satisfactory results, partial fulfillment, and/or compromise. Case sees it as pleasure, liberality, fulfillment, and/or happiness. Clearly, then, this card lacks a standard meaning as defined by these interpreters. The nine of pentacles provides a further example of meanings attributed to the minor arcana of the tarot. Kaplan interprets it as accomplishment, discernment, discretion, foresight, safety, prudence, material well-being, and/or love of nature. From Case's perspective it means prudence, material gain, and/or completion. While these authorities exhibit greater agreement on the meaning of this card, at least as partly defined by the general theme of this suit, a considerable range of meanings is attributed to the nine of pentacles.

Dictionary meanings attributed to individual cards provide at most a very fluid basis for using the language of tarot. In many instances the meanings attributed to the cards are connected, though rarely literally, with the images and symbols portrayed. This is not unlike the objects named by language. Sometimes there is an observable or rational connection between the object named and its label, once one learns the association, but oftentimes there is not. The meaning of the label and its appropriate use, furthermore, necessarily depends on some larger body of knowledge. While tarot is much more fluid and less definitive than a formal language, it nevertheless is facilitated by knowledge pertinent to the production of meaning and its use. Just as it is possible to create one's own vocabulary for things, tarot meanings may be, and sometimes are, invented subjectively, typically by freely associating symbols with meanings. Yet, behind and implicit in the dictionary of meanings discussed above are many different systems or theosophies for attributing meaning and defining its usage.

Occult interpretations of the minor arcana, as illustrated above, reflect a tacit theory of human existence. This implicit theory envisions human life in terms of certain essential sociocultural and psychological realms: creativity, inner strength, and spirituality (wands, rods, batons); emotions, especially love, pleasure, and successful activities (cups); misfortune, force, and intellectual power (swords); and economic activity (pentacles, coins). Complementing and expanding these basic features of human existence are the characteristics attributed to the major arcana. These basic features of human existence include: the quest for human, spiritual meaning; human creative power and intelligence; femininity, and balance between opposites of good and evil, fertility and infertility, life and death; nature, fruitfulness, motherhood, and love; fatherhood, order, authority; spiritual power, morality; human union, knowledge, choice; moral triumph; force and strength; prudence; justice; change and rebirth; temperance; evil; destruction; divine guidance; self-criticism; enlightened consciousness; judgment; and the cosmos. Occult theosophies of the tarot further structure these meanings by way of grammars whereby they are interconnected and interrelated to form elaborate interpretations of human existence and related environments.

GRAMMARS OF OCCULT MEANING

The language of tarot provides grammars whereby the vocabulary represented by particular cards may be organized into more cohesive wholes. The grammars of tarot generally are ill-defined and commonly embedded within specific theosophic occult systems. Tarot card interpreters oftentimes build upon primitive grammatical systems or devices, and they sometimes construct unique grammars for themselves. The major arcana, for instance, may organize these cards ordinally from simplicity to complexity, highest to lowest (in priority, significance, abstraction, and so on), and/or may be envisioned in terms of sets of cards (those depicted as personages, heavily bodies, states or qualities) as related and interrelated to one-another in simple and complex ways. Since it is not too difficult for the interpreter to retain a meaning or set of meanings attached to each of the 22 cards of the major arcana in memory, these cards may be allowed to float unencumbered by grammatical structures.

It is much more difficult, however, to memorize additional meanings of the 56 cards composing the minor arcana. Partly for this reason, some grammar generally is used to organize the vocabulary of this set of tarot cards. The simplest grammars of the minor arcana organize meanings in terms of the ordinal position of the cards in each suit, as in from least to most serious, weak to strong, negative to positive (or the reverse), and so on, defined in terms of the basic characteristics (emotions, spirituality, intellect, economics) of the suits. More complex grammatical systems are constructed: The tarot has been related to alchemy by endowing the four suits with characteristics of the four elements (earth, air, water, fire); and many linkages have been established with astrology, numerology and the Kabala, as well as other occult arts (see, for example, Waite, 1971; Crowley, 1944; Douglas, 1972). As a text, then, the tarot offers an elaborate body of knowledge, an almost infinite range of possible meanings, and techniques for arranging these meanings into more cohesive wholes.

Possible grammars for deriving, attributing, and structuring the meanings of the tarot cards and their symbols are limited only by human imagination and its collective expression. Put differently, virtually any collection or system of ideas, such as Christianity, Jungian archtypes, psychoanalysis, Campbellian symbolism, astrology, alchemy, physics, or mythology, may be used to derive the meanings of tarot symbols and fashion significance for particular purposes (see, for example, Geer, 1988; Heline, 1969; Nichols, 1980; Campbell and Roberts, 1979; Pollack, 1986). Some grammars of the occult tarot are defined by esoteric traditions culminating in the grand syncretism of the Golden Dawn, as reflected through the writings of its creators, such as Mathers, and its later interpreters, Waite, Case, Crowley, Regardie, Cavendish, and Wang. Subsequent writers have greatly expanded this tendency to link the tarot with other systems for constructing meaning. These systems, furthermore, may be combined and syncretized in complex and confounding ways.

In sketching out some of the theosophical frameworks they developed, I do not aim to reconstruct them exhaustively or comprehensively in anything like pure form, if there is such a thing, or to judge among rival claims and interpretations of arcane traditions. My purpose, instead, is to illustrate grammars of the occult tarot selectively, based on some of its central and most intriguing traditions. I begin with a review of some of the correspondences between the tarot and various occultisms, like astrology and alchemy, and the natural environment, followed by an attempt to illustrate the ornate association between the tarot and Kabalistic mysticism.

The Tarot and Alchemy

The occult tarot and the exceptionally obtuse occult theosophy of alchemy commonly are interrelated. Crowley (1969:17-25) followed the syncreticism of the Golden Dawn in illustrating one of the ways in which the tarot and alchemy have been connected and interrelated. The Ancients, he argued, divided the **universe** into three "pure elements," or entirely spiritual forms of pure energy, called **fire**, **water**, and **air**. The fourth element, **earth**, is said to be "crystallized" from the other three. These elements, he emphasized, are alchemical, not chemical: They refer to spirit or ideas, not to qualities or properties of nature. In this view, the qualities of the elements pervade the entire universe and its symbolization by way of the occult tarot. The universe, Crowley contended, essentially operates by way of analysis (division) and synthesis (unity) and these operations are pertinent to the alchemical elements and derivative properties of them.

As discussed by Crowley, the most pure and active element, fire, corresponds to the image of father, pure but passive; the element of water symbolizes mother; while the union of these elements results in the distinctive quality of air (son) and earth (daughter). In the Corwleyian system the three elements, fire, water, air, further correspond to qualities of being, knowledge, and bliss; the Guanas, Sttvas, Rajas and Tamas of Hinduism; and principles of energy, sulphur, mercury, and salt. In this schema sulphur is activity, energy, and desire; mercury is fluidity, intelligence, and the power of transmission; and salt is the vehicle of the other two forms of energy which reacts to them while possessing its own qualities. Fire, water, and air also are attributed to the Hebrew letters of Shin, Mem and Aleph, while earth is represented by the Hebrew letter Tau. In these and even more complex ways Crowley draws on occult alchemy which is intermingled with Eastern religion, occult kabalism, numerology, astrology, magic, animism, paganism, and other symbolic systems to produce attributes and correspondences to the occult tarot.

More specifically, Crowley (1969:19-20) envisioned the universal, alchemical elements as related in exceptionally complex ways to all of the major tarot trumps. The Fool, for instance, reflects all of the properties of the basic, pure elements, fire, water, especially air, and their correspondences, and it is called the "gold of air" (Crowley, 1969:68). Other specific correlations between the major arcana and alchemy include the Hanged Man with water, and Judgment with fire (see Table 11, below). In more specific ways, Crowley related alchemy and the minor cards. The tarot suits are interpreted by relating wands to fire, cups to water, swords to air, and disks (pentacles or coins) to earth. Each of the court cards are presented in terms of alchemical elements. In other words, each element itself is subdivided by the properties fire, water, air, and earth, such that the knights correspond to fire, queens correspond to water, princes reflect air, and princesses refer to earth. By this method a matrix is produced whereby, for instance, the princess of wands is interpreted as earth of fire; the prince of cups refers to air of water; the queen of swords corresponds to water of air; and, the knight of disks is attributed as fire of earth. This schema enables the interpreter to derive specific attributes of these cards from the occult theosophy of alchemy.

Tarot Correspondences to Mythology, Nature, and Other Phenomena

Crowley's interpretation of the tarot trumps, as described by Cavendish (1975:58), provided for an almost bewildering array of correspondences with deities, animals, and plants. Some of these relationships are summarized in Table 10. The correspondences illustrated in Table 10 provide an elementary framework for elaborating meanings of the major arcana in relationship with mythology and specific gods, as well as prominent characteristics of nature, particularly animals and plants. Specified in this way, the definitions of the tarot trumps is amplified, and their meanings may be related in terms of an increasingly complex matrix and system of human significance.

The possibility of connecting the tarot to an infinite array of meaningful grammars is illustrated further in Table 11. It shows each of the major arcana in relationship to particular colors, sounds, and various qualities attributed to them by occultists. The Empress, for example, is shown as corresponding to the color emerald green, the sound F#, and the binary qualities of peace and war. These relationships, at least in principle, permit translations back and forth between the

TABLE 10:
TAROT CORRESPONDENCES TO DEITIES, ANIMALS, PLANTS

Tarot Trumps	Deities	Animals	Plants
Fool	Zeus, Jupiter	man, eagle	aspen
Magician	Thoth, Hermes	swallow, ibis, ape, cynoephalus	vervain, palm
High Priestess	Artemis, Diana,Hecate	dog	almond, moonwort
Empress	Hathor, Aphrodite, Venus	dove, swan, sparrow	myrtle, rose
Emperor	Athena, Mars, Minerva	owl, ram	tiger lily, geranium
Hierophant	Apis, Venus	bull	mallow
Lovers	Castor and Pollux, Pollux	magpie	orchids, hybrids
Chariot	Khepera, Apollo	crab, turtle, sphinx	lotus
Strength	Bastet, Skhmet	lion	sunflower
Hermit	Adonis, Attis	anchorite, virgin, eagle	lily, narcissus, snowdrop
Wheel	Amon, Zeus, Jupiter	eagle	oak, fig, popular
Justice	Maat, Vulcan	elephant	aloe
Hanged Man	Poseidon, Neptune	snake, scorpion	water plants
Death	Seth, Mars	beetle, lobster, scorpion, wolf	cactus
Temperance	Artemis, Diana	centaur, horse, dog	rush
Devil	Khem, Pan, Priapus	goat, ass	thistle
Tower	Horus	bear, wolf	absinthe, rue
Star	Juno, Ganvmede	eagle, peacock	coconut
Moon	Khepera, Poseidon, Neptune	fish, dolphin, beetle	opium
Sun	Re, Hellos	lion, sparrowhawk	sunflower, laurel, heliotrope
Judgment	Hades, Pluto	lion	poppy, nettle, hibiscus
World	Sebek, Saturn	crocodile	ash, cypress, yew, hellebore

tarot and music as well as manifestations and representations of color. Such a grammar of meaning may be connected and even synthesized with alchemy, as described above, as well as other occult systems, such as astrology.

Tarot and Astrology

Occult thought relates the tarot with astrology. In other words, astrology provides a theosophy whereby the tarot cards are linked with the signs of the Zodiac and other aspects of astrological thought. Table 12 illustrates occult correspondences between the major arcana and astrological images of the planets, houses, and signs of the zodiac. The Magician, for instance, is connected in this way to Mercury as well as to whatever it signifies in terms of an occult astrology. Three of the major arcana of the tarot, namely the Fool, the Hanged Man, and Judgment, are not attributed with specific astrological significance. Instead, they retain a primary association with the grammar of alchemy. Occult theosophies of the tarot consequently tend to be seen as complementary. This reinforces the occult contention that

**TABLE 11:
MAJOR ARCANA RELATIONS TO COLOR, SOUND, QUALITIES**

Major Arcana	Color	Sound	Qualities
Fool	luminous pale yellow	E	air, spirit, origins
Magician	yellow	E	life/death
High Priestess	blue	G#	wisdom/folly
Empress	emerald green	F#	peace/war
Emperor	scarlet	C	sight
Hierophant	red-orange	C#	sound
Lovers	tangerine	D	smell
Chariot	amber	D#	speech
Strength	yellow, greenish	E#	taste
Hermit	green, yellowish	F	touch, sexual love
Wheel	violet	A#	wealth/poverty
Justice	chartreuse green	F#	work
Hanged Man	deep blue	G#	water, matter
Death	green blue	G	change, variation, transformation
Temperance	azure	G#	anger
Devil	indigo	A	jocularity
Tower	scarlet	C	grace/indignation
Star	violet	A#	imagination
Moon	crimson	B	tranquility, sleep, lassitude
Sun	orange	D	fertility/infertility
Judgment	fiery orange-scarlet	C	fire, union
World	cobalt	A	domination/submission

the tarot is the key to all arcane knowledge. A comprehensive knowledge of such a theosophy of the tarot necessarily requires the fluent user to acquire some understanding of multiple occult grammars for deriving human meaning.

The astrological attribution of meanings to the tarot is illustrated further in Table 13 by way of correspondences between the minor arcana and specific signs of the zodiac. Each of the astrological houses, as depicted in the left-hand column of Table 13, is associated with sets of numbered cards, certain court cards, as well as the princesses and aces. Each of the houses of the zodiac, as shown in Table 13, is divided into specific periods of time (days of months) corresponding to the associated cards of the minor arcana. Aries, for example, corresponds to the two, three, and four of wands, defined by the temporal periods of March 21 to 30, March 31 to April 10, and April 11 to 20, respectively, as well as the queen of wands, prince, princess and ace of pentacles. In this way, particular cards may be used chronologically in relationship to very specific historical dates or periods. The occult tarot thereby may be interpreted as fully integrated with theosophies of astrology in mutually elaborating ways.

TABLE 12:
MAJOR ARCANA CORRESPONDENCES TO PLANETS/ZODIAC

Major Arcana	Planets and Houses/Signs
Fool	[Air]
Magician	Mercury
High Priestess	Moon
Empress	Venus
Emperor	Aries
Hierophant	Taurus
Lovers	Gemini
Chariot	Cancer
Strength	Leo
Hermit	Virgo
Wheel	Jupiter
Justice	Libra
Hanged Man	[Water]
Death	Scorpio
Temperance	Sagittarius
Devil	Capricorn
Tower	Mars
Star	Aquarius
Moon	Pisces
Sun	Sun
Judgment	[Fire]
World	Saturn

The Occult Kabala and the Tarot

The syncretic theosophy of the occult tarot developed by the Golden Dawn fundamentally was based on the occult Kabala as filtered through Renaissance Hermeticism. It central teachings are summarized symbolically in the **Tree of Life**, its ten emanations and 22 paths. A principal link between this mystical model of creation and the tarot is provided by the Hebrew alphabet and a related numerology. Kabalistic interpretations of the tarot commonly are at least partly integrated with the ornate and enigmatic correspondences briefly described above to alchemy (earth, fire, wind, air), astrology (planets and signs of the zodiac), mythology (gods, goddesses, related entities and symbols), nature (plants, animals, colors, stones, smells, sounds), and mathematical systems (geometric designs, number systems), among other possibilities (like the Holy Grail and Celtic paganism).

The Kabala used by the Golden Dawn was an occult one, loosely derived historically from a diffuse and recondite body of Jewish mysticism (see Wang, 1983; Cavendish, 1975; Douglas, 1972; Kaplan, 1978, 1986). Its origins are obscure. Some occultists believe it originally was taught by God to a company of angel initiates comprising an elite thaumaturgical school in heaven. Other occultists hold that God gave the Kabala to Moses on Mount Sinai, who in turn initiated seventy Elders. The Kabala is thought to have been broadcast orally from generation to generation, though Kings David and Solomon. According to occult traditions, it eventually was written down and collected in the *Book of Splendors* or *Zohar*. The principal sources of the occult Kabala were the *Sepher Yezirah* or *Book of Creation*, a collection of medieval works. These mystical teachings were amplified during the middle ages, filtered through Renaissance humanism (gnosticism and Neoplatonicism) as well as German traditions of Rosicrucianism, and then appropriated, disseminated, and syncretized by French and British occultism.

The teachings of this occult Kabala envision a universe emanating from the godhead, En Soph. It forms a unity of macrocosm and microcosm, and means whereby Ascension to divinity may be achieved. It thereby emphasizes the experience of the Divine, not an unattainable knowledge of God. It presents pathways to a divine source, but not creation itself. This exceptionally ethereal and multifarious doctrine is summarized symbolically by the Tree of Life.

The Tree of Life is represented by ten circles and 22 connecting lines, as shown in Figure 4. It is read, like Hebrew, from the right to the left of the viewer. The circles (spheres) represent aspects of God called sephiroth. The names of the sephiroth and their meanings are: 1) Kether, the Crown; 2) Chokmah, Wisdom; 3) Binah, Understanding; 4) Chesed, Mercy; 5) Geburah, Severity; 6) Tiphareth, Beauty; 7) Netzach, Victory; 8) Hod, Splendor; 9) Yesod, Foundation; and 10) Malkuth, Kingdom. An invisible Sephira, Daath or Knowledge, sometimes is envisioned, but not visibly represented as a bridge between Binah and Chesed. Connections between the sephiroth, as represented by twenty-two numbered lines in Figure X, are considered paths on the tree of life. Each path is identified by a letter of the Hebrew alphabet: 1) Aleph; 2) Beth; 3) Gimel; 4) Daleth; 5) He; 6) Vau; 7) Zyin (zain); 8) Heth; 9) Teth; 10) Yod; 11) Kaph; 12) Lamed; 13) Mem; 14) Nun; 15) Smekh; 16) Ayin; 17) Pe; 18) Tzaddi; 19) Qoph; 20) Resh; 21) Shin; and 22) Tau. Collectively, the Sephiroth and Paths commonly are referred to by occultists as "the thirty-two paths of wisdom."

Vertically, each set of sephiroth (2, 4, 7; 1, 6, 9, 10; 3, 5, 8), as illustrated in Figure 4, may be envisioned as pillars or columns. The right-hand pillar is called Mercy, the middle pillar is named Mildness, and the left-hand pillar is referred to as Judgment (or Severity). Each sephira is thought to balance its opposite, while each path is thought to balance the connected sephira, as well as the opposite path. The Pillar of Mercy generally is understood as masculine, active or force, while the Pillar of Judgment (severity) is regarded as feminine, passive, or form. The opposites of Mercy (force, masculine, active, positive) and Judgment (form, feminine, passive, negative) are thought to be balanced by the Pillar of Mildness and it consequently is said to reflect unity and equilibrium.

Correspondences between the Kabala as represented by the Tree of Life and the occult tarot are presented in Table 14. Part I of Table 14 illustrates the sephiroth in relationship to particular tarot cards. The left-hand column of this table shows the sephiroth and their related meanings while the right-hand column lists corresponding tarot cards.

TABLE 13:
MINOR ARCANA CORRESPONDENCES TO THE ZODIAC

Houses	Numbered Cards	Days	Court Cards	Princesses/Aces
	2 Wands	3/21-30	Queen of Wands	
Aries	3 Wands	3/31-4/10	Queen of Wands	
	4 Wands	4/11-20	Prince of Pentacles	Princess of Pentacles
	5 Pentacles	4/21-30	Prince of Pentacles	
Taurus	6 Pentacles	5/1-10	Prince of Pentacles	
	7 Pentacles	5/11-20	King of Swords	Ace of Pentacles
	8 Swords	5/21-31	King of Swords	
Gemini	9 Swords	6/1-10	King of Swords	
	10 Swords	6/11-20	Queen of Cups	
	2 Cups	6/21-7/1	Queen of Cups	
Cancer	3 Cups	7/2-11	Queen of Cups	
	4 Cups	7/12-21	Prince of Wands	Princess of Wands
	5 Wands	7/21-8/1	Prince of Wands	
Leo	6 Wands	8/2-11	Prince of Wands	
	7 Wands	8/11-22	King of Pentacles	Ace of Wands
	8 Pentacles	8/23-9/1	King of Pentacles	
Virgo	9 Pentacles	9/2-11	King of Pentacles	
	10 Pentacles	9/12-22	Queen of Swords	
	2 Swords	9/23-10/2	Queen of Swords	
Libra	3 Swords	10/3-12	Queen of Swords	
	4 Swords	10/13-22	Prince of Cups	Princess of Cups
	5 Cups	10/23-11/1	Prince of Cups	
Scorpio	6 Cups	11/2-12	Prince of Cups	
	7 Cups	11/13-22	King of Wands	Ace of Cups
	8 Wands	11/23-12/2	King of Wands	
Sagittarius	9 Wands	12/3-12	King of Wands	
	10 Wands	12/13-21	Queen of Pentacles	
	2 Pentacles	12/22-30	Queen of Pentacles	
Capricorn	3 Pentacles	12/31-1/9	Queen of Pentacles	
	4 Pentacles	1/10-19	Prince of Swords	Princess of Swords
	5 Swords	1/20-29	Prince of Swords	
Aquarius	6 Swords	1/30-2/8	Prince of Swords	
	7 Swords	2/9-18	King of Cups	Ace of Swords
	8 Cups	2/19-28	King of Cups	
Pisces	9 Cups	3/1-10	King of Cups	
	10 Cups	3/11-20	Queen of Wands	

Not shown in Table 14 is occult association of the tarot suits with the divine name, TETRAGRAMMATON, and the letters Yod, Heh, Vau, Heh (Wang, 1978:31-34). Wands are represented by the letter Yod; cups are associated with the letter Heh; swords are represented by the letter Vau; and pentacles reflect the second letter Heh. By this Kabalistic reading of the tarot, furthermore, wands are connected with Chokmah (Wisdom), cups are related to Binah (understanding), swords reflect the characteristics of Tiphareth (Beauty), and pentacles are pertinent to Malkuth (the Kingdom). Even more complexly, occult interpretations of the kabala divides the universe into four basic worlds: Atziluth, an archetypal reality; Briah, a world of creativity; Yetzirah, the formative reality; and Assiah, the active world or reality (see Wang, 1978:34, 1983:40). These realities reflect a hierarchy on the Tree of Life and thereby correspond to the Sephiroth and Paths, as well as to various tarot suits and cards. From this standpoint, wands represent Atziluth (archetypical reality), cups reflect Briah (the creative world), swords signify Yetzirah (formative reality), and pentacles stand for Assiah (active reality).

TABLE 14:
TAROT CORRESPONDENCES TO THE TREE OF LIFE

Part I: The Sephiroth

Sephiroth (meaning)	Corresponding Tarot Cards
1. Kether: Crown	aces
2. Binah: Wisdom	twos, kings
3. Chokmah: Understanding	threes, queens
4. Chesed: Mercy	fours
5. Geburah: Severity	fives
6. Tiphareth: Beauty	sixes, princes
7. Netzach: Victory	sevens
8. Hod: Splendor	eights
9. Yesod: Foundation	nines
10. Malkuth: Kingdom	tens, princesses

This schema suggests a spiritual journey from mundane, earthly existence through various levels, ultimately to divinity. Spiritual evolution or progression, as shown in Table 14, involves a corresponding sequence of tarot cards: from the tens to aces, and from the princesses to princes, then queens to kings (or knights). From this standpoint particular sets of tarot cards (tens, princes, aces, and so on) may be attributed significance in terms of the corresponding qualities of beauty, wisdom, understanding, and the like. Some basic knowledge of the occult kabala and corresponding tarot cards thereby enables a user to reproduce definitions and meanings of particular cards in a reasonably systematic way without depending on a mechanical dictionary of meanings. Put differently, whatever meaning is ascribed to a particular tarot card is accomplished in terms of an occult theosophy of the kabala. In this way the meaning of a specific card is fluid and interconnected with a much larger, more elaborate schema of interpretation.

Part II of Table 14 illustrates each of the twenty-two paths of the Tree of Life and corresponding tarot trumps. The left-hand column represents each path by number and the Hebrew letter associated with it, while the right-hand column lists the corresponding tarot card of the major arcana.

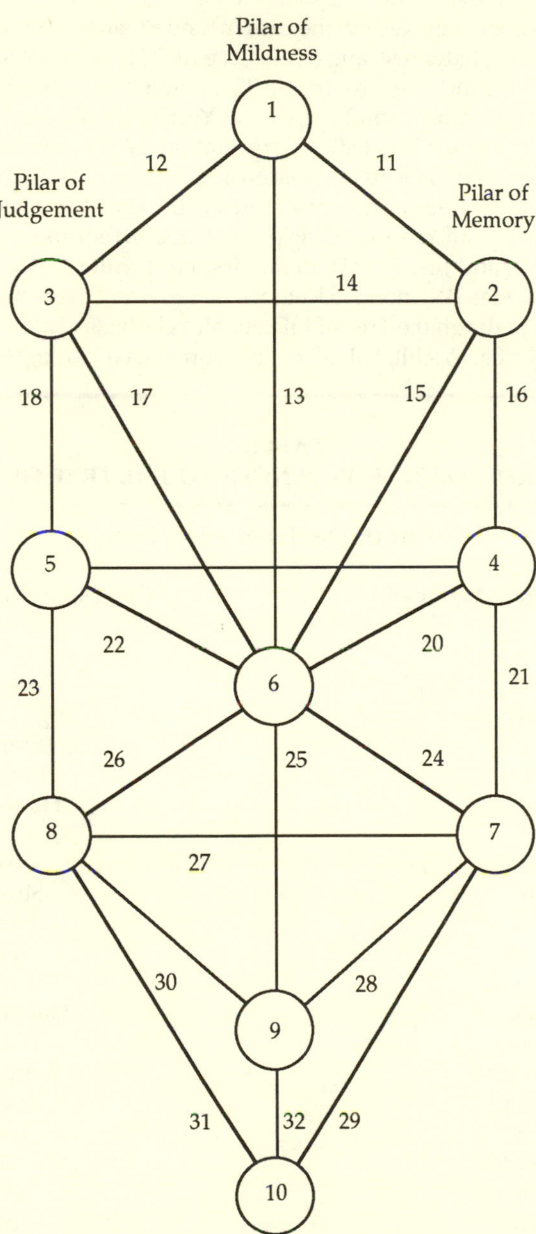

Figure 4. The Tree Of Life

In reviewing this part of Table 14 it is important to keep in mind that each of the twenty-two paths reflects a relationship between particular sephiroth, as shown in Figure 4. For example: the Magician which corresponds to the letter beth represents path 12 between Kether (the Crown) and Binah (Understanding); the Sun is associated with the letter resh and it reflects path 30 between Yesod (Foundation) and Hod (Splendor); and, the tarot trump Temperance is associated with the letter samech and it represents path 25 between Yesod (Foundation) and Tiphareth (Beauty). Like with occult kabalistic interpretations of the minor arcana, the tarot trumps also are ordered in terms of an ascension to the godhead. In this schema, the last tarot trump, the world (or universe) reflects the start of the journey to enlightenment. This journey follows ascending paths, through the other major arcana, such as Judgement (31), and Justice (22), to the first tarot trump, the Fool representing path 11 from Chokmah (Wisdom) to Kether (the Crown). Correspondences between the tarot trumps paths on the Tree of Life enable occultists to attribute meanings to the cards by way of an occult, kabalistic theosophy (see Wang, 1983).

TABLE 14:
TAROT CORRESPONDENCES TO THE TREE OF LIFE

Part II: The Twenty-two Paths

Number/Path/Letter	Corresponding Tarot Cards
1 (11). Aleph	Fool
2 (12). Beth	Magician
3 (13). Gimel	High Priestess
4 (14). Daleth	Empress
5 (15). Heh	Emperor
6 (16). Vau	Hierophant
7 (17). Zain	Lovers
8 (18). Cheth	Chariot
9 (19). Teth	Strength
10 (20). Yod	Hermit
11 (21). Kaph	Wheel
12 (22). Lamed	Justice
13 (23). Mem	Hanged Man
14 (24). Num	Death
15 (25). Samekh	Temperance
16 (26). Ayin	Devil
17 (27). Peh	Tower
18 (28). Tzaddi	Star
19 (29). Qoph	Moon
20 (30). Resh	Sun
21 (31). Shin	Judgment
22 (32). Tau	World

Take for example, the path (32) of Tau, as represented by the World (or universe). From the perspective of an occult kabalism, the universe represents a beginning; the material world joined with pathways to higher levels of spiritual development; the dualism of body and mind; and primitive consciousness. Similarly, from the perspective of an occult kabalism, the tarot's Temperance is understood as the path of Smekh (path 25) connecting Yesod (the Foundation) and Tiphareth (Beauty), signifying a physical process involving oppositional forces or energies, along the path to greater awareness of a higher spiritual self. To illustrate further, the Magician represents the path (12) of Beth from Binah (Intelligence) to Kether (the Crown). It is the path of "transparent intelligence," a channel for "one pure source of all," or a process of change and transformation (Wang, 1983:240).

In the theosophy of the Golden Dawn, the tarot and kabalistic mysticism are joined and connected with all manners of occultism. For instance, the major arcana, as Cavendish (1975:58-59) observed, is attributed by Crowley in relationship to the twenty-two paths defined by the Kabalistic tree of life, the letters of the Hebrew alphabet (a kabalistic numerology), alchemical elements, astrological planets and the zodiac, as well as animal and plant symbolisms. The Magician (Magus, Juggler), for instance, is attributed by Crowley [1976 (1944):69-72), as "...Wisdom, the Will, the Word, the Logos by whom the worlds were created." In the Crowleyian system this card corresponds to the path on the tree of life from Kether to Binah; the Hebrew letter beth, creative and dualistic; the planet Mercury, the messenger of the gods, continuous creation, the unconscious will, and cunning; the god Thoth, Hermes, Egyptian Mercury; the ape, monkey, ibis, cynocephalus; as well as the plants, vervain and palm. Lust (Strength), to illustrate further, is defined as the joy of strength exercised, vigor, the rapture of vigor, original marriage in nature, divine drunkenness, ecstasy, primitive, creative, and irrational [Crowley, 1976 (1944):91-94]. Lust corresponds to the nineteenth path of the tree of life; the Hebrew letter, teth; the zodiacal sign Leo, the kerub of fire ruled by the sun; the deities Bastet, Sekhmet; the lion, serpent, lion-serpent; and the sunflower plant.

HORIZONS OF OCCULT THEOSOPHY

The occult tarot, I have argued, is an intricate body of socially and historically constructed knowledge. Use of this knowledge by occultists may be analyzed as a sort of language. The language of tarot contains vocabulary defined by rather indeterminate dictionaries of meaning traditionally associated with the seventy-eight tarot cards, as well as the ordering of this text in terms of sequences of numbered cards and higher order court cards as minor secrets, and twenty-two sequentially ordered greater secrets. Although dictionaries of the tarot sometimes exhibit a more or less consistent range of meanings, oftentimes they do not. In other words, definitions of tarot cards ultimately are quite ambiguous and indistinct, such that any effort to tarot talk on this basis would resemble babble. Furthermore, taken alone, dictionaries specifying tarot vocabulary are insufficient for arranging these meanings into coherent processions.

Tarot vocabularies, I argued, are derived from and ordered by various grammatical devices for arranging these meanings systematically into more cohesive wholes. Various grammars for structuring the meaning of tarot talk were noted and illustrated. Some of these grammars are relatively simple, mostly mechanical devices for producing astringent phrases, such as procedures for reading the meaning of particular cards in numerical succession as representing simplicity to complexity. Other grammatical devices, such as rendering each suit with essential meaning, though relatively modest, furnish more powerful ways for deriving occult significance from the cards and arranging these messages into larger units.

Even more powerful tarot grammars are nourished by occult theosophies of lesser and greater complexity. Occult theosophies such as astrology and kabalistic mysticism dispense exceptionally multifarious and powerful ways of interpreting the significance of the tarot cards and arranging them into elaborate systems of meaning. They commonly have been viewed as complementary, leading to the development of remarkably ornate, composite occult theosophies. Traditions derived from the Hermetic Order of the Golden Dawn, for example, fashion significance out of the tarot cards by way of various combinations of alchemy, astrology, the kabala, mythology, and related occult theories of color, music, society, and nature. Some contemporary students of the tarot have expanded traditional occult theosophies of the tarot, while others devotees have developed new interpretations based on traditional religion and exoteric bodies of thought, such as psychology. The horizon of occult theosophies of the tarot thereby appears to be unlimited.

My central aim in reviewing meanings and theosophies of the occult tarot has been to illustrate some of these possibilities, rather than to endorse any particular system or develop it in a fully comprehensive fashion. While meanings and theosophies of the occult tarot are a necessary part of the application of this knowledge for particular purposes, they fail to describe adequately the procedures whereby a knowledge of the tarot actually is used. A treatment of this issue is the topic of the next chapter.

Chapter 8

Interpreting the Occult Tarot

The occult tarot, as described in Chapters Six and Seven, represents a book of esoteric knowledge, a sacred theosophical text, which ultimately may be seen as the key to all arcane wisdom. Wang (1978:8), for instance, observed that: "**The Tarot is a system of enlightenment, a system whose ultimate aim is assisting the individual in understanding his relationship to the Cosmos**" (emphasis in the original). What does this knowledge mean to contemporary occult practitioners? For what purposes is it used? How do occultists use it? Are occult claims to knowledge and related practices understandable sociologically?

Much like conventional, socially legitimated philosophical, scientific, or religious texts, the occult tarot may be used for **scholarly-like studies**. Employed in this way the tarot serves as the basis for collective and individual theosophies which are thought to reveal for students the hidden secrets of the universe: a religiophilosophical model of nature, human existence, and the cosmos. As a comprehensive body of knowledge, study of the occult tarot serves its users as a form of education, personal enlightenment, as well as the basis for individual and collective thought, action, and feeling. More specifically, the tarot is used by contemporary occultists as a religiophilosophical foundation for individual and sometimes group **meditation** and **ritual**. The occult tarot probably is best known and most visible to the general public as a source for the **divination** of past, present, and future events; or more crudely, from an occult standpoint, as a means of fortunetelling.

With the proliferation of the printed literature on the tarot over the last twenty years, many additional uses of this knowledge have been enumerated (see, for example, Wang, 1978; Geer, 1984, 1988; Denning and Phillips, 1988; Pollack, 1986; Anonymous, 1985). Contemporary practitioners advocate use of the tarot for physical and psychological healing, creative and autobiographical writing, painting, song writing, creating and enacting dance, and performing dramas. The contemporary literature on the tarot also expands and amplifies many aspects of its more traditional uses. Students, for instance, have been encouraged to maintain journal records of their experiences with tarot studies, meditations, rituals, and divination. In addition to the increasingly public rituals of the Hermetic Order of the Golden Dawn which incorporated the tarot into its elaborate ceremonial structure, contemporary occult, pagan, and especially witchcraft groups have developed formal and informal ceremonial and ritual uses for the tarot (see, for instance, Adler, 1986; Luhrmann, 1989).

In this chapter I describe, analyze, and interpret sociologically several principal uses of the tarot as it is employed by contemporary occultists. I proceed by briefly developing a theoretical perspective, based on a **sociology of knowledge**, for analyzing and interpreting occult practices. Interpretative use of the tarot by believers, I contend, may be understood sociologically from the standpoint of an **ethnomethodological** perspective as constituted by interactional procedures whereby members creatively fashion and enact what they regard as an extraordinary knowledge of reality (see Garfinkel, 1967; O'Neill, 1974). Occult practitioners of the tarot, in other words, socially accomplish a knowledge of what is envisioned by them as an uncommon reality. I briefly discuss the use of the tarot for learned contemplation and meditation. My analysis and interpretation of the tarot concentrates specifically on the occult practice of tarot divination.

I do not hold that my reading of occult knowledge is the **only** way of understanding these hermeneutic techniques, or that it exhausts the realities of practices like tarot divination. Unlike much of contemporary Religion and Science, I insist on taking occult claims to knowledge seriously as what societal members think, feel, and do. I therefore reject as overly reductionistic and sociologically uninformative those interpretations of occult practices which regard them as an illusion, delusion, absurd, or somehow as a reflection of societal problems or evil. While I find it sociologically unacceptable to summarily dismiss occult claims to knowledge, it is equally inappropriate, in my view, to endorse them at face value. Whether or not occult claims to a knowledge of reality ultimately are True, simply cannot be adjudicated sociologically.

A SOCIOLOGICAL PERSPECTIVE ON OCCULT PRACTICES

The occult tarot, viewed as a theosophical text used for pedantic study, ritual, meditation, and/or divination, is represented by practitioners claims to an **extraordinary** knowledge of reality. Its proponents, in other words, claim by way of their use of the occult tarot to acquire a knowledge and understanding of reality or realities which generally are not discernable or knowable by more ordinary means, such as by mere sensory perception, reason, or common sense. Like most occultisms, the claims to knowledge formed by the occult tarot and its use rarely have been taken seriously by religious or scientific elites within the larger context of Western culture. In spite of the widespread historical popularity of occultisms among the masses (as discussed in Chapter Two), societal elites and other interested groups increasingly have rejected and disparaged occult claims to knowledge. From the standpoint of orthodox Religion and Science, contemporary occult claims generally have been seen as unwarranted. The proponents of socially legitimated bodies of knowledge, moreover, sometimes have perceived occult claims, such as those of the tarot, to be badly misguided and even dangerous to practitioners and the larger collective condition of humanity.

The occult tarot has been viewed from the standpoint of Religion as at least inconsistent with and frequently contradictory to orthodox conceptions of a sacred reality. In rather extreme instances, the occult tarot has been identified as the "devil's picture book," and associated with evil. Similarly, occult practices derived from the tarot have been viewed as a form of "magic" linked with misguided or evil forces and persons. From the standpoint of a fundamentalist American religiosity, the occult tarot frequently has been associated with popular, mass communicated images of "cults" (as discussed in Chapter Three). Its practitioners thereby have been regarded as "brainwashed" or mindless people whose activities are controlled by evil leaders and/or forces. Insofar as the occult tarot is linked with Aliester Crowley as well as other persons and groups prototypically and symbolically identified as "demonic" by the contemporary anti-cult movement in America, associated beliefs, practices, and adherents commonly have been labeled "Satanists." From an anti-cult perspective use of the tarot thereby represents a critical social problem, the evil of which justifies all possible legal and extra-legal means of eradication.

The views of religionists and anti-cultists are immensely functional, psychologically and socially, for advocates. They serve to: distinguish symbolically between good and evil; label and identify what is regarded as socially deviant and evil, focusing attention on beliefs, practices, and people who are so defined; socially discredit evil beliefs, practices, people, and related organizations; reinforce the definers' self-images as good versus evil, as well as their images of themselves as combatants of evil; and define public opinion, rally public support against evil, as well as sustain anti-evil social movements. An evaluation of the social and psychological consequences of such an image and approach to occult practices is beyond the scope of this study. It is clear, however, that this view of occult practices contributes little to scholarly understanding. Few, if any, of the religious fundamentalists and anti-cultists claims to a knowledge of occult beliefs, practices, adherents, or groups are sustained by even a modest degree of familiarity with contemporary occultists, what they believe and practice, and how they act or organize their activities.

Occult claims to knowledge, similarly, rarely have been taken seriously by orthodox science. Instead, they have been attributed to anxiety, deficient reasoning, gullibility, and trickery (Felson and Gmelch, 1979; Weiman, 1982; Benassi et al., 1980; Hyman, 1977; Stachnik and Stachnik, 1980), alone or in combination with social deprivation, marginality, conflict, alienation, and false consciousness (Adorno, 1974; Quarentelli and Wenger, 1973; Withnow, 1978). Occult practices are dismissed without being subjected to detailed description or examination from the standpoint of would-be scientific perspectives. These views of occult practices presuppose that such claims are absurd since they do not conform to orthodox scientific principles of reality and because they cannot be verified by conventional scientific methods of study. From the standpoint of conventional science, occult claims therefore are explained away by factors and conditions attributed to practitioners and/or their social circumstances.

The ability of scientists to explain occult claims to knowledge in these ways, like the explanations of religionists and anti-cultists, necessarily depends on ignoring what occults say and do, or construing what they say and do as something entirely different from what practitioners intend. In many instances, the arguments of scientists are tautological. Certain that occultists are frauds, illogical, and/or socially deprived, orthodox scientists have little difficulty in finding these conditions and constructing their explanations accordingly (see Gurney and Tierney, 1982). Insofar as occult claims to knowledge have been perceived as contradictory to the principles of science, the resulting explanations are functional for scientists. Scientific explanations serve to: discredit potentially rival claims to knowledge, thereby protecting the privileged status of scientific claims; reinforce popular images of the occult as a social problem; enhance scientists' records of publication, and lead to further studies; stimulate a need for finding solutions; and sometimes eventuate in related forms of employment and income for scientists.

A sociological concern for the symbolic construction of what people take to be reality (Berger and Luckmann, 1966; Blumer, 1969; Schutz, 1973), particularly through social interactional processes like conversation (Cicourel, 1973; Garfinkel, 1967; Goffman, 1959, 1967, 1974, 1981; Lyman and Scott, 1975; O'Neill, 1972, 1974; Schenkein, 1978; Sudnow, 1972) provides another perspective on esoteric and occult knowledge (also see Chapter Two). From the standpoint of a sociology of knowledge, occult beliefs and practices are supported by adherents' abilities to sustain some sense of having accomplished a knowledge of reality. The sociological perspective of ethnomethodology, in particular, focuses attention on the interpretative procedures societal members employ to maintain the sense of having achieved a knowledge of reality. Whether or not occult knowledge is true (or True) is less important sociologically than the careful, systematic investigation of how occultists acquire and sustain their sense of reality. Societal members' images of reality, even when they are demonstrably "mistaken," still have very real consequences for them (Thomas, 1928).

A modest body of sociological literature on occult practices illustrates this viewpoint. In analyzing the occult literature on alchemy, Eglin (1974, 1986) found that occult knowledge was internally consistent and coherent. Contrary to some historians of science, Eglin (1986) observed, alchemy is not a mistakenly poor chemistry or psychology. Its essentially Hermetic doctrine, "as above, so below," reveals a "unique phenomenology" whereby an alchemical reality is made observable and accountable by its practitioners' methods "as a rationally defensible enterprise" (Eglin, 1986:155). Alchemy, in other words, contains distinctive ontological and epistemological vantage points which practitioners use to produce realities that are observable and accountable to them. The logic of its production, according to Eglin, is internally consistent, coherent, and real to its producers.

Similarly, through an ethnographic study of contemporary astrology, Wedow (1976) showed that divination by astrology is sustained by astrologers' use of interpretative procedures. Astrological divination, she observed, was accomplished by practitioners through a highly indexical and reflexive process. The meaning or reality of astrological divination, in other words, was established by the practitioners' ability to use the interactional context, interpretatively, to make sense out of otherwise vague, ambiguous, absurd, and meaningless statements about past, present, and future events. Jones' (1981) analysis of the conversational structure of tea leaf readings provided additional support for the contention that occult meanings are interactionally negotiated in concrete ways. Indexicality and reflexivity are not unique to occult practices. These basic properties of interactional interpretation are abundantly evident in common sense activities, doctor/patient interactions, prison convict subcultures, clinics, education, and other human settings (Leiter, 1980:Chapter V; Cicourel et al., 1974).

On the basis of an ethnographic study of contemporary English magic and witchcraft, Luhrmann (1989) evaluated extraordinary claims to knowledge. She argued that: magical beliefs, like beliefs generally, are not inherently ordered and coherent (rational), but fluid, sometimes inconsistent, and regularly open to believers' doubtfulness; esoteric beliefs are not necessarily prior to action, rather magical practices serve to reinforce and justify occult beliefs; and a magical worldview is not simply a different language for expressing reality, but instead it involves fundamentally different assumptions about and ways of seeing the world. On the basis of her participant observational experiences with magical beliefs and practices, Luhrmann theorizes that an occult worldview, much like any specialized interpretative perspective, is acquired gradually by a process she described as "interpretative drift." Through a slow, commonly unplanned, processual transformation of interpretative perspectives, she argued, magicians acquire esoteric knowledge, learn to use it to restructure their interpretative frames of reference, and through practice begin to gain mastery of this knowledge. On this basis, she (1989:313) observed, the magician experiences the world as different from before and interprets these experiences from a magical standpoint:

> [T]here are the new feelings and responses, which need to be comprehended; imaginative intensity which gives experiential content to otherwise contentless words; self-manipulation in ritual practice which makes the other world realistic; and symbolism, which dominates the magician's imagination, surrounds his practice with secretive mystery, and provides a mythology when one seems lacking. Symbolism is the most diversely slippery of these different involvements. But they all make the magic dramatic, exciting, appealing.

Much like the ethnomethodologists, Luhrmann argued that magical beliefs, experiences, and practices are interdependent. In other words, the "rationalization" and defense of magic reinforces the practitioners commitment; experiences deemed to be extraordinary give magical beliefs sense and meaning; and magic beliefs provide ways of understanding experience. Finally, she noticed, believers explanations of magic are not inherently different from orthodox theological explanations of a conventional, sacred, religious reality.

Furthermore, studies of professional cultures (Hughes, 1958; Becker, 1970; Clarke and Gerson, 1990; Crane, 1967; Freidson, 1970) have confirmed the idea that what passes for "knowledge" is controlled by and otherwise dependent on interactional processes within communities of experts. Studies of the social production of knowledge in contexts as diverse as bureaucratic organizations, psychotherapy, and art worlds to astronomy, mathematics, and physics have indicated that truth and meaning are negotiated and interpreted (Althiede and Johnson, 1980; Becker, 1982; Garfinkel et al., 1981; Knorr-Cetina, 1981; Knorr-Cetina and Mulkay, 1983; Labov and Fanshell, 1977; Latour, 1987; Latour and Woolgar, 1979; Livingston, 1982; Lynch, 1985; Pickering, 1984; Pinch, 1982a, 1982b). Scientific thinking, as the ethnomethodologists have demonstrated, is not a substitute for common-sense rationality in everyday life (Garfinkel, 1967; Leiter, 1980), and scientific theories and methods depend on common-sense interpretations (Cicourel, 1974; Johnson, 1977a). Psychosocial theorizing about socially marginal claims to knowledge aside, occult claims to knowledge, I intend to demonstrate, are not categorically inferior to other knowledge claims in any of these ways.

HERMETIC STUDY AND MEDITATION

Contemporary occultists exhibit highly varied degrees of interest in esoteric scholarship. The tarot, according to Wang (1978:15), "must be viewed as a pedagogical tool, intended to lead to a deep-rooted understanding of the human condition." Yet, for the majority of tarot devotees, serious, intensive, systematic study is at most a very occasional activity. Earnest students of the occult, however, almost always claim to own significant theosophical works on the tarot and related subjects, possess at least an elementary understanding of these basic systems of thought, and use this knowledge for practical results. Students of the tarot commonly are able to describe their appropriation of classic theosophical traditions, and they fondly display personalized innovations on standard themes. Users of the tarot not uncommonly maintain personal journals or records of their occult studies.

Most of the literature on the tarot provides some interpretation of the symbolism of the cards; although most of these discussions are concerned directly and indirectly with divination. In rare instances students of the tarot publish the results of their meditative, scholarly research in dissertation-like works without relating them to divination (see Anonymous, 1985). Formal scholarly study of the tarot exhibit distinctive strategies and procedures. Research on the tarot typically begins with some consideration of the symbolism of the pictorial cards. The next step is to provide a summary of what the symbolic images represent. Then the researcher interprets and derives some meaning for the cards which have been examined and analyzed. Finally, these meanings are interpreted further in terms of exoteric and/or esoteric thought whereby the scholar endeavors to contribute new insights to the arcane text. Tarot meanings may be interpretatively compared and contrasted with the Bible and various other texts of world religions, ancient and modern philosophies (Plato, Nietzsche, Marxism, Leninism), various theories of art and symbolism, and so on (see Anonymous, 1985).

Occultists who teach classes on the tarot generally include some discussion of related theosophical systems, but they usually concentrate on divinatory interpretations. In my experience, teachers of the tarot rarely were able to respond to questions about related theosophies comprehensively or, in most cases, with more than modest competency. Some students of the tarot have acquired extensive knowledge of occult thought. A very few people in the esoteric community were generally acknowledged as experts on the occult tarot, and some of them were in demand as public lecturers. In a very few cases, these elites in the esoteric community claimed to have written texts describing their studies, commonly in the form of mimeographed or photocopied versions; yet none of them, to the best of my knowledge, actually published their results. In spite of the relatively recent proliferation of published literature on the tarot, an interest in and ability to sustain original scholarship and disseminate it to other occultists and the general public clearly is restricted to a very few contemporary specialists.

Occult interpretations of the tarot, like magical beliefs and practices generally, tend to stress practical results. While scholarly studies are valued and widely advocated publicly, the willingness of tarot devotees to engage in concerted intellectual activities is mediated by a preoccupation with magical work and its rewards. Scholarly investigations of tarot theosophy are mitigated further by the tendency for occultists to see their claims to truth as more or less relativistic. Luhrmann (1989:283), for instance, observed that: "Magicians often argue indirectly for the value of believing in magic, rather than for the truth of magical ideas." Occultists generally do not argue that magic is superior to science as an explanation of physical reality, she elaborated; instead they "tend to explain why the normal rules of truth-testing do not apply to magic." According to Luhrmann (1989:283-303), occult claims to knowledge are "rationalized" in four basic ways, which she labeled "realist," "two worlds," "relativist," and "metaphorical."

> The realist position says that the magician's claims are of the same status as those of "science"; the two worlds position says that they are true, but cannot be evaluated by rational means; the relativist position says that it is impossible even to ask questions about their "objective" status; and the metaphorical position asserts that the claims themselves are objectively false but valid as myth.

All of these folk epistemologies, even the realist view, avoid absolutism and thereby resemble forms of relativism.

Luhrmann insightfully acknowledged that these occult epistemologies are intermingled and rather fluidly invoked by believers. Occult claims to truth, as discussed in Chapter Two, commonly are advanced on non-rationalistic and non-objectivistic, or even anti-rationalistic and anti-objectivistic grounds. Occult knowledge frequently is justified on the bases of aesthetic, ethical or moral (freedom), intuitive, emotional or psychic (non-sensory feelings), and/or spiritual judgments of truth, among other possibilities. An important consequence of these characteristically relativistic occult epistemologies is to temper an intellectual interest in highly formal occult theosophies and divert attention away from a fundamentalist preoccupation with hermetic study of particular systems as encompassing absolute truth. Occultists, in other words, generally do not share the positivistic interests of exoteric science in formal, propositional theorizing as a means to absolutely certain principles of the universe.

Use of the occult tarot for hermetic, scholarly-like studies assumes a variety of at least slightly different forms among contemporary practitioners. Among the most devoted students of the tarot it may involve efforts to become familiar with the history of Western occultism, especially as it is related to the tarot, and the principal tarot theosophies, as described in Chapter Seven. Investigations of the history and theosophy of the tarot necessarily tend to be informal and individualistic. Perhaps obviously, there are few, if any, esoteric colleges or universities which offer formal programs of study leading to mastery of the occult arts and sciences. Occult societies, typically modeled after the Golden Dawn system of initiation which involved intensive programs of study leading to hierarchical degrees, provide the nearest approximation to exoteric studies (see Wang, 1978:41ff); however, even these more formal methods of occult study and initiation generally are based on master/apprentice relationships which tend to be highly individualized. Formal classes on the tarot, such as the ones I observed in the esoteric community, mostly were devoted to divinatory practices; they rarely involved extensive study of tarot theosophies; and they also tended to be personalized by the particular relationship between a teacher and student. While I was never discouraged from casually or systematically investigating the history and theosophy of the tarot, my teachers did not encourage these interests, and I felt as if they did not consider them to be essential for divinatory practices.

In the Valley, students of the occult frequently devoted casual interest to investigating a particular theosophy of the tarot. Most teachers and readers were conversant with several classic works on the tarot, and many of them sought to combine casual study of the tarot with other occultisms, such as numerology and astrology. For most of these occult practitioners, however, theosophical inquiries were a means for conducting divinatory readings of the tarot, rather than ends in-and-of themselves. In the esoteric community, students of the tarot sometimes combined their occult studies with informal and even formal training in exoteric disciplines, especially psychology and counseling. Some of these people devoted considerable study time to detailed examinations of the tarot in terms of psychological theories and principles. Their esoteric and exoteric studies commonly involved serious efforts to work out personal systems of meaning. Their explorations of occult theosophies also were aimed at employing the tarot as a resource or tool, therapeutically, for themselves as well as clientele.

A very common form of tarot scholarship in the esoteric community was to focus specifically on interpretations of the tarot deck and particular cards mostly independently of formal theosophies. Tarot devotees regularly provided spontaneous reports of their studies of a certain card, sets of cards, such as the aces or court cards of a particular suit, or different packs. Analyses of tarot cards, according to their reports, focused on such matters as color schemes, symbolism, the representation of figures, symbols, and images, relations among symbols, colors, and personages, as well as similarities and differences between suits, oppositional cards in the deck, and tarot packs. They also exhibited a scholarly-like concern for integrating knowledge and practice of the tarot with other occult theosophies. Some of these interpreters of the tarot regularly or periodically recorded their results, and they used their findings as a topic of conversation with other readers and students. As a consequence of these studies, occultists claimed to acquire enhanced familiarity with the tarot, new insights into the significance of particular cards, sequences, and decks, as well as extraordinary senses or feelings of awe, inspiration, intuition, and power.

These highly individualistic experiences with the tarot sometimes take the form of more stylized and self-conscious **tarot meditations**. The tarot, Douglas (1972:213) argued, "display a powerful array of psychic images" which may serve as "focal points of consciousness during individual or group meditations." Occultists commonly provide theories of tarot meditation and how it works. Douglas claimed, for instance, that the tarot provides symbols which may be regarded as "psychic transmitters." These symbolic images "bring into focus the primordial images of the psyche and channel their power through into consciousness." He envisioned them as "seeds of new life" the nourishment of which "bear the fruits of fresh insights." These images are unconscious and consequently unapproachable by way of rationality; they pertain to a level between "ego" and the "inner self." Through tarot meditation "awareness of the inner realities of the whole self" are enlarged, and consciousness is greatly expanded. According to Douglas' theory, the tarot thereby provides a "language by which the inner worlds make themselves known."

In principle tarot meditations are not substantially different from many other forms of intense concentration, reflection, and contemplation. "The aim of Tarot meditation," according to Douglas (1972:214-215), "is to project oneself in the imagination into each card" thereby "exploring its imagery, getting the 'feel' of its symbolism." Through this process meaning is revealed "in terms of one's own psychic structure." Meditators commonly are instructed to: choose a quiet location free from distraction; physically and mentally relax by taking deep breaths and closing one's eyes, for example; and otherwise structure the environment, for instance by controlling light and sound. The basic aim of these preliminary activities of course is to facilitate intense but comfortably relaxed concentration. Meditations may last for a very few minutes or extend over longer periods of time, perhaps lasting several hours.

The focus of meditation may be a single tarot card or several cards arranged in some series or pattern. The major arcana and court cards commonly are used for this purpose. "After a few sessions you should be able to picture the card clearly in your mind's eye" (Douglas, 1972:215-216). The method and goal of meditation may take many slightly different forms. The meditator, for instance, may concentrate intensely on the card by simply staring at it without any preconceived observational plan. Although it is not necessary, the eventual aim of meditation may be to achieve a hypnotic trance-like state. By way of some altered state of consciousness, occultists report greatly expanded experiences of time, space, feeling, visual sensation and imagery, as well as enhanced appreciation for the tarot resulting in greater understanding of self, the worldly environment, and the cosmos.

Luhrmann (1989:319), for instance, reported using the tarot in a meditative fashion when contemplating "a complex relationship or a difficult choice." Although fully aware of the arbitrary, random order of the tarot cards, she maintained that this very feature of meditation facilitated an ability to "impose structure upon the slippery ambiguity of my particular problem," and it thereby assisted her interpretation. Furthermore, she reported being "repeatedly astonished" by the "pertinence" of the tarot cards. According to occultists, meditation on the tarot commonly results in a greatly expanded consciousness long after the immediate experiential episode. In spite of her intellectual commitment to anthropology, Luhrmann (1989:319), much like occultists in the esoteric community, reported subsequently having extraordinary experiences: "I woke early one morning to see six druids beckoning to me from the window. This was not a dream, but a hypnopompic vision." She further described this "vision" as "on the borders of sleep and awareness—not quite a dream, but not reality."

Meditation on the tarot sometimes is used by occultists deliberately for the purpose of radically transforming ordinary consciousness and projecting themselves beyond an earthly plane of existence (see Wang, 1978:39-41). The meditator may imaginatively see herself as the Queen of Wands, for instance, and seek to experience the Queen's throne, garments, crowns, symbols, consorts, personality, cosmic domain, and so on. Douglas (1972:216) suggested that the meditator "mentally clothe the figures and scenery in bright, living colours; endow them with weight and solidity." The tarot cards also may be used as "doorways" through which the meditator visually and imaginatively projects himself, becoming part of scene, and "traveling" back and forth to alternative realities. "Step in your imagination over the threshold of the card as if through an open door, and stand with the characters in their own world" (Douglas, 1972:216). By way of tarot meditation, in other words, occultists claim to have fantastic visionary and out of earthly-body experiences. "New symbols might be discovered...or the characters might move and perform various actions or even speak."

Occultists hold that practices, like meditation, are potentially dangerous. Entering into and leaving a meditative state is thought to require practice and experience. Practitioners generally are warned to exercise caution and develop their skills gradually. While steps or procedures commonly are recommended, occultists usually recognize that there are many different ways to achieve the same results. Douglas (1972:217) recommended reversing the steps to tarot meditation to avoid "psychic leakage." He insisted that: "The powers which can be invoked during the visualisation process **must be dismissed thoroughly** before you return to everyday consciousness" (original emphasis). True self knowledge commonly is viewed as requiring months and years of practice.

Although I regularly used the tarot for the purposes of scholarly-like studies and meditation, I never experienced anything which seemed to me as especially extraordinary. My study of the tarot focused on the meanings of the symbols and cards; comparing and contrasting interpretations of the tarot cards found in the published literature; and learning various theosophies. These experiences were illuminating, and I gradually became more knowledgeable about the occult tarot. I did not define these experiences as any more extraordinary, however, than my exoteric scholarship. My occult studies were no more perplexing than my effort to comprehend German sociology, French structuralism, or philosophical existentialism. Just as reading Garfinkel, Gadamer, Habermas, and Levi-Strauss sometimes resulted in flashes of insight and inspiration, so too my occult studies ocassionally opened up a line of thinking which I theretofore had not been able to acknowledge.

Similarly, I experienced my meditations on the tarot as pretty ordinary. I found it difficult and time consuming to do meditations regularly. Sometimes it was rather boring. When I was able to sustain meditations on the tarot over a regular period of time, generally with some purpose in mind, it seemed beneficial. My ability to project with the tarot never progressed beyond a fairly primitive stage. It never became a vivid visual experience. For me it was at the very best like an exceptionally fuzzy dream. Like a vague dream, I commonly found it difficult to discern particular people or events beyond a rather inarticulate awareness of them. The emotional experience of meditation on the tarot was better for me, however. I found that it tended to reduce anxiety and calm my mind. Sometimes I experienced rather intense emotions, feeling shifts and swings of mood. Even these experiences, however, did not seem especially extraordinary to me. They were not as intense or sensory stimulating as psychedelic drugs; no more or less moving than many of my religious experiences. In many respects, they more closely resembled the feelings provoked by watching a good movie, or the feelings of quiet, wonder, charm, and awe produced by nature.

TAROT DIVINATION

Tarot divination is a social interactional process whereby a reader interprets past, present and future events commonly for a querent through the medium of the cards. The querent must participate in this interaction and engage in interpretation in order to sustain a sense of having accomplished extraordinary knowledge. Even though divination by the tarot is a particular occult practice, it is a principal form of occultism, and very much like other practices, such as alchemy, astrology, numerology, and forms of magic, particularly those derived from the Hermetic-Kabbalistic tradition. It also is similar to scrying, divination by sticks and stones, hypnosis, and many forms of psychic (clairvoyant, telepathic) reading. I see this occult practice as a dramatistic performance. My attention focuses on social interactional processes whereby occult meanings are structured and applied, and certain interpretative procedures used by interactants to advance and sustain extraordinary claims to knowledge.

My description and analysis of tarot divination is based on participant observational experiences as a seeker, client, and tarot card reader. It is supported and supplemented by similar experiences which Lin shared with me, as well as informal discussions with seekers, clients, and readings in the Valley. In the course of fieldwork I collected a variety of tarot card readings, most of which were tape-recorded with the permission of the reader. The use of audio-recording equipment for this purpose is a common practice in the esoteric community and among the various professional practitioners. Querents therefore were able to collect this information unobtrusively, and without having to reveal my research interests. In all cases the querents anticipated using the audio-recordings for themselves as well

ILLUSTRATION NINETEEN: **Schwert-Kônig,** ***Zigeuner Tarot.*** Reproduced by permission of AGMüller, Neuhausen am Rheinfall, Switzerland. Copyright ©AGMüller. Further reproduction prohibited.

as permitting me to use them for this research. The querents included myself, Lin, and four assistants, Lee Bennett, Debbie Bradshaw, David Kurtz and Tina Walton. These people ranged in age from 21 to 35 years, and they reflected a variety of other social characteristics including gender. The readings described here include several illustrations from divinatory interpretations performed by Lin or myself, but the majority of these readings were conducted by various professional practitioners in the community. The readers reflected a full range of social variation of these people in the community, including age, gender, and their orientation (metaphysical, hermetic, psychic) to occultism. Information collected elsewhere and by other people support the contention that these readings are representative of divinatory activity (see Jones, 1981; Wedow, 1976; Luhrmann, 1989).

For analytic purpose fifteen audio recordings of divinatory readings of the tarot were transcribed. Insofar as it was possible, the aim was to produce a literal transcription of these materials (see Jefferson and Schenkein, 1977; Sacks, Schegloff and Jefferson, 1974; Schenkein, 1978). I employed linguistic-type procedures for analyzing these materials. Unlike the conversational analysts, however, I am not interested in the structure of conversation as such; rather I have employed some of these techniques loosely in seeking the manner in which divinatory meaning is accomplished socially. In some cases, the transcribed readings presented here have been edited for greater readability, but only when this could be done without altering fundamental meanings.

The Divinatory Context

Divination, from an occult standpoint, is an appropriate use of the tarot when it is employed with reverence and respect as a sacred tool for self-enlightenment, as in readings performed for one's self, or for helping other people develop an esoteric knowledge of themselves and their circumstances. Just as exoteric religious functionaries accept pay for their services, performing tarot divination for a fee, particularly when it is regarded as a donation, is not deemed inappropriate from an occult perspective. Divination is regarded as profane, however, when the sacred tarot is used crassly and irreverently as a mere fortune-telling instrument. Tarot divination performed for a general public as a commercial activity commonly is seen as profane, and it requires the reader to exercise skill in managing this delicate situation to avoid being defined as a fortune-teller, or worse yet as a gypsy or con artist. Divination as entertainment generally is regarded by occult insiders as disrespectful, irreverent, sacrilegious, and even blasphemous.

Divination may be performed for anyone rather than someone in particular, as illustrated by computerized readings, newspaper astrology, and telephone tarot services. Although occultists do not see such readings as necessarily invalid, they are regarded widely as inferior to face-to-face divination. Readings for anyone may be discredited because of their highly commercial, exploitative character. In reading for anyone, as will be discussed in detail, the social interactional process whereby occult meaning is fashioned, negotiated, and appropriated is bypassed. Occultists therefore see them as less valid, compelling, and legitimate, and they much prefer to read to someone rather than anyone.

In performing divination readers discriminate among different types of clients, and they understand that the kind of client influences the reading (as was briefly discussed in Chapter Five). Occultists tend to see novice outsiders as the most difficult type of client. These strangers are most likely to be encountered in public situations, at events like psychic fairs. The reader therefore generally knows nothing about the querent, making it difficult to read for someone rather than anyone. Uninitiated outsiders commonly have little knowledge about what to expect, how to conduct themselves, or how to participate in a reading. Strange clients who insist on revealing too much of themselves in a reading tend to spoil the magical character of a reading. Similarly, novice clients who refuse to participate actively in a reading are regarded by occultists as the worst type of client since they make it difficult, if not impossible, to negotiate meaning and generate a sense of satisfactory divinatory accomplishment. Unknown querents are preferable to intimate friends, however, when they have been properly socialized in divinatory practices. They know how to appropriate occult knowledge interactionally, and because their biographies are unknown to the reader, the magical character of acquiring an extraordinary knowledge thereby is enhanced.

Occultists generally report difficulty in reading the tarot in a divinatory fashion for themselves rather than for other people. When they use the tarot for themselves, it tends to be defined as "meditation" or self-study, rather than divination or portending. Divinatory self-readings require the practitioner to separate roles, as reader and as querent, and constantly switch back and forth if occult meaning is to be appropriated in a satisfactory fashion. Since readers know themselves very well, reading for self tends to diminish the experience of sharp, sudden, and highly dramatic insights and revelations.

Partly for this reason, many occultists also dislike performing divination for close and especially intimate friends. Too great a knowledge of the querent may hinder divinatory activity and otherwise spoil the magical character of a divinatory performance. This point, however, should not be overemphasized. Occultists frequently do perform divination for one another, as well as for close friends. Reading for a friend, moreover, is made easier if the person is knowledgeable about the occult and therefore knows what to expect and how to employ and understand extraordinary knowledge.

Scripting a Reading

When used for divinatory performances, occult knowledge of the tarot is structured around three interrelated components. The occult tarot provides a body of knowledge in the form of meanings historically attributed to the cards, and theosophies for arranging these meanings into cohesive wholes. As discussed in Chapter Seven, the tarot may be seen as a kind of language with a vocabulary and grammar, and in this sense it is a text. The occult significance of a divinatory reading is structured by conventions for laying out or spreading a sample of tarot cards. Used in conjunction with available information about the querent's identity, the spread provides a script for enacting a particular divinatory drama (see Jorgensen, 1984).

Arranging the tarot cards in some pattern makes the occult text available as a script for a divinatory performance. This organization of the cards, commonly referred to as a "spread," limits and links the meanings of particular cards by placing them in relationship to other cards forming a gestalt or whole. Readers generally use more or less standard spreads, although they frequently innovate on these structures. Figures 5 through 9 illustrate various ways of spreading the tarot for a divinatory performance. Most spreads structure the cards in such a way as to produce a temporal order of events. Temporal ordering may be simple or more complex. Most spreads also organize the cards such that they deal with a problem, issue, or set of basic events in the life of the querent. More complex arrangements mix temporal ordering and problems to be discovered, and they sometimes introduce additional features for the reader to interpret.

Figure 5, for instance, provides a very simple organization of the cards defining a temporal order from past to present. This spread facilitates a reading of the cards in sequence, card by card, row by row, representing a progression from the distant past to the near past to the more recent past, then to the distant present, more recent present, and so on, through the distant future. The tarot diviner anticipates discovering some problem, theme or set of issues within each time frame. Furthermore, tarot card readers commonly endeavor to connect and relate these themes with one another. In other words, past events commonly are connected interpretively as contingent features of the present which, in turn, form the thematic and temporal context for the client's future. Conducted in this way, tarot divination forms an emergent narrative story about the client's existence.

Figure 6 reflects a variation on the theme of temporal ordering. The last card to be placed up, card thirteen as shown in Figure 6, is the most important card. It provides some overall tone of the reading, and it generally is interpreted first. The remaining cards represent months of the coming year, and they are read in sequence from one through twelve in a counterclockwise fashion. In this way the spread facilitates the identification of some generally problematic issue in the querent's life, the specific features of which may be discovered on a monthly basis. The divinatory spread illustrated by Figure 6 is particularly useful for integrating the occult tarot with related astrological theosophies because of the manner in which time is ordered by months of the year and thereby related to signs of the zodiac.

The Horseshoe spread, shown in Figure 7, structures time, and it explicitly provides a problem structure. Cards one to three, in this spread, pertain to past, present, and future influences on the problem to be divined. Cards four to seven deal with aspects of the problem or issue to be discovered: a recommended course of action (four); attitudes of other people (five); obstacles (six); and a probable or final outcome (seven). Hence, unlike the divinatory spreads illustrated by Figures 5 and 6, the Horseshoe spread serves to define concrete features (past events, a course of action, other's attitudes, obstacles) of existentially problematic situations.

The Celtic Cross, as shown in Figure 8, is one of the most popular divinatory spreads used by professional readers in the Valley and elsewhere. It structures the reading by focusing on a problem or question while more implicitly than explicitly providing for temporal order. The Celtic Cross spread, partly due to its apparent complexity, contributes to the mystique of a divinatory performance. Each card in

1	2	3	4	5	6	7
8	9	10	11	12	13	14
15	16	17	18	19	20	21

Figure 5.–Past-Present-Future Spread

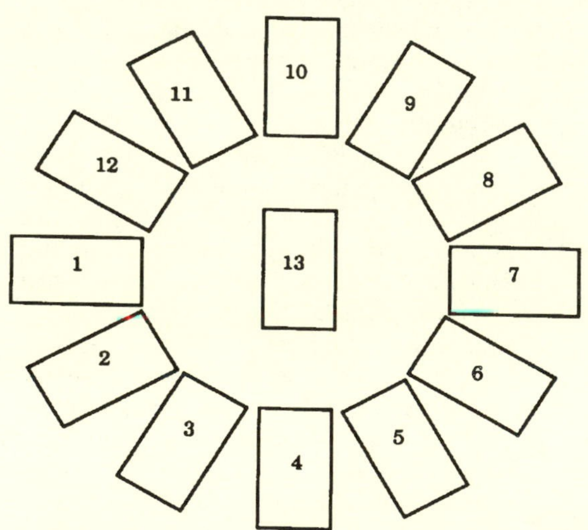

Figure 6.–Circular Spread-Forecast

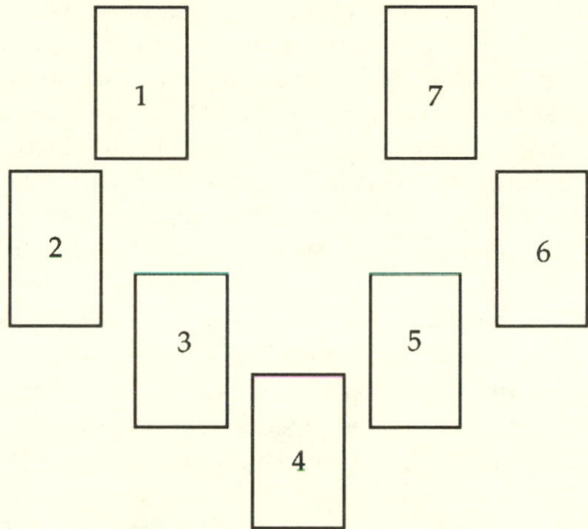

Figure 7.–Horseshoe Spread

this spread stands for a different phase or aspect of the querent's problem or the question to be addressed: the overall situation, mood, or motivation (one); source of difficulty or failure (two); the basis of the seeker's present condition (three); past events (four); the merit of the question or problem (five); immediate influences (six); the seeker's attitude toward the reading, question, or reader (seven); sources of power or energy (eight); the querent's hopes or fears about the problem (nine); and, the outcome or result (ten). Temporal ordering, it should be noted, is de-emphasized by the Celtic Cross spread in favor of a much more concerted focus on the querent's presumed problem or question. Like other divinatory spreads, it also contains an implicit theory of human action and existence. That is: People act on the basis of moods and motivations in particular situations; their actions are influenced by temporal sequences of events beyond and within their control, including their emotions and pre-dispositions to act; human existence is experienced as problematic; problematic action situations have consequential outcomes; and occult divination is useful for learning about and influencing human action, retrospectively and prospectively.

The Tree of Life spread, as depicted in Figure 9, does not structure time and it does not focus specifically on a problem or issues in the querent's life. Instead, this way of arranging the tarot cards for divinatory purposes principally deals with the seeker's life as a totality. In the Tree of Life spread the cards are read according to the following pattern: one's highest ideals (one); creative powers (two); wisdom (three); virtues (four); forces or obstacles (five); health, beauty, or altruism (six); instincts, lust, love, or arts (seven); procreation, science, crafts, design (eight); vision, psychic powers, engineering (nine); and, the querent's embodiment or earthly home (ten). Like the previous illustrative spread, the Tree of Life arrangement clearly involves a tacit theory of human existence as expressed by the features identified. The totalistic character of this tarot spread strongly encourages esoteric or spiritual readings of the tarot in relation to the querent's existence. It therefore is more likely to be used for divining self-understanding, or used in the context of a spiritually oriented cult than as a professional service for strangers for pay.

The tarot text, socially fashioned script, and querent's identity, viewed together, provide a **structure of psychosocial relevance** adaptable to almost any setting, situation, cast of characters, and occasion. This structure of relevance provides the basic resources for a divinatory performance. It also provides practitioners with implicitly acknowledged grounds for objecting to the critical contention that a divinatory reading of the tarot is so general that it might apply to anyone. Readers agree that divinatory renderings, like all signs are ambiguous and ripe with meaning. Tarot card readers, however, feel strongly that what they say is tailored to particular people on particular occasions. The referential categories of a reading may apply to anyone fitting the particular characteristics of a given class: for example, a physically attractive, college aged female of neat appearance, along with everything else implied by collective, commonsense understandings of such a type of person.

Readers argue that they perform divination for someone in particular, not anyone. A particular typification or normal form (see Sudnow, 1965; Leiter, 1980), they note, carries more or less certain expectations: Romance, marriage, sexual activity, children, career decisions, money problems are implicit in the aforementioned example. These expectations, they argue, are markedly different from other normal forms. As a human type, the college aged female differs significantly, for example, from such a type as a middle aged, professional-looking, slightly-rounding, middle-class male, along with all else which it implies. Furthermore, readers point out, the particular expectations for any given normal form differentiated and particularized further by the script provide a structure of relevances at hand in which topics like death, marriage, romance, careers, and spirituality are to be discussed in particular ways, instead of other sets of possibilities, such as birth, health, athletics, travel, child rearing, or UFO's.

When confronted with the question of whether or not tarot divination works or how it works, tarot card readers provide a variety of different answers. Some subscribe literally to occult theories; others believe in psychic senses and powers; some provide naturalistic explanations based on psychological theories; and still others see it as a metaphorical process or candidly admit that they do not know the answer. No matter how it is explained, occultists agree that divination somehow works. Lin's fieldnotes on this subject are instructive:

> Many people have asked me how the cards work. I don't know, really. I do know that its a process; a process of opening up and reaching out. When someone asks me to do a reading, I can usually assume correctly that they are involved in a situation that is confusing to them, a situation in which they appreciate advice and/or direction. There are, of course, people who are immersed in occult activities and use the Tarot (and other divinatory techniques) for routine guidance. But, on the most part, people who request an occasional reading seem to be asking for help. So how does the

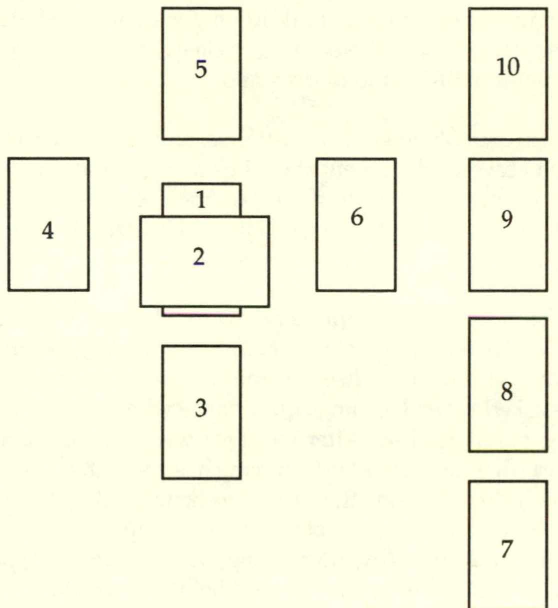

Figure 8.–Celtic Cross Spread

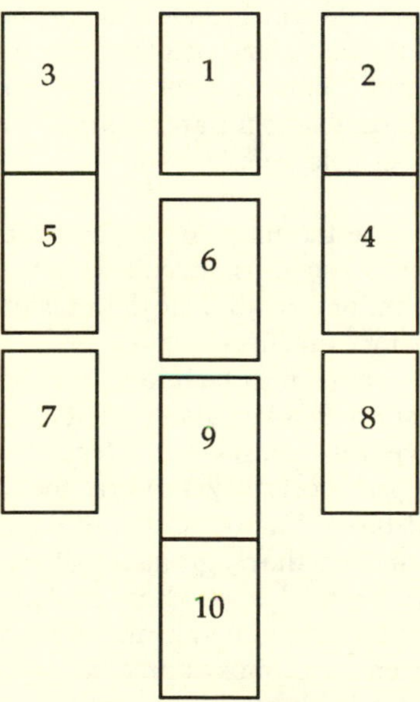

Figure 9.–Tree of Life Spread

> Tarot help? Well, for most people, just talking about a situation assists them in clarifying their thinking; if a suggestion is made, even its rejection can make the path more clear. The psychological aspects are not too difficult to understand.

Occultists also are able to supply endless examples of seemingly extraordinary events which serve to document their belief in divination. Their examples inevitably are framed as challenges to rival, exoteric explanations. In other words, what they illustrate defies ordinary explanation. Lin's fieldnotes contained the following account:

> What is difficult for me to comprehend and explain is the fact that even when a problem is not stated before the reading begins, it somehow manages to show itself in the cards. For example, last night I was asked to read for an acquaintance who stated she just wanted a "general" reading. After the cards were spread, my first statement was that she seemed to be having hassles with a romantic relationship. Indeed this was the situation she wished to discuss. I had met this woman only once before and was not aware of any details of her private life. Why, after seeing the cards, did I not speak to aspects of her job, or her physical well-being, or any number of other topics that could just as well have been on her mind? Because I saw it in the cards. Or at least I believe I did. Perhaps I was telepathically receiving signals that this relationship was foremost in her mind at that time. Maybe I made a lucky guess. But I don't think so—my use of the Tarot has been too accurate (even statistically significant) to put it on that level. The question of how the Tarot works is unanswerable to me at this time. I just know that it does work. And it does help people.

Documentary examples, such as the one provided by Lin, are pervasively employed by occultists in the Valley. Even those occultists who express doubts, exhibit skepticism, and otherwise endorse relativistic folk epistemologies, sustain a rather incorrigible belief in divinatory practices.

Uninitiated querents sometimes have and express reservations about the objective validity of divination. Readers also exhibit a concern for whether or not querents are able to discover for themselves the truth and meaning of divination. Yet, to participate in a magical worldview requires that interactants are able to at least temporarily suspend these doubts. As the divinatory process unfolds, the participants generally assume that the magic has greater and greater plausibility. In the divinatory readings of the tarot described and analyzed below, the participants exhibit little concern that indicative generalizations based on normal forms commonly fail to conform to scientific canons of predictions. In this respect, divinatory readings of the tarot are remarkably similar to commonsense reasoning, as well as psychotherapy, the use of personality inventories, and many other largely taken-for-granted interactional processes characteristic of contemporary human existence (see, for instance, Delaney and Woodyard, 1974; Jones, 1981; Leiter, 1980; Labov and Fanshell, 1977; Seperson, 1981; Stachnik and Stachnik, 1980; Truzzi, 1975).

Divinatory Discourse

In a divinatory performance of the tarot a beginning, a body of utterance sequences, and an ending are observable features. The following transcription of a tarot card reading illustrates its occult practice in the esoteric community. The reader, Nellie, is regarded as one of the best tarot diviners in the community; although she rarely interacts publicly with other members of the community. Her divinatory performances generally are conducted privately in her home. She is about sixty years of age, and one of the longest practicing tarot card readers in the Valley. The querent is a thirty-four year old female graduate student. She also reads the tarot and therefore is an unusually knowledgeable client. This reading was recorded following a lengthy conversation between these women.

Reader: Cut this way, three wishes to perform.
Client: See, I keep cutting those good cards.
Reader: I told you there's good coming around. Make three stacks with your left hand. After you make....
Client: Oh dear. I don't know whether that one wanted to come or go.
Reader: Is your husband dark-headed?
Client: That's [pointing to a card] my husband?
Reader: That's what I said. Is he dark-headed? Well, you see, that is why I'm wondering. Not knowing you, that shows a great deal of love and shows there's an awful lot of good coming up around your husband. But it also shows you've been very worried and Hierophant says, "Quit it!" And you know the cards, so there's no way I can fool you. It shows there's a deep love here.
Client: I try not to read the cards when someone's doing a reading for me.
Reader: Well, I know, but this is what it shows and there's alot of good coming up around your husband. Put them [the cards] together with your left hand, how ever you want. Because there's a good offer around. You know the two of cups is a good offer of love, or a good offer. You know that, don't you?
Client: Sounds good.
Reader: Don't get negative or I'll give you a knight. I want twelve cards, one on top of the other, and you can use your right hand if you want to. Pick them carefully. Face down. This shows that the answer to your prayers on money matters is some friend and that you should use your wisdom because some very good is coming in, cause this is what you're thinking: The Finances, the mind, the home, the love affair with the children, the help in the work. This is the first partner and the partner in money, and this is the second partner and around. This is the tenth card, or what you're aspiring to be. And this is the

hopes and the wishes. And this is the good or the bad, the twelfth card, which ever you're thinking, or how you're using your mind at this time. Now it shows here you do worry a great deal about children and shows you haven't been up to health physically, and it shows you're worried about work. And it shows the answer here to your prayers so far. But it shows you keep worrying on marriage too. You should sort of clear your head and know all marriage is good. Don't worry about anything coming up in your marriage, because you are kind of worried about it.

Client: Sometimes I think you shouldn't take people for granted.

Reader: I'm not saying to take people for granted, but take your own self to be sure and stand in the light and know that you can have it, because you do have an inferiority complex and you do cut yourself down. And this is where you're wrong. Don't do that. Cause you're very worried about those kids. You get very worried. Shows it's good, but there's a change coming around. Alot of good around those kids.

Client: They're very special and a big part of our lives.

Reader: There's alot of good news coming in to you. But it shows that there have been alot of people that sort of done you in and alot of problems around different people too. Alot of times you take people....

Client: Which house is this?

Reader: That's the hopes and the wishes. There's been alot of good around you, but there are some people that have caused some upsets and one of your friends is about to get a divorce or something.

Client: Oh yeah!

Reader: Here's the home, OK? It shows you worry too much and too much tension. Alot of good, but there are problems around in your early life. And alot of times you do...You're really quite negative, honey. You've come a long way. Your vibrations show that, so does your hand.

Client: Well you know, I was about twenty-seven before I realized how good my parents are.

Reader: Ya. But you see, when you was little, you didn't feel that there was that much love around you. See, your hand shows it and so you have to take that into consideration. And this shows it. That when you were little you didn't feel there was that much love around.

Client: My parents are not demonstrative at all. They don't give hugs and kisses and say I love you.

Reader: I know that, and this is what you missed when you was a kid. And it shows that you do constantly, alot of times, feel very insecure if your husband doesn't come in and do this. It also shows as a health sign. Your father's living, isn't he?

Client: Yes.

Reader: And it shows here that you're gonna get what you want, but quit worrying about money, quit worrying about it, because you're stopping all the good by worrying. Here is the good coming in around you. But you are very worried. I know money is a necessary part of our lives, but it does show that if you can let go of that thought, you can have it made. Because there's alot of good coming around you. And there will be a change shows here. See here. This is the everyday mind worrying's doing the strutting. See what I mean? But here you see the Tower and you're afraid it won't change quick enough. This is the line. Here's your husband. Here's the long travel that you're gonna be taking with the three of pentacles. Temperance says it will be, remember that. Don't worry about the money because there's some deep thought about money. There will be a situation where they'll be talking on money or wages, or what have you. So it will work. But you've got to take your mind off of it. Cause money's been quite an uptight part of you. Cause this is the House of Finances and you think, Geez, what are we going to do? There's good news on the money situation too, and it will come from a distance. It will be a change. Cause you know how these cards run. But you've been worried for quite some time on the money situation. But you see you didn't have to be. Justice shows up and there's gonna come in.

Client: Alright! Which house was that?

Reader: This was the eighth house, the direct finances. And it shows alot of times you worry too much. It shows it! Cause this is ruining your personality. And there's a whole lot of good changes coming up. Please take your mind off being negative and please start feeling that you are....

Client: That's my husband's card. He identifies with the Magician.

Reader: This shows that the marriage is good and that your wish is granted and there's been alot of deep thought. And it shows that he does care a great deal about you. And it shows that this marriage is good, so you have got to quit being so negative.

Client: That's his card and my card. I don't feel negative, I just feel wary.

Reader: This is as negative as you can get. Don't ever do that. Count your blessings daily, multiplied, build your dreams. Put him and the kids all around you. You have a snapshot of the family, use it. It shows you've not been up to par recently either.

Client: I'm dieting.

Reader: It shows. If you're gonna diet, be sure to use the right....

Client: I went cold turkey off of coke [the soft drink] a week ago, and I've already lost five pounds.

Reader: Was your first husband kind of tall and brown-headed? Light brown? Well, he's cut in there. Not that great a guy.

Client: No. He's very violent and nasty.

Reader: Well, it shows in your hand. I told you. This shows that you let go of all the upsets, the whole new change will be good around you, lady. So I don't know why you're worrying. You see what I'm trying to say is you're not using things the way you should. You are

> letting too many outside.... Interferences build health signs around your father. And your mother's had a great deal of upsets in her life that nobody knows about because she holds alot in.
> *Client*: Yes, she's told me about some of them.
> *Reader*: I'm gonna use that card for you. She gets what she wants and I change cards for people. And I read different ways to get all the answers. I was reading backwards for this part.

More than many divinatory readings of the tarot, Nellie's readings tend to be highly indexical of the particulars of the situation at hand. From an exoteric perspective she is vague. From an esoteric standpoint, she provides dense, arcane, spiritual readings of the tarot. It also should be noted that she incorporates palmistry into her readings, as well as directly and indirectly makes references to an astrological theosophy of the cards.

My discussion with the Nellie's client indicated that she experienced the reading as rather nonspecific; however, she did not find it to be inaccurate. My knowledge of the client confirmed Nellie's contention that the repetitively themes of worry about marriage, children, and money were accurate reflections of the situation. Nellie's concern that the client think more positively about herself also was insightful advice from my vantage point. Within the next five years the client's father began to experience serious health problems, eventually resulting in his death. His wife constantly worried about his health even before the onset of serious problems. In less than a year the client's husband found good job and they moved across the United States. The move resulted in financial stability and rather dramatic changes in their lives.

At the beginning of a reading the diviner and querent verbally and nonverbally size up one another; negotiate a fee, if any; engage in familiarizing small talk; and briefly discuss problems, issues, or questions the client may wish to have examined. This social interaction between the reader and client sets the stage, frames, and facilitates an emergent definition of the situation. It involves, furthermore, a variety of subtle and not so subtle techniques of impression management. The reader, for instance, may strategically manage props and conversation to convey the impression that s/he is an expert and about to perform something extraordinary. In dealing with novice clients, readers sometimes present elaborate performances aimed at convincing the querent of the practitioner's expertise and the magical character of the situation. Much of this front work is omitted when readers deal with more experienced clients. The initial interaction between reader and querent conveys the sense that this is a relationship between a superordinate expert and a subordinate client. What everyone knows about role specific performances of this type thereby is applied to these situations (see Jones, 1981; Bateson, 1972; Seperson, 1981). These features of divinatory readings sometimes are viewed as discrediting esoteric claims to knowledge on scientific grounds (Hyman, 1977; Jones, 1981). They differ, however, only in degree, if at all, from the fronting-out performances of exoteric experts, like physicians, attorneys, corporate executives, politicians, and college professors.

The main portion of a reading, the body of it, includes the start of divinatory activity, the divinatory reading, and some ending. At the outset of divination, the reader generally provides the client with basic information about what is likely to happen, how he or she will proceed, the tarot pack to be used, techniques for spreading the cards, as well as any special instructions the reader may have about where the client should or should not sit, how the querent should hold themselves, what to do with the cards, what to look for, and so on. Keying activity of this sort is compelling for both the reader and the client since it helps mark and accent the boundary between the ordinary and extraordinary. In short, it portends an important shift of consciousness.

Occult knowledge, as briefly discussed above with respect to tarot meditation, is characterized by a cognitive style and shift of consciousness. The "paramount" reality of everyday life, as described by Schutz (1967), is characterized by the "natural attitude." It includes wide-awake consciousness, suspension of doubt, practicality, a total self, intersubjectivity, and a sense of time as durée. Important modifications in these features of the natural attitude serve to define the cognitive style of occult thought as a "finite province of meaning."

Occult practices, as briefly discussed in Chapter Five, greatly expand wide-awake consciousness, not in the nonconscious or inattentive style of dreaming or the disorganized style of insanity, but in the sense of a heightened awareness of things unavailable to mundane consciousness. Unlike dreaming, fantasy, or insanity, esoteric practices like hypnosis, trance, clairvoyance, and so on, increase tremendously the world available to perception. Occult consciousness, in this regard, is similar to scientific consciousness of objects like the id, ego, superego, atoms, germs, black holes, anomie, or deprivation for example, most of which likewise are unavailable to ordinary consciousness.

Normal consciousness of time, self, and sociability, similarly are extended. While the natural attitude of everyday life is oriented to the past, present, and future organized in terms of a biographical self located in an intersubjective world, esoteric time alter this orientation, sometimes radically. The total self becomes a historically boundless soul, and the intersubjective world includes other souls, spirits, and entities without historical limitation. Freed from the here-and-now of everyday life, the past, present, and future of esoteric time is truly cosmic; that is, a temporal orientations in which the past may be a reference not to a historical self located in the here-and-now of an intersubjective world of other biographical selves, but a cosmic past in which the individual, along with "others," may be viewed, for example, as an extra-terrestrial ancestor of earthly human-kind.

Esoteric knowledge in practice is practical in its own way. A powerful feature of tarot divination is the assumption that querents have a problem or purpose. I once set an assistant to receive a reading with the instructions that the was not to admit or reveal any problem for the reader to discover or solve. The reading proceeded, as usual, with the diviner presenting potentially problems and situations for the querent to find meaningful, and for which the reader might offer advice and perhaps a solution. The querent rejected an denied each problem in turn, producing with each rejection an intense search by the reader for the querent's problem(s). Ultimately the reader's visible trauma was resolved when the querent, unable to resist the discovery of sense, and contrary to my instructions, relented, confirming a problem and interactively participating in the solution.

The pragmatic character of divinatory activity is intertwined with a certain suspension of doubt in the existence of occult objects and events. The uninitiated almost always approach occultism with the skepticism of the natural attitude for things beyond ordinary, everyday life experience. Participation in occult knowledge, however, requires that the plausibility of occult reality be assumed. If the querent is unable to suspend disbelief, or otherwise accept the activity as plausible, then occult knowledge is impossible. The importance of plausibility was vividly demonstrated to me, accidently, when I endeavored to discuss my research with a graduate student, Chris, by performing tarot divination for him. As I began reading the tarot, after explaining the situation, providing instructions, and spreading the cards, Chris began laughing and shortly we were both laughing uncontrollably at the common sense and scientific absurdity of what we were doing. Twice more, after regaining our composure and appropriate repair on my part, I proceeded to attribute occult significance. In both cases the results were the same, Chris erupted in almost hysterical laughter. I did not realize until later, as I reflected on and attempted to make sense of this frustrating episode, that Chris had been unable to suspend doubt and accept our activity as plausible. He thereby rendered the accomplishment of tarot divination impossible. Once this cognitive leap has been made, almost anything becomes possible.

The body of a divinatory reading of the tarot has an identifiable set of verbalizations employed by the reader and the querent, as well as related sequences of utterance chains. Practitioners of tarot divination use five basic types of utterances. These expressions reflect their superordinate location in the interaction (see Jones, 1981).

One, I call the most common type of locutions used by readers theoretical or hypothetical **statements of possible fact**. They function to provide and/or request information from the querent. I find that two fundamental statements of possible fact are used. **Questions** serve as direct inquiries or requests for information about the querent, such as "are you divorced?" or "have you started a new job recently?" **Declarations** are quizzical comments, exploratory expressions, or statement of fact intended to elicit a response from the client. Declarations may be predictions like: "You're going to feel better about this shortly"; or "In the very near future you're going to meet a new guy you really like."

Two, **interpretative statements**, as I define them, provide the flavor, significance, purpose, cause, or motive of some circumstance, object, or encounter. Interpretative statements give meaning to statements of possible fact. I find that they come in several forms, such as evaluations, proscriptions/prescriptions, advice, elaborative expressions, explanations, and attributions of esoteric significance. For example: "I hope you're planning on taking a trip because you're going to have a great time"; "I think I see a career move for you and it's going to turn out fine"; "You're into astrology with strong water sign characteristics, which basically means you'd be a person with a lot of feelings."

Three, depositions providing assignments, directions or information about esoteric techniques, messages, or programs characteristically are **instructive statements**, in my view. I find that these educational comments include: "Ok, and shuffle the cards until you feel a sense of vibration between you and the cards"; "Please don't cross your arms, it's unlucky"; or "now, concentrate on the images until they feel right."

Four, expressions formed in answer to or acknowledgement of direct or implied questions of the querent are identified here as **responsive statements**. These expressions, such as "yes," "o.k," or "yeh" oftentimes are transformed into interpretive comments.

Five, **qualifying statements**, by my analysis, modify, change, regulate, or adjust comments of possible fact or interpretations. I find that readers qualify, disclaim, or change earlier or later expressions. For example: "It's hard to gauge extremes with the cards, ya know? You can get a general idea. Ah, it looks like..."; "I don't know anything about art, but there's something or other that you are going to be doing, which somebody or other could call artistic..."; or "I think this means that you're a very spiritual, psychic person, but I'm not exactly sure what this refers to, or ...."

As subordinate parties to divinatory interaction, I observed that querents also utilize a limited range of utterances. Querents' expressions frequently are formed as responses to actual or implied statements of possible fact or interpretations of the reader. At least three types of responsive utterances by querents are observable.

One, my analysis suggests that querents commonly **confirm** (or **verify**), and **reject** (or **deny**) statements of supposed facts by readers, or they **request** more specific information, or additional illumination of a particular topic. They say, for example: "Yes, I understand"; "No, I don't feel that way at all"; "Could it involve a child"; or, "Can you tell if it's going to be a long distance or a short distance?"

Two, according to my analysis, clients sometimes provide **translations** of statements made by the reader. In other words, they rephrase, interpret, clarify, or render meaningful what the reader says. For example: "I think that already happened"; I have a mother-in-law and a mother...I don't have problems with either one"; or, "Yeh, you must be thinking of my brother, he has red hair."

Three, my analysis indicates that querents also help readers by providing **revelations** about themselves or particular situations pertinent to a reading of the tarot. In other words, they supply the specific sense and meaning to what is being said by telling something about themselves or the situation in question. To illustrate: "Is this negative relating to my more recent relationship then? Because I probably haven't been telling her the whole truth?"; "I'm dieting"; or, "Well, I have an extra tooth, and because of that I've always had lots of problems with decay and stuff like that."

Tarot card readers and their clients, I contend, use these utterances to form sequences of talk. The prototypical sequence takes the form of question/answer. A typical sequence is structured as follows. First, the reader makes a statement of possible fact formed as a question: "Are you married?" Second, the querent provides confirmation of the question: "yes, I've been married for 6 years." Third, the reader then furnishes the querent with an interpretative statement: "Well, stand by for a wee bit of friction of some sort on the home front." The body of a divinatory reading of the tarot contains endless variations of this sequence. For example, the sequence may be a statement of possible fact/interpretation, marked by silence or an implied affirmative response on the part of the querent. Or, to illustrate further, the divinatory sequence of talk may take the form: statement of possible fact; acknowledgement; interpretation; translation; interpretation; revelation; interpretation; acknowledgment, through which the significance of a particular expression of fact is negotiated actively by the reader and client. These sequences, as will be discussed below, provide a social interactional framework for sense-making activities.

The endings of divinatory readings of the tarot, unlike many forms of conversational exchange, sometimes appear to conclude abruptly. The reading may be over once the diviner finishes interpreting the spread of the cards. The card arrangement, however, tacitly prestructures and predetermines an end of sorts to the interaction. Since both parties understand that this will happen by design, it may not be necessary to negotiate any other conclusion to the interaction. Yet, many practitioners implicitly recognize that social interaction endings require more gradual closure so that interactants may actively participate in it and bring things to an end. Readers, for instance, usually permit and frequently request that querents ask concluding questions. To avoid drawn out endings, many readers will suggest that the client ask "one more" question before leaving.

Negotiating Meanings

Discovering the occult meanings of a divinatory performance is structured through social interaction. Tarot divination, however, is not fastidiously automated or mechanical. The occult meanings of divination are skillfully and artfully accomplished by interactants in concrete situations. Divinatory performances, as discussed in Chapter 5, involve a substantial shift in consciousness so that all parties are prepared to appropriate occult knowledge, and a sense of having accomplished an extraordinary knowledge of reality (see Jorgensen, 1984, Wedow, 1976). This process is not just a con-job (Hyman, 1977), or even simply a sometimes sincere effort to convince the client of the esoteric importance of readers' statements (Jones, 1981). A truly satisfactory divinatory reading, one that **feels good** to the reader and querent, requires them to negotiate actively meaning and discover the sense of what otherwise is absurd. Occult "truth," in this sense, is as much affective as it is cognitive. It, in other words, depends on feeling as well as thinking. This notion of truth conflicts, of course, with the idealized standards of science and its epistemologies; but in actual practice science also depends on values and feelings (see Johnson, 1977a).

In occult practice sense making plays off the relationship between more or less general and more or less particular statements. This relationship is part of what ethnomethodologists (see Garfinkel, 1967; Mehan and Wood, 1975; Leiter, 1983) call "indexicality" and "reflexivity." There are at least two ways of conceptualizing the general/particular relationship as it appears in divinatory discourse (as illustrated by the conversational sequences presented above). One, the reader may suggest a general for which the querent is expected to supply the particular. Two, the client may provide the particular for the reader to relate to some more general state of affairs. Generality and particularity are extremely relative or contingent conditions of social life. A particular of one moment may become a general of a later moment, and then be transformed into a particular and once again connected to some general matter, and so on, as well as the reverse.

A distinctive feature of divinatory readings of the tarot is that the parties assume, unless otherwise noted, that the querent will be able to supply the particular to which the reader's general statements of possible fact refer. The general statements of possible fact, for a variety of possible reasons, may not be negotiated in the course of a reading. It commonly is assumed by both parties without further remark that the client will at some time and in some way uncover the sense of things. Much the same assumption is made in psychotherapy (see Seperson, 1981).

The social interactionally constructed and negotiated character of tarot divination is evident in the following simple examples.

> *Reader*: In your future, there is one of two things; either you have a younger sister or a daughter. I don't know which. Do you have a younger sister?
> *Querent*: [shakes head no] I do have a daughter.
> *Reader*: Does she have blond hair or dark [hair]?
> *Querent*: Yeh, one of them does.
> *Reader*: Yeh, I see her in your future.
> *Querent*: The one with blonde hair?
> *Reader*: Yeh, ah, she seems to be a really happy sort of person.
> *Querent*: Yeh.
> *Reader*: Ah, she, it seems that when she gets older she'll be the type that can kinda charm people into doing things she wants them to. Ya know, kinda flirt with them and that sort of thing. But I see her more in your future than she is at present and she doesn't seem to have as much bearing or as much influence at present as she will have in the future.
> *Querent*: Can you tell what's going to happen with her in relation to me in the future?
> *Reader*: Looks like there is goin' [to] be a more, ah, it's like a closer feeling. But I don't know if it's a closer physical or a closer, ah, ya know, emotionally.

In this illustration, the reader's proposition of possible fact refers to a vague "daughter" or "sister." A particular "daughter," one with blond hair, then is located and confirmed by the querent. The ability of the querent to confirm the reader's declaration about the particular indicates that meaning is being appropriated by both parties. Thereafter meaning flows as the reader and client continue making sense in a particular fashion. In other words, once the initially ambiguous daughter with blond hair has been identified, the reader and querent act as if this is what they have been taking about all along. The querent confirms the statement that she is a "happy sort of person." The querent's request for additional information about the future strongly suggests that what the reader is saying is not absurd but meaningful.

The next example of tarot divination displays a similar process of making sense and negotiating reality.

> *Reader*: Getting into the present—Do you have any friend that lives either in the military or police or still is ah...
> *Querent*: I have a close friend that was at one time in the military, yeh.
> *Reader*: Look, it looks like he may be having some problems at present or something.
> *Querent*: Can you tell what kind of a problem?
> *Reader*: Possibly with a—looks like with a female who's older than he is. May be kinda dragging him down or ah not letting him; he may not think he's being held down but it seems like he's not really doing as much as he could be doing because of the [untranscribable].
> *Querent*: Is there any advice that I could give him?
> *Reader*: Ah, you might tell him that not really to worry as far as being afraid of losing a friend by what actions he might take, like losing that person or something, because if she or any other people he happens to know, don't ya know, want to keep holding him down, and restricting him, he's better off to probably find new friends. 'Cause it looks like he could be going a lot more and enjoying himself a lot more if he wasn't as, as tied down and restricted and this sort of thing.

Again, the reader and querent interactionally negotiate meaning by way of the movement between general and particular expressions. The particular meaning of a general statement (about some friend) was ambiguous from the standpoint of an outsider observer. Yet, this is in no discernable way disturbing to these divinatory participants. My participation as a querent and discussions with other querents strongly suggests that these parties are largely unaware of this feature once the plausibility of divinatory knowledge has been assumed. In order words, they assume that the activity is plausible and look for opportunities to make sense. Even if a particular expression becomes a source of trouble, fails somehow to make sense, both parties assume the meaning of it is discoverable, not that the process is defective (see Wedow, 1976; also see Garfinkel, 1967; Leiter, 1980).

Sense making in divinatory readings of the tarot closely resemble what Garfinkel (1967), following Mannheim (1952) and Schutz (1967), called the "documentary method of interpretation." In this view, societal members treat appearances as the document of some presupposed, underlying pattern or state of affairs. The pattern both is derived from and refers to the documentary evidence. In this way document and pattern are mutually elaborative. By way of the documentary method of interpretation, societal members attribute facticity to the social world which they have created, and in this way they also sustain their creations. Put still differently, occultists create extraordinary realities, and by way of occult practices make reality accountable to their practices.

On this basis, I propose that a rather crude set of instructions which cover divinatory activities may be outlined. Written as directions for a reader, tarot divination might be described as follows. First, make a statement of possible fact, X1. Second, wait for the client's reaction. If the querent confirms X1, then provide an interpretation of it, or elaborate on it somehow. If the querent does not confirm X1, find other grounds for making sense of it. Third, if the querent confirms X1, then continue to offer possible facts (X2, X3, X4, and so on), linking these statements when possible. If the querent fails to confirm X1 and you cannot make sense of it immediately, continue anyway looking for further grounds in later statements of possible fact that might reveal the meaning of X1. Similar directions might be written for a querent. First, listen to the reader's statement, X1. Second, search your biographical experience and the social context for its subjective meaning. Third, respond to the reader. If the meaning of X1 is uncovered, signal the reader to continue; that is, confirm the hit by an affirmative response, provide a revelation, and so on, or ask for further information that might clarify X1. If the sense of X1 is not discovered, refute it and drop the matter, search for more information about it, or redirect the matter. Clearly, even more intricate instructions might be constructed for tarot divination or other kinds of interaction, like psychotherapy.

DECIPHERING OCCULT CLAIMS TO KNOWLEDGE

My view of the occult tarot and its uses stands opposed to widespread public, religious, and scientific images which see occult knowledge and practices as somehow illegitimate and reducible to defective reasoning, people, or social organizations. The occult tarot is not unlike many other bodies of sociohistorically created knowledge which have been subjected to constant interpretation and serve as the basis for certain human practices. Unlike ordinary, commonsense knowledge, the occult tarot represents extraordinary knowledge claims. My aim in this chapter has been to describe some of the ways in which contemporary occultists use the occult tarot, and to analyze and interpret its use for divinatory purposes.

Tarot divination was viewed interpretatively as a dramatic performance by a reader for a querent. The general structure and context of this interactional situation is understandable sociologically. It consists of a script, structures of relevance, and discourse. Through complex sequences of interaction, parties to tarot divination generate a set of predictions about the past, present, and future of the querent. Expressions of possible fact may remain as discrete observations. Yet, participants commonly come to see them as connected and interrelated in a meaningful whole or totality. This happens in several ways.

In the course of a reading, the client and/or the reader may explicitly make connections among the many sequences of conversation. The temporality implicit or explicit in a reading and the stream of symbolic images provided by the tarot cards provide grounds for envisioning continuity and unity. The assumption that clients have problems recommends that the reader's advice should be interpreted as connected to some focus or foci. The assumption of plausibility indicates that advice will be meaningful and interrelated, even if it does not seem to be at the outset. Social actors constantly employ their social biographies and social contexts reflexively to seek meaning, even in the face of apparent absurdity.

My analysis and interpretation supports the contention that the meaning and sense of occult practices like tarot divination are produced and sustained by societal members through a complex but otherwise ordinary process of social interactional negotiation. This documentary method of interpretation also applies to common sense activity, psychotherapy, and many other aspects of human existence, such as science. Because of the "magical" character of **social interaction**, serious occultists have little need for self-conscious trickery. If they perpetrate deceptions, these deceits are part of recognizable strategies of impression management, and thereby routine features of human interaction. Clients and readers may exhibit gullibility and engage in "deficient" reasoning. Yet, these are not discriminating properties of occult practices. The supposed defects of tarot divination are pervasive features of face-to-face interaction. Occultists and common sense actors inappropriately use causal, probabilistic, and correlational thinking. But, truth and meaning are negotiated by these folks in spite of these defects. Just as science necessarily depends on common sense and is not substitutable for it, so too it seems unlikely that occultists would find scientific thinking or ritual to be a satisfactory substitute for tarot divination. If nothing else, occult practices are affectively satisfying, while scientific practices apparently are not.

Does tarot divination work? Yes, of course, it works or people would not do it. Is it possible to foretell future events by way of the tarot? I do not know. Probably not in any kind of a scientifically observable way, if by "foretell" one means objectively and fully to envision events which have not yet happened. Although it has not happened to me very often, I have experienced occult demonstrations by way of the tarot and otherwise which I cannot explain or interpret adequately from a sociological or otherwise scientific standpoint. Does this mean that magic works? Once again, I do not know. I do know, as my occult friends argue, that the world is most wondrous; more fantastic than our present ability to account for it. Were it not, at the very least many of us would be very bored.

Chapter 9

Esoteric Culture and a Postmodern World

I have described, analyzed, and interpreted esoteric culture, the cultic milieu, and the occult tarot sociologically. From the standpoint of a sociology of knowledge, esoteric culture and occult knowledge of the tarot were defined and located within the context of sociohistorical processes characteristic of larger changes and movements within Western culture. Employing a methodology of participant observation I focused specifically on a contemporary esoteric scene in the form of a cultic milieu and community of practitioners and groups in a large southwestern American urban center. The Valley setting, it was argued, is much like other large cities in the United States today.

The esoteric scene and cultic milieu in the Valley were described in terms of members' beliefs and practices, as well as the manner in which their activities were organized socially through networks and groups. The geographically dispersed collection of occultists in the Valley envisioned themselves as a "community" of like-minded practitioners of arcane wisdom. Their activities were organized socially through overlapping relationships of practitioners and cultic groups constituting factions with somewhat different perspectives on esotericism. In the Valley some contemporary adherents see their esoteric beliefs and practices as a form of scholarly enlightenment and they commonly emphasize metaphysical healing; other believers stress the science-like quality of psychic research and practices; and still other contemporary participants in the esoteric scene see themselves as essentially religious or spiritual. Community-wide psychic fairs provide members with a basis for collective consciousness and solidarity.

Members of the esoteric community in the Valley employed an occult knowledge of the tarot for the purpose of meaningfully making existential sense of the everyday life world. The tarot they use is a product of the sociohistorical production of this pack of seventy-eight cards as an occult text and related theosophies. The occult tarot was viewed interpretatively as a text which is employed like a language for scholarly study, meditation, and discerning past, present, and future events.

Esoteric community members' sense-making activities commonly included occult practices like tarot divination whereby they accomplished an extraordinary knowledge of reality. Members of the community reflexively make these practices work for them. Whether or not occult practices are seen as somehow objectively real, they manifest a coherence and utility in the experiences and practices of esoteric community members.

In this chapter I provide a summary of my research findings and I draw conclusions about their relevance for human life in a contemporary world. What, I ask, is the contemporary significance of esoteric culture, the cultic milieu, and occult knowledge and practices as illustrated by the tarot? Is esotericism anything more than a relic of the premodern epoch? If so, what is the role of esoteric culture in a modern or postmodern context? What are the implications of the cultic milieu for its participants and some larger organization of human existence? How do occult knowledge and related practices serve contemporary adherents?

I proceed by briefly reflecting on the strengths and limitations of the methodology of participant observation I employed to study esoteric culture, the cultic milieu, and the occult tarot. What claims to sociological knowledge and understanding does this methodology support? Are these strategies and methods sufficient for sustaining the reported findings? What is the status of these findings? What issues remain for further study? How might these unanswered issues be addressed?

I then discuss the notion of esoteric culture and its implications for contemporary American culture. What is the status of esotericism and occultism in relationship to the historical production of modern culture? Why and how have these forms of premodernism persisted in the sociocultural context of modernism? Are the cultic milieu, esoteric community, and networks of practitioners and groups somehow a reflection of esoteric culture and knowledge? Finally, I consider some of the implications of esoteric culture for the future of believers in the occult, their practices, organizations, and collective existence, as well as the larger exoteric culture in which they are located. Is esoteric culture, I wonder, capable of sustaining human existence in some future, postmodern world? Is esoteric culture destined to remain socially and culturally marginal? Or is it capable of exerting some larger influence over contemporary sociocultural existence?

REFLECTIONS ON METHODOLOGY

Based on a methodology of participant observation I reported on a sociology of esoteric culture, the cultic milieu, and the occult tarot in the United States today. Beginning in 1975 I participated with and observed Americans who subscribed to esoteric beliefs, engaged in occult practices, and organized their activities by way of overlapping networks of interaction, relationship, and small cultic groups. During the next three years I became deeply involved with a geographically dispersed collection of American urbanites composing a cultic milieu in the Valley. I initially was defined by members as a "seeker" of esoteric enlightenment in what they experienced as an "esoteric community" within the Valley's cultic milieu. As I participated more intensively and extensively in the esoteric community and received tarot card readings from members, they came to see me as a "client" of people who were defined as "professional" practitioners.

I subsequently embarked on serious, intensive, participational study of the occult tarot and its divinatory use. Becoming a "student" of two prominent tarot card readers resulted in the community's recognition of me as a serious devotee of occult knowledge, my involvement in local psychic fairs as a tarot diviner, and eventually my identification by community members as a professional practitioner. My participant observation was facilitated and supported by a fellow researcher and companion, Lin, who also became a professional practitioner of tarot divination in the Valley's esoteric community. In the course of our inquiry, we opportunistically collected artifacts, printed communications, published literature on esotericism, and audio tape-recorded divinatory readings of the tarot. We also engaged in casual, informal conversations, and conducted more formally structured interviews to supplement our participant observational experiences and direct observations. These materials enabled me to describe the insiders' world of meaning, practice, and interaction.

Although I **passed** as a fully participating member of the esoteric community in the Valley, I experienced an occult identity as personally conflictual, and I sustained my self-identity as a sociologist rather than as an occultist. My inability fully to internalize an occult knowledge of reality as personally meaningful limited direct access to the subjective significance of the most intimate aspects of occultists' experiences. Since I did not **verstehen** intrapsychic occult experience as more than a curious possibility, I was unable to report, except weakly, on this extremely important, affective dimension of contemporary esotericism. My experiences of extraordinary reality, in other words, were less than existentially genuine, and many of them were vicarious and, thereby, indirect. Consequently, I generally found it difficult to frame and ask insiders meaningful questions which were appropriate for revealing these experiences; and I regularly neglected to record potentially important information about members' intimately subjective experiences of occultism. These limitations suggest an important area of future study, and they reveal a certain threshold, perhaps the **abyss** between exotericism and esotericism. I am uncertain about the possibilities of apprehending and sociologically interpreting the most profound, intrapsychic depths of an emotive experience of the esoteric and occult from the standpoint of exoteric, ethnographic strategies and methods. Clearly this area of inquiry merits further scholarly attention.

My participant observational research in the esoteric community was not guided by any effort systematically to examine specific hypotheses. While I certainly held preconceptions about what to observe and how to participate, I self-consciously endeavored to remain intellectually flexible and open to my immediate research experiences and direct observation of the insiders' world of meaning and interaction. My initial naivete about American esotericism greatly limited an adroitness in moving directly and efficiently toward observing matters which probably would have been obvious to a more knowledgeable researcher; yet my inexperience also facilitated proficiency with discerning and observing matters which otherwise might have been largely taken for granted, deemed unproblematic, and neglected. I thereby experienced the members' world of meaning and action with a certain sense of discovery, uncovering issues which I defined as problems for further study, analysis, and interpretation. Although participant observation provides an unequaled methodology for generating novel insights, its utility is not limited to preliminary, pre-scientific stages of inquiry.

Throughout my fieldwork I constantly encountered issues of personal, practical, and sociological interest, defining, analyzing, and interpreting them repeatedly on the basis of previous information and tentative, preliminary conclusions. My definition of study problems, and their analysis and interpretation accelerated toward the end of my fieldwork as I more systematically reviewed relevant scholarly literatures and endeavored to write up certain findings for presentation to professional audiences. As I became more distanced from the experiences of fieldwork and labored to reconcile my discoveries with seemingly pertinent scholarly contentions, it became less difficult for me to locate ethnographic products within a sociological framework, and to engage in the processes of analysis and interpretation. Over the last fifteen years I have endeavored to analyze and interpret my fieldwork materials further by way of scholarly literature and information collected in other regions of the country. Inevitably, analysis and interpretation of ethnographic materials results in a certain objectification of the members' world and, thereby, a certain distortion of the lived experience of everyday life. Societal members also objectify and reify the world of daily experience, sometimes in ways informed by sociology and other intellectual traditions. Insofar as the interests of social actors and scholars differ, the manner in which our objectifications of it construct and reconstruct reality thereby also differ. Scholarly interpretation is not the same as everyday life or it would not be scholarship. Whatever the value of scholarly sense making, this is not to say that it is superior to the human realities that it seeks to understand.

My participant observation in the esoteric community was a largely unobtrusive strategy for directly experiencing and observing the insiders' meanings and interactions as they were constituted and enacted within an ordinary, natural, everyday life social world. My findings, consequently, are reflections of what community members routinely feel, think, say, and do. Although largely unintentional, the process whereby I became a seeker, client, student, and professional tarot card reader within the community enabled me to experience and observe the members' world from different vantage points. Lin's experiences and observations provided additional participant-membership perspectives on the esoteric community. Our transition from outsiders to insiders constituted an entirely ordinary process whereby other Americans become involved in the cultic milieu and esoteric community. Our findings describe occult meanings and interactions, even if they do not exhaust them.

Our experiences, like those of any other particular person, clearly were "subjectively" unique, as well as socially and temporally bound in concrete ways; but there is little reason to think that what we experienced and observed was atypical, uncommon, or radically different from what someone else might have experienced and observed in similar situations. Conclusions about the ontological status of these findings depend in part on different scholarly evaluations of the extent to which human experiences, cultures, and collectivities are or are not shared by members. Some human experiences, as briefly noted above, are embedded within profoundly intrapersonal processes. While I am willing to acknowledge that people's experiences are somewhat different, I also am convinced that human beings generally interpret their experiences in terms of sociocultural bodies of knowledge and frameworks as essentially similar and intersubjectively shareable. My findings, moreover, clearly were influenced by interpretative judgments grounded in contemporary sociological thinking about what was significant, appropriate procedures for analysis, as well as the ways in which I rendered these materials sociologically problematic and presented them. They, consequently, unavoidably objectify and reify the members' social world.

What, then, may be claimed on the basis of my findings? They are not, on the one hand, somehow objective, timelessly realistic representations of some abstractly detached anybody. There is no single, unified, purely objective, externally real, ahistorical American occultism. Sociological observations always are somebody's interpretations in concrete situations at particular moments in time and never nobody's timeless, nonsituational interpretations. My findings, on the other hand, are not completely subjective, impressionistic, unrepeatedable and unpatterned fictions of some absolutely idiosyncratic somebody. Social realities are intersubjectively available and observable as what societal members feel, say, and do. The members of society reproduce and reconstruct culture socially, even though they do so in existentially meaningful and creative ways through interaction with one another.

The truth value of my findings is dependent on the judgments and procedures whereby I experienced, observed, described, analyzed, interpreted, and presented the always emergent and somewhat ambiguous members' world of meaning and interaction. These findings and their truth value also are dependent on the reader's experiences and evaluation of my methods and findings. In displaying my methods in relationship to what they produced, I have endeavored to be "reflexively accountable" for what I claim is true (see Johnson and Altheide, 1990a). Different, truthful interpretations of the esoteric scene and community in the Valley clearly are possible. Some of my descriptions and interpretations are specific to esotericism and occultism in the Valley between 1976 and 1978. Although all sociological interpretations are historically dependent on concrete social situations and settings, my observations and other studies of different American settings discussed here suggest that many of these findings have considerable generalizability. The ways in which my contentions are similar to and different from other observations of contemporary American occultism make a worthy topic of further study. The similarities and differences between Americans and other practitioners of the occult in contemporary societies also is a largely neglected research topic.

ESOTERIC CULTURE AND MODERNIZATION

The scholarly literature on the apparent American revival of esotericism and occultism of the late 1960's and the 1970's commonly treated these events as faddish and collective behavioral in character. This literature, furthermore, generally has failed to locate esotericism within larger social, cultural, and historical contexts. It commonly was assumed that popular interest in esotericism and occultism bloomed almost overnight and without the support of previous American practitioners, groups, networks, or subcultures. As late as 1980 sociologists like Stark and Bainbridge still were arguing that American occultism was not supported by groups, networks, or organizations.

An emergent body of scholarly research on the sociocultural history of esotericism in Western societies and particular American groups and movements has contributed to a much more balanced appreciation for the significance of esoteric culture. The mass, popular cultural aspects of esotericism is itself part of much larger sociohistorical processes. These aspects reflect a level of participation in which esotericism sometimes is largely a matter of popular entertainment, yet this very popularity supports and reinforces multiple layers of more serious, devoted participation in the esoteric and occult. They also reflect the very conditions of the larger contemporary culture and organization of society in which esoteric culture exists. Even so, current scholarly understandings of esoteric culture have not yet provided a sharp picture or story line of this social scene.

The esoteric community in the Valley was described, analyzed, and interpreted from the perspective of a sociology of culture and knowledge. It thereby was treated as a product of societal members' efforts to recreate a humanly meaningful world. Like Religion and Science, esotericism mediates existential anxiety, and it creates an orderly, trustworthy, dependable, accessible world. These human products were located within the contexts of social, cultural, and historical processes whereby esoteric culture and knowledge increasingly have been constituted as a socially marginal feature of Western culture. Although esoteric culture appears to have had little influence on economic, political, conventionally scientific, or traditionally religious American cultures and institutions, historically it has influenced artistic worlds and movements in ways largely unrecognized by social scientists.

Occult knowledge in particular was a product of the very cultural renaissance which contained the seeds of modernism (Tiryakian, 1973, 1974; Yates, 1964). Drawing on a massive reservoir of meanings borrowed from previous civilizations, occultism provided a more or less distinctive constellation of culturally available, premodern options for achieving and enacting knowledge, meaning, and truth. Whether it was manifest as Religion or Science, the thought categories of modernism identified the cosmos and nature as discrete realities, leaving human existence in an ambiguous relationship to one, the other, or both of them. Modernism complicated and blurred the distinction between the sacred and profane. It discriminated radically between sacred and secular, object and subject, public and private, collectivism and individualism, rationalism and irrationalism, the visible and invisible, material and nonmaterial, senses and feelings, as well as other thought categories. Modernism thereby substantially destroyed manifold premodern unities and orders of thought which esotericism and occultism aimed to preserve and use.

ILLUSTRATION TWENTY: Empress, Justice, Tens of Wands, Cups, *Salvador Dali's Tarot*. Reproduced by permission of Naipes y Especialidades Garficas, S.A., Barelona, Spain. Copyright © Naipes y Especialidades Garficas, S.A.. Further reproduction prohibited.

The Marginality of Esoteric Culture

Modernization is the historical process whereby the exoteric culture of Western societies was created and established its dominance (see Giddens, 1990). It thereby provides the sociocultural context for sociologically interpreting and understanding the marginality of esoteric culture and occultism (see Douglas 1966, 1970, 1973; Douglas and Wildavsky, 1982). Modernism, especially its emphasis on rationality, created and shaped the thought categories of a modern, exoteric culture (see Douglas, 1986). The rationalistic disenchantment of cultural realities, as Weber (1952; 1956; 1958) and Berger (1967) have argued, is inherent in Old Testament traditions which provided the foundation for Western religion. Yahweh is radically transcendent, ethically demanding, and he acts historically (Berger, 1967: Chapter Five). The transmission of these thought categories through early Christianity, especially in its eventual Catholic form, partly arrested the propensity for rationalization. Esotericism and occultism, particularly Gnosticism and Kabbalism along with magics and astrologies, thereby co-existed with and partly were transmitted by exoteric religious cultures for a considerable period of time.

Although Western occultism was a product of the Renaissance, its sociocultural prominence was short-lived. The Protestant Reformation and the Counter-Reformation constituted serious challenges to magics and occultism. Early Protestantism generally advanced the cause of rationality, while admitting multiple exceptions to it, challenging Catholicism to respond in kind (see Becker, 1991). Magics and occultism increasingly were defined and labeled socially as heresy from the standpoint of tradition Western Religion. The Enlightenment accelerated the rationalization of Protestantism, partly by creating the rival sciences of nature which eventually encompassed human domains (see Merton, 1936, 1938). The emergence of a rationalistic cultural paradigm was socially supported, reinforced, and reflected in the very structure of modern societies as the basis for religious, educational, political, legal, scientific, and economic institutions. These institutions provided their human representatives with massive social power for defining and treating rival claims to knowledge.

Through modernization larger and larger portions of what was defined as reality were claimed by rational culture and its institutions. Rival claims to knowledge, consequently, were rejected, purged and treated as esoteric and occult. Claims which survived were excluded from the center of sociocultural existence and, thereby, encapsulated and relegated to the **periphery** of modern life. For bodies of knowledge so defined this meant that all subsequent challenges to modernism necessarily would be advanced from a **subordinate** location on the sociocultural margins against the sociocultural center. The ability of esotericism and occultism to compete successfully with modernism thereby was severely limited and constrained. Its claims to knowledge were delegitimated and sometimes treated as deviant and even criminal; its practitioners and their organizations were forced to adjust and accommodate to an alien cultural context; it no longer enjoyed social prestige or power; and it appeared to be incoherent in a modern context.

The occult metaphor of reality, "as above so below" was forced to compete, for example, in terms of a dominate sociocultural image of reality as segregated by distinctive domains into the supernatural, natural, social, psychological, and so on. From a modernist standpoint, occult claims to knowledge had to be of the character of religion or science, not both. If they were advanced as scientific, then occult claims had to be judged by the appropriate canons as empirical and rational to be true. Similarly, if they were advanced as religious, then occult claims had to be evaluated on the basis of orthodox religious ontologies and epistemologies.

From a modernist standpoint the occult claim to be both science and religion simply is conceptually illegitimate and, thereby, it is incomprehensible. It consequently is understandable that occult claims to knowledge would be advanced or perceived to be advanced as forms of a science or a religion. Nor is it surprising that occult claims to knowledge and truth would be regarded from the standpoint of modernist ontologies and epistemologies as bad science and bad religion. In spite of the inability of occultism to rally widespread public support within a sociocultural context dominated by modernism, it also is understandable that from an occult standpoint the claims of Religion and Science are seen as incomplete and thereby deficient. The occult is a language game which ultimately is completely different from the language games of Religion and Science; however, the occult generally is forced to compete in terms of the rules and moves defined by the games of Religion and Science. The social consequences of this situation are that occult moves are seen as illegitimate in the games of Religion and Science, and it is only with great difficulty that occultism is constituted as a coherent game in its own right. Even insiders to esoteric culture find it difficult to remove themselves sufficiently from the influence of exoteric culture to compose and enact occultism as a distinctive game in its own right.

The Persistence of Esoteric Culture

Since modernism was victorious over rival esoteric and occult claims to knowledge and truth, why and how did esoteric thought and the occult arts and sciences remain a part of modern societies? There are several ways of addressing this question, all of which revolve around the inability or failure of modern rationality to eliminate absolutely its substantially defeated rivals. In spite of suffering repeated losses to modernism, esotericism and occultism survived, commonly through substantial bodies of cultural lore and literature, sometimes supported by collectivities and organizations, which served as the basis for subsequent revivals and revitalization. Ironically, perhaps, the modernist quest for knowledge facilitates the preservation of nonmodernist worldviews. Premodern occultisms and traditional religion, among many other nonmodernists forms of knowledge consequently linger and sometimes thrive under the general conditions of modernity.

The sociocultural definition of esoteric and occult thought as religious heresy defined it as deviant and even criminal. The viability of such a definition, however, presupposes some monopoly of religious orthodoxy on truth claims and related images of reality. When religion does not exercise such a monopoly, alternative claims and images are possible. Esotericism and occultism consequently have persisted in Western culture as alternative forms of religion. The lore and literature survived, dispersed and sustained by mass communications. Esotericism and occultism also were formulated and/or perceived as science rather than religion. Religious definitions of Hermeticism as heresy, for instance, did not eliminate the possibility of treating it as science, or its revival and revitalization as an alternative form of religion in a different sociohistorical context. Similarly, the rejection of alchemy and astrology as natural sciences did not eliminate them as religions or forms of other sciences, such as psychology. Even after alchemy and astrology were discredited as in any way scientific, they still were employed to account for natural and psychological phenomena not explained by science. And, unlike science, even rationalistic religion is ill prepared to eliminate its rivals totally when the larger cultural environment acknowledges rival possibilities and religion lacks corresponding political-legal power.

Although largely victorious, modernism has been unable exhaustively to subsume and account for all humanly meaningful experiences of the world. Whereas the range of human experiences subsumed by rationalistic accounts has become smaller and smaller historically, some experiences resist and even defy rational interpretation. So long as modernism is unable exhaustively to provide meaningful accounts of **all** human experiences, esotericism and occultisms will persist in some form as alternative ways of accounting for otherwise ambiguous experiences and realities. Furthermore, insofar as esotericism and occultism persist they will provide bases for human beings to create, recreate, and enact meaningful versions of reality founded on such grounds. Revivals and revitalizations of the esoteric and occult are more or less likely depending on particular sociocultural circumstances and institutional arrangements.

Changes in and transitions between modernist paradigms provide a fertile environment for new challenges from old, revitalized rivals, sometimes as a result of rationalism's creation and identification of anomalous phenomena. Whenever Religion or Science is seen as moving between all encompassing interpretations of reality it leaves some opening for rival, perhaps esoteric or occult interpretations. In spite of a propensity for absolutism, modernism resulted in cultural pluralism, and it commonly acknowledges relativistic epistemologies. Transitions in modernist paradigms, moreover, sometimes create anomalies which are pregnant with possible esoteric and/or occult accounts.

The delegitimation of esotericism and occultism left previously valued literatures in its wake. While modernization sometimes discredited and even eliminated the collectivities sustaining esotericism and occultism, the literatures survived. When believers persisted, they commonly were defined as outsiders to the dominant institutional collectivities and, thereby, ideological minorities. In some instances this resulted in the elimination of esoteric and occult beliefs among certain social strata and classes. Yet, their treatment as ideological minorities served as bases for social solidarity and countercultural movements. Folk beliefs, furthermore, rarely were extinguished. Rather, they sustained and even perpetuated esotericism and occultism, oftentimes in different and novel constellations.

Even after modernism become dominant, however, anti-modernist counterattacks periodically were mounted from the outside as well as within Science and Religion. In the process, even discredited views were sustained and persisted as minority viewpoints, sometimes represented by substantial bodies of previously valued literatures. Over the long run modernist Religion and Science secured greater and greater control over larger and larger domains of knowledge, supporting social institutions, and publics. Occult claims to knowledge consequently persisted in many areas, until such time as they were subsumed by Science or Religion. Occult thinking about human personality, for instance, persisted long after it was banished from astronomy, physics, and biology. During periods when the modernist paradigms reflected widely accepted theories of Science and Religion, counterattacks rarely were successful. Stated differently, when scientific and religious consensus exists, all manner of would-be challenges to orthodoxy are more easily dismissed. Transitions and changes in religious or scientific thought commonly are accomplished by way of radical challenges to existing paradigms. When there is a lack of consensus and orthodoxy, rival claims, including those of the occult, are more difficult to dismiss or explain away, and therefore they are more likely to be taken seriously by insiders and especially by outsiders.

Esotericism and occultism in the form of previous literatures, traditions, and collectivities generally provide for little more than the preservation and persistence of a socially marginal culture. While they may contain ideas of contemporary relevance, they derive from and reflect sociocultural contexts whose significance for contemporary, collective existence rarely is self-evident. Esoteric and occult revivals always imply a certain revitalization whereby existing ideas are translated into beliefs and practices which speak meaningfully to the contemporary existence of would-be adherents. The revival and popularity of the occult tarot, for instance, was not manifest, except in very limited ways, with the replication of secretive orders patterned after the theosophy and organization of the Golden Dawn. Rather, the recent popularity of the tarot commonly has been its use as a sort of psychotherapy, an instrument of otherwise widespread counseling rituals, sometimes with spiritual or religious overtones formed after its exoteric, science-like counterparts. Large numbers of contemporary Americans, for whatever reasons, apparently do not find secretive orders to be appealing as ways of addressing problematic aspects of their existence. They do, however, find existential meaning through tarot card readings enacted as counseling sessions.

Similarly, the apparent social success of new religious groups, such as Scientology, is not based on any simplistic revival of esoteric or occult thought. While Scientology contains important elements of Western occultism, their appeal derives from the manner in which they have been reshaped to deal significantly with human existence in a contemporary, modern world. The recent, and more than likely continued growth of magic and witchcraft in the United States and elsewhere further illustrates this point (see Adler, 1986; Luhrmann, 1989). Contemporary magic and witchcraft movements commonly borrow extensively from existing occult traditions and literature. The social meanings of these traditions and literatures have been extensively reinterpreted and revitalized around significant contemporary concerns for human spirituality, gender roles, environmental issues, human relationships, and the creation of new ritual meanings. Among contemporary practitioners of the Craft, use of the tarot is hardly conservative, even when it is historically grounded in occult traditions.

THE SOCIAL ORGANIZATION OF ESOTERIC CULTURE

Esoteric culture was portrayed here as exceptionally multidimensional, particularly in terms of the ways in which contemporary Americans employ it to enact collective, human associations. Admittedly, much of the culture of esotericism is almost entirely collective behavioral; that is, it is not socially supported or sustained by groups or organizations as they are defined by sociologists. The esoteric scene in the Valley, however, was described and analyzed in terms of spheres of overlapping human networks and associations. A core portion of the esoteric scene in the Valley was depicted in terms of what members called the esoteric community. My efforts to describe this geographically dispersed Valley community revealed a multiplicity of socially recognized roles and relationships, networks of practitioners and collectivities, and loosely affiliated collections of practitioners and groups composing social segments. The esoteric scene in the Valley may be seen sociologically as **organized** in all of these ways.

The social organization of the esoteric scene and community in the Valley may be interpreted, it seems to me, as in some large part a reflection of the very ethos of contemporary esoteric culture. One of the central features of this ethos is what was called epistemological individualism. It is an extreme form of cultural pluralism whereby orthodoxy and absolutism are rejected, and toleration for widely varied and even divergent beliefs are valued and encouraged. Significantly, the highly pluralistic character of esoteric culture is intertwined with quests for knowledge which advocate a reliance on human feelings, intuition, subjectivity, irrationality, mysticism, magic, and the like. Such a style of human thought has important social organizational implications for human existence.

The ethos of esoteric culture mitigates against the formation of tightly organized, authoritarian, absolutist, sectarian groups. Its very thought style prohibits these forms of social organization. The people who subscribe to esoteric knowledge as a part of their basic beliefs and practices are uninclined to create groups or organizations which might limit their freedom of belief and practice or otherwise extract normative compliance to the collectivity over and against their personal freedom. Their very beliefs in esoteric and occult knowledge lead them to fashion and perform roles creatively, alter their role performances frequently, affiliate casually and informally with one another, form collectivities on the basis of shared interests (but little else), and reform them as their interest change, as well as move from group to group. Differences in their levels of interest, belief, and practice do serve to differentiate among them. Yet most of these differences, among seekers, clients, students, practitioners, and cult members are relatively unimportant except for the core membership whose social location within the cultic milieu remains more or less stable. The esoteric scene and the cultic milieu, consequently, organizationally reflect and embody the ethos and cognitive style of esoteric culture.

The esoteric community in the Valley is a somewhat more stable manifestation of the ethos of esoteric culture. Its members have a still somewhat vague, but more standard image of what constitutes their range of mutual interests, beliefs, practices, ethics, politics, economics, appropriate roles, and boundaries. It exists primarily in the consciousness of its members and by way of overlapping networks of friendships, business interests, professional relationships, and cultic groups. Psychic fairs provide a social context in which community members interact, sustain, and enact mutual interests and collective awareness. Even so, the esoteric community in the Valley is composed of three somewhat distinctive orientations to esotericism and occultism. These different images, in turn, are manifest by way of specific linkages among practitioners and groups, as well as in terms of the ways in which they organize collective relationships.

Community members who define themselves as spiritual or religious tend to form church-like groups; those who see themselves as practitioners of psychic arts and sciences form professional practices and associations; while members who stress esoteric medicine and healing establish clinics and study groups. Occult practices composed as counseling-like efforts at self-understanding or healing socially produce would-be professional practitioners, clientele, and students. Religious self-imagery results at least weakly in exoteric-like ministers and congregations of believers.

The social organization of esoteric culture exhibits its social marginality, limits its social success, influence, and power, and supports its persistence within the larger, exoteric society. The premodern origins of esoteric culture socially define and locate it within the contemporary sociohistorical and cultural context of modernity as part of the past rather than the present or future. Its loss of widespread institutional influence probably is insurmountable. It has been confined by modernism and its own ethos to a feature of popular culture, collective behavioral audiences, cultic milieus, like-minded urban collectivities such as the esoteric community, and loosely organized groups and associations. All of these social organizational features of esoteric culture reflect and exhibit its marginality, its location on the periphery but not the center of the human organizations and institutions of modernity.

The social organization of esoteric culture, particularly its lack of influence over modern institutions, severely limits its ability to mobilize resources or exercise social power. Its lack of institutional bases of support and legitimacy, in other words, is a profound obstacle to acquiring the collective, social organizational grounds for changing this situation. Its fate consequently is controlled by the exoteric society. So long as the exoteric society is dominated by modernity, esoteric society will remain unable to transform itself and establish effective bases for securing support and influence.

The rather weak, loose, diffuse, multidimensional social organization of esoteric culture may be seen, however, as a source of strength. Because of these very characteristics, esoteric culture remains flexible and potentially viable within highly varied and recurrent social and historical contexts. It is exceptionally difficult for modernity or its particular agents to eliminate more than a few features of esoteric culture or its social organization at any given moment. Parts of the esoteric and occult remain popular and receive social support even during periods of seemingly little activity. Discredited esotericisms and occultisims rarely go away once they have been defeated within a particular context. Rather, they commonly are preserved among some collection of believers and subsequently revived and revitalized at a later historical moment under somewhat different sociocultural circumstances. Cultic collections of believers, furthermore, generally reflect at least slightly different versions of esotericism and occultism. When a particular cult ceases to exist, its members commonly are redistributed among existing cults and/or they create new ones.

The cultic milieu consequently is an inherently stable and resilient form of social organization, even though the concrete ways in which it is manifest, as unstable, loosely organized cults and social networks are inherently fragile and transitory. It also is in some sense a potentially robust form of social organization. Because new cults constantly are being created, the cultic milieu routinely generates novel adaptation to concrete social and historical circumstances. While most of them will be unsuccessful in the short run, in relatively rare instances some of them are successful. And in a very few cases, successful cults become significant social movements of lasting influence.

Highly successful cults and movements eventually develop more stable organizations generally in conjunction with the formulation of more orthodox beliefs. Through this process they also tend to become increasingly removed from the cultic milieu. Even so, they symbolize for participants in the cultic milieu the possibility of achieving greater popularity and success. Modestly successful cults, furthermore, tend to maintain connections with the cultic milieu and its basic networks. Hence, even if only a very small proportion of new cults attains any degree of success, they contribute to the social organizational stability of the cultic milieu and esoteric culture.

THE FUTURE OF ESOTERIC CULTURE

What then is the future of esoteric culture? At the present moment Western culture and society seem to be undergoing a potentially drastic transition. Some contemporary scholars envision it as a radical alteration of modernity which has or will eventually result in postmodernity. Like Giddens (1990), I am not at all certain that modernity has been transposed, even if it has been substantially radicalized. Some of the features of what is being hailed as postmodernism resemble characteristics of premodern culture and, thereby, suggest an affinity between postmodern and esoteric cultures. If culture is not progressive, neither is it regressive. In other words, I do not see Western culture as any more likely to move backwards than it is to move forward. What culture, and thereby society, does is change. It becomes different from what it was before, and it does so in part at least on the basis of previous patterns, current conditions, and future innovations.

The future of esoteric culture, as noted above, depends in some large part on changes in exoteric culture. If the postmodernists are correct, then the exoteric culture of the future probably will create an environment which is much more receptive to esotericism and occultism in some form than were modern culture and society. Esotericism and occultism are unlikely to become more influential and successful, in my view, simply on the basis of contemporary formulations and organizations. What will be required are new and highly innovative developments in which past and present esotericisms and occultisms are themselves radically transformed in such a way as to reflect the existentially meaningful conditions of substantial numbers of the human inhabitants of a postmodern world.

Appendix A

Esoteric Community Survey Form

NAME: ____
ADDRESS: ____
____
PHONE: ____

1. Basically what are your beliefs? (Supplementary: which of the following terms best describe the beliefs of your group—spiritual,psychic, occult, metaphysical, esoteric?).

2. Is your group/organization/church a charter or affiliate of any larger (national) organization?

3. When do you meet?

	a. time	b. type of meeting	c. average attendance	d. cost
(1)				
(2)				
(3)				

4. Do you have any leaders? Are they paid?

	a. name	b. title	c. degrees
(1)			
(2)			
(3)			

5. Is your group/organization/church affiliated with any local groups (such as SAC, Omega, APRC, etc.)?

6. Any other relevant information:

Appendix B

Tarot Card Reader Interview Schedule

This questionnaire has been devised by Danny and Lin Jorgensen (The Ohio State University and Arizona State University) as part of a larger project designed to explore contemporary interest in the esoteric/occult/mystical/meta-physical/ psychic/spiritual field. Your cooperation in answering this questionnaire will be helpful in determining and documenting the nature and extent of this social movement. The collection of valid information depends on your cooperation and honesty. Please be advised that your responses will be completely confidential. If you do not wish to participate or if you object to answering any of the following questions please tell us. Thank you very much.

PART I

Please check the appropriate answer:

1. What is your age? ___years ___months

2. What is your sex? ___male ___female

3. How many years of "formalized schooling" have you completed?

4 5 6 7 8/	9 10 11 12/	13 14 15 16/	17 18 19 20
Jr. High	Sr. High	College	Grad. School

4. Have you received degrees other than those from "formalized schooling"?
   a. no b. yes
   If yes, what degrees?
   Where were they granted?

5. Do you have an occupation other than reading tarot cards?
   a. no b. Yes (specify)

6. What was your income last year from reading tarot cards? $

7. What was your personal income last year before taxes? (Include all sources.)

a.	less than $5,000	f.	$15,000 - $17,499
b.	$5,900 - $7,499	g.	$17,500 - $19,999
c.	$7,500 - $9,999	h.	$20,000 - $24,999
d.	$10,000 - $12,499	i.	above $25,000
e.	$12,500 - $14,999		

8. What is your present religious preference?

9. In an average month, how many times do you attend church?

a.	never	d.	three times a month
b.	once a month	e.	four times a month
c.	twice a month	f.	five or more times a month

10. Other than going to church, how religious minded would you say you are?
    a. not religious minded at all
    b. not very religious minded
    c. somewhat religious minded
    d. fairly religious minded
    e. very religious minded

11. What is the strength of your present religious affiliation?
    a. very week
    b. fairly weak
    c. middling
    d. fairly strong
    e. very strong

12. Do you classify yourself as
    a. devout
    b. moderately devout
    c. inactive

13. How would you describe your political views on this continuum?

1	2	3	4	5	6	7	8	9
very conservative				moderate				very liberal

14. Do you use any of the following drugs?
    a. tobacco
    b. alcohol
    c. caffine
    d. marijuana
    e. cocaine
    f. "ups"
    g. "downs"
    h. heroin
    i. others (specify)

15. How long have you lived in the Valley area? ___years ___ months

16. Where did you live before you came to the Valley area?

17. Do you have any children?
    a. no b. yes (how many?)
    Are your children presently living with you?
    a. no b. yes

18. What is your present marital status?
    a. never married (skip to question 23)
    b. divorced (skip to question 23)
    c. widowed (skip to question 23)
    d. presently married for the first time (go to question 19)
    e. remarried (go to question 19)

19. How many years of "formalized schooling" has your wife completed?

4 5 6 7 8/	9 10 11 12/	13 14 15 16/	17 18 19 20
Jr. High	Sr. High	College	Grad. School

20. What is your spouse's occupation?

21. What was your spouse's personal income last year, before taxes?
    a. less than $5,000
    b. $5,900 - $7,499
    c. $7,500 - $9,999
    d. $10,000 - $12,499
    e. $12,500 - $14,999
    f. $15,000 - $17,499
    g. $17,500 - $19,999
    h. $20,000 - $24,999
    i. above $25,000

22. What is your spouse's present religious affiliation?

23. With whom did you spend the majority of your growing-up years?
    a. mother and father
    b. mother and stepfather
    c. stepmother and father
    d. mother only
    e. father only
    f. other (specify)

24. How many years of "formalized schooling" did your father complete?

4	5	6	7	8/	9	10	11	12/	13	14	15	16/	17	18	19	20
Jr. High					Sr. High				College				Grad. School			

25. What is/was your father's occupation?

26. What is/was your father's religious affiliation?

27. How many years of "formalized schooling" did your mother complete?

4	5	6	7	8/	9	10	11	12/	13	14	15	16/	17	18	19	20
Jr. High					Sr. High				College				Grad. School			

28. What is/was your mother's occupation?

29. What is/was your mother's religious affiliation?

30. Are any members of your family involved in occult/esoteric/psychic activities?
    a. no
    b. yes - if yes, who? (circle all that apply)
    a. spouse
    b. daughter(s)
    c. son(s)
    d. mother
    e. father
    f. grandmother(s)
    g. grandfather(s)
    h. uncle(s)
    i. aunt(s)
    j. cousin(s)
    k. others (specify)

PART II

1. What is the average number of hours per week that you spend on
   a. readings (for money)
   b. readings (not for money)

2. Where do you do your readings?
   a. home
   b. office
   c. church
   d. bookstore
   e. other (specify)

3. How much do you charge for a reading?

4. What is the average length of time it takes you to do a reading?

5. Which spreads do you use in your readings?

6. Which tarot decks do you own?

7. Which tarot decks do you use for readings?

8. What type of client usually requests your services (e.g., age, sex, SES)?

9. What type of questions are most frequently asked of the tarot in your readings?

10. What, to you, would constitute an "ideal" querent (client)?

11. What was the "worst type" of client you've had?

12. Do you read the tarot cards for yourself?

13. Do you ask others to read tarot cards for you?
    If so, whom?

14. What is your estimate of the number of tarot readers in the Valley?
    Non-professional?

15. Do you associate with other tarot readers
    professionally?
    socially?

16. Do you use tarot cards for any purpose other than divinatory readings?
    If so, what?

17. Basically, what is your philosophy regarding the cards (and readings)?

18. How did you first get involved with reading tarot cards?

19. Have you ever had any out-of-the-ordinary psychic experiences?
    Please descirbe (i.e., type, intensity)

20. Are you a member of any occult/psychic groups?
    If so, which?

21. Do you practice any of the following? (circle all that apply)
    a. witchcraft
    b. alchemy
    c. numerology
    d. palmistry
    e. astrology
    f. mediumship
    g. scrying
    h. tea leaf readings
    i. others (specify)

22. Do you employ any of the above practices in your tarot readings?
    If so, which?

References

Adler, Patricia A., and Peter Adler. 1987. *Membership Roles in Field Research*. Beverly Hills, CA: Sage.

Adler, Margot. 1986 (1979). *Drawing Down the Moon: Witches, Druids, Goddess-Worshippers and Other Pagans in America Today*. NY: Viking.

Adorno, Theodore. 1974. "The Stars Down to Earth," *Telos* 19: 13-91.

Agar, Michael H. 1986. *Speaking of Ethnography*. Beverly Hills, CA: Sage.

Agassi, Joseph. 1979. "Toward a Rational Theory of Superstition. *Zetetic Scholar* 3-4: 107-120.

_______, and I. C. Jarvie. 1977. "Magic and Rationality Again," *British Journal of Sociology* 26: 236-245.

Ahlstrom, Sydney E. 1972. *A Religious History of the American People*. New Haven: Yale University Press.

Altheide, David. 1976. *Creating Reality*. Beverly Hills, CA: Sage.

____, and John M. Johnson. 1979. *Bureaucratic Propaganda*. Boston: Allyn and Bacon.

Anderson, John P. 1977. "Practical Reasoning in Action," pp. 174-198 in Jack D. Douglas and John M. Johnson (eds.), *Existential Sociology*. Cambridge, MA: Cambridge University Press.

Anonymous. 1985. *Meditations on the Tarot: A Journey Into Christian Hermeticism*. Amity, NY: Amity House.

Anthony, D. and T. Robbins. 1974. "The Meher Baba Movement: Its Effect on Post-Adolescent Social Alienation," pp. 479-511 in I. I. Zaretsky and M. P. Leone (eds.), *Religious Movements in Contemporary America*. Princeton, NJ: Princeton University Press.

Appel, Willa. 1983. *Cults in America*. NY: Holt, Rinehart and Winston.

Bainbridge, William S. 1978. *Satan's Power: A Deviant Psychotherapy Cult*. Berkeley, CA: University of California Press

_______, and Rodney Stark. 1979. "Cult Formation: Three Compatible Models," *Sociological Analysis* 40 (4): 285-293.

Baker, Eileen (ed.). 1982. *New Religious Movements: A Perspective for Understanding Society*. NY: Edwin Mellen.

Balch, Robert. W. 1978. "Two Models of Conversion and Commitment in a UFO Cult," paper presented to the Pacific Sociological Association, Anaheim, CA.

____. 1980. "Looking Behind the Scenes in a Religious Cult," *Sociological Analysis* 41 (2): 137-143.

____, and David Taylor. 1976. "Salvation in a UFO," *Psychology Today* 10 (October): 58-66, 106.

_____. 1977a. "Seekers and Saucers: The Role of the Cultic Milieu in Joining a UFO Cult," *American Behavioral Scientist* 20: 839-860.

________. 1977b. "Becoming a Sect," Paper presented at the Pacific Sociological Association Meetings, Sacramento, CA.

Bateson, Gregory. 1972. *Steps to an Ecology of Mind*. NY: Chandler.

Becker, George. 1991. "Pietism's Confrontation with Enlightenment Rationalism: An Examination of the Relation between Ascetic Protestantism and Science," *Journal for the Scientific Study of Religion* 30 (3): 139-158.

Becker, Howard S. 1970. *Sociological Work*. Chicago: Aldine.

_____. 1982. *Art Worlds*. Berkeley: University of California Press.

_____. 1986. *Doing Things Together*. Evanston: Northwestern University Press.

______, and Michal M. McCall. 1990. *Symbolic Interaction and Cultural Studies*. Chicago: University of Chicago Press.

Beckford, James A. 1985. *Cult Controversies: The Societal Response to New Religious Movements*. NY: Tavistock.

_____, and Melanie Cole. 1987. "British and American Responses to New Religious Movements," paper presented to the Association for the Sociology of Religion, Chicago, IL.

Bellah, Robert. 1970. *Beyond Belief*. NY: Harper and Row.

Benassi, Victor A., Barry Singer, and Craig B. Reynolds. 1980. "Occult Belief," *Journal for the Scientific Study of Religion* 80 (4): 337-349.

Berger, Bennet M. 1981. *The Survival of a Counterculture*. Los Angeles: University of California Press.

Berger, Peter L. 1961. *The Precarious Vision*. NY: Doubleday.

_____. 1967. *The Sacred Canopy*. NY: Doubleday.

_____. 1974. *Religion in a Revolutionary Society*. Washington, D.C.: American Enterprise Institute for Public Policy Research.

_____, B. Berger, and H. Kellner. 1974. *The Homeless Mind*. NY: Doubleday.

______, and Thomas Luckmann. 1963. "Sociology of Religion and Sociology and Knowledge," *Sociology and Social Research* 47 (4): 417-427.

_____. 1966. *The Social Construction of Reality*. Englewood Cliffs, NJ: Prentice-Hall.

Beyon, E. 1938. "The Voodoo Cult Among Negro Migrants in Detroit," *American Journal of Sociology* 43 (May): 894-907.

Biezais, Haralds (ed.). 1975. *New Religions*. Stockholm: Almqvist and Wiksel.

Blumer, Herbert. 1957. "Collective Behavior," pp. 127-158 in J. B.Gultler (ed), *Review of Sociology*. NY: Wiley.

_____. 1969. *Symbolic Interactionism*. Englewood Cliffs, NJ: Prentice-Hall.

_____ 1990 (David R. Maines and Thomas J. Morrione, eds.). *Industrialization as an Agent of Social Change: A Critical Analysis*. Hawthorne, NY: Aldine de Gruyter.

Bourguignon, Erika (ed.). 1973. *Religion, Altered States of Consciousness, and Social Change*. Columbus: The Ohio State University Press.

Boyne, Roy. 1990. *Foucault and Derrida: The Other Side of Reason*. Boston: Unwin Hyman.

Bromley, David G., and Phillip H. Hammond. 1987. *The Future of New Religious Movements*. Macon, GA: Mercer University.

Bromley, David G., and Anson D. Shupe. 1981. *Strange Gods: The Great American Cult Hoax*. Boston: Beacon.

______. 1987. "The Future of the Anit-Cult Movement," pp. 221-234 in David G. Bromley and Phillip H. Hammond (ed.), *The Future of New Religious Movements*. Macon, GA: Mercer University.

Brown, Richard Harvey. 1989. *Social Science As Civic Discourse*. Chicago: University of Chicago Press.

Bruyn, Severyn T. 1966. *The Human Perspective in Sociology: The Methodology of Participant Observation*. Englewood Cliffs, NJ: Prentice-Hall.

Buckner, H. T. 1965. "The Flying Saucerians: An Open Door Cult," pp. 223-230 in M. Truzzi (ed.), *Sociology and Everyday Life*. Englewood Cliffs, NJ: Prentice-Hall.

Butler, Jon. 1978. "The People's Faith in Europe and America: Four Centuries in Review," *Journal of Social History* 12 (Fall): 159-167.

_____. 1979 "Magic, Astrology, and the Early American Religious Heritage, 1600-1760," *American Historical Review* 84 (April): 317-346.

_______. 1983. *The Huguenots in America: A Refugee People in New World Society*. Cambridge, MA: Harvard University Press.

Butterfield, Herbert. 1948. *Origins of Modern Science*. London: Bell.

Campbell, Colin. 1972. "The Cult, the Cultic Milieu and Secularization," *A Sociological Yearbook of Religion in Britain* 5: 119-136.

Campbell, Joseph and Richard Roberts. 1979. *Tarot Revelations*. San Anselma, CA: Vernal Equinox Press.

Campiche, Roland J. 1987. "Sectes et Nouveaux Movements Religieux," paper presented at the First Latin American Conference on Popular Religion, Identity and Ethnology, Mexico City.

Case, Paul Foster. 1947. *The Tarot*. Richmond, VA: Macoy.

Catton, W.R. 1957. "What Kind of People Does A Religious Cult Attract?" *American Sociological Review* 22: 561-566.

Cavendish, Richard. 1975. *The Tarot*. NY: Harper and Row.

Cicourel, Aaron V. 1973. *Cognitive Sociology: Language and Meaning in Social Interaction*. NY: The Free Press.

_____. 1974. *Theory and Method in a Study of Argentine Fertility*. NY: Wiley.

____, K.H. Jennings, S.H.M. Jennings, K.C.W. Leiter, Robert MacKay, Hugh Mehan, and D.R. Roth. 1974. *Language Use and School Performance*. NY: Academic Press.

Clarie, Thomas C. 1978. *Occult Bibliography: An Annotated List of Books Published in English, 1971 through 1975*. Metuchen, NJ: Scarecrow Press.

Clarke, Adele E., and Elihu M. Gerson. 1990. "Symbolic Interactionism in Social Studies of Science," pp. 179-214 in Howard S. Becker and Michal M. McCall (eds.), *Symbolic Interaction and Cultural Studies*. Chicago: University of Chicago Press.

Clifford, James, and George E. Marcus (eds.). 1986. *Writing Culture: The Poetics and Politics of Ethnography*. Berkeley: University of California Press.
Collins, Randall. 1977. "Toward a Modern Science of the Occult," *Consciousness and Culture* 1 (1): 43-58.
_____. 1978. *The Case of the Philosophers' Ring*. NY: Crown.
Crane, Diana. 1972. *Invisible Colleges: The Diffusion of Knowledge in Scientific Communities*. Chicago: University of Chicago Press.
Cross, Whitney R. 1944. "Mormonism in the 'Burned-over District,'" *New York History* 25 (July): 326-338.
Crowley, Aleister. 1974 (1944). *The Book of Thoth*. York Beach, ME: Samuel Weiser.
Damrell, Joseph. 1977. *Seeking Spiritual Meaning*. Beverly Hills, CA: Sage.
_____. 1978. *Search for Identity*. Beverly Hills, CA: Sage.
DeFrance, Philippe, et al. 1971. *Le retour des astrologues*. Paris: Les Cahiers du Club de Novel Observateur.
Delaney, James G., and Howard D. Woodyard. 1974. "Effects of Reading an Astrological Description on Responding to a Personality Inventory," *Psychological Reports* 34: 1214.
Demos, John P. 1982. *Entertaining Satan: Witchcraft and the Culture of Early New England*. NY: Oxford University Press.
Denning, Melita, and Osborne Phillips. 1988. *The Magic of the Tarot*. St. Paul, MN: Llewellyn.
Denzin, Norman K. 1986. "Postmodern Social Theory," *Sociological Theory* 4 (Winter): 194-204
_____. 1989a. *Interpretative Interactionism*. Newbury Park, CA: Sage.
_____. 1989b. *Interpretative Biography*. Newbury Park, CA: Sage.
_____. 1989c. *The Research Act*. Englewood Cliffs, NJ: Prentice-Hall (Third Edition).
_____. 1991. *Images of Postmodern Society*. Newbury Park, CA: Sage.
Dohrman, H. T. 1958. *California Cult*. Boston: Beacon.
Douglas, Alfred. 1972. *The Tarot*. London: Gollancz.
Douglas, Jack. 1976. *Investigative Social Research*. Beverly Hills, CA: Sage.
_______, and John M. Johnson (eds). 1977. *Existential Sociology*. NY: Cambridge University Press.
Douglas, Mary. 1966. *Purity and Danger: An Analysis of Concepts of Pollution and Taboo*. NY: Routledge and Kegan Paul.
_____. 1970. *Natural Symbols*. NY: Pantheon.
_____. 1973. *Rules and Meanings*. NY: Penguin.
_____. 1986. *How Institutions Think*. Syracuse: Syracuse University Press.
____, and Aaron Wildavsky. 1982. *Risk and Culture*. Berkeley: University of California Press.
Dummett, Michael. 1980a. *The Game of Tarot from Ferrara to Salt Lake City*. London: Duckworth.
_____. 1980b. *Twelve Tarot Games*. London: Duckworth.
_____. 1986. *The Visconti-Sforza Tarot Cards*. NY: Braziller.
Durkheim, Emile (Joseph W. Swain, trans). 1965 (1915). *The Elementary Forms of the Religious Life*. NY: The Free Press.

Eglin, Trent. 1974. "Introduction to a Hermeneutics of the Occult: Alchemy," pp. 323-358 in E. A. Tiryakian (ed.), *On the Margin ofthe Visible*. NY: Wiley.

_____. 1986. "Introduction to a Hermeneutics of the Occult: Alchemy," pp. 123-159 in Harold Garfinkel (ed.), *Ethnomethodological Studies of Work*. NY: Routledge and Kegan Paul.

Ellwood, Robert S., and Harry B. Partin. 1988. *Religious and Spiritual Groups in Modern America*. Englewood Cliffs, NJ: Prentice Hall.

Eister, Allan W. 1972. "An Outline of a Structural Theory of Cults," *Journal for the Scientific Study of Religion* 11 (4): 319-333.

Eliade, Mircea (Willard R. Trask, trans). 1964. *Shamanism: Archaic Techniques of Ecstasy*. Princeton: Princeton University Press.

_______. 1976. *Occultism, Witchcraft, and Cultural Fashion*. Chicago: University of Chicago Press.

Evans-Pritchard, E.E. 1973 (1937). *Witchcraft, Oracles and Magic Among the Azande*. NY: Oxford University Press.

Faivre, Antoine. 1989a. "What is Occultism," pp. 3-9 in Lawrence E. Sullivan (ed.), *Hidden Truths: Magic, Alchemy, and the Occult*. NY: Macmillan.

_____. 1989b. "Esotericism," pp. 38-48 in Lawrence E. Sullivan (ed.), *Hidden Truths: Magic, Alchemy, and the Occult*. NY: Macmillan.

_____. 1989c. "Hermetism," pp. 49-62 in Lawrence E. Sullivan (ed.), *Hidden Truths: Magic, Alchemy, and the Occult*. NY: Macmillan.

Featherstone, Mike (ed.). 1988. *Postmodernism: Explorations in Critical Social Science*. London: Sage.

Felson, Richard B., and George Gmelch. 1979. "Uncertainty and the Use of Magic," *Current Anthropology* 20 (3): 587-589.

Festinger, Leon, Henry W. Riecken, and Stanley Schachter. 1956. *When Prophecy Fails*. NY: Harper Torchbooks.

Feyerabend, Paul. 1978. *Against Method: Outline of An Anarchistic Theory of Knowledge*. London: Verso.

Fischler, Claude. 1974. "Astrology and French Society," pp. 281-293 in E. A. Tiryakian (ed.), *On the Margin of the Visible*. NY: Wiley.

Flanders, Robert B. 1965. *Nauvoo: Kingdom on the Mississippi*. Urbana: University of Illinois Press.

Foranaro, R. J. 1973. "Neo-Hinduism in America," *Journal of Social Research* 16 (March).

Frazer, James G. 1922. *The Golden Bough*. NY: Macmillan.

Freedland, N. 1972. *The Occult Explosion*. NY: G. P. Putnam.

French, Peter J. 1972. *John Dee*. NY: Routledge and Kegan Paul.

Freidson, Eliot. 1970. *Professional Dominance*. Chicago: Aldine.

Gadamer, Hans-Georg. 1975. *Truth and Method*. NY: Seabury.

Galbreath, Robert (ed.). 1972. "The Occult," *Journal of Popular Culture* 5 (Winter): 629-736.

____. 1983. "Explaining Modern Occultism," pp. 11-37 in Howard Kerr and Charles L. Crow (eds.), *The Occult in America*. Urbana: University of Illinois Press.

Gallup, George. 1978. "Belief in Occult is Common in U.S.," Princeton, NJ: Gallup Poll.

Garfinkel, Harold. 1967. *Studies in Ethnomethodology*. Englewood Cliffs, NJ: Prentice-Hall.

____, Michael Lynch, and Eric Livingston. 1981. "The Work of Discovering Science Construed with Materials from the Opitically Discovered Pulsar," *Philosophy of the Social Sciences* 11: 131-158.

Geertz, Clifford. 1964. "Ideology as a Cultural System," pp. 47-77 in D. Apter (ed.), *Ideology and Discontent*. London: Collier-Macmillan.

_____. 1973. *The Interpretation of Cultures*. NY: Basic.

_____. 1988. *The Anthropologist as Author*. Stanford: Stanford University Press.

Gellner, E. 1973. "The Savage and the Modern Mind," pp. 162-181 in R. Horton and R. Finnegan (eds.), *Modes of Thought*. London: Faber.

Gidden, Anthony. 1990. *The Consequences of Modernity*. Stanford: Stanford University Press.

Gilbert, R. A. (ed.). 1983. *The Sorcerer and His Apprentice*. Wlllingborough: Aquarian.

Glazer, Barney, and Anselm L. Strauss 1967. *The Discovery of Grounded Theory*. Chicago: Aldine.

Glock, Charles Y. 1964. "The Role of Deprivation in the Origin and Evolution of Religious Groups," pp. 24-36 in Robert Lee and Martin Marty (eds.), *Religion and Social Conflict*. NY: Oxford University Press.

_____, and Robert N. Bellah (eds.). 1976. *The New Religious Consciousness*. Berkeley: University of California Press.

Goffman, Erving. 1959. *The Presentation of Self in Everyday Life*. NY: Doubleday.

_____. 1967. *Interactional Ritual*. NY: Doubleday

_____. 1974. *Frame Analysis*. NY: Harper and Row.

_____. 1981. *Forms of Talk*. Philadelphia: University of Pennsylvania Press.

Gold, Raymond L. 1958. "Roles in Sociological Field Observations," *Social Forces* 36: 217-223.

_______. 1969. "Roles in Sociological Field Observations," pp. 30-39 in George J. McCall and J.L. Simmons (eds.), *Issues in Participant Observation*. Reading, MA: Addison-Wesley.

Gottschalk, Stephen. 1988. "Christian Science and Harmonalism," pp. 901-916 in Charles H. Lippy and Peter W. Williams (eds.), *Encyclopedia of the American Religious Experience*. NY: Scribner's Sons.

Gray, Eden. 1972. *A Complete Guide to the Tarot*. NY: Bantam.

Greeley, Andrew. 1974. "Implications for the Sociology of Religion of Occult Behavior in Youth Culture," pp. 295-302 in E. A.Tiryakian (ed.), *On the Margin of the Visible*. NY: Wiley.

_____. 1975. *The Sociology of the Paranormal*. Beverly Hills, CA: Sage.

____. 1989. *Religious Change in America*. Cambridge, MA: Harvard University Press.

_______, and W. C. McCready. 1974. "Some Notes on the Sociological Study of Mysticism," pp. 303-322 in E. A. Tiryakian (ed.), *On the Margin of the Visible*. NY: Wiley.

Greer, Mary K. 1984. *Tarot for Yourself: A Workbook for Personal Transformation*. San Bernardino, CA: Borgo Press.

_____. 1988. *Tarot Mirrors: Reflections on Personal Meaning*. North Hollywood, CA: Newcastle Publishing.

Grim, Patrick (ed.). 1982. *Philosophy of Science and the Occult*. Albany: State University of New York Press.

Gurney, Joan Neff, and Kathleen J. Tierney. 1982. "Relative Deprivation and Social Movements," *Sociological Quarterly* 23: 33-47.

Hall, David D. 1984. "A World of Wonders: The Mentality of the Supernatural in Seventeenth-Century New England," in Gary B. Nash and Cynthia J. Shelton (eds.) *The Private Side of American History*. NY: Harcourt, Brace, Javanovich.

Harder, Mary W., James T. Richardson, and R. B. Simmonds. 1972. "Jesus People," *Psychology Today* 6 (December): 45-50, 110-113.

Hargrave, Catherine P. 1966. *A History of Playing Cards and a Bibliography of Cards and Gaming*. NY: Dover.

Harper, Charles L. 1982. "Cults and Communities: The Community Interfaces of Three Marginal Religious Communities," *Journal for the Scientific Study of Religion* 21 (1): 26-36.

Hartman, Patricia A. 1973. "Social Variations in Magical Belief." Ph.D. dissertation, University of Minnesota.

_____. 1976. "Social Dimensions of Occult Participation," *British Journal of Sociology* 27: 169-183.

Heenan, Edward (ed.). 1973. *Mystery, Magic and Miracles*. Englewood Cliffs, NJ: Prentice-Hall.

Heline, Corinne. 1969. *The Bible and the Tarot*. Marina del Rey, CA: DeVorss.

Hervieu-Leger, Daniéle 1986. *Ver un Nouveau Christianisme?* Paris: Cerf.

Higgins, Paul C., and John M. Johnson (eds.) 1988. *Personal Sociology*. NY: Praeger.

Hine, Virginia H. 1974. "The Deprivation and Disorganization Theories of Social Movements," pp. 646-661 in I. I. Zaretsky and M. P. Leone (eds.), *Religious Movements in Contemporary America*.Princeton, NJ: Princeton University Press.

Hughes, Everett C. 1958. *Men and Their Work*. Glencoe, IL: The Free Press.

Hyman, Ray. 1977. "Cold Reading," *Zetetic* 1: 18-37.

Isaacs, Ernest. 1983. "The Fox Sisters and American Spiritualism," pp. 79-110 in Howard Kerr and Charles L. Crow (eds.), *The Occult in America*. Urbana: University of Illinois Press.

Irwin, John. 1977. *Scenes*. Beverly Hills, CA: Sage.

Jackson, Carl T. 1975. "The New Thought Movement and the Nineteenth-Century Discovery of Oriental Philosophy," *Journal of Popular Culture* 8 (Spring): 523-548.

Jackson, John, and Ray Jobling. 1968. "Toward an Analysis of Contemporary Cults," D. Martin (ed.), *A Sociological Yearbook of Religion in Britain*, 94-105.

Jacobs, David M. 1983. "UFO's and the Search for Scientific Legitimacy," pp. 218-231 in Howard Kerr and Charles L. Crow (eds.), *The Occult in America*. Urbana: University of Illinois Press.

Jarvie, E. C., and J. Agassi. 1967. "The Problem of the Rationality of Magic," *British Journal of Sociology* 18: 55-74.

Jefferson, Gail, and Jim Schenkein. 1977. "Some Sequential Negotiations in Conversation," *Sociology* 11 (1): 87-103.

Johnson, Benton. 1957. "A Critical Appraisal of the Church-Sect Typology," *American Sociological Review* 22 (1): 88-92.

_____. 1963. "On Church and Sect," *American Sociological Review* 28: 589-599.

____. 1971. "Church and Sect Revisited," *Journal for the Scientific Study of Religion* 10: 124-137.

Johnson, John M. 1975. *Doing Field Research*. NY: The Free Press.

_____. 1977a. "Behind the Rational Appearances," pp. 201-228 in Jack D. Douglas and John M. Johnson (eds.), *Existential Sociology*. Cambridge, MA: Cambridge University Press.

____. 1977b. "Occasioned Transcendence," pp. 229-253 in Jack D. Douglas and John M. Johnson (eds.), *Existential Sociology*. Cambridge, MA: Cambridge University Press.

_______, and David L. Altheide. 1990a. "Reflexive Accountability," pp. 25-33 in Norman K. Denzin (ed.), *Studies in Symbolic Interaction* (Vol. 11). Greenwich, CT: JAI Press.

_____. 1990b. "The Ethnographic Ethic," unpublished paper.

Jones, Funmilayo M. 1981. "Strategies and Techniques Used in Occasion Maintenance." Ph.D. dissertation, Boston University.

Jordan, David K. 1982. "Taiwanese Poe Divination," *Journal for the Scientific Study of Religion* 21(2):114-118.

Jorgensen, Danny L. 1978. "The Esoteric Community in the Valley of the Sun: An Ethnographic Study of Social Structure and Organization," paper presented to the American Socioogical Association, San Francisco, CA.

_____.1979. "Tarot Diviantion in the Valley of the Sun: An Existential Sociology of the Esoteric and Occult," Ph.D. dissertation, The Ohio State University.

______. 1980. "The Social Construction and Interpretation of Deviance: Jonestown and the Mass Media," *Deviant Behavior* 10 (1): 309-332.

____. 1981. "Networks of Occultists: Comment on Stark and Bainbridge," *American Journal of Sociology* 87 (2): 427-429.

_____.1982. "The Esoteric Community: An Ethnographic Investigation of the Cultic Milieu," *Urban Life* 10 (4): 383-332.

____. 1983. "Psychic Fairs: A Basis for Solidarity and Networks Among Occultists," *California Sociologist* 6 (1): 57-75.

_____. 1984. "Divinatory Discourse," *Symbolic Interaction* 7 (2): 135-153.

______. 1989. *Participant Observation: A Methodology for Human Studies*. Newbury Park, CA: Sage.

______.1990a. "Some Implications of Postmodernism for Sociological Participant Observation," paper presented at the Gregory Stone Symbolic Interaction Symposium, St. Petersburg Beach, FL.

___.1990b. "The Fiery Darts of the Adversary: An Interpretation of Early Cutlerism," *The John Whitmer Historical Association Journal* 10: 67-83.

____. 1990c. "Antecedents of the Cutlerite Schism," paper presented to the Mormon History Association, Hawaii.

____.1991. "The Church of Jesus Christ (Cutlerite): A Sociological Interpretation of a Mormon Schism," *AAR/SBL Book of Abstracts* (A34): 199.

____, and Lin Jorgensen. 1977. "Reading the Tarot: Observing Participants and Participating Observers," paper presented to the Pacific Sociological Association, Sacramento, CA.

____. 1982. "Social Meanings of the Occult," *Sociological Quarterly* 23 (3): 373-389.

Judah, J. Stillson. 1967. *The History and Philosophy of the Metaphysical Movements in America*. Philadelphia: Westminster Press.

____. 1974. "The Hare Krishna Movement," pp. 463-478 in I. I. Zaretsky and M. P. Leone (eds.), *Religious Movements in Contemporary America*. Princeton, NJ: Princeton University Press.

Jules-Rosette, Bennetta. 1975. *African Apostles: Ritual and Conversion in the Church of John Maranke*. Ithaca: Cornell University Press.

Jung, C. G. (H. Reed. M. Fordham, and G. Adler, eds.). 1953. *Collected Works of C. G. Jung*. NY: Pantheon.

____ (R.F.C. Hull, trans.). 1963. *Essays on a Science of Mythology*. NY: Harper and Row.

____. 1967. *Analytical Psychology: Its Theory and Practice*. NY: Pantheon.

____. 1968. *The Archetypes and the Collective Unconscious*. Princeton, NJ: Princeton University Press.

Junker, B. H. 1960. *Field Work*. Chicago: University of Chicago Press.

Kaplan, Stuart R. 1970. *Tarot Cards for Fun and Fortune Telling*. New York: U. S. Games Systems.

____. 1972. *Tarot Classic*. New York: Grosset and Dunlop.

____. 1975a. *The American Historical Playing Card Deck: Portraits in American History*. NY: U.S.Games Systems.

____. 1975b. *The Royal Fez Moroccan Tarot Deck Instructions*. NY: U.S. Games Systems.

____. 1975c. *The Visconti-Sforza Tarocchi Deck Instructions*. NY: U.S. Games Systems.

____.1978. *The Encyclopedia of Tarot*. Volume I. NY: U. S. Games Systems.

____. 1986. *The Encyclopedia of Tarot*. Volume II. NY: U.S. Games Systems.

Kearney, Hugh. 1971. *Science and Change, 1500-1700*. NY: McGraw-Hill.

Kelley, I. W. 1979. "Astrology and Science," *Psychological Reports* 44: 1231-1240.

Kerr, Howard. 1972. *Mediums, and Spirit-Rappers, and Roaring Radicals: Spiritualism in American Literature, 1850-1900*. Urbana: University of Illinois Press.

____, and Charles L. Crow (eds.). 1983. *The Occult in America: New Historical Perspectives*. Urbana: University of Illinois Press.

Kilbourne, Brock K., and James T. Richardson 1984. "Psychotherapy and New Religions in a Pluralistic Society," *American Psychologists* 39 (3): 237-251.

Knorr-Cetina, Karen. 1981. *The Manufacture of Knowledge: An Essay on the Constructivist and Contextual Nature of Science*. Oxford: Pergamon Press.

____, and Michael Mulkay (eds.). 1983. *Science Observed: Perspectives on the Social Study of Science*. London: Sage.

Krieger, S. 1985. "Beyond Subjectivity," *Qualitative Sociology* 8: 309-324.

Kroker, Arthur, and David Cook. 1987. *The Postmodern Scene*. NY: St. Martin's.

Kuhn, Thomas. 1970 (1962). *The Structure of Scientific Revolutions*. Chicago: University of Chicago Press.

Labov, William, and D. Fanshell. 1977. *Therapeutic Discourse*. NY: Academic Press.

Lakoff, George, and Mark Turner. 1989. *More Than Cool Reason: A Field Guide to Poetic Metaphor*. Chicago: University of Chicago Press.

Latour, Bruno. 1987. *Science in Action*. Cambridge, MA: Harvard University Press.

_____, and Steve Woolgar. 1979. *Laboratory Life: The Social Construction of Scientific Facts*. Beverly Hills, CA: Sage.

Leiter, Kenneth. 1980. *A Primer on Ethnomethodology*. NY: Oxford University Press.

Leventhal, Herbert. 1976. *In the Shadow of the Enlightenment: Occultism and Renaissanced Science in Eighteenth-Century America*. NY: New York University Press.

Levi-Strauss, Claude. 1963. *Structural Anthropology*. NY: Doubleday.

Livingston, Eric. 1982. "Mathematicians' Work and the Relationship Between Mathematics and Theoretical Physics." Ph.D. dissertation, University of California, Los Angeles.

Lloyd, Susannah M. 1978. "The Occult Revival: Witchcraft in the Contemporary United States." Ph.D. dissertaion, University of Missouri.

Lofland, John. 1966. *Doomsday Cult*. Englewood Cliffs, NJ: Prentice Hall.

_____, and R. Stark. 1965. "Becoming a World Saver," *American Sociological Reivew* 10 (3): 128-134.

Loyotard, Jean-François. 1984. *The Postmodern Condition: A Report on Knowledge*. Minneapolis: University of Minnesota Press.

Luhrmann, T.M. 1989. *Persuasions of the Witch's Craft: Ritual Magic in Contemporary England*. Cambridge, MA: Harvard University Press.

Lyman, Stanford M., and Marvin B. Scott. 1970. *A Sociology of the Absurd*. NY: Meredith.

Lynch, Frederick R. 1977. "Field research and Future History: Problems Posed for Ethnographic Sociologists by the 'Doomsday Cult' Making Good," *American Sociologist* 12: 80-88.

____. 1978. "Toward A Theory of Conversion and Commitment to the Occult," pp. 91-112 in James T. Richardson (ed.), *Conversion Careers: In and Out of the New Religions*. Beverly Hills, CA: Sage.

Lynch, Michael. 1985. *Art and Artifact in Laboratory Science: A Study of Shop Work and Shop Talk in a Research Laboratory*. NY: Routledge and Kegan Paul.

Macklin, June. 1974. "Belief, Ritual, and Healing," pp. 383-417 in I. I. Zaretsky and M. P. Leone (eds.), *Religious Movements in Contemporary America*. Princeton, NJ: Princeton University Press.

Malinowski, B. 1948. *Magic, Science and Religion, and Other Essays*. Boston: Beacon Press.

Mannheim, Karl. 1952 (1936). *Ideology and Utopia*. NY: Routledge and Kegan Paul.

Marcus, George E. and Michael M. J. Fischer. 1986. *Anthropology as Cultural Critique*. Chicago: University of Chicago Press.

Marty, Martin. 1970. "The Occult Establishment," *Social Research* 37: 212-230.
_____. 1985. "Transpositions: American Religion in the 1980's," *Annals of the Academy of Political and Social Sciences* 480 (July): 11-23.
Marx, John J., and B. Holzner. 1977. "The Social Construction of Strain and Ideological Models of Grievance in Contemporary Movements," *Pacific Sociological Reveiw* 20 (July): 411-438.
Mauss, Armand L., and D. W. Peterson. 1973. "Prodigals as Preachers," Paper presented to the Society for the Scientific Study of Religion, San Francisco.
Mauss, M. 1915. *A General Theory of Magic*. NY: W. W. Norton.
McCarthy, John D., and M. N. Zald. 1977. "Resource Mobilization and Social Movements," *American Journal of Sociology* 82 (May): 1212-1246.
McClenon, James. 1984. *Deviant Science: The Case of Parapsychology*. Philadelphia: University of Pennsylvania Press.
McGuire, Meredith B. 1988. *Ritual Healing in Suburban America*. New Brunswick, NJ: Rutgers University Press.
McHugh, Peter. 1968. *Defining the Situation*. Indianapolis: Bobbs-Merrill.
McIntosh, Christopher. 1972. *Eliphas Lévi and the French Occult Revival*. London: Rider.
Mehan, Hugh, and H. Wood. 1975. *The Reality of Ethnomethodology*. NY: Wiley.
Melton, J. Gordon. 1978. *Encyclopedia of American Religions*. Wilmington, NC: Consortium.
____. 1982. *Magic, Witchcraft, and Paganism in America: A Bibliography*. NY: Garland.
_____. 1986. *Encyclopedic Handbook of Cults in America*. NY: Garland.
____, and Robert L. Moore. 1982. *The Cult Experience: Responding to the New Religious Pluralism*. NY: Pilgrim.
Merton, Robert K. (ed.). 1936. *Social Theory and Social Structure*. NY: Free Press.
_______. 1938. *Science, Technology and Society in Seventeenth Century England*. NY: Fertig.
Mills, C. Wright. 1959. *The Sociological Imagination*. NY: Oxford University Press.
Moore, R. Laurence. 1977. *In Search of White Crows: Spiritualism, Parapsychology, and American Culture*. NY: Oxford University Press.
_____. *Religious Outsiders and the Making of Americans*. NY: Oxford University Press.
Murphy, John W. 1989. *Postmodern Social Analysis and Criticism*. NY: Greenwood.
Needleman, Jacob. 1970. *The New Religions*. NY: Doubleday.
_____. 1975. *A Sense of the Cosmos*. NY: Doubleday.
____, and George Baker (eds.). 1978. *Understanding the New Religions*. NY: Seabury.
Nelson, Geoffrey K. 1968. "The Concept of Cult," *Sociological Review* 16 (November): 351-362.
____. 1969. "The Spiritualist Movement: A Need for the Redefinition of the Concept of Cult," *Journal for the Scientific Study of Religion* 8: 152-160.
____. 1972. "The Membership of a Cult," *Review of Religious Research* 13 (3): 170-177.
______. 1975. "Toward a Sociology of the Psychic," *Review of Religious Research* 16 (Spring): 166-173.
Nelson, R. A. 1971. *The Art of Cold Reading*. Calgary: Micky Hades Enterprises.

Nichols, Sallie. 1980. *Jung and Tarot: An Archetypical Journey*. NY: Weiser.

Oberschall, A. 1973. *Social Conflict and Social Movements*. Englewood Cliffs, NJ: Prentice-Hall.

O'Keefe, Daniel Lawrence. 1982. *Stolen Lighting: The Social Theory of Magic*. NY: Continuum.

O'Neill, John. 1972. *Sociology as a Skin Trade*. NY: Harper and Row.

_____. 1974. *Making Sense Together*. NY: Harper and Row.

O'Neill, Robert V. 1986. *Tarot Symbolism*. Lima, OH: Fairway Press.

Papus (translated by A. P. Morton, with preface by Arthur E. Waite). 1975 (1889). *The Tarot of the Bohemians*. Hollywood, CA: Wilshire.

Petersen, D. W., and A. Mauss. 1973. "The Cross and the Commune," pp. 261-280 in C. Y. Glock (ed.), *Religion in SociologialPerspective*. Belmont, CA: Wadsworth.

Pickering, Andrew. 1984. *Constructing Quarks: A Sociological History of Particle Physics*. Chicago: University of Chicago Press.

Pinch, Trevor. 1982a. "The Development of Solar-Neutrino Astronomy." Ph.D. Thesis, University of Bath.

_______. 1982b. "Theory testing in science—the Case of Solar Neutrinos," paper presented to the combined Meeting of HSS, PSA, SHOT, and 4S, Philadelphia.

Pollack, Rachel. 1985. *Salvador Dali's Tarot*. Salem, NH: Salem House.

_____. 1986. *Tarot: The Open Labyrinth*. Wellingborough: Aquarian.

Prince, R. H. 1974. "Cocoon Work," pp. 255-271 in I. I. Zaretsky and M. P. Leone (eds.), *Religious Movements in Contemporary America*. Princeton, NJ: Princeton University Press.

Quarantlli, E. L., and Dennis Wenger. 1973. "A Voice from the Thirteenth Century," *Urban Life and Culture* 1 (January): 379-400.

Quinn, D. Michael. 1987. *Early Mormonism and the Magic World View*. Salt Lake City: Signature.

Rambo, Carol A. 1987. "Turn-Ons for Money." M.A. Thesis, University of South Florida.

Rambo-Roni, Carol, and Carolyn S. Ellis. 1989. "Turn-ons for Money: Interactional Strategies of the Table Dancer," *Journal of Contemporary Ethnography* 18 (3): 271-298.

Regardie, Israel. 1972 (1932). *The Tree of Life: A Study in Magic*. NY: Weiser.

_____. 1989 (1937-1940). *The Golden Dawn*. St. Paul, MN: Llewellyn.

Richardson, James T. 1975. "From Cult to Sect," Paper presented to the Pacific Sociologial Association Meetings, San Diego, CA.

Robbins, Thomas. 1969. "Esastern Mysticism and the Resocialization of Drug Users," *Journal for the Scientific Study of Religion* 8 (Fall): 308-317.

_____. 1973. "The Jesus Movement, Eastern Cults, and the Contemporary Crisis of Values," Paper presented to the Society for the Scientific Study of Religion, San Francisco.

_____. 1988. *Cults, Converts and Chrisma: The Sociology of New Religious Movements*. Newbury Park, CA: Sage.

______, and Dick Anthony (eds.). 1981. *In Gods We Trust: New Patterns of Religious Pluralism in America*. New Bruswick: Tranaction Books.

Robbins, Thomas, D. Anthony, and T. Curtis. 1975. "Youth Culture Religious Movements," *Sociological Quarterly* 16 (Winter): 48-64.

Robbins, Thomas, William Shepherd, and James McBride (eds.). 1985. *Cults, Culture and the Law*. Chico, CA: Scholars Press.

Roberts, Jane. 1970. *The Seth Material*. NY: Frederick Hall.

Rochford, E. Burke. 1985. *Hare Krishna in America*. New Brunswick, NJ: Rutgers University Press.

Roszak, Theodore. 1988. *Fool's Cycle/Full Cycle: Reflections on the Great Trumps of the Tarot*. San Francisco: Robert Briggs Associates.

Rowley, Peter. 1970. *New Gods in America*. NY: McKay.

Russell, Jeffery B. 1974. *A History of Witchcraft*. London: Thames and Hudson.

Sacks, Harvey, Emmanuel Schegloff, and Gail Jefferson. 1974. "A Simplest Systematics for the Analysis of Turn Taking in Conversations," *Language* 50: 696-735.

Schatzman, Leonard, and Anselm L. Strauss. 1973. *Field Research*. Englewood Cliffs, NJ: Prentice-Hall.

Schenkein, Jim (ed.). 1978. *Studies of Conversational Interaction*. NY: Academic Press.

Schutz, Alfred (Maurice Natanson, ed.). 1967. *Collected Papers I: The Problem of Social Reality*. The Hague: Martinus Nijhoff.

Scott, Gini G. 1980. *Cult and Countercult: A Study of a Spiritual Growth Group and a Witchcraft Order*. Westport, CT: Greenwood.

Seperson, Susanne B. 1981. "The Language of Psychotherapy." Ph.D. dissertation, The City University of New York.

Settle, Tom. 1971. "The Rationality of Science versus the Rationality of Magic," *Philosophy of the Social Sciences* 1: 171-194.

Shepherd, William C. 1972. "Religion and the Counter-Culture—A New Religiosity," *Sociological Inquiry* 42 (1): 3-9.

Shupe, Anson D., Jr. 1981. (ed.). *Six Perspectives on New Religions: A Case Study Approach*. Lewiston, NY: Edwin Mellen.

____. 1985. "The Routinization of Conflict in Modern Cult/Anticult Controversy," *Nebraska Humanist* 8 (2): 26-40.

____, and David G. Bromley. 1980. *The New Vigilantes: Deprogrammers, Anti-Cultists and the New Religions*. Beverly Hills, CA: Sage.

Shweder, Richard A. 1977. "Likeness and Likelihood in Everyday Thought," *Current Anthropology* 18 (4): 637-658.

Simmons, J. L. 1969. *Deviants*. Berkeley, CA: The Glendessary Press.

Smart, Ninian. 1976. *The Religious Experience of Mankind*. NY: Scribner.

Smelser, N. D. 1963. *Theory of Collective Behavior*. NY: The Free Press.

Speier, M. 1973. *How to Observe Face-to-Face Communication*. Pacific Palisades, CA: Goodyear.

Stacknik, Thomas, and Harry Stachnik. 1980. "Acceptance of Non-Specific Astrological Personality Descriptions," *Psychological Reports* 47: 537-538.

Staniford, Phillip. 1982. "On Psi and Magic," *Current Anthropology* 23 (3): 348.

Stark, Rodney (ed.). 1985. *Religious Movements: Genesis, Exodus, and Numbers*. NY: Paragon.

____, and William S. Bainbridge. 1979. "Of Churches, Sects and Cults: Preliminary Concepts for a Theory of Religious Movements," *Journal for the Scientific Study of Religion* 18 (2): 117-133.

____. 1980a. "Networks of Faith: Interpersonal Bonds and Recruitment to Cults and Sects," *American Journal of Sociology* 85 (6): 1376-1395.

____. 1980b. "Toward A Theory of Religion: Religious Commitment," *Journal for the Scientific Study of Religion* 19 (2): 114-128.

______. 1980c. "Secularization, Revival and Cult Formation," *Annual Review of the Social Sciences of Religion* 4: 85-119.

_____. 1981. "Reply to Jorgensen," *American Journal of Sociology* 87 (2): 430-432

_____. 1985. *The Future of Religion: Secularization, Revival and Cult Formation.* Berkley: University of California Press.

_____. 1987. *A Theory of Religion.* NY: Peter Lang.

______, and D.P. Doyle. 1979. "Cults in America: A Roconnaissance in Time and Space," *Sociological Analysis* 40 (4): 347-359.

Staude, John R. 1970. "Alienated Youth and the Cult of the Occult," pp. 86-95 in M. L. Medley and J. E. Congress (eds.), *Sociology for the Seventies.* New York: Wiley.

Straus, Roger. 1976. "Changing Oneself: Seekers and the Creative Transformation of Life Experience," pp. 251-273 in John Lofland (ed.), *Doing Social Life.* NY: Wiley.

Stupple, David. (ed). 1975. "The Occult," *Journal of Popular Culture* 8(Spring):856-932.

Sudnow, David. 1965. "Normal Crimes," pp. 174-185 in Earl Rubington and Martin Weinberg (eds.), *Deviance: The Interactionist Perspective.* NY: Macmillan.

_____ (ed.). 1972. *Studies in Social Interaction.* NY: The Free Press.

Sullivan, Lawrence E. (ed.). 1989. *Hidden Truths: Magic, Alchemy, and the Occult.* NY: Macmillan.

Tambiah, S.J. 1973. "Form and Meaning of Magical Acts," pp. 230-248 in R. Horton and R. Finnegan (eds.), *Modes of Thought.* London: Faber.

Tatro, C. 1974. "Cross my Palm with Silver," pp. 286-299 in C. D. Bryant (ed.), *Deviant Behavior.* Chicago: Rand McNally.

Taylor, Alan. 1986. "The Early Republic's Supernatural Economy: Treasure Seeking in the American Northeast, 1780-1830," *American Quarterly* 38 (Spring): 6-34

Tecther, David. 1972. "Psi: Past, Present, Future," *Journal of Popular Culture* 5 (Winter): 647-654, 26.

Thomas, Keith. 1971. *Religion and the Decline of Magic.* NY: Scribner's.

Thomas, W. I. (with D. S. Thomas). 1928. *The Child in America.* NY: Alfred A. Knopf.

Thorndike, Lynn. 1958 (1923). *History of Magic and Experimental Science.* NY: Macmillan.

Tiryakian, Edward A. 1973. "Toward a Sociology of Esoteric Culture," *American Journal of Sociology* 78: 491-512.

_____ (ed). 1974. *On the Margin of the Visible.* New York: Wiley.

Truzzi, Marcello. 1972a. "Definitions and Dimensions of the Occult: Toward a Sociological Perspective," *Journal of Popular Culture* 5 (Winter): 635-645.

_____. 1972b. "The Occult Revival as Popular Culture," *Sociological Quarterly* 13 (Winter): 16-36.

____. 1974. "Toward a Sociology of the Occult: Notes on Modern Witchcraft," pp. 628-645 in I. I. Zaretsky and M. P. Leone (eds.), *Religious Movements in Contemporary America*. Princeton, NJ: Princeton University Press.

_____. 1975. "Astrology as Popular Culture," *Journal of Popular Culture* 8 (Spring): 906-911.

_____. 1978. "Sociology of Deviant Science," Paper presented at the 73rd Annual Meeting of the American Sociological Association, San Francisco.

Turner, Frank M. 1974. *Between Science and Religion*. New Haven, CT: Yale University Press.

Turner, Ralph H. 1969. "The Public Perception of Protest," *American Sociologial Review* 34 (December): 815-831.

Tylor, E. B. 1871. *Primitive Culture*. London: Murry.

Van Maanen, John. 1988. *Tales of the Field: On Writing Ethnography*. Chicago: University of Chicago Press.

Vogt, Evon Z., and Ray Hyman. 1959. *Water Witching U.S.A.* Chicago: University of Chicago Press, 1959.

Waite, Alfred Edward. 1975. "Preface," pp. v-xviii in Papus, *The Tarot of the Bohemians*. Hollywood, CA: Wilshire.

_____. 1989 (1986, 1910). *The Pictorial Key to the Tarot: Being Fragments of a Secret Tradition Under the Veil of Divination*. York Beach, Maine: Weiser.

Walker, D.P. 1975 (1958). *Spiritual and Demonic Magic*. Notre Dame, IN: University of Notre Dame Press.

Wallis, Roy. 1974. "The Altherius Society: A Case Study in the Formation of a Mystologic Congregation," *Sociological Review* 22 (February): 27-45.

_____. 1975. *Sectarianism*. NY: Wiley.

______. 1977. *The Road to Total Freedom: A Sociological Analysis of Scientology*. NY: Columbia University Press.

_____. 1984. *Elementary Forms of the New Religious Life*. NY: Routledge and Kegan Paul.

____. 1986. "Figuring Out Cult Recepivity," *Journal for the Scientific Study of Religion* 25 (4): 494-503.

_____. 1987. "Hostages to Fortune: Thoughts on the Future of Scientology and the Children of God," pp. 80-90 in David Bromley and Phillip Hammond (eds.), *The Future of New Religious Movements*. Macon, GA: Mercer University.

______, and Steven Bruce, 1986. *Sociological Theory, Religion and Collective Action*. Belfast: The Queen's University.

Wang, Robert. 1978. *An Introduction to the Golden Dawn Tarot*. York Beach, Maine: Weiser.

____. 1983. *The Qabalistic Tarot: A Textbook of Mystical Philosophy*. York Beach, Maine: Samuel Weiser.

Wax, R.H. 1971. *Doing Fieldwork*. Chicago: University of Chicago Press.

_______. 1979. Gender and Age in Fieldwork and Fieldwork Education," *Social Problems* 26: 509-22.

Weber, Max (Hans Gerth and Don Martindale, trans.). 1952. *Ancient Judaism*. NY: Free Press.

_____ (Talcott Parsons, trans.). 1958 (1904-5). *The Protestant Ethic and the Spirit of Capitalism*. NY: Scriber's Sons.

_______ (Ephraim Fischoff, trans.). 1963 (1922). *The Sociology of Religion*. Boston: Beacon.

_____. 1971. "The Three Types of Legitimate Rule," pp. 169-179 in M. Truzzi (ed.), *Sociology: The Classic Statements*. NY: Random House.

Wedow, Suzanne. 1976. "The Strangeness of Astrology," pp. 181-193 in W. Areno and Susan P. Montague (eds.). *The American Dimension*. NY: Alfred.

Weiman, Gabriel. 1982 "The Prophecy that Never Fails," *Sociological Inquiry* 52 (4): 274-290.

Weisman, Richard. 1984. *Witchcraft, Magic, and Religion in 17th-Century Massachusetts*. Amherst: University of Massachusetts Press.

Westrum, Ron. 1977. "Scientists as Experts," *Zetetic* 1 (1): 34-46.

_____. 1983. "Crypto-science Rides Again," *Zetetic Scholar* 11: 109-122.

White, Rhea A. 1973. *Parapsychology: Sources of Information*. Metuchen, NJ: Scarecrow Press.

Whitehead, Harriet. 1974. "Reasonably Fantastic," pp. 547-587 in I. I. Zaretsky and M. P. Leone (eds.), *Religious Movements in Contemporary America*. Princeton, NJ: Princeton University Press.

Wilkinson, Ronald Sterne. 1962. "New England's Last Alchemists," *Ambix* 10 (October): 128-138.

Wilson, Bryan. 1961.*Sects and Society*. Berkeley: University of California Press.

_____. 1970. *Religious Sects*. New York: McGraw-Hill.

Winch, Peter. 1958. *The Idea of a Social Science and Its Relation to Philosophy*. NY: Humanities Press.

Winkelman, Michael. 1982. "Magic," *Current Anthropology* 23: 37-66.

Wittgenstein, L. 1968. *Philosophical Investigations*. NY: Macmillan.

Wood, Gordon S. 1980. "Evangelical America and Early Mormonism," *New York History* 61 (October): 359-386.

Wuthnow, Robert. 1978. *Experimentation in American Religion*. Berkeley: University of California Press.

_____. 1987. *Meaning and Moral Order*. Berkeley: University of California Press.

Yates, Frances A. 1964. *Giordano Bruno and the Hermetic Tradition*. Chicago: University of Chicago Press.

_____. 1972. *The Rosicrucian Enlightenment*. Bolder: Shambhala.

_____. 1979. *The Occult Philosophy in the Elizabethan Age*. NY: Routledge and Kegan Paul.

Yinger, Milton J. 1970. *The Scientific Study of Religion*. NY: Macmillan.

Zaretsky, Irving I. 1974. "In the Beginning was the Word: The Relationship of Language to Social Organization in Spiritualist Churches," pp. 166-219 in I. I. Zaretsky and M. P. Leone (eds.), *Religious Movements in Contemporary America*. Princeton, NJ: Princeton University Press.

____, and Mark P. Leone (eds.). 1974. *Religious Movements in Contemporary America*. Princeton, NJ: Princeton University Press.

Index

P

Q

R

S

T

V

W

About the Author

Danny L. Jorgensen is an Associate Professor in the Department of Religious Studies, and the Associate Director of the Center for Interdisciplinary Studies in Culture and Society at the University of South Florida, St. Petersburg. He was awarded a Ph.D. in sociology from The Ohio State University in 1979. His research and writing on qualitative methodology and new religious movements in America have resulted in *Participant Observation: A Methodology for Human Studies* (Newbury Park, California: Sage Publications, 1989), as well as articles in *Kansas History, The John Whitmer Historical Association Journal, Symbolic Interaction*, the *California Sociologist, The Sociological Quarterly, Urban Life* (now the *Journal of Contemporary Ethnography*), and *Deviant Behavior.* He currently is working on an indepth study of the Church of Jesus Christ (Cutlerite), a Mormon schism, and a biographical study of early Mormon women on the American frontier. Dr. Jorgensen is married, the father of five children, and an impetuous tennis player.